I0005920

A New Collection of Voyages, Discoveries and Travels

George Sandby

(Knox)

K

A NEW
COLLECTION

OF

VOYAGES,

DISCOVERIES and TRAVELS:

CONTAINING

Whatever is worthy of Notice, in

EUROPE, ASIA,

AFRICA and AMERICA:

IN RESPECT TO

The Situation and Extent of Empires, Kingdoms, and
Provinces; their Climates, Soil, Produce, &c.

WITH

The Manners and Customs of the several Inhabitants;
their Government, Religion, Arts, Sciences,
Manufactures, and Commerce.

The whole confifting of fuch ENGLISH and FOREIGN Authors
as are in moſt Eſteem; including the Deſcriptions and Remarks
of fome celebrated late Travellers, not to be found in any
other Collection.

Illuſtrated with a Variety of accurate
MAPS, PLANS, and elegant ENGRAVINGS.

VOL. VII.

LONDON:

Printed for J. KNOX, near Southampton-Street,
in the Strand. MDCCLXVII.

ρ

C O N T E N T S

OF THE

SEVENTH VOLUME.

A

COLLECTION

OF

VOYAGES and TRAVELS.

Of GREAT BRITAIN in general.

GREAT BRITAIN, the largeſt iſland in
Europe, comprehends the two kingdoms of
England and Scotland, with the principality
of Wales. Its latitude, at the Lizard Point in Cornwall, according to Moll, is 50° north, and at the
head-land at Caithneſs in Scotland, 58° 30′; ſo that,
according to the geometrical meaſure of Engliſh ſtatute miles, which is 69 miles and 864 feet to a
degree, the length of the iſland, meaſured in a
direct line, without attending to the hills and winding of the roads, is 587 miles. Its longitude, Te-
neriffe being the firſt meridian, is 9° 45′ at the
Land's-End in Cornwall, and at the South Foreland
in Kent, 17° 15′. Now every degree of longitude
in this latitude being about 38 ſtatute miles, the
breadth therefore between theſe two extremities will
be 285 miles.

As an iſland, this country has ſome peculiar natural advantages and diſadvantages: it is ſubject
to perpetual varieties of heat and cold, wet and dry;
but the heats in ſummer, and the colds in winter,
are more temperate than in any part of the Continent that lies in the ſame latitude: the harbours in
Holland, Germany, and Denmark, are blocked up

with ice, while ours, which lie in the fame latitude, are open. To this moderation of the climate is attributed the long lives of many of the inhabitants; and to the fame caufe is owing that almoft perpetual verdure, in a manner peculiar to this country; which in the fummer is frequently refrefhed by feafonable fhowers, and by the warm vapours of the fea, in winter, is generally fecured from any long continuance of froft and fnow.

This happy fituation of our ifland can never be fufficiently valued, as it renders Great Britain a world, as it were, within itfelf, intirely independent of other nations; and furnifhes her with all the neceffaries of life, in fuch abundance, as enables her to fupply other nations.

That part of Great Britain which lies toward the Weftern Ocean, is mountainous, as Cornwall, Wales, and Cumberland; likewife fome of the interior counties, as part of Derbyfhire, Yorkfhire, Weftmorland, Northumberland, and near one half of Scotland. The eaftern and fouthern parts of the country, chiefly confift of little fruitful hills and vallies, champaign fields, inclofed grounds of arable, pafture, and meadow lands; agreeably intermixed with wood and water; and being much inclofed and cultivated, it abounds with profpects that in beauty can fcarcely be exceeded, even by the fictions of imagination.

It has on all fides very convenient harbours, and many extenfive navigable rivers, that convey the riches of all the nations of the known world into the very centre of the kingdom. The moft confiderable rivers in England are the Thames, Severn, and Humber; in Scotland, the Forth, Clyde, and Tay.

Various are the names by which this ifland hath been known, and as different are the reafons affigned for them. It was called Albion by the Greeks, Bretanica by the Phœnicians, and Brittannia by the Romans,

STONE HENGE, a celebrated Monument of the Druids on Salisbury Plain.

mans, who diftinguifhed that part, now the Highlands of Scotland, by the name of Caledonia.

The inhabitants of Great Britain and Ireland, according to fome calculations, fo late as the year
1758, allowing fix perfons to each houfe, are computed at eight millions; viz. in England and Wales
5,700,000; in Scotland 1,300,000; and in Ireland
1,000,000; to thefe may be added near 2,000,000
fuppofed to be in the Britifh fettlements in Afia,
Africa, and America.

With refpect to the perfons and character of the
English, they are generally of a ftrong active make,
well fhaped, and of good ftature. They are industrious, lovers of the liberal arts, and capable of carrying them to the greateft perfection. They are neither fo heavy as the Germans, nor fo exceedingly
mercurial as the French; but are obferved to be generally open and blunt in their behaviour, and particularly averfe to fervility and cringing. Their good
nature, generofity and humanity, have been frequently fhewn to their enemies, in fuch a manner as
to do honour even to human nature. The lenity
of their laws in capital cafes; their compaffion for
convicted criminals; even the general humanity of
highwaymen and robbers of this nation, compared
with thofe of other countries; are all convincing
proofs that the fpirit of humanity is natural to them.
The many noble foundations for the relief of the
miferable and the friendlefs; the large annual fupplies from voluntary charities to thefe foundations,
and on every other occafion where their benevolence
is folicited, are alfo ftriking proofs of true goodnefs
of heart and greatnefs of foul, for which this nation has been always diftinguifhed.

In point of courage no people exceed, and very
few equal the English; who are remarkable for this
particular, that no people fhew a more refolute obftinacy in battle, though under the greateft difadvan-
tages. Their valour and bravery, both by fea and

land,

land, hath been so frequently exerted in many parts of the world, that the most formidable kingdoms have been constrained to yield to the superior force of their arms: so that Great Britain, at this time, by their courage and prudence, gives liberty to Europe, and has acquired an extent of territory equal to the Roman empire when in its meridian of power, and infinitely more useful to the mother country.

The women, beside their natural beauty, which is such as not to need the assistance of paint, so common in other countries, are still more to be valued for their prudent behaviour, thorough cleanliness, and a tender affection for their husbands and children. As to the faults of the English; foreigners have remarked that they are somewhat passionate, melancholy, fickle and unsteady; one moment applauding, what they detest in the next; and that the lower sort of people have too contemptible an idea of other nations; and are thence apt to treat strangers with rudeness. But this latter accusation seems rather to have been founded on particular instances, which a great relish for, and propensity to humour, so observable among the common people, may sometimes betray them into; than to belong to them as a national character.

Of the Government and Civil Policy of
BRITAIN.

In all states there is an absolute supreme power, to which the right of legislation belongs; and which, by the singular constitution of these kingdoms, is vested in the king, lords, and commons.

Of the King.

The supreme executive power of Great Britain, and Ireland, is vested by our constitution in a single person, king or queen; for it is indifferent to
which

which fex the crown defcends: the perfon entitled to
it, whether male or female, is immediately invefted
with all the enfigns, rights, and prerogatives of fovereign power.

The grand fundamental maxim upon which the
right of fucceffion to the throne of thefe kingdoms
depends, is: " that the crown, by common law and
conftitutional cuftom, is hereditary; and this in a
manner peculiar to itfelf: but that the right of inheritance may from time to time be changed or limited by act of parliament: under which limitations
the crown ftill continues hereditary."

King Egbert, king Canute, and king William I.
have been fucceffively conftituted the common ftocks,
or anceftors, of this defcent.

On the death of queen Elizabeth, without iffue,
the line of Henry VIII. became extinct. It therefore became neceffary to recur to the other iffue of
Henry VII. by Elizabeth of York his queen: whofe
eldeft daughter Margaret having married James IV.
king of Scotland, king James the Sixth of Scotland,
and of England the Firft, was the lineal defcendant
from that alliance. So that in his perfon, as clearly as
in Henry VIII. centered all the claims of the different
competitors from the conqueft downward; he being
indifputably the lineal heir of the conqueror. And,
what is ftill more remarkable, in his perfon alfo centered the right of the Saxon monarchs, which had
been fufpended from the conqueft till his acceffion.
For, Margaret the fifter of Edgar Atheling, the
daughter of Edward the Outlaw, and granddaughter
of king Edmund Ironfide, was the perfon in whom
the hereditary right of the Saxon kings, fuppofing
it not abolifhed by the conqueft, refided. She
married Malcolm king of Scotland; and Henry II.
by a defcent from Matilda their daughter, is generally called the reftorer of the Saxon line. But it
muft be remembered, that Malcolm by his Saxon
queen had fons as well as daughters; and that the

B 3

royal

royal family of Scotland, from that time downward, were the offspring of Malcolm and Margaret. Of this royal family king James I. was the direct lineal descendant; and therefore united in his person every possible claim, by hereditary right, to the English as well as Scottish throne, being the heir both of Egbert and William the Conqueror.

At the revolution, the convention of estates, or representative body of the nation, declared, that the misconduct of king James II. amounted to an abdication of the government, and that the throne was thereby vacant.

In consequence of this vacancy, and from a regard to the ancient line, the convention appointed the next Protestant heirs of the blood royal of king Charles I. to fill the vacant throne, in the old order of succession; with a temporary exception, or preference, to the person of king William III.

On the impending failure of the Protestant line of King Charles I. (whereby the throne might again have become vacant) the king and parliament extended the settlement of the crown to the Protestant line of King James I. viz. to the princess Sophia of Hanover, and the heirs of her body, being Protestants: and she is now the common stock, from whom the heirs of the crown must descend.

The true ground and principle, upon which the revolution proceeded, was an entirely new case in politics, which had never before happened in our history; the abdication of the reigning monarch, and the vacancy of the throne thereupon. It was not a defeazance of the right of succession, and a new limitation of the crown, by the king and both houses of parliament: it was the act of the nation alone, upon a conviction that there was no king in being. For in a full assembly of the lords and commons, met in convention upon the supposition of this vacancy, both houses came to this resolution;

" that

" that king James II. having endeavoured to fubvert the conftitution of the kingdom, by breaking the original contract between king and people; and, by the advice of jefuits and other wicked perfons, having violated the fundamental laws; and having withdrawn himfelf out of this kingdom; has abdicated the government, and that the throne is thereby vacant." Thus ended at once, by this fudden and unexpected vacancy of the throne, the old line of fucceffion; which from the conqueft had lafted above 600 years, and from the union of the heptarchy in king Egbert, almoft 900.

Though in fome points (owing to the peculiar circumftances of things and perfons) the revolution was not altogether fo perfect as might have been wifhed; yet from thence a new æra commenced, in which the bounds of prerogative and liberty have been better defined, the principles of government more thoroughly examined and underftood, and the rights of the fubject more explicitly guarded by legal provifions, than in any other period of the Englifh hiftory. In particular, it is worthy obfervation, that the convention, in this their judgment, avoided with great wifdom the wild extreams into which the vifionary theories of fome zealous republicans would have led them. They held that this mifconduct of king James amounted to an endeavour to fubv rt the conftitution, and not to an actual fubverfion, or total diffolution of the government. They therefore very prudently voted it to amount to no more than an abdication of the government, and a confequent vacancy of the throne; whereby the government was allowed to fubfift, though the executive magiftrate was gone; and the kingly office to remain, though king James was no longer king. And thus the conftitution was kept intire; which upon every found principle of government muft otherwife have fallen to pieces, had fo principal and conftituent a

part

part as the royal authority been abolished, or even
suspended *.

Hence it is easy to collect, that the title to the
crown is at present hereditary, though not quite so
absolutely hereditary as formerly; and the common
stock or anceftor, from whom the descent muft be
derived, is also different. Formerly the common
stock was king Egbert; then William the Conqueror; afterward in James the Firft's time the two common stocks united, and so continued till the vacancy
of the throne in 1688: now it is the princefs Sophia,
in whom the inheritance was vefted by the new king
and parliament. Formerly the descent was absolute,
and the crown went to the next heir without any re-

* The constitution of England, says Dr. Smollet, had now af-
sumed a new aspect. The maxim of hereditary, indefeasible right,
was at length renounced by a free parliament. The power of the
crown was acknowledged to flow from no other fountain than that
of a contract with the people. Allegiance and protection were
declared reciprocal ties depending upon each other. The reprefentatives of the nation made a regular claim of rights in behalf of
their conftituents; and William III. afcended the throne in confequence of an exprefs capitulation with the people. Yet, on this
occafion, the parliament, toward their deliverer, feems to have
overfhot their attachment to their own liberty and privileges: or,
at leaft, they neglected the faireft opportunity that ever occurred,
to retrench those prerogatives of the crown to which they imputed all the late and former calamities of the kingdom. Their
new monarch retained the old regal power over parliaments, in
its full extent: he was at liberty to convoke, adjourn, prorogue,
and diffolve them at his pleafure; he was enabled to influence
elections, and opprefs corporations: he poffeffed the right of
chufing his own council; of nominating all the great officers of the
ftate, and of the houfhold, of the army, the navy, and the church.
He referved the abfolute command of the militia: fo that he remained mafter of all the inftruments and engines of corruption and
violence, without any other reftraint than his own moderation, and
prudent regard to the claim of rights and principle of refiftance
on which the revolution was founded. In a word, the fettlement
was finished with fome precipitation, before the plan had been
properly digefted and matured; and this will be the cafe in every
eftablifhment, formed upon a fudden emergency in the face of oppofition.

striction;

ftriction: but now, upon the new fettlement, the inheritance is conditional; being limited to fuch heirs only, of the body of the princefs Sophia, as are Proteftant members of the church of England, and are married to none but Proteftants.

And in this due medium confifts the true confti-tutional notion of the right of fucceffion to the im-perial crown of thefe kingdoms. The extreams, between which it fteers, are each of them equally deftructive of thofe ends for which focieties were formed and are kept on foot. Where the magiftrate, upon every fucceffion, is elected by the people, and may by the exprefs provifion of the laws be depofed (if not punifhed) by his fubjects, this may found like the perfection of liberty, and look well enough when delineated on paper; but in practice will be ever productive of tumult, contention, and anarchy. And, on the other hand, divine indefeafible heredi-tary right, when coupled with the doctrine of unli-mited paffive obedience, is furely of all conftitutions the moft thoroughly flavifh and dreadful. But when fuch an hereditary right, as our laws have created and vefted in the royal ftock, is clofely interwoven with thofe liberties, which are equally the inheri-tance of the fubject; this union will form a confti-tution, in theory the moft beautiful of any, in prac-tice the moft approved, and, in all probability, will prove in duration the moft permanent. This con-ftitution, it is the duty of every good Englifhman to underftand, to revere, and to defend.

The principal duties of the king are expreffed in his oath at the coronation, which is adminiftered by one of the archbifhops, or bifhops of the realm, in the prefence of all the people; who on their parts do reciprocally take the oath of allegiance to the crown. This coronation oath is conceived in the following terms:

" *The archbifhop or bifhop fhall fay*, Will you fo-" lemnly promife and fwear to govern the people
" of

" of this kingdom of England, and the dominions
" thereunto belonging, according to the statutes in
" parliament agreed on, and the laws and customs
" of the same?——*The king or queen shall say,* I
" solemnly promise so to do.

" *Archbishop or bishop.* Will you to your power
" cause law and justice, in mercy, to be executed in
" all your judgments?——*King or queen.* I will.

" *Archbishop or bishop.* Will you to the utmost of
" your power maintain the laws of God, the true
" profession of the gospel, and the Protestant re-
" formed religion established by the law? And will
" you preserve unto the bishops and clergy of this
" realm, and to the churches committed to their
" charge, all such rights and privileges as by law
" do or shall appertain unto them, or any of them?
" ——*King or queen.* All this I promise to do.

" *After this the king or queen, laying his or her hand*
" *upon the holy gospels, shall say,* The things which
" I have here before promised I will perform and
" keep: so help me God. *And then shall kiss the*
" *book.*"

This is the form of the coronation oath, as it is
now prescribed by our laws: and we may observe,
that in the king's part in this original contract, are
expressed all the duties that a monarch can owe to
his people; viz. to govern according to law: to execute judgment in mercy: and to maintain the established religion. With respect to the latter of these
three branches, we may farther remark, that by the
act of union, 5 Ann. c. 8. two preceding statutes
are recited and confirmed; the one of the parliament of Scotland, the other of the parliament of
England: which enact; the former, that every king
at his accession shall take and subscribe an oath, to
preserve the Protestant religion and Presbyterian
church government in Scotland; the latter, that at
his coronation he shall take and subscribe a similar
oath, to preserve the settlement of the church of
England

England within England, Ireland, Wales, and Berwick, and the territories thereunto belonging.

The king of Great Britain, notwithstanding the limitations or the power of the crown, already mentioned, is one of the greatest monarchs reigning over a free people. His person is sacred in the eye of the law, which makes it high treason so much as to imagine or intend his death; neither can he, in himself, be deemed guilty of any crime, the law taking no cognizance of his actions, but only in the persons of his ministers, if they infringe the laws of the land. As to his power, it has no bounds, (except where it breaks in upon the liberty and property of his subjects, as in making new laws, or raising new taxes) for he can make war or peace; send and receive ambassadors; make treaties of league and commerce; levy armies, fit out fleets, employ them as he thinks proper; grant commissions to his officers both by sea and land, or revoke them at pleasure; dispose of all magazines, castles, &c. summon the parliament to meet, and, when met, adjourn, prorogue, or dissolve it at pleasure; refuse his assent to any bill, though it hath passed both houses; which, consequently, by such a refusal, has no more force than if it had never been moved. He possesseth the right of chusing his own council; of nominating all the great officers of state, of the houshold, and the church; and, in fine, is the fountain of honour, from whom all degrees of nobility and knighthood are derived. Such is the dignity and power of a king of Great Britain.

Of the Parliament.

Parliaments, in some shape, are of as high antiquity as the Saxon government in this island; and have subsisted, in their present form, at least five hundred years.

The parliament is assembled by the king's writs, and it's sitting must not be intermitted above three

years.

years. Its constituent parts are, the king sitting there in his royal political capacity, and the three estates of the realm; the lords spiritual, the lords temporal, (who sit, together with the king, in one house) and the commons, who sit by themselves in another. The king and these three estates, together, form the great corporation or body politic of the kingdom, of which the king is said to be *caput, principium, et finis*. For upon their coming together the king meets them, either in person or by representation; without which there can be no beginning of a parliament; and he also has alone the power of dissolving them.

It is highly necessary for preserving the balance of the constitution, that the executive power should be a branch, though not the whole, of the legislature. The crown cannot begin of itself any alterations in the present established law; but it may approve or disapprove of the alterations suggested and consented to by the two houses. The legislative therefore cannot abridge the executive power of any rights which it now has by law, without it's own consent: since the law must perpetually stand as it now does, unless all the powers will agree to alter it. And herein indeed consists the true excellence of the English government, that all the parts of it form a mutual check upon each other. In the legislature, the people are a check upon the nobility, and the nobility a check upon the people; by the mutual privilege of rejecting what the other has resolved: while the king is a check upon both, which preserves the executive power from encroachments.

The lords spiritual consist of two archbishops and twenty-four bishops. The lords temporal consist of all the peers of the realm, the bishops not being in strictness held to be such, but meerly lords of parliament. Some of these sit by descent, as do all antient peers; some by creation, as do all the new-made ones; others, since the union with Scotland, by election, which is the case of the sixteen peers, who

represent

reprefent the body of the Scots nobility. Their number is indefinite, and may be encreafed at will by the power of the crown.

A body of nobility is more peculiarly neceffary in our mixed and compounded conftitution, in order to fupport the rights of both the crown and the people; by forming a barrier to withftand the encroachments of both. It creates and preferves that gradual fcale of dignity, which proceeds from the peafant to the prince; rifing like a pyramid from a broad foundation, and diminifhing to a point as it rifes. The nobility therefore are the pillars, which are reared from among the people, more immediately to fupport the throne; and if that falls, they muft alfo be buried under it's ruins. Accordingly, when in the laft century the commons had determined to extirpate monarchy, they alfo voted the houfe of lords to be ufelefs and dangerous.

The commons confift of all fuch men of any property in the kingdom, as have not feats in the houfe of lords; every one of which has a voice in parliament, either perfonally, or by his reprefentatives. In a free ftate, every man, who is fuppofed a free agent, ought to be, in fome meafure, his own governor; and therefore a branch at leaft of the legiflative power fhould refide in the whole body of the people. In fo large a ftate as ours, it is very wifely contrived, that the people fhould do that by their reprefentatives, which it is impracticable to perform in perfon: reprefentatives, chofen by a number of minute and feparate diftricts, wherein all the voters are, or eafily may be, diftinguifhed. The counties are therefore reprefented by knights, elected by the proprietors of lands; the cities and boroughs are reprefented by citizens and burgeffes, chofen by the mercantile part or fuppofed trading intereft of the nation. The number of Englifh reprefentatives is 513, and of Scots 45; in all 558. And every member, though chofen by one particular diftrict, when elected and

6   returned,

returned, ferves for the whole realm. For the end
of his coming thither is not particular, but general;
not barely to advantage his conftituents, but the common wealth, and to advife his majefty, as appears
from the writ of fummons.

These are the conftituent parts of a parliament, the
king, the lords fpiritual and temporal, and the commons. Parts, of which each is fo neceffary, that the
confent of all three is required to make any new law
that fhould bind the fubject. Whatever is enacted
for law by one, or by two only, of the three, is no
ftatute; and to it no regard is due, unlefs in matters
relating to their own privileges.

The power and jurifdiction of parliament, fays Sir
Edward Coke, is fo tranfcendent and abfolute, that
it cannot be confined, either for caufes or perfons,
within any bounds. It hath fovereign and uncon-
trolable authority in making, confirming, enlarging,
reftraining, abrogating, repealing, reviving, and ex-
pounding of laws, concerning matters of all poffible
denominations, ecclefiaftical, or temporal, civil, military, maritime, or criminal: this being the place
where that abfolute defpotic power, which muft in
all governments refide fomewhere, is entrufted by the
conftitution of thefe kingdoms. All mifchiefs and
grievances, operations and remedies, that tranfcend
the ordinary courfe of the laws, are within the reach
of this extraordinary tribunal. It can regulate or
new model the fucceffion to the crown; as was done
in the reign of Henry VIII. and William III. It can
alter the eftablifhed religion of the land; as was done
in a variety of inftances, in the reigns of king
Henry VIII. and his three children. It can change
and create afrefh even the conftitution of the kingdom and of parliaments themfelves; as was done by
the act of union, and the feveral ftatutes for triennial
and feptennial elections. It can, in fhort, do every
thing that is not naturally impoffible; and therefore
fome have not fcrupled to call it's power, by a figure
rather

rather too bold, the omnipotence of parliament. True it is, that what the parliament doth, no authority upon earth can undo. So that it is a matter most effential to the liberties of this kingdom, that fuch members be delegated to this important truft, as are moft eminent for their probity, their fortitude, and their knowlege; for it was a known apothegm of the great lord treafurer Burleigh, " that England " could never be ruined but by a parliament:" and, as Sir Matthew Hale obferves, this being the higheft and greateft court, over which none other can have jurifdiction in the kingdom, if by any means a mifgovernment fhould any way fall upon it, the fubjects of this kingdom are left without all manner of remedy.

In order to prevent the mifchiefs that might arife, by placing this extenfive authority in hands that are either incapable, or elfe improper, to manage it, it is provided that no one fhall fit or vote in either houfe of parliament, unlefs he be twenty-one years of age. To prevent innovations in religion and government, it is enacted, that no member fhall vote or fit in either houfe, till he hath in the prefence of the houfe taken the oaths of allegiance, fupremacy, and abjuration; and fubfcribed and repeated the declaration againft tranfubftantiation, the invocation of faints, and the facrifice of the mafs. To prevent dangers that may arife to the kingdom from foreign attachments, connexions, or dependencies, it is enacted, that no alien, born out of the dominions of the crown of Great Britain, even though he be naturalized, fhall be capable of being a member of either houfe of parliament.

Some of the more notorious privileges of the members of either houfe are, privilege of fpeech, of perfon, of their domeftics, and of their lands and goods. As to the firft, privilege of fpeech, it is declared by the ftatute of 1 W. & M. ft. 2. c. 2. as one of the liberties of the people, " that the freedom of
" fpeech,

" fpeech, and debates, and proceedings in parlia-
" ment, ought not to be impeached or queftioned in
" any court or place out of parliament." And this
freedom of fpeech is particularly demanded of the
king in perfon, by the fpeaker of the houfe of commons, at the opening of every new parliament. So
likewife are the other privileges, of perfon, fervants,
lands and goods. This includes not only privilege
from illegal violence, but alfo from legal arrefts, and
feifures by procefs from the courts of law. To affault
by violence a member of either houfe, or his menial
fervants, is a high contempt of parliament, and there
punifhed with the utmoft feverity. Neither can any
member of either houfe be arrefted and taken into
cuftody, nor ferved with any procefs of the courts of
law; nor can his menial fervants be arrefted; nor can
any entry be made on his lands; nor can his goods be
diftrained or feized; without a breach of the privilege
of parliament.

Thefe privileges however, which derogate from
the common law, being only indulged to prevent the
members being diverted from the public bufinefs,
endure no longer than the feffion of parliament, fave
only as to the freedom of his perfon: which in a peer
is for ever facred and inviolable; and in a commoner
for forty days after every prorogation, and forty days
before the next appointed meeting; which is now in
effect as long as the parliament fubfifts, it feldom
being prorogued for more than fourfcore days at
a time. As to all other privileges which obftruct the
ordinary courfe of juftice, they ceafe immediately
after the diffolution or prorogation of the parliament,
or adjournment of the houfes for above a fortnight:
and during thefe receffes a peer, or member of the
houfe of commons, may be fued like an ordinary
fubject, and in confequence of fuch fuits may be difpoffeffed of his lands and goods. Likewife, for the
benefit of commerce, it is provided, that any trader,
having privilege of parliament, may be ferved with
legal

legal procefs for any just debt, to the amount of 100 l. and unlefs he makes fatisfaction within two months, it fhall be deemed an act of bankruptcy; and that commiffions of bankrupt may be iffued againft fuch privileged traders, in like manner as againft any other.

The houfe of lords have a right to be attended, and confequently are, by the judges of the court of king's bench and common-pleas, and fuch of the barons of the exchequer as are of the degree of the coif, or have been made ferjeants at law; as likewife by the mafters of the court of chancery; for their advice in point of law, and for the greater dignity of their proceedings.

The fpeaker of the houfe of lords is generally the lord chancellor, or lord-keeper of the great feal, which dignities are commonly vefted in the fame perfon.

Each peer has a right, by leave of the houfe; when a vote paffes contrary to his fentiments, to enter his diffent on the journals of the houfe, with the reafons for fuch diffent; which is ufually ftiled his proteft.

The houfe of commons may be properly ftiled the grand inqueft of Great Britain, impowered to enquire into all national grievances, in order to fee them redreffed.

The peculiar laws and cuftoms of the houfe of commons relate principally to the raifing of taxes, and the elections of members to ferve in parliament.

With regard to taxes: it is the antient indifputable privilege and right of the houfe of commons, that all grants of fubfidies or parliamentary aids do begin in their houfe, and are firft beftowed by them; altho' their grants are not effectual to all intents and purpofes, until they have the affent of the other two branches of the legiflature. The general reafon, given for this exclufive privilege of the houfe of commons, is, that the fupplies are raifed upon the body of the people, and therefore it is proper that they alone should have the right of taxing themselves. And so reasonably jealous are the commons of this privilege, that herein they will not suffer the other house to exert any power but that of rejecting; they will not permit the least alteration or amendment to be made by the lords to the mode of taxing the people by a money bill. Under this appellation are included all bills, by which money is directed to be raised upon the subject, for any purpose or in any shape whatsoever; either for the exigencies of government, and collected from the kingdom in general, as the land tax; or for private benefit, and collected in any particular district, as by turnpikes, parish rates, and the like.

The method of making laws is much the same in both houses. In each house the act of the majority binds the whole: and this majority is declared by votes openly and publicly given: not as at Venice, and many other senatorial assemblies, privately or by ballot. This latter method may be serviceable, to prevent intrigues and unconstitutional combinations: but is impossible to be practised with us; at least in the house of commons, where every member's conduct is subject to the future censure of his constituents, and therefore should be openly submitted to their inspection.

To bring a bill into the house of commons, if the relief sought by it is of a private nature, it is first necessary to prefer a petition; which must be presented by a member, and usually sets forth the grievance desired to be remedied. This petition (when founded on facts that may be in their nature disputed) is referred to a committee of members, who examine the matter alleged, and accordingly report it to the house; and then (or, otherwise, upon the meer petition) leave is given to bring in the bill. In public matters the bill is brought in upon motion made to the house, without any petition. (In the house of lords, if the bill begins there, it is, when of a private nature, referred

to

to two of the judges, to examine and report the state of the facts alleged, to fee that all neceffary parties confent, and to fettle all points of technical propriety.) This is read a firft time, and at a convenient diftance a fecond time; and after each reading the fpeaker opens to the houfe the fubftance of the bill, and puts the queftion, whether it fhall proceed any farther. The introduction of the bill may be originally oppofed, as the bill itfelf may at either of the readings; and, if the oppofition fucceeds, the bill muft be dropt for that feffions; as it muft alfo, if oppofed with fuccefs in any of the fubfequent ftages.

After the fecond reading it is committed, that is, referred to a committee; which is either felected by the houfe in matters of fmall importance, or elfe, upon a bill of confequence, the houfe refolves itfelf into a committee of the whole houfe. A committee of the whole houfe is compofed of every member; and, to form it, the fpeaker quits the chair, (another member being appointed chairman) and may fit and debate as a private member. In thefe committees the bill is debated claufe by claufe, amendments made, the blanks filled up, and fometimes the bill entirely new modelled. After it has gone through the committee, the chairman reports it to the houfe with fuch amendments as the committee have made; and then the houfe reconfider the whole bill again, and the queftion is repeatedly put upon every claufe and amendment. When the houfe have agreed or difagreed to the amendments of the committee, and fometimes added new amendments of their own, the bill is then ordered to be engroffed, or written in a ftrong grofs hand, on one or more long rolls of parchments fewed together. When this is finifhed, it is read a third time, and amendments are fometimes then made to it; and, if a new claufe be added, it is done by tacking a feparate piece of parchment on the bill, which is called a ryder. The fpeaker then again opens the contents; and, holding it up

in

in his hands, puts the question, whether the bill
shall pass. If this is agreed to, the title to it is then
settled. After this, one of the members is directed
to carry it to the lords, and desire their concurrence;
who attended by several more, carries it to the bar
of the house of peers, and there delivers it to their
speaker, who comes down from his woolsack to receive it. It there passes through the forms as in the
other house, (except engrossing, which is already
done) and, if rejected, no more notice is taken, but
it passes *sub silentio*, to prevent unbecoming alterca-
tions. But if it is agreed to, the lords send a message by two masters in chancery (or sometimes two of
the judges) that they have agreed to the same:
and the bill remains with the lords, if they have
made no amendment to it. But if any amendments
are made, such amendments are sent down with the
bill to receive the concurrence of the commons. If
the commons disagree to the amendments, a confe-
rence usually follows between members deputed from
each house; who for the most part settle and adjust
the difference: but, if both houses remain inflexible,
the bill is dropped. If the commons agree to the
amendments, the bill is sent back to the lords by one
of the members, with a message to acquaint them
therewith. The same forms are observed, *mutatis
mutandis*, when the bill begins in the house of lords.
But, when an act of grace or pardon is passed, it is
first signed by his majesty, and then read once only in
each of the houses, without any new engrossing or
amendment. And when both houses have done with
any bill, it always is deposited in the house of peers,
to wait the royal assent; except in the case of a
money-bill. which after receiving the concurrence of
the lords is sent back to the house of commons.

The royal assent may be given two ways: 1. In
person: when the king comes to the house of peers,
in his crown and royal robes, and sending for the
commons to the bar, the titles of all the bills that
have

have paffed both houfes are read; and the king's anfwer is declared by the clerk of the parliament in
Norman-French: a badge, it muft be owned, (now
the only one remaining) of conqueft; and which one
could wifh to fee fall into total oblivion; unlefs it be
referved as a folemn *memento* to remind us that our
liberties are mortal, having once been deftroyed by
a foreign force. If the king confents to a public bill,
the clerk ufually declares, *le roy le veut*, "the king
wills it fo to be;" if to a private bill, *foit fait come il
eft defirè*, "be it as it is defired." If the king refufes
his affent, it is in the gentle language of *le roy f' avi-
fera*, "the king will advife upon it." When a money-
bill is paffed, it is carried up and prefented to the king
by the fpeaker of the houfe of commons, and the
royal affent is thus expreffed, *le roy remercie fes loyal
fubjects, accepte lour benevolence, et auffi le veut*, "the
king thanks his loyal fubjects, accepts their benevolence, and wills it fo to be." In cafe of an act of
grace, which originally proceeds from the crown, and
has the royal affent in the firft ftage of it, the clerk of
the parliament thus pronounces the gratitude of the
fubject; *les prelats, feigneurs, et commons, en ce prefent
parliament affemblees, au nom de touts vous autres fubjects, remercient tres humblement votre majefte, et prient
a Dieu vous donner en fante bone vie et longue*; "the
prelates, lords, and commons, in this prefent parliament affembled, in the name of all your other fubjects, moft humbly thank your majefty, and pray to God
to grant you in health and wealth long to live."
2. By the ftatute 33 Hen. VIII. c. 21. the king may
give his affent by letters patent under his great feal,
figned with his hand, and notified, in his abfence, to
both houfes affembled together in the high houfe.
And, when the bill has received the royal affent in
either of thefe ways, it is then, and not before, a
ftatute or act of parliament.

This ftatute or act is placed among the records of
the kingdom; there needing no forma lpromulgation

C 3   to

to give it the force of a law, as was neceſſary by the
civil law with regard to the emperors edicts : becauſe
every man in England is, in judgment of law, party
to the making of an act of parliament, being preſent
thereat by his repreſentatives.   However, a copy
thereof is uſually printed at the king's preſs, for the
information of the whole land.

An act of parliament, thus made, is the exerciſe of
the higheſt authority that this kingdom acknowleges
upon earth. It hath power to bind every ſubject in
the land, and the dominions thereunto belonging ;
nay, even the king himſelf, if particularly named
therein.   And it cannot be altered, amended, dif-
penſed with, ſuſpended, or repealed, but in the ſame
forms and by the ſame authority of parliament : for
it is a maxim in law, that it requires the ſame ſtrength
to diſſolve, as to create an obligation.

Such is the parliament of Great Britain, the ſource
and guardian of our liberties and properties, the
ſtrong cement which binds the foundation and ſuper-
ſtructure of our government, and the wiſely concerted balance maintaining an equal poiſe, that no one
part of the three eſtates overpower or diſtreſs either
of the other.

Privy counſellors are made by the king's nomina-
tion, without either patent or grant ; and, on taking
the neceſſary oaths, they become immediately privy
counſellors during the life of the king that chooſes
them, but ſubject to removal at his diſcretion.

The duty of a privy counſellor appears from the
oath of office, which conſiſts of ſeven articles : 1. To
adviſe the king according to the beſt of his cunning
and diſcretion.   2. To adviſe for the king's honour
and good of the public, without partiality through
affection, love, meed, doubt, or dread.   3. To keep
the king's counſel ſecret.   4. To avoid corruption.
5. To help and ſtrengthen the execution of what
ſhall be there reſolved   6. To withſtand all perſons
who would attempt the contrary.   And, laſtly, in
                                          general,

general, 7. To obferve, keep, and do all that a good and true counfellor ought to do to his fovereign lord.

The two principal fecretaries of ftate (one of whom is generally prefent whenever the council is held) are entrufted with the cuftody of the king's fignet. They jointly tranfact the king's affairs relating to Great Britain; but as to thofe concerning foreign nations, they are divided between them; the eldeft fecretary having the fouthern province, containing Flanders, France, &c. affigned to his management; and the younger fecretary manages the northern province, containing fuch nations as lie north of thofe already mentioned.

Of the Courts of Law, &c.

The court of Chancery, which is a court of equity, is next in dignity to the high court of parliament, and is defigned to relieve the fubject againft frauds, breaches of truft, and other oppreffions; and to mitigate the rigour of the law. The lord high chancellor fits as fole judge, and in his abfence the mafter of the Rolls. The form of proceeding is by bills, anfwers, and decrees, the witneffes being examined in private: however, the decrees of this court are only binding to the perfons of thofe concerned in them, for they do not affect their lands and goods; and confequently, if a man refufes to comply with the terms, they can do nothing more than fend him to the prifon of the Fleet. This court is always open; and if a man be fent to prifon, the lord chancellor, in any vacation, can, if he fees reafon for it, grant a *babeas corpus*.

The clerk of the crown likewife belongs to this court, being obliged, or by his deputy, always to attend on the lord chancellor as often as he fits for the difpatch of bufinefs; through his hands pafs all writs for fummoning the parliament or chufing of members; commiffions of the peace, pardons, &c.

The King's Bench, fo called either from the kings of England fometimes fitting there in perfon, or be-

C 4

caufe

caufe all matters determinable at common law between
the king and the fubject, are here tried; except
fuch affairs as properly belong to the court of Exchequer. This court is, likewife, a kind of cheque
upon all the inferior courts, their judges and juftices
of the peace. Here prefide four judges, the firft of
whom is ftiled lord chief juftice of the king's bench,
or by way of eminence, lord chief juftice of England, to exprefs the great extent of his jurifdiction
over the kingdom: for this court can grant prohibitions in any caufe depending either in fpiritual or
temporal courts; and the houfe of peers does often
direct the lord chief juftice to iffue out his warrant
for apprehending perfons under the fufpicion of high
crimes. The other three judges are called juftices,
or judges, of the king's bench.

- The court of Common Pleas takes cognizance of
all pleas debateable between fubject and fubject; and
in it, befide all real actions, fines and recoveries are
tranfacted, and prohibitions are likewife iffued out of
it, as well as from the King's Bench. The firft judge
of this court is ftiled lord chief juftice of the common
pleas, or common bench; befide whom there are likewife three other judges, or juftices, of this court. None
but ferjeants at law are allowed to plead here.

The court of Exchequer was inftituted for managing the revenues of the crown, and has a power
of judging both according to law and according to
equity. In the proceedings according to law, the
lord chief baron of the Exchequer, and three other
barons, prefide as judges. They are ftiled barons,
becaufe formerly none but barons of the realm were
allowed to be judges in this court. Befide thefe, there
is a fifth called curfitor baron, who has not a judicial
capacity, but is only employed in adminiftring the
oath to fheriffs and their officers, and alfo to feveral of
the officers of the Cuftom-houfe.—But when this court
proceeds according to equity, then the lord treafurer
and the chancellor of the Exchequer prefide, affifted
by the other barons. All matters touching the king's

treafury, revenue, cuftoms, and fines, are here tried
and determined.——Befide the officers already mentioned, there belong to the Exchequer, the king's
remembrancer, who takes and ftates all accounts of
the revenue, cuftoms, excife, parliamentary aids and
fubfidies, &c. except the accounts of the fheriffs and
their officers. The lord treafurer's remembrancer,
whofe bufinefs it is to make out proceffes againft
fheriffs, receivers of the revenue, &c.

For putting the laws effectually in execution, an
high fheriff is annually appointed for every county
(except Weftmorland and Cumberland) by the king;
whofe office is both minifterial and judicial. He is
to execute the king's mandates, and all writs directed
to him out of the king's courts of juftice; to impan-
nel juries, to bring caufes and malefactors to trial, to
fee the fentences both in civil and criminal affairs,
executed. And at the affize to attend on the judges,
and guard them all the time they are in his county.
It is alfo part of his office to collect all public fines,
diftreffes, and amerciaments, into the Exchequer, or
where the king fhall appoint, and to make fuch pay-
ments out of them as his majefty fhall think proper.

As his office is judicial, he keeps a court, called
the county court, which is held by the fheriff, or his
under-fheriffs, to hear and determine all civil caufes
in the county under forty fhillings; this however is
no court of record; but the court, formerly called
the fheriff's turn, was one; and the king's leet, thro'
all the county: for in this court, enquiry was made
into all criminal offences againft the common law,
where by the ftatute law there was no reftraint. This
court, however, has been long fince abolifhed.

Under the fheriff are various officers, as the under-
fheriff, clerks, ftewards of courts, bailiffs, (in London called ferjeants) conftables, gaolers, beadles, &c.

The next officer to the fheriff, is the juftice of
peace, feveral of whom are commiffioned for each
county: and to them is intrufted the power of putting great part of the ftatute law in execution in relation

tion to the highways, the poor, vagrants, treasons, felonies, riots, the prefervation of the game, &c. &c. and they examine and commit to prifon all who break or difturb the peace, and difquiet the king's fubjects. In order to punish the offenders, they meet every quarter at the county-town, when a jury of 12 men, called the grand inqueft of the county, is fummoned to appear. This jury, upon oath, is to enquire into the cafes of all delinquents, and to prefent them by bill guilty of the indictment, or not guilty: the juftices commit the former to gaol for their trial at the next affizes, and the latter are acquitted. This is called the quarter-feffions for the county. The juftice of peace ought to be a perfon of great good fenfe, fagacity, and integrity, and to be not without fome knowlege of the law; for as much power is lodged in his hands, and as nothing is fo intoxicating, without thefe qualifications he will be apt to make miftakes, and to ftep beyond his authority, for which he is liable to be called to an account at the court of king's bench.

There are alfo in each county two coroners, who are to enquire by a jury of neighbours, how and by whom any perfon came by a violent death, and to enter it on record as a plea of the crown.

The civil government of cities is a kind of fmall independent policy of itfelf; for every city hath, by charter from the king, a jurifdiction within itfelf to judge in all matters civil and criminal; with this reftraint only, that all civil caufes may be removed from their courts to the higher courts at Weftminfter; and all offences that are capital, are committed to the judge of the affize. They are conftituted with a mayor, aldermen, and burgeffes, who together make the corporation of the city, and hold a court of judicature, where the mayor prefides as judge. They likewife, when affembled in council, can make laws, called bye-laws, for the government of the city. And here the mayor, aldermen, and common-council refemble the king, lords and commons in parliament.

The

The government of incorporated boroughs is much after the fame manner; in fome there is a mayor, and in others two bailiffs. All which, during their mayoralty or magiftracy, are juftices of the peace within their liberties, and confequently efquires.

For the better government of villages, the lords of the foil or manor (who were formerly called barons) have generally a power to hold courts, called courts-leet, and courts baron, where their tenants are obliged to attend and receive juftice. The bufinefs of courts-leet is chiefly to prefent and punifh nuifances; and at courts baron, the conveyances and alienations of the copyhold tenants are enrolled, and they are admitted to their eftates on a defcent or purchafe.

There are alfo high conftables appointed for the divifions called hundreds, and petty conftables in every parifh; whofe bufinefs it is to keep the peace, and in cafe of quarrels to fearch for and take up all rioters, felons, &c. and to keep them in the prifon or in fafe cuftody, till they can be brought before a juftice of the peace; and in this he is affifted by another officer, called the tithing-man. It is likewife the bufinefs of thefe officers to put in execution within their diftrict, all warrants that are brought them from the juftice of the peace.

Befide thefe, there are courts of confcience fettled in many parts of England for the relief of the poor, in the recovery or payment of fmall debts, not exceeding forty fhillings.

The rights of individuals are fo attentively confidered under the Britifh government, that the fubject may, without the leaft danger, fue his fovereign, or thofe who act in his name, and under his authority; he may do this in open court, where the king may be caft, and be obliged to pay damages to his fubject. He cannot take away the liberty of the leaft individual, unlefs he has by fome illegal act forfeited his right to liberty, or except when the ftate is in danger, and the reprefentatives of the people think the public

safety

safety makes it neceffary that he fhould have the
power of confining perfons, on a fufpicion of guilt:
but this power is always given him only for a limited
time.   The king has a right to pardon, but neither
he nor the judges, to whom he delegates his authority, can condemn a man as a criminal, except he be
firft found guilty, by twelve men, who muft be his
peers or his equals.   That the judges may not be influenced by the king, or his minifters, to mifrepre-
fent the cafe to the jury, they have their falaries for
life, and not during the pleafure of their fovereign.
Neither can the king take away, or endanger the life
of any fubject, without trial, and the perfons being
firft chargeable with a capital crime, as treafons, murder, felony, or fome other act injurious to fociety:
nor can any fubject be deprived of his liberty for the
higheft crime, till fome proof of his guilt be given
upon oath before a magiftrate; and he has then a
right to infift upon his being brought, the firft opportunity, to a fair trial, or to be reftored to liberty
on giving bail for his appearance. If a man is charged
with a capital offence, he muft not undergo the ignominy of being tried for his life, till the evidences
of his guilt are laid before the grand jury of the
town or county in which the fact is alleged to be
committed, and not without twelve of them agreeing
to a bill of indictment againft him.   If they do this,
he is to ftand a fecond trial before twelve other men,
whofe opinion is definitive. In fome cafes, the man
(who is always fuppofed innocent till there is fufficient proof of his guilt) is allowed a copy of his indictment, in order to help him to make his defence. He
is alfo furnifhed with the pannel, or lift of the jury,
who are his true and proper judges, that he may learn
their characters, and difcover whether they want
abilities, or whether they are prejudiced againft him.
He may in open court peremptorily object to twenty
of the number *, and to as many more as he can give

---

* The party may challenge thirty-five in cafe of treafon.

reafon for their not being admitted as his judges; till
at laft twelve unexceptionable men, the neighbours
of the party accufed, or living near the place where
the fuppofed fact was committed, are fworn, to give
a true verdict according to the evidence produced in
court. By challenging the jury, the prifoner prevents
all poffibility of bribery, or the influence of any fuperior power: by their living near the place where
the fact was committed, they are fuppofed to be men
who know the prifoner's courfe of life, and the credit of the evidence. Thefe only are the judges,
from whofe fentence the prifoner is to expect life or
death, and upon their integrity and underftanding,
the lives of all that are brought in danger ultimately
depend; and from their judgment there lies no appeal: they are therefore to be all of one mind, and
after they have fully heard the evidence, are to be
confined without meat, drink, or candle, till they
are unanimous in acquitting or condemning the prifoner. Every juryman is therefore invefted with a folemn and awful truft: if he without evidence fubmits
his opinion to that of any of the other jury, or yields
in complaifance to the opinion of the judge; if he
neglects to examine with the utmoft care; if he quef-
tions the veracity of the witneffes, who may be of an
infamous character; or after the moft impartial hearing has the leaft doubt upon his mind, and yet joins
in condemning the perfon accufed; he will wound his
own confcience, and bring upon himfelf the compli-
cated guilt of perjury and murder. The freedom of
Englifhmen confifts in its being out of the power of
the judge * on the bench to injure them, for declaring

* " Some jurymen, fays Mr. Clare, in his Fnglifh Liberties,
" may be apt to fay, that if we could not find as the judge directs,
" we may come into trouble, the judge may fine us, &c.. I an-
" fwer, no judge dares offer any fuch thing; you are the proper
" judges of the matters before you, and your fouls are at ftake;
" you ought to act freely, and are not bound, though the court de-
" mand

ing a man innocent, whom he wishes to be brought in
guilty. Was not this the case, juries would be useless;
so far from being judges themselves, they would only
be the tools of another, whose province it is not to
guide, but to give a sanction to their determination. Tyranny might triumph over the lives and liberties of the subject, and the judge on the bench
be the minister of the prince's vengeance.

These are the glorious privileges which we enjoy
above any other nation upon earth. Juries have always been considered as giving the most effectual
check to tyranny; for in a nation like this, where a
king can do nothing against law, they are a security
that he shall never make the laws, by a bad administration, the instruments of cruelty and oppression.
Was it not for juries, the advice given by father
Paul, in his maxims of the republic of Venice, might
take effect in its fullest latitude. " When the offence
" is committed by a nobleman against a subject, says
" he, let all ways be tried to justify him; and if that
" is not possible to be done, let him be chastised with
" greater noise than damage. If it be a subject that
" has affronted a nobleman, let him be punished with
" the utmost severity, that the subject may not get
" too great a custom of laying their hands on the
" patrician order." In short, was it not for juries,

" mand it, to give the reason why you bring it in thus or thus; for
" you of the grand jury are sworn to the contrary, viz. to keep
" secret your fellows counsel and your own; and you of the petty
" jury are no way obliged to declare your motives, for it may not
' be convenient. In queen Elizabeth's days, a man was arraigned
" for murder before justice Anderson; the evidence was so strong,
" that eleven of the twelve were presently for finding him guilty,
" the twelfth man refused, and kept them so long that they were
" ready to starve, and at last made them comply with him, and
" bring in the prisoner not guilty. The judge, who had seve-
" ral times admonished him to join with his fellows, being surpris-
" ed, sent for him, and discoursed him privately; to whom, upon
" promise of indemnity, he at last owned, that he himself was the
" man that did the murder, and the prisoner was innocent, and
" that he was resolved not to add perjury, and a second murder to
" the first."

a corrupt nobleman might, whenever he pleafed, act the tyrant, while the judge would have that power which is now denied to our kings. But by our happy conftitution, which breathes nothing but liberty and equity, all imaginary indulgence is allowed to the meaneft, as well as the greateft. When a prifoner is brought to take his trial, he is freed from all bonds; and though the judges are fuppofed to be counfel for the prifoner, yet, as he may be incapable of vindicating his own caufe, other counfel are allowed him; he may try the validity and legality of the indict-ment, and may fet it afide, if it be contrary to law. Nothing is wanting to clear up the caufe of innocence, and to prevent the fufferer from finking under the power of corrupt judges, and the oppreffion of the great. The racks and tortures that are cruelly made ufe of in other parts of Europe, to make a man accufe himfelf, are here unknown, and none punifhed without conviction, but he who refufes to plead in his own defence.

As the trial of malefactors in England is very different from that of other nations, the following account thereof may be ufeful to foreigners and others, who have not feen thofe proceedings.

The court being met, and the prifoner called to the bar, the clerk commands him to hold up his hand, then charges him with the crime of which he is accufed, and afks him whether he is *guilty* or *not guilty*. If the prifoner anfwers *guilty*, his trial is at an end; but if he anfwers *not guilty*, the court proceeds on the trial, even tho' he may before have confeffed the fact: for the law of England takes no notice of fuch confeffion; and unlefs the witneffes, who are upon oath, prove him guilty of the crime, the jury muft acquit him, for they are directed to bring in their verdict according to the evidence given in court. If the prifoner refufes to plead, that is, if he will not fay in court, whether he is *guilty* or *not guilty*, he is by the law of England to be preffed to death.

When

When the witnesses have given in their evidence, and the prisoner has, by himself or his counsel, cross examined them, the judge recites to the jury the substance of the evidence given against the prisoner, and bids them discharge their conscience; when, if the matter be very clear, they commonly give their verdict without going out of court; and the foreman, for himself and the rest, declares the prisoner *guilty*, or *not guilty*, as it may happen to be. But if any doubt arises among the jury, and the matter requires debate, they all withdraw into a room with a copy of the indictment, where they are locked up, till they are unanimously agreed on the verdict; and if any one of the jury should die during this their confinement, the prisoner will be acquitted.

When the jury have agreed on the verdict, they inform the court thereof by an officer who waits without, and the prisoner is again set to the bar, to hear his verdict. This is unalterable, except in some doubtful cases, when the verdict is brought in special, and is therefore to be determined by the twelve judges of England.

If the prisoner is found guilty, he is then asked what reason he can give why sentence of death should not be passed upon him? If it be the first fault, and his offence be within the statute made for that purpose, he may demand the benefit of the clergy, which saves his life, and he will be only burnt in the hand. But where the benefit of the clergy is not admitted, the sentence of death, after a summary account of the trial, is pronounced on the prisoner, in these words: *The law is, That thou shalt return to the place from whence thou camest, and from thence be carried to the place of execution, where thou shalt hang by the neck, till thy body be dead, and the Lord have mercy on thy soul:* whereupon the sheriff is charged with the execution.

All prisoners found *not guilty* by the jury, are immediately acquitted and discharged, and in some cases obtain a copy of their indictment from the court to proceed at law against their prosecutors.

Of

Of Punishments.

Though the laws of England are esteemed more merciful, with respect to offenders, than those which at present subsist in any other part of the known world; yet the punishment of such who at their trial refuse to plead guilty or not guilty, is here very cruel. In this case the prisoner is laid upon his back, and his arms and legs being stretched out with cords, and a considerable weight laid upon his breast, he is allowed only three morsels of barley bread, which is given him the next day without drink, after which he is allowed nothing but foul water till he expires. This, however, is a punishment which is scarcely inflicted once in an age; but some offenders have chose it to preserve their estates for their children. Those guilty of this crime are not now suffered to undergo such a length of torture, but have so great a weight placed upon them, that they soon expire. In case of high treason, though the criminal stands mute, judgment is given against him as if he had been convicted, and his estate is confiscated.

The law of England includes all capital crimes under high treason, petty treason, and felony. The first consists in plotting, conspiring, or rising up in arms against the sovereign, or in counterfeiting the coin. The traitor is punished by being drawn on a sledge to the place of execution, when, after being hanged upon a gallows for some minutes, the body is cut down alive, the heart taken out and exposed to public view, and the entrails burnt: the head is then cut off, and the body quartered, after which the head is usually fixed on some conspicuous place. All the criminal's lands and goods are forfeited, his wife loses her dowry, and his children both their estates and nobility.

But though coining of money is adjudged high treason, the criminal is only drawn upon a sledge to the place of execution, and there hanged.

Vol. VII.   D   Though

. Though the fentence paffed upon all traitors is the fame, yet with refpect to perfons of quality, the punifhment is generally altered to beheading : a fcaffold is erected for that purpofe, on which the criminal placing his head upon a block, it is ftruck off with an axe *.

The punifhment for mifprifion of high treafon, that is, for neglecting or concealing it, is imprifonment for life, the forfeiture of all the offender's goods, and of the profits arifing from his lands.

Petty treafon is when a child kills his father, a wife her hufband, a clergyman his bifhop, or a fervant his mafter or miftrefs. This crime is punifhed by being drawn in a fledge to the place of execution, and there hanged upon a gallows till the criminal is dead. Women guilty both of this crime, and of high treafon, are fentenced to be burnt alive, but inftead of fuffering the full rigour of the law, they are ftrangled at the ftake before the fire takes hold of them.

Felony includes murders, robberies, forging notes, bonds, deeds, &c. Thefe are all punifhed by hanging, only murderers are to be executed foon after the fentence is paffed ; and then delivered to the furgeons in order to be publicly diffected. Perfons guilty of robbery, when there are fome alleviating circumftances, are fometimes tranfported for a term of years to his majefty's plantations. And in all fuch felonies where the benefit of the clergy is allowed, as it is in many, the criminal is burnt in the hand with a hot iron.

Other crimes punifhed by the laws are,

Manflaughter, which is the unlawful killing of a perfon without premeditated malice, but with a prefent intent to kill ; as when two who formerly meant no harm to each other, quarrel, and the one kills the

---

* This is not to be confidered as a different punifhment; but as a remiffion of all the parts of the fentence mentioned before, excepting the article of beheading.

other.

other; in this cafe, the criminal is allowed the benefit of his clergy for the firft time, and only burnt in the hand.

Chance-medley, is the accidental killing of a man without an evil intent, for which the offender is alfo to be burnt in the hand; unlefs the offender was doing an unlawful act, which laft circumftance makes the punifhment death.

Shop-lifting, and receiving goods knowing them to be ftolen, are punifhed with tranfportation to his majefty's colonies, or burning in the hand.

Perjury, or keeping diforderly houfes, are punifhed with the pillory and imprifonment.

Petty-larceny, or fmall theft, under the value of twelve-pence, is punifhed by whipping.

Libelling, ufing falfe weights and meafures, and foreftalling the market, are commonly punifhed with ftanding on the pillory, or whipping.

For ftriking, fo as to draw blood, in the king's court, the criminal is punifhed with lofing his right-hand.

For ftriking in Weftminfter-hall while the courts of juftice are fitting, is imprifonment for life, and forfeiture of all the offender's eftate.

Drunkards, vagabonds, and loofe, idle, diforderly perfons, are punifhed by being fet in the ftocks, or by paying a fine.

Of the Religion of England.

Chriftianity was very early planted in England, but when, or by whom, is very uncertain; probably in the latter end of the firft, or the beginning of the fecond century. The reformation in England, begun in the reign of Henry VIII. was greatly promoted under his fon Edward VI. It was, however, checked by queen Mary, but compleated by queen Elizabeth. This reformation being conducted by the bifhops, the eftablifhed church of England became Epifcopal.

Calvin

Calvin indeed ufed many endeavours to obtain a fhare in the advancement and direction of this ecclefiaftical reformation ; but being defirous of depriving the bifhops of their temporal grandeur, of banifhing all external ornaments and pomp from divine worfhip, and introducing the Genevan conftitution ; the bifhops declined his offers of affiftance. Many, however, approving of Calvin's doctrine, formed an ecclefiaftical government on his plan. Thefe were afterward termed Puritans, from their avowed defire of freeing the church from the impurities ftill retained in it, and Nonconformifts, from their not conforming to the rules of the eftablifhed church. Agreeably to Calvin's model, they inftituted prefbyters without bifhops, from whence they obtained the name of Prefbyterians ; inftituting alfo church-laws among themfelves, and being governed by fynods compofed of the minifters of feveral different churches. Others maintaining, that every Chriftian congregation ought to be free, and fubject neither to bifhops nor fynods, thefe were termed Independents.

The Epifcopalians and Prefbyterians are the two principal parties, and differ the leaft from each other ; the firft form the eftablifhed religion of England and Ireland, and the latter of Scotland. The moft numerous of the other religious fects are the Baptifts, who do not believe that infants are the proper fubjects of baptifm, and in the baptifm of adults practife immerfion. It is here proper to obferve, that the Englifh Prefbyterians differ almoft as much from the church of Scotland, as from the church of England ; fynods growing gradually out of ufe, each feparate congregation is become, in a manner, independent of the reft : they have moft of them forfaken the opinions of Calvin, and believing univerfal redemption, maintain that the univerfal Parent has excluded none of his offspring from a poffibility of falvation ; while the Independents, and many congregations of the Baptifts, agree with the church of Scotland

Scotland in the doctrines of particular election and reprobation. It must also be added, that the presbyterians, with the church of England, receive the facrament of the Lord's fupper at noon, while the Independents and Baptifts receive it after the conclufion of the afternoon fervice.

One of the principal of the other fects is the Quakers, who profefs to be guided by an internal revelation dictated by the Spirit of God : they have no regular minifters, and neither practife baptifm, nor commemorate the death of Chrift in the Lord's Supper.

The Methodifts have lately arifen, and now form a very numerous body ; moft of them are alfo members of the church of England, and profefs to adhere more clofely than the other members of that church to the thirty-nine articles ; and the greateft part of them are rigid Calvinifts.

The number of Papifts here is alfo very confiderable, particularly in Lancafhire, Staffordfhire, and Suffex.

Many authors have exclaimed, with great heat, of the many fects in England ; but let it be confidered, that civil and religious liberty are clofely connected ; and that it does not become any church, who makes no pretenfions to infallibility, to fet up the ftandard of perfecution.

But to return : the church of England is under the government of two archbifhops and twenty-five bifhops, who are fubject to the king as fupream temporal head of the church. The archbifhop of Canterbury is ftiled the firft peer and metropolitan of the kingdom ; he takes place immediately after the royal family, and confequently precedes not only all dukes, but likewife the great officers of ftate. In addreſies to him he enjoys the title of Your grace, in common with dukes, and alfo that of moft reverend father in God. He has the power of holding juridical courts in church affairs, with many other privileges relating to the granting of licenfes and difpenfations, in all

D 3 cafes

cases formerly sued for at the court of Rome, where they are not repugnant to the law of God, or the king's prerogative. He has also within his province, by common law, the probate of all wills, where the party dying is worth upward of five pounds. He has under him twenty-one bishops, beside his own particular diocese; these are the bishops of London, Winchester, Ely, Lincoln, Rochester, Litchfield and Coventry, Hereford, Worcester, Bath and Wells, Salisbury, Exeter, Chichester, Norwich, Gloucester, Oxford, Peterborough, Bristol; and in Wales, St. David's, Landaff, St. Asaph, and Bangor.

The archbishop of York likewise takes the precedence of all dukes who are not of the blood royal; as also of all the great officers of state, excepting the lord chancellor, who is immediately next in rank to the archbishop of Canterbury. In his diocese he is stiled primate of England and metropolitan; he also enjoys the title of his grace, and most reverend father in God. Exclusive of his own diocese, in his province are Durham, Carlisle, Chester, and Sodor and Man. In Northumberland he has the power of a palatine, and jurisdiction in all criminal proceedings.

The twenty-five bishops are stiled right reverend, and your lordship; all these walk next after the viscounts, and precede the barons. In parliament they sit in a double capacity, as bishops and barons; they also enjoy many other privileges, as freedom from arrests, outlawries, &c. They live in great state; their revenues are also considerable; but where the income is not very large, some other lucrative preferment, as a deanry, is generally annexed to it.

The business of a bishop is to examine and ordain priests and deacons, to consecrate churches and burying-places, and to administer the rite of consecration. The jurisdiction of a bishop relates to the probation of wills; he is to grant administration of goods to such as die intestate; to take care of perishable
able

5

able goods, when no one will adminifter; to collate to benefices; to grant inftitutions to livings; to defend the liberties of the church; and to vifit his own diocefe once in three years.

Next to the bifhops are the deans and prebends of cathedrals, out of whom the bifhops are chofen. After thefe are the archdeacons, of which every diocefe has one or more, the whole number in the kingdom of England amounting to fixty. Their office is to vifit the churches twice or thrice every year. The archdeacons are followed by the rural deans, who were formerly ftiled archi-prefbyters, and fignify the bifhop's pleafure to his clergy, the lower clafs of which confifts of priefts and deacons.

With refpect to the ecclefiaftical government and courts, it is proper to obferve, that the principal part of the ecclefiaftical government was formerly lodged in the convocation, which is a national fynod of the clergy, affembled to confider of the ftate of the church, and to call thofe to an account who have advanced new opinions, inconfiftent with the doctrines of the church of England: but in the reign of his late majefty, they being thought to proceed with too much heat and feverity againft fome learned divines, and to be too great a check upon free inquiry, they have not been permitted to fit for any long time fince. However, they are affembled at the fame time with the parliament, by the authority of the king, who directs his writs to the archbifhop of each province to fummon all bifhops, deans, archdeacons, &c. to meet at a certain time and place.

The court of arches is the moft ancient confiftory of the province of Canterbury, and all appeals in church matters, from the judgment of the inferior courts, are directed to this. The proceffes run in the name of the judge, who is called dean of the arches; and the advocates who plead in this court muft be doctors of the civil law. The court of audience has the fame authority with this, to which the

D 4 archbifhop's

archbifhop's chancery was formerly joined. The prerogative court is that wherein wills are proved, and adminiftrations taken out. The court of peculiars, relating to certain parifhes, have a jurifdiction among themfelves for the probate of wills, and are therefore exempt from the bifhop's courts. The fee of Canterbury has no lefs than fifteen of thefe peculiars. The court of delegates receives its name from its confifting of commoners, delegated or appointed by the royal commiffion ; but it is no ftanding court. Every bifhop has alfo a court of his own, called the confiftory court. Every archdeacon has likewife his court, as well as the dean and chapter of every cathedral.

Of the Revenues of the Britifh Government.

The king's ecclefiaftical revenue confifts in, 1. The cuftody of the temporalities of vacant bifhoprics. 2. Corodies and penfions. 3. Extra-parochial tithes. 4. The firft fruits and tenths of benefices.

The king's ordinary temporal revenue confifts in, 1. The demefne lands of the crown. 2. The hereditary excife ; being part of the confideration for the purchafe of his feodal profits, and the prerogatives of purveyance and pre-emption. 3. An annual fum iffuing from the duty on wine licences ; being the refidue of the fame confideration. 4. His forefts. 5. His courts of juftice, &c.

The extraordinary grants are ufually called by the fynonimous names of aids, fubfidies, and fupplies ; and are granted, as has been before hinted, by the commons of Great Britain, in parliament affembled : who, when they have voted a fupply to his majefty, and fettled the *quantum* of that fupply, ufually refolve themfelves into what is called a committee of ways and means, to confider of the ways and means of raifing the fupply fo voted. And in this committee every member (though it is looked upon as the peculiar

culiar province of the chancellor of the exchequer) may propofe fuch fcheme of taxation as he thinks will be leaft detrimental to the public. The refolutions of this committee (when approved by a vote of the houfe) are in general efteemed to be (as it were) final and conclufive. For, though the fupply cannot be actually raifed upon the fubject till directed by an act of the whole parliament, yet no monied man will fcruple to advance to the government any quantity of ready cafh, on the credit of a bare vote of the houfe of commons, though no law be yet paffed to eftablifh it.

The annual taxes are, 1. The land tax, or the antient fubfidy raifed upon a new affeffment. 2. The malt tax, being an annual excife on malt, mum, cyder, and perry.

The perpetual taxes are, 1. The cuftoms, or tonnage and poundage of all merchandize exported or imported. 2. The excife duty, or inland impofition, on a great variety of commodities. 3. The falt duty. 4. The * poft office, or duty for the carriage of letters. 5. The ftamp duty on paper, parchment, &c. 6. The duty on houfes and windows. 7. The duty on licences for hackney coaches and chairs. 8. The duty on offices and penfions.

The clear neat produce of thefe feveral branches of the revenue, after all charges of collecting and management paid, amounts annually to about feven millions and three quarters fterling; befide two millions and a quarter raifed annually, at an average, by the land and malt tax. How thefe immenfe fums are appropriated, is next to be confidered. And this is, firft and principally, to the payment of the intereft of the national debt.

In order to take a clear and comprehenfive view of the nature of this national debt, it muft firft be

* From the years 1715 to 1763, the annual amount of franked letters gradually increafed from 23,000 l. to 170,700 l.

premifed,

premifed, that after the revolution, when our new connections with Europe introduced a new fyftem of foreign politics; the expences of the nation, not only in
fettling the new eftablifhment, but in maintaining
long wars, as principals, on the continent, for the fecurity of the Dutch barrier, reducing the French monarchy, fettling the Spanifh fucceffion, fupporting
the houfe of Auftria, maintaining the liberties of the
Germanic body, and other purpofes, increafed to an
unufual degree: infomuch that it was not thought
advifeable to raife all the expences of any one year
by taxes to be levied within that year, left the un-
accuftomed weight of them fhould create murmurs
among the people. It was therefore the policy of
the times, to anticipate the revenues of their pofterity, by borrowing immenfe fums for the current fervice of the ftate, and to lay no more taxes upon the
fubject than would fuffice to pay the annual intereft
of the fums fo borrowed: by this means converting
the principal debt into a new fpecies of property,
transferable from one man to another at any time
and in any quantity. A fyftem which feems to have
had its original in the ftate of Florence, *A. D.* 1344:
which government then owed about 60,000 l. fterling: and, being unable to pay it, formed the principal into an aggregate fum, called metaphorically
a mount or bank; the fhares whereof were transferable like our ftocks. This laid the foundation of what is called the national debt: for a
few long annuities created in the reign of Charles II.
will hardly deferve that name. And the example
then fet has been fo clofely followed, during the
long wars in the reign of queen Anne, and fince;
that the capital of the national debt (funded and
unfunded) amounted in January 1765, to upward
of 145,000,000 l. to pay the intereft of which, and
the charges for management, amounting annually
to about four millions and three quarters, the extraordinary revenues juft now enumerated (excepting
only

only the land-tax and annual malt-tax) are in the firft place mortgaged, and made perpetual by parliament; but ftill redeemable by the fame authority that impofed them: which, if it at any time can pay off the capital, will abolifh thofe taxes which are raifed to difcharge the intereft.

It is indifputably certain, that the prefent magnitude of our national incumbrances very far exceeds all calculations of commercial benefit, and is productive of the greateft inconveniencies. For, firft, the enormous taxes that are raifed upon the neceffaries of life for the payment of the intereft of this debt, are a hurt both to trade and manufactures; by raifing the price, as well of the artificer's fubfiftence, as of the raw material, and of courfe, in a much greater proportion, the price of the commodity itfelf. Secondly, if part of this debt be owing to foreigners, either they draw out of the kingdom annually a confiderable quantity of fpecie for the intereft; or elfe it is made an argument to grant them unreafonable privileges, in order to induce them to refide here. Thirdly, if the whole be owing to fubjects only, it is then charging the active and induftrious fubject, who pays his fhare of the taxes, to maintain the indolent and idle creditor who receives them. Laftly, and principally, it weakens the internal ftrength of a ftate, by anticipating thofe refources which fhould be referved to defend it in cafe of neceffity. The intereft we now pay for our debts would be nearly fufficient to maintain any war, that any national motives could require. And if our anceftors in king William's time had annually paid, fo long as their exigencies lafted, even a lefs fum than we now annually raife upon their accounts, they would, in time of war, have borne no greater burdens than they have bequeathed to, and fettled upon, their pofterity in time of peace; and might have been eafed the inftant the exigence was over.

The

The produce of the several taxes before-mentioned were originally separate and distinct funds; being securities for the sums advanced on each several tax, and for them only. But at last it became necessary, in order to avoid confusion, as they multiplied yearly, to reduce the number of these separate funds, by uniting and blending them together; superadding the faith of parliament for the general security of the whole. So that there are now only three capital funds of any account: the aggregate fund, and the general fund, so called from such union and addition; and the South Sea fund, being the produce of the taxes appropriated to pay the interest of such part of the national debt as was advanced by that company and its annuitants. Whereby the separate funds, which were thus united, are become mutual securities for each other; and the whole produce of them, thus aggregated, liable to pay such interest or annuities as were formerly charged upon each distinct fund; the faith of the legislature being moreover engaged to supply any casual deficiencies.

The customs, excises, and other taxes, which are to support these funds, depending on contingencies, upon exports, imports, and consumptions, must necessarily be of a very uncertain amount: but they have always been considerably more than was sufficient to answer the charge upon them. The surplusses therefore of the three great national funds, the aggregate, general, and South Sea funds, over and above the interest and annuities charged upon them, are directed by statute 3 Geo. I. c. 7. to be carried together, and to attend the disposition of parliament; and are usually denominated the sinking fund, because originally destined to sink and lower the national debt. To this have been since added many other intire duties, granted in subsequent years; and the annual interest of the sums borrowed on their respective credits, is charged on, and payable out of the produce of the sinking fund. However the neat
surplusses

furpluffes and favings, after all deductions paid, amount annually to a very confiderable fum ; particularly in the year ending at Chriftmas 1764, to about two millions and a quarter. For, as the intereft on the national debt has been at feveral times reduced, (by the confent of the proprietors, who had their option either to lower their intereft, or be paid their principal) the favings from the appropriated revenues muft needs be extreamly large. This finking fund is the laft refort of the nation ; its only domeftic refource, on which muft chiefly depend all the hopes we can entertain of ever difcharging or moderating our incumbrances. And therefore the prudent application of the large fums, now arifing from this fund, is a point of the utmoft importance, and well worthy the ferious attention of parliament; which was thereby enabled, in the year 1765, to reduce above two millions fterling of the public debt.

But, before any part of the aggregate fund (the furpluffes whereof are one of the chief ingredients that form the finking fund) can be applied to diminifh the principal of the public debt, it ftands mortgaged by parliament to raife an annual fum for the maintenance of the king's houfhold and the civil lift. For this purpofe, in the late reigns, the produce of certain branches of the excife and cuftoms, the poft-office, the duty on wine licences, the revenues of the remaining crown lands, the profits arifing from courts of juftice, (which articles include all the hereditary revenues of the crown) and alfo a clear annuity of 120,000 l. in money, were fettled on the king for life, for the fupport of his majefty's houfhold, and the honour and dignity of the crown. And, as the amount of thefe feveral branches was uncertain, (though in the laft reign they were computed to have fometimes raifed almoft a million) if they did not arife annually to 800,coo l. the parliament engaged to make up the deficiency. But his prefent majefty having, foon after his acceffion, fpontaneoufly

taneoufly fignified his confent, that his own hereditary revenues might be fo difpofed of, as might beft
conduce to the utility and fatisfaction of the public;
and having gracioufly accepted the limited fum of
800,000 l. *per annum*, for the fupport of his civil lift,
(and that alfo charged with three life annuities, to
the princefs of Wales, the duke of Cumberland, and
princefs Amelia, to the amount of 77,000 l.) the
faid hereditary, and other revenues, are now carried
into, and made a part of, the aggregate fund; and
the aggregate fund is charged with the payment of
the whole annuity to the crown of 800,000 l. *per
annum*. Hereby the revenues themfelves, being put
under the fame care and management as the other
branches of the public patrimony, will produce more,
and be better collected than heretofore; and the public is a gainer of upward of 100,000 l. *per annum*, by
this difinterefted bounty of his majefty. The civil lift,
thus liquidated, together with the four millions and
three quarters, intereft of the national debt, and the
two millions and a quarter produced from the finking fund, make up the feven millions and three quarters *per annum*, neat money, which were before ftated
to be the annual produce of our perpetual taxes : befide the immenfe, though uncertain fums, arifing
from the annual taxes on land and malt, but which, at
an average, may be calculated at more than two millions and a quarter; and which, added to the preceding
fum, make the clear produce of the taxes, exclufive
of the charge of collecting, which are raifed yearly
on the people of this country, amount to upward of
ten millions fterling.

The expences defrayed by the civil lift are thofe
that in any fhape relate to civil government; as the
expences of the houfhold, all falaries to officers of
ftate, to the judges, and every of the king's fervants;
the appointments to foreign ambaffadors, the maintenance of the queen and royal family, the king's private expences, or privy purfe, and other very nume-

rous outgoings; as secret service-money, pensions, and other-bounties. These sometimes have so far exceeded the revenues appointed for that purpose, that application has been made to parliament, to discharge the debts contracted on the civil list; as particularly in 1724, when one million was granted for that purpose by the statute 11 Geo. I. c. 17.

The civil list is indeed properly the whole of the king's revenue in his own distinct capacity; the rest being rather the revenue of the public, or its creditors, though collected, and distributed again, in the name, and by the officers of the crown; it now standing in the same place, as the hereditary income did formerly; and, as that has gradually diminished, the parliamentary appointments have encreased.

Of the Military and Marine strength of Great Britain.

The military state includes the whole of the soldiery; or, such persons as are peculiarly appointed among the rest of the people, for the safeguard and defence of the realm.

In a land of liberty it is extreamly dangerous to make a distinct order of the profession of arms. In such, no man should take up arms, but with a view to defend his country and its laws: he puts not off the citizen when he enters the camp; but it is because he is a citizen, and would wish to continue so, that he makes himself for a while a soldier. The laws therefore, and constitution of these kingdoms know no such state as that of a perpetual standing soldier, bred up to no other profession than that of war: and it was not till the reign of Henry VII. that the kings of England had so much as a guard about their persons.

It seems universally agreed by all historians, that king Alfred first settled a national militia in this kingdom, and by his prudent discipline, made all the subjects of his dominions soldiers.

In

In the mean time we are not to imagine that the kingdom was left wholly without defence, in cafe of domeftic infurrections, or the profpect of foreign invafions. Befide thofe, who by their military tenures, were bound to perform forty days fervice in the field, the ftatute of Winchefter obliged every man, according to his eftate and degree, to provide a determinate quantity of fuch arms as were then in ufe, in order to keep the peace : and conftables were appointed in all hundreds, to fee that fuch arms were provided. Thefe weapons were changed by the ftatute 4 and 5 Ph. and M. c. 2. into others of more modern fervice ; but both this and the former provifion were repealed in the reign of James I. While thefe continued in force, it was ufual from time to time, for our princes to iffue commiffions of array, and fend into every county officers in whom they could confide, to mufter and array (or fet in military order) the inhabitants of every diftrict : and the form of the commiffion of array was fettled in parliament in the 5 Hen. IV. But at the fame time it was provided, that no man fhould be compelled to go out of the kingdom at any rate, nor out of his fhire, but in cafes of urgent neceffity ; nor fhould provide foldiers unlefs by confent of parliament. About the reign of king Henry VIII. and his children, lord lieutenants began to be introduced, as ftanding reprefentatives of the crown, to keep the counties in military order ; for we find them mentioned as known officers in the ftatute 4 and 5 Ph. and M. c. 3. though they had not been then long in ufe ; for Camden fpeaks of them in the time of queen Elizabeth, as extraordinary magiftrates, conftituted only in times of difficulty and danger.

Soon after the reftoration of king Charles II. when the military tenures were abolifhed, it was thought proper to afcertain the power of the militia, to recognize the fole right of the crown to govern and command them, and to put the whole into a more

regular

regular method of military fubordination: and the order in which the militia now ftands by law, is principally built upon the ftatutes which were then enacted. It is true, the two laft of them are apparently repealed; but many of their provifions are re-enacted, with the addition of fome new regulations, by the prefent militia laws; the general fcheme of which is to difcipline a certain number of the inhabitants of every county, chofen by lot for three years, and officered by the lord lieutenant, the deputy lieutenants, and other principal landholders, under a commiffion from the crown. They are not compellable to march out of their counties, unlefs in cafe of invafion or actual rebellion, nor in any cafe compellable to march out of the kingdom. They are to be exercifed at ftated times: and their difcipline in general is liberal and eafy; but, when drawn out into actual fervice, they are fubject to the rigours of martial law, as neceffary to keep them in order. This is the conftitutional fecurity which our laws have provided for the public peace, and for protecting the realm againft foreign or domeftic violence; and which the ftatutes declare, is effentially neceffary to the fafety and profperity of the kingdom.

But, as the fafhion of keeping ftanding armies has univerfally prevailed over all Europe of late years (though fome of its potentates, being unable themfelves to maintain them, are obliged to have refource to richer powers, and receive fubfidiary penfions for that purpofe) it has alfo for many years paft been annually judged neceffary by our legiflature, for the fafety of the kingdom, the defence of the poffeffions of the crown of Great Britain, and the prefervation of the balance of power in Europe, to maintain, even in time of peace, a ftanding body of troops, under the command of the crown; who are however, *ipfo facto*, difbanded at the expiration of every year, unlefs continued by parliament. The land forces of thefe kingdoms, in time of peace, amount to about 40,000 men, including troops and garrifons in Ireland, Gibraltar, Minorca, and America; but in time of war, there have been in Britifh pay, natives and foreigners, above 150,000! The regiftered militia in England confifts of near 200,000.

The maritime ftate is nearly related to the former; though much more agreeable to the principles of our free conftitution. The royal navy of England hath ever been its greateft defence and ornament; it is its ancient and natural ftrength; the floating bulwark of the ifland; an army, from which, however ftrong and powerful, no danger can ever be apprehended to liberty: and accordingly it has been affiduoufly cultivated, even from the earlieft ages. To fo much perfection was our naval reputation arrived in the twelfth century, that the code of maritime laws, which are called the laws of Oleron, and are received by all nations in Europe, as the ground and fubftruction of all their marine conftitutions, was confeffedly compiled by our king Richard I. at the ifle of Oleron on the coaft of France, then part of the poffeffions of the crown of England. And yet, fo vaftly inferior were our anceftors in this point, to the prefent age, that even in the maritime reign of queen Elizabeth, Sir Edward Coke thinks it matter of boaft, that the royal navy of England then confifted of 33 fhips. The prefent condition of our marine is in great meafure owing to the falutary provifions of the ftatutes, called the navigation-acts; whereby the conftant increafe of Englifh fhipping and feamen was not only encouraged, but rendered unavoidably neceffary. The moft beneficial ftatute for the trade and commerce of thefe kingdoms is that navigation-act, the rudiments of which were firft framed in 1650, with a narrow partial view: being itended to mortify the fugar iflands, which were difaffected to the parliament, and ftill held out for Charles II. by ftopping the gainful trade which they then carried on with the Dutch; and at the fame time to clip the wings of those our opulent and aspiring neighbours. This prohibited all ships of foreign nations from trading with any English plantations without licence from the council of state. In 1651, the prohibition was extended also to the mother country; and no goods were suffered to be imported into England, or any of its dependencies, in any other than English bottoms; or in the ships of that European nation, of which the merchandize imported was the genuine growth or manufacture. At the restoration, the former provisions were continued, by statute 12 Car. II. c. 18. with this very material improvement, that the master and three fourths of the mariners shall also be English subjects.

The complement of seamen, in time of peace, usually amounts to twelve or fifteen thousand. In time of war, they have amounted to no less than sixty thousand men. See at the end of this volume a list of the royal navy of England, as it stood at the end of the late war.

This navy is commonly divided into three squadrons, namely, the red, white, and blue, which are so termed from the difference of their colours. Each squadron has its admiral; but the admiral of the red squadron has the principal command of the whole, and is stiled vice-admiral of Great Britain. Subject to each admiral is also a vice and a rear-admiral. But the supreme command of our naval force is, next to the king, in the lords commissioners of the admiralty. We may venture to affirm that the British navy, during the late war, was able to cope with all the other fleets in Europe. In the course of a few years it entirely vanquished the whole naval power of France, disabled Spain, and kept the Dutch in awe.

For the protection of the British empire, and the annoyance of our enemies, it was then divided into several powerful squadrons, and so judiciously stationed, that while one fleet was successfully battering walls,

hitherto

hitherto reckoned impregnable, others were employed in fruſtrating the deſigns of France, and eſcorting home the riches of the eaſtern and weſtern worlds.

Notwithſtanding our favourable ſituation for a maritime power, it was not until the vaſt armament ſent to ſubdue this nation by Spain, in 1588, that the nation, by a vigorous effort, became fully ſenſible of its true intereſt and natural ſtrength, which it has ſince ſo happily cultivated. This appears more fully by the ſhort view of our naval tranſactions, which cloſes this volume; and which, beginning with the reign of queen Elizabeth, is carried down to the peace of Verſailles in 1763.

An Hiſtorical Account of the Policy and Trade of Great Britain.

The preſent ſyſtem of Engliſh politics may properly be ſaid to have taken riſe in the reign of queen Elizabeth. At this time the Proteſtant religion was eſtabliſhed, which naturally allied us to the reformed ſtates, and made all the Popiſh powers our enemies.

We began in the ſame reign to extend our trade, by which it became neceſſary for us alſo to watch the commercial progreſs of our neighbours; and, if not to incommode and obſtruct their traffic, to hinder them from impairing ours.

We then likewiſe ſettled colonies in America, which was become the great ſcene of European ambition; for, ſeeing with what treaſures the Spaniards were annually enriched from Mexico and Peru, every nation imagined, that an American conqueſt or plantation would certainly fill the mother country with gold and ſilver.

The diſcoveries of new regions, which were then every day made, the profit of remote traffic, and the neceſſity of long voyages, produced, in a few years,

a great

a great multiplication of fhipping. The fea was confidered as the wealthy element; and, by degrees, a new kind of fovereignty arofe, called naval dominion.

As the chief trade of Europe, fo the chief maritime power was at firft in the hands of the Portuguefe and Spaniards, who, by a compact, to which the confent of other princes was not afked, had divided the newly difcovered countries between them : but the crown of Portugal having fallen to the king of Spain, or being feized by him, he was mafter of the fhips of the two nations, with which he kept all the coafts of Europe in alarm, till the Armada, he had raifed at a vaft expence for the conqueft of England, was deftroyed; which put a ftop, and almoft an end, to the naval power of the Spaniards.

At this time the Dutch, who were oppreffed by the Spaniards, and feared yet greater evils than they felt, refolved no longer to endure the infolence of their mafters; they therefore revolted; and after a ftruggle, in which they were affifted by the money and forces of Elizabeth, erected an independant and powerful commonwealth.

When the inhabitants of the Low Countries had formed their fyftem of government, and fome remiffion of the war gave them leifure to form fchemes of future profperity, they eafily perceived that, as their territories were narrow, and their numbers fmall, they could preferve themfelves only by that power which is the confequence of wealth; and that by a people whofe country produced only the neceffaries of life, wealth was not to be acquired, but from foreign dominions, and by the tranfportation of the products of one country into another.

From this neceffity, thus juftly eftimated, arofe a plan of commerce, which was for many years profecuted with induftry and fuccefs, perhaps never feen in the world before; and by which the poor tenants of mud-walled villages and impaffable bogs, erected

E 3   them-

themfelves into high and mighty ftates, who fet the greateft monarchs at defiance, whofe alliance was courted by the proudeft, and whofe power was dreaded by the fierceft nations. By the eftablifh-ment of this ftate, there arofe to England a new ally, and a new rival.

At this time, which feems to be the period def-tined for the change of the face of Europe, France began firft to rife into power, and from defending her own provinces with difficulty and fluctuating fuc-cefs, to threaten her neighbours with incroachments and devaftations. Henry IV. having, after a long ftruggle, obtained the crown, found it eafy to go-vern nobles, exhaufted and wearied with a long ci-vil war; and having compofed the difputes between the Proteftants and Papifts, fo as to obtain, at leaft, a truce for both parties, was at leifure to accumu-late treafure, and raife forces which he propofed to have employed in a defign of fettling for ever the balance of Europe. Of this great fcheme he lived not to fee the vanity, or feel the difappointment; for he was murdered in the midft of his mighty pre-parations.

The French, however, were in this reign taught to know their own power; and the great defigns of a king, whofe wifdom they had fo long experienced, even though they were not brought to actual expe-riment, difpofed them to confider themfelves as maf-ters of the deftiny of their neighbours: and from that time he that fhall nicely examine their fchemes and conduct, will find that they began to take an air of fuperiority, to which they had never pretended be-fore; and that they have been always employed more or lefs openly, upon fchemes of dominion, though with frequent interruptions from domeftic troubles.

When Queen Elizabeth entered upon the govern-ment, the cuftoms produced only 36,000 l. a year; at the reftoration, they were lett to farm for 400,000 l. and produced confiderably above double that fum

before

before the revolution. The people of London, before we had any plantations, and but very little trade,
were computed at about 100,000; at the death of
queen Elizabeth, they were increased to 150,000,
and are now about six times that number. In those
days, we had not only our naval stores, but our
ships from our neighbours. Germany furnished us
with all things made of metal, even to nails; wine,
paper, linen, and a thousand other things came from
France. Portugal furnished us with sugars; all the
produce of America was poured upon us from Spain;
and the Venetians and Genoese retailed to us the commodities of the East Indies at their own price. In
short, the legal interest of money was 12 per cent.
and the common price of our land ten or twelve years
purchase. We may add, that our manufactures
were few, and those but indifferent; the number of
English merchants very small, and our shipping much
inferior to what now belong to the northern colonies.

Such was the state of our trade when this great
princess came to the throne; but as the limits of our
undertaking does not permit us to give a detail of the
gradual progress of commerce, we flatter ourselves
that the British reader will not be displeased with the
following view of our extensive trade, at present carried on through the various nations of the globe.

Great Britain is, of all other countries, the most
proper for trade; as well from its situation, as an
island, as from the freedom and excellency of its constitution, and from its natural products, and considerable manufactures. For exportation: our country
produces many of the most substantial and necessary
commodities, as butter, cheese, corn, cattle, wool,
iron, lead, tin, copper, leather, copperas, pitcoal,
alum, saffron, &c. Our corn sometimes preserves
other countries from starving. Our horses are the
most serviceable in the world, and highly valued by
all nations for their hardiness, beauty, and strength.

E 4   With

With beef, mutton, pork, poultry, bifcuit, we victual not only our own fleets, but all foreigners that come and go. Our iron we export manufactured in great guns, carcafes, bombs, &c. Prodigious, and almoft incredible, is the value likewife of other goods from hence exported; viz. hops, flax, hemp, hats, fhoes, houfhold-ftuff, ale, beer, red-herrings, pilchards, falmon, oyfters, faffron, liquorice, watches, ribbands, toys, &c.

There is fcarce a manufacture in Europe, but what is brought to great perfection in England; and therefore it is perfectly unneceffary to enumerate them all. The woollen manufacture is the moft confiderable, and exceeds in goodnefs and quantity that of any other nation. Hard-ware is another capital article; locks, edge-tools, guns, fwords, and other arms, exceed any thing of the kind; houfhold utenfils of brafs, iron, and pewter, alfo are very great articles; our clocks and watches are in very great efteem. There are but few manufactures we are defective in. In thofe of lace and paper we do not feem to excel; but we import much more than we fhould, if the duty on Britifh paper was taken off. As to foreign traffic, the woollen manufacture is ftill the great foundation and fupport of it.

The commerce between Great Britain and the countries fubject to the grand fignior is carried on by the merchants incorporated into the Levant or Turkey company; but now opened in fuch a manner by a late ftatute, as to be more capable of anfwering national purpofes, without leffening the particular advantages, which Turkey merchants ought in juftice to enjoya. The commodities we export are chiefly lead, tin, and iron, watches and clocks; and of our woollen manufactures, broad cloth and long ells. It is alfo faid, that our merchants fend thither French and Lifbon fugars, as well as bullion. We take in return raw filk in great quantities; which however is only proper for the fhute of our damafk, and other

coloured

coloured filks; it will alfo ferve for making ftockings, galloons, and filver and gold lace; but it is not proper for the warp of any filk, nor even for the woof of fome of the finer forts. We import alfo grogram yarn, dying ftuffs of various kinds, drugs, foap, leather, cotton, fruit, oil, &c. While the war continued, it was a great help to us in this trade, as the French are our principal competitors therein; and as they fuffered very feverely, not only by captures, but by the high infurance they paid on all the goods they exported; fo they could not but come very dear to markets, and perhaps we preferve ftill fome of the advantages then acquired.

We export to Italy, of our own commodities, tin and lead, great quantities of fifh, fuch as pilchards, herrings, falmond, cod, &c. various kinds of Eaft India goods; and of our own manufactures, broad cloths, long ells, Bays, druggets, camblets, and other ftuffs; as alfo leather and other things. We import from thence prodigious quantities of filk, raw, thrown, and wrought; wine, oil, foap, olives, dying ftuffs, &c. It is from this country, and more efpecially from the dominions of his Sardinian majefty, that we have the fine filk called organzine, which is thrown by an engine, much truer than it can be by hand, of which we have one, and but one, at Derby. That prince, however, has taken care to preferve to his fubjects this precious commodity in its full extent; for we have no Piedmont filk raw, and what we have we pay for in ready money, at a very high rate. This therefore makes the balance of power, and the change of mafters, at leaft in the maritime parts of Italy, a thing of very great confequence to Great Britain; and as fuch, it ought always to be confidered by our minifters, and if poffible, in no other light.

We export to Spain, tin, lead, corn, &c. pilchards, herrings, cod, and other kinds of fifh; of our manufactures broad cloth, druggets, bays, and ftuffs, of various kinds; as alfo a great variety of different goods,

goods, which are re-shipped by them from Cadiz to
their colonies in America. On the other hand, we
import from Spain, wine, oil, and fruit, wool, indigo, cochineal, and other drugs. It appears from
hence, that if the Spaniards are good customers to
us, we are also the best customers they have; for it
is thought we take off two-thirds of their commodities: so that considering them as a nation, nothing
can distress the Spaniards so much as a war with the
English. It is very true, that in time of peace we
draw a considerable balance from thence in specie or
in bullion; but at the same time, we furnish them
with the commodities that are most necessary, with
the manufactures that bring them this bullion, and
take also vast quantities of commodities that must
otherwise lie upon their hands; whereas the French
furnish them with many trifles, as well as some costly
manufactures, for which they are paid wholly in
silver. Hence it appears, that it is the mutual interest of Spain and Britain to deal with each other;
and if this was thoroughly inculcated, it would en-
rich us and serve them.

We export to Portugal, tin, lead, corn, fish, and
almost all of our commodities, as also broad cloths,
druggets, bays, stuffs, leather, and many other manufactures; we take from them wine, oil, salt, and
fruit; so that though it is generally supposed the
balance of this trade is as much in our favour as any,
yet the Portuguese find their account in it: for in the
first place, we take almost all the commodities they
export, and for which, if we did not take them, they
could hardly find another market; and we furnish
them with the best part of those things they export
to the Brazils, and thereby draw that immense treasure
yearly, which, for its bigness, renders Portugal one
of the richest countries in Europe. Beside, these
reciprocal advantages have made such a connection
between our interests, that upon all occasions we have
been ready to espouse those of Portugal, and to protect

tect her from the only power she has reason to fear, by the timely interposition of our maritime force.

We export to France, tin, lead, corn, horn plates, and great quantities of tobacco, some flannels; but very little else of our manufactures. We take from thence, in time of peace, wine, brandy, linen, lace, cambrics, lawns, (unless our late acts can keep them out) and an infinite number of other things which are run in upon us, and whatever else the French are pleased to direct: whence it appears, that of all others, the French commerce is to us the most dangerous and destructive.

We export to Flanders, tin, lead, and some iron ware, as also sugar and tobacco; of our manufactures, serges, some flannels, and a few stuffs. On the other hand, we take from them fine lace, cambrics, lawns, linen, tape, inkles, and other goods of that kind, to a very great value; so that there seems to be no doubt that the balance of this trade is considerably against us, which is chiefly owing to the prohibition of our cloth: therefore if any thing be worthy our seeking on the continent, it is the port of Ostend, with a small district about it, which at the same time would be of service to our allies, and might contribute to repair the expences we have been at in our several land wars. This is mentioned only incidentally.

We send to Germany, tin, lead, and many other commodities; tobacco, sugar, ginger, and all kinds of East-India goods. Of our woollen manufactures, some of almost every kind we make. On the other hand, we take from them tin plates, linen, kid skins, and several other things. The balance of this trade is looked upon to be very much in our favour, but it might be made still more; for in many places of late they have prohibited different kinds of our manufactures, and in some they have prohibited all. But in our treaties of subsidy, if we had an article to prevent or remove such prohibitions, it would be but reasonable: for as we pay the Germans for fighting
their

their own battles, they might methinks in return allow a free vent to our manufactures; and as they are sure of taking our money, should give us a chance at least for seeing some of theirs.

We have a great trade with Denmark and Norway, but we export very little; a small quantity of tobacco, and a few coarse woollen goods is all; but we are forced to tack to these crown-pieces and guineas, to pay for timber and iron; and the matter is not all mended, but on the contrary grows worse; if instead of exporting our wealth, we stay till the Danes come and fetch it, for then we not only pay for their goods, but the freight also; and this evil it seems is not in our power to cure at present.

We carry on the same kind of losing trade to Sweden, where it is a maxim of state to beat out as much as possible all our commodities and manufactures; and this has been so steadily pursued, that it is now pretty near done, and gold and silver are almost our only exports. Copper, iron, and naval stores, are the goods we bring from thence, to the amount of about three hundred thousand pounds a year. We were formerly under a necessity of doing this; because their goods must be had, and could be had no where else. At present it is otherwise, we might have all these at much more reasonable rates from our own plantations, which is much the same thing as having them at home.

We export to Russia, tin, lead, and other commodities, a great quantity of tobacco; and of our manufactures, coarse cloths, long ells, worsted stuffs, &c. On the other hand, we import from thence, tallow, furrs, iron, pot-ashes, hemp, flax, linen, Russia leather, &c. Our trade to this country is managed by a company, the best constituted, and the best conducted of any that we have; for any merchant may be admitted into it for a very small consideration, and the measures they pursue are such as prove highly beneficial, and never can do any harm. The trade through

this

this empire into Perfia, may become a thing of great confequence, as it will furnifh us with that fort of filk which we want moft, at an eafy price, and may be attended with other advantages that we have not room to explain.

We export to Holland almoft all the commodities and manufactures that we have, as well as moft of our plantation goods, and of thofe we bring from the Levant and the Eaft Indies. We import prodigious quantities of fine linen, threads, tapes, inkles, whale-fins, brafs battery, cinnamon, mace, cloves, drugs, and dying ftuffs, &c. yet with refpect to the fair trade we have a large balance: the only doubt is, how far this may be abated by the great induftry of fmug-lers, who gain their bread and raife fortunes by a fteady purfuit of their private interefts, at the expence of the public.

With refpect to our African trade, it is certainly of the higheft importance to the nation, for it creates a vaft exportation of our commodities and manufac-tures, and produces a large balance in bullion from the Spaniards, as well as in gold-duft, red-wood, ivory, and other valuable commodities, fome of which are re-exported; but above all it fupplies our plan-tations with negroes, which is a thing of prodigious confequence. The old African company of Eng-land, once the moft flourifhing and profitable of all our companies, and but for bad management within, and party prejudice without, might have continued fo, has been at length diffolved by parliament, and the commerce put into a new channel; which either anfwers, or will be made to anfwer national purpofes; fince no commerce can more nearly concern Great Britain and her colonies than this does, and fcarcely any is fo much the fubject of foreign envy.

The Eaft-India trade is a prodigious thing, and of great benefit to the nation, though we export chiefly bullion; and though it is carried on by a company. But the goods we bring home are bought at low prices,

prices, are fold at high rates, and what we export is believed to produce a balance equivalent at leaft to the bullion that is fent out to buy them. It has been of late fuggefted, and not without good reafon, that this commerce is capable of great improvements, by extending it to the north-eaft; for in that cafe, we might hope to vend large quantities of our manufactures, which would at once remove the only reafonable exception that was ever taken to this trade, would augment our navigation, and hinder the northern nations from interfering with us, by employing the very money we pay for naval ftores, in beating us out of a very confiderable branch of commerce, for the carrying on of which thofe ftores are purchafed.

As for the plantation trade, we have already fpoken of it elfewhere, and without doubt it is by far the moft confiderable of any that we have, and is notwithftanding this, far lefs confiderable than it might be; for with a little pains and encouragement, it might be made in its favings and in its produce, twice or thrice as beneficial at it is : for it has been computed, that by encouraging hemp and flax, pot-afhes, timber, iron, other naval ftores, and filk, we might either get or keep confiderably above a million annually; and by making other regulations it is demonftrable, that within a few years we might gain as much more.

In fhort, the advantages are infinite that redound to us from our American empire, where we have at leaft a million of Britifh fubjects, and between fifteen hundred and two thoufand fail of fhips conftantly employed.

The annual exports of Englifh and foreign goods amount to between fix and feven millions fterling, and our imports do not exceed five millions. As a confiderable part of this is again exported, the annual iffues from England for foreign merchandize, has been eftimated at four millions. Yet our foreign trade does not amount to one fixth part of the inland;

land; the annual produce of the natural products and manufactures of England amounting to above forty-two millions. The gold and silver of England is received from Portugal, Spain, Jamaica, the American colonies, and Africa; but great part of this gold and silver we again export to Holland, and the East Indies; and it is supposed that two-thirds of all the foreign traffic of England is carried on in the port of London.

We shall conclude this account of our trade with the following comparative view of shipping, which, till a better table can be formed, may have its uses.

If the shipping of Europe be divided into twenty parts, then;

Great Britain, &c. is computed to have	6
The United Provinces — —	6
The subjects of the northern crowns —	2
The trading cities of Germany, and the Austrian Netherlands — — —	1
France — — — —	2
Spain and Portugal — — —	2
Italy, and the rest of Europe — —	1

A short View of the Stocks, or public Funds in England, with an historical Account of the East India, the Bank, and South Sea Companies.

As there are few subjects of conversation more general than the value of stocks, and hardly any thing so little understood, nothing can be more useful than a short account of them, which we shall here give in as clear and concise a manner as possible; presenting our readers with the rationale of the stocks, and a short history of the several companies, describing the nature of their separate funds, the uses to which they are applied, and the various purposes they answer, both with respect to the government, the companies themselves, and the community in general.

In

In order to give a clear idea of the money transactions of the several companies, it is proper we should say something of money in general, and particularly of paper money, and the difference between that and the current specie. Money is the standard of the value of all the necessaries and accommodations of life, and paper-money is the representative of that standard to such a degree, as to supply its place, and to answer all the purposes of gold and silver coin. Nothing is necessary to make this representative of money supply the place of specie, but the credit of that office or company, who delivers it; which credit consists in its always being ready to turn it into specie whenever required. This is exactly the case of the bank of England, the notes of this company are of the same value as the current coin, as they may be turned into it, whenever the possessor pleases. From hence, as notes are a kind of money, the counterfeiting them is punished with death as well as coining.

The method of depositing money in the bank, and exchanging it for notes (though they bear no interest) is attended with many conveniencies; as they are not only safer than money in the hands of the owner himself; but as the notes are more portable and capable of a much more easy conveyance: since a bank note for a very large sum, may be sent by the post, and to prevent the designs of robbers, may, without damage, be cut in two and sent at two several times. Or bills, called bank post bills, may be had by application at the bank, which are particularly calculated to prevent losses by robberies, they being made payable to the order of the person who takes them out at a certain number of days after sight; which gives an opportunity to stop bills at the bank, if they should be lost, and prevents their being so easily negotiated by strangers as common bank notes are: and whoever considers the hazard, the expence and trouble there would be in sending large sums of

gold

gold and silver to and from distant places, must also consider this as a very singular advantage. Beside which another benefit attends them; for if they are destroyed by time, or other accidents, the bank will, on oath being made of such accident, and security being given, pay the money to the person who was in possession of them.

Bank notes differ from all kinds of stock in these three particulars. 1. They are always of the same value. 2. They are paid off without being transferred; and, 3. They bear no interest; while stocks are a share in a company's funds, bought without any condition of having the principal returned. India bonds indeed (by some persons, though erroneously, denominated stock) are to be excepted, they being made payable at six months notice, either on the side of the company or of the possessor.

By the word *stock* was originally meant, a particular sum of money contributed to the establishing a fund to enable a company to carry on a certain trade, by means of which the person became a partner in that trade, and received a share of the profit made thereby in proportion to the money employed. But this term has been extended farther, though improperly, to signify any sum of money which has been lent to the government, on condition of receiving a certain interest till the money is repaid, and which makes a part of the national debt. As the security both of the government and of the public companies is esteemed preferable to that of any private person, as the stocks are negotiable and may be sold at any time, and as the interest is always punctually paid when due, so they are thereby enabled to borrow money on a lower interest than what might be obtained from lending it to private persons, where there must be always some danger of losing both principal and interest.

But as every capital stock or fund of a company is raised for a particular purpose, and limited by parliament to a certain sum, it necessarily follows, that

when that fund is compleated, no ftock can be
bought of the company; though fhares already purchafed, may be transferred from one perfon to another. This being the cafe, there is frequently a
great difproportion between the original value of the
fhares, and what is given for them when transferred;
for if there are more buyers than fellers, a perfon who
is indifferent about felling will not part with his fhare
without a confiderable profit to himfelf; and on the
contrary, if many are difpofed to fell, and few inclined
to buy, the value of fuch fhares will naturally fall, in
proportion to the impatience of thofe who want to
turn their ftock into fpecie.

The fe obfervations may ferve to give our readers
fome idea of the nature of that unjuftifiable and
difhoneft practice called *ftock-jobbing*, the myftery of
which confifts in nothing more than this: the perfons concerned in that practice, who are denominated
ftock-jobbers, make contracts to buy or fell, at a certain diftant time, a certain quantity of fome particular ftock, againft which time they endeavour,
according as their contract is, either to raife or lower
fuch ftock, by raifing rumours and fpreading fictitious ftories in order to induce people either to fell
out in a hurry, and confequently cheap, if they are
to deliver ftock, or to become unwilling to fell, and
confequently to make it dearer, if they are to receive
ftock.

The perfons who make thefe contracts are not in
general poffeffed of any real ftock, and when the
time comes that they are to receive or deliver the
quantity they have contracted for, they only pay fuch
a fum of money as makes the difference between the
price the ftock was at when they made the contract,
and the price it happens to be at when the contract is
fulfilled, and it is no uncommon thing for perfons not
worth 100 l. to make contracts for the buying or felling 100,000 l. ftock. In the language of Exchange
Alley,

Alley, the buyer in this cafe is called the Bull, and the feller the Bear.

Befide thefe, there are another fet of men, who though of a higher rank, may properly enough come under the fame denomination. Thefe are your great monied men, who are dealers in ftock and contractors with the government whenever any new money is to be borrowed. Thefe indeed are not fictitious, but real buyers and fellers of ftock; but by raifing falfe hopes, or creating groundlefs fears, by pretending to buy or fell large quantities of ftock on a fudden, by ufing the fore-mentioned fet of men as their inftruments, and other like practices, are enabled to raife or fall the ftocks one or two per cent. at pleafure.

However, the real value of one ftock above another, on account of its being more profitable to the proprietors, or any thing that will really, or only in imagination, affect the credit of a company, or endanger the government, by which that credit is fecured, muft naturally have a confiderable effect on the ftocks. Thus, with refpect to the intereft of the proprietors, a fhare in the ftock of a trading company which produces 5 l. or 6 l. per cent. per ann. muft be more valuable than an annuity with government fecurity, that produces no more than 3 l. or 4 l. per cent. per annum; and confequently fuch ftock muft fell at a higher price than fuch an annuity. Though it muft be obferved, that a fhare in the ftock of a trading company producing 5 l. or 6 l. per cent. per annum, will not fetch fo much money at market as a government annuity producing the fame fum, becaufe the fecurity of the company is not reckoned equal to that of the government, and the continuance of their paying fo much per annum, is more precarious, as their dividend is, or ought to be, always in proportion to the profits of their trade.

As the ftocks of the Eaft India, the bank, and South-Sea companies, are diftinguifhed by different

denomi-

denominations, and are of a very different nature; we shall give a short history of each of them, together with an account of the different stocks, each is possessed of, beginning with the East India company, as the first established.

Of the East India Company.

There is no trading company in Europe, the Dutch East India company excepted, which can be put in competition with this. Its was first established in the latter end of the reign of queen Elizabeth ; and its privileges have been enlarged, or confirmed, by almost every monarch since. Its shares, or subscriptions, were originally only 50 l. sterling; and its capital only 369,891 l, 5 s. but the directors having a considerable dividend to make in 1676, it was agreed to join the profits to the capital, by which the shares were doubled, and consequently each became of 100 l. value, and the capital 739,782 l. 10 s. to which capital, if 963,639 l. the profits of the company to the year 1685, be added, the whole stock will be found to be 1,703,402 pounds.

However, this company having sustained several losses by the Dutch, and the subjects of the great Mogul, was in a declining way at the revolution, when the war with France reduced it so low, that it appearing scarcely possible to be supported, a new one was erected. The merchants forming the new East India company, received their charter in 1698, having in consideration of the grant thereof, lent to the government two millions at 8 per cent. per annum, and pushing their trade with vigour, they soon carried on twice the business that was ever done by the old company. But after the two companies had subsisted a few years in a separate state, means were contrived to unite them, which was effected in 1702, when a new charter was granted them under the title of the United Company of Merchants trading to the East Indies.

To

To the two millions advanced by the new company, the united company in the 6th of queen Anne, lent the government 1,200,000 l. which made their whole loan amount to 3,200,000 l. a further sum was also lent by the company in 1730, on a renewal of their charter, the interest of which is reduced to 3 per cent. and called the India 3 per cent. annuities.

As to India stock, it is of a quite different nature; for as that is not money put out to interest, but the trading stock of the company, and the proprietors of the shares, instead of receiving a regular annuity, have a dividend of the profits arising from the company's trade; which, as it is more valuable, these shares generally sell at a price much above the original value.

As to the management of this united company, all persons without exception, natives and foreigners, men and women, are admitted members of it, and 500 l. in the stock of the company, gives the owner a vote in the general court, and 2000 l. qualifies him to be chosen a director. The directors are 24 in number, including the chairman, and deputy chairman, who may be re-elected for four years. successively. The chairman has a salary of 200 l. a year, and each of the directors 150 l. The meetings or courts of directors, are to be held at least once a week; but are commonly oftener, being summoned as occasion requires.

Out of the body of directors are chosen several committees, who have the peculiar inspection of certain branches of the company's business; as the committee of correspondence, a committee of buying, a committee of treasury, a house-committee, a committee of warehouses, a committee of shipping, a committee of accompts, a committee of law-suits, and a committee to prevent the growth of private trade, &c. who have under them a secretary, cashier, clerks, warehouse-keepers, &c.

F 3

Other

Other officers of the company are governors and factors abroad, some of whom have guards of soldiers, and live in all the state of sovereign princes.

Of the Bank of England.

The company of the bank was incorporated by parliament, in the 5th and 6th years of king William and queen Mary, by the name of the Governor and Company of the Bank of England; in confideration of the loan of 1,200,000 l. granted to the government; for which the fubfcribers received almoft 8 per cent. By this charter, the company are not to borrow under their common feal, unlefs by act of parliament; they are not to trade, or fuffer any perfon in truft for them, to trade in any goods, or merchandize; but they may deal in bills of exchange, in buying or felling bullion, and foreign gold and filver coin, &c.

By an act of parliament paffed in the 8th and 9th year of king William III. they were impowered to enlarge their capital ftock to 2,201,171 l. 10 s. It was then alfo enacted, that bank ftock fhould be a perfonal, and not a real eftate; that no contract either in word or writing, for buying or felling bank ftock, fhould be good in law, unlefs regiftered in the books of the bank within feven days; and the ftock transferred in 14 days, and that it fhould be felony, without benefit of clergy, to counterfeit the common feal of the bank, or any fealed bank bill, or any bank note, or to alter or erafe fuch bills or notes.

By another act paffed in the 7th of queen Anne, the company were impowered to augment their capital to 4,402,343 l. and they then advanced 400,000 l. more to the government, and in 1714, they advanced another loan of 1,500,000 l.

In the third year of the reign of king George I. the intereft of their capital ftock was reduced to 5 per cent, when the bank agreed to deliver up as many exchequer bills as amounted to 2,000,000 l. and to
accept

accept an annuity of 100,000 L. and it was declared lawful for the bank to call from their members, in proportion to their interefts in the capital ftock, fuch fums of money as in a general court fhould be found neceffary. If any member fhould neglect to pay his fhare of the monies fo called for, at the time appointed by notice in the London Gazette, and fixed upon the Royal exchange, it fhould be lawful for the bank, not only to ftop the dividend of fuch member, and to apply it toward payment of the money in queftion; but alfo to ftop the transfers of the fhare of fuch defaulter, and to charge him with an intereft of 5 l. per cent. per annum, for the money fo omitted to be paid: and if the principal and intereft fhould be three months unpaid, the bank fhould then have power to fell fo much of the ftock belonging to the defaulter as would fatisfy the fame.

After this, the bank reduced the intereft of the 2,000,000 l. lent to the government, from 5 to 4 per cent. and purchafed feveral other annuities, which were afterward redeemed by the government, and the national debt due to the bank reduced to 1,600,000 l. But in 1742, the company engaged to fupply the government with 1,600,000 l. at 3 per cent. which is now called the 3 per cent. annuities, fo that the government was now indebted to the company 3,200,000 L. the one half carrying 4, and the other 3 per cent.

In the year 1746, the company agreed that the fum of 986,800 l. due to them in the exchequer bills unfatisfied, on the duties for licences to fell fpirituous liquors by retail, fhould be cancelled, and in lieu thereof to accept of an annuity of 39,442 l. the intereft of that fum at 4 per cent. The company alfo agreed to advance the further fum of 1,000,000 l. into the exchequer, upon the credit of the duties arifing by the malt and land-tax, at 4 per cent. for exchequer bills to be iffued for that purpofe; in confideration of which the company were enabled to

augment

———— ———— with 986,800 l. the interest of
———— —— that of the other annuities, was re-
———— —— ——— per cent. till the 25th of Decem-
——— —— from that time to carry only 3 per cent.
——— —— —— to enable them to circulate the said
——— —— —— they established what is now called
——— —— ——. The nature of which, not being
—— ——, we shall take the liberty to be a
—— —— particular in its explanation than we have
—— —— regard to the other stocks.

—— company of the bank are obliged to keep cash
—— to answer not only the common, but also
—— ordinary demand that may be made upon
—— and whatever money they have by them, over
—— above the sum supposed necessary for these pur-
—— they employ in what may be called the trade
—— company; that is to say, in discounting bills
—— exchange, in buying of gold and silver, and in
government securities, &c. But when the bank entered into the above-mentioned contract, as they did
not keep unemployed a larger sum of money than
what they deemed necessary to answer their ordinary
and extraordinary demands, they could not conveni-
ently take out of their current cash so large a sum as
a million, with which they were obliged to furnish
the government, without either lessening that sum
they employed in discounting, buying gold and silver, &c. (which would have been very disadvanta-
geous to them) or inventing some method that should
answer all the purposes of keeping the million in cash.
The method which they chose, and which fully an-
swers their end, was as follows.

They opened a subscription, which they renew
annually, for a million of money; wherein the
subscribers advance 10 per cent. and enter into a
contract to pay the remainder, or any part thereof,
whenever the bank shall call upon them, under the
penalty of forfeiting the 10 per cent. so advanced; in
consideration of which, the bank pays the subscribers

4 per

4 per cent. intereſt for the money paid in, and ¼ per cent. for the whole ſum they agree to furniſh; and in caſe a call ſhould be made upon them for the whole, or any part thereof, the bank farther agrees to pay them at the rate of 5 per cent. per annum for ſuch ſum till they repay it, which they are under an obligation to do at the end of the year. By this means the bank obtains all the purpoſes of keeping a million of money by them; and though the ſub-ſcribers, if no call is made upon them (which is in general the caſe) receive 6¼ per cent. for the money they advance, yet the company gains the ſum of 23,500 l. per annum by the contract; as will appear by the following account.

	£.
The bank receives from the government for the advance of a million —	30,000
The bank pays to the ſubſcribers who advance 100,000 l. and engage to pay (when called for) 900,000 l. more	6,500
The clear gain to the bank therefore is	23,500

This is the ſtate of the caſe, provided the com-pany ſhould make no call on the ſubſcribers, which they will be very unwilling to do, becauſe it would not only leſſen their profit, but affect the public cre-dit in general.

Bank ſtock may not improperly be called a trading ſtock, ſince with this they deal very largely in foreign gold and ſilver, in diſcounting bills of exchange, &c. Beſide which, they are allowed by the government very conſiderable ſums annually for the management of the annuities paid at their office. All which advan-tages render a ſhare in their ſtock very valuable, tho' it is not equal in value to the Eaſt India ſtock. The company make dividends of the profits half yearly, of which notice is publicly given; when thoſe who have occaſion for their money may readily receive it; but private perſons, if they judge convenient, are

permitted

permitted to continue their funds, and to have their interest added to the principal.

This company is under the direction of a governor, deputy-governor, and 24 directors, who are annually elected by the general court, in the same manner as in the East India company. Thirteen, or more, compose a court of directors for managing the affairs of the company.

The officers of this company are very numerous.

Of the South Sea Company.

During the long war with France in the reign of queen Anne, the payment of the sailors of the royal navy being neglected, and they receiving tickets instead of money, were frequently obliged by their necessities to sell these tickets to avaritious men at a discount of 40 l. and sometimes 50 l. per cent. By this and other means the debts of the nation unprovided for by parliament, and which amounted to 9,471,321 l. fell into the hands of these usurers. On which, Mr. Harley, at that time chancellor of the exchequer, and afterward earl of Oxford, proposed a scheme to allow the proprietors of these debts and deficiencies 6 l. per cent. per annum, and to incorporate them in order to their carrying on a trade to the South Sea; and they were accordingly incorporated under the title of the Governor and Company of Merchants of Great Britain, trading to the South Seas, and other parts of America, and for encouraging the Fishery, &c.

Though this company seem formed for the sake of commerce, it is certain the ministry never thought seriously during the course of the war, about making any settlements on the coast of South America, which was what flattered the expectations of the people; nor was it indeed ever carried into execution, or any trade ever undertaken by this company, except the Assiento, in pursuance of the treaty of Utrecht, for furnishing the Spaniards with negroes, of which this.

company

company was deprived by the late convention between the courts of Great Britain and Spain, soon after the treaty of Aix la Chapelle in 1748.

After this, some other sums were lent to the government in the reign of queen Anne at 6 per cent. In the third of George I. the interest of the whole was reduced to 5 per cent. and they advanced two millions more to the government at the same interest. By the statute of the 6th of George I. it was declared, that this company might redeem all or any of the redeemable national debts, in consideration of which the company were empowered to augment their capital according to the sums they should discharge: and for enabling the company to raise such sums for purchasing annuities, exchanging for ready money new exchequer bills, carrying on their trade, &c. the company might by such means as they should think proper, raise such sums of money as in a general court of the company should be judged necessary. The company were also impowered to raise money on contracts, bills, bonds or obligations under their common seal, on the credit of their capital stock. But if the sub-governor, deputy-governor, or other members of the company should purchase lands or revenues of the crown, upon account of the corporation, or lend money by loan or anticipation, on any branch of the revenue, other than such part only on which a credit of loan was granted by parliament, such sub-governor, or other member of the company, should forfeit treble the value of the money so lent.

The fatal South Sea scheme transacted in the year 1720, was executed upon the last-mentioned statute. The company had at first set out with good success, and the value of their stock for the first five years had risen faster than that of any other company, and his majesty, after purchasing 10,000 l. stock, had condescended to be their governor. Things were in this situation, when taking advantage of the above statute, the South Sea bubble was projected. The

pretended

pretended defign of which was to raife a fund for carrying on a trade to the South Seas, and purchafing annuities, &c. paid to the other companies: and propofals were printed and diftributed fhewing the advantages of the defign, and inviting perfons into it. The fum neceffary for carrying it on, together with the profits that were to arife from it, were divided into a certain number of fhares, or fubfcriptions to be purchafed by perfons difpofed to adventure therein. And the better to carry on the deception, the directors engaged to make very large dividends, and actually declared, that every 100 l. original ftock would yield 50 l. per annum, which occafioned fo great a rife of their ftock, that a fhare of 100 l. was fold for upward of 1000 l. This was in the month of July, but before the end of September it fell to 150 l. by which multitudes were ruined, and fuch a fcene of diftrefs occafioned as is fcarcely to be conceived. But the confequences of this infamous fcheme are too well known. We fhall pafs over all the other tranfactions of this company in the reign of king George I. as not material to our prefent purpofe.

By a ftatute of the 6th of his late majefty, it was enacted, that from and after the 24th of June 1733, the capital ftock of this company, which amounted to 14,651,103 l. 8 s. 1 d. and the fhares of the refpective proprietors, fhould be divided into four equal parts, three-fourths of which fhould be converted into a joint ftock, attended with annuities, after the rate of 4 per cent until redemption by parliament, and fhould be called, the new South Sea annuities, and the other fourth part fhould remain in the company as a trading capital ftock, attended with the refidue of the annuities or funds payable at the exchequer to the company for their whole capital, till redemption; and attended with the fame fums allowed for charges of management, and with all effects, profits of trade, debts, privileges and advantages belonging to the South Sea company. That
the

the accomptant of the company fhould twice every year, at Chriftmas and Midfummer, or within one month after, ftate an account of the company's affairs, which fhould be laid before the next general court, in order to their declaring a dividend : and all dividends fhould be made out of the clear profits, and fhould not exceed what the company might reafonably divide, without incurring any farther debt ; provided that the company fhould not at any time divide more than 4 per cent. per annum, until their debts were difcharged; and that the South Sea company, and their trading ftock, fhould, exclufively from the new joint ftock of annuities, be liable to all the debts and incumbrances of the company; and that the company fhould caufe to be kept within the city of London, an office and books, in which all transfers of the new annuities fhould be entered and figned by the party making fuch transfer, or his attorney, and the perfon to whom fuch transfer fhould be made, or his attorney, fhould under-write his acceptance, and no other method of transferring the annuities fhould be good in law.

The annuities of this company, as well as the other, are now reduced to 3 l. per cent.

This company is under the direction of a governor, fub-governor, deputy-governor, and 21 directors; but no perfon is qualified to be governor, his majefty excepted, unlefs fuch governor has in his own name and right, 5000 l. in the trading ftock; the fubgovernor is to have 4000 l. the deputy 3000 l. and a director 2000 l. in the fame ftock. In every general court, every member having in his own name and right 500 l. in trading ftock, has one vote; if 2000 l. two votes; if 3000 l. three votes, and if 5000 l. four votes.

The Eaft India company, the bank of England, and the South Sea company, are the only incorporated bodies to which the government is indebted, except the million bank, whofe capital is only one million

million, conftituted to purchafe the reverfion of the
long exchequer orders.

The intereft of all the debts owing by the government is now reduced to 3 per cent. excepting only the
annuities for the years 1756, and 1758, the life annuities, and the exchequer orders: but the South Sea
company ftill continues to divide four per cent. on
their prefent capital ftock, which they are enabled to
do from the profits they make on the fums allowed
to them for management of the annuities paid at their
office, and from the intereft of annuities which are
not claimed by the proprietors.

As the prices of the different ftocks are continually fluctuating above and below par; fo when a perfon who is not acquainted with tranfactions of that
nature, reads in the papers the prices of ftocks, where
bank ftock is marked perhaps 127 l. India ditto
134 a 134 $\frac{1}{4}$. South Sea ditto 97 $\frac{1}{2}$, &c. he is to underftand that a 100 l. of thofe refpective ftocks fell at
fuch a time for thofe feveral fums.

In comparing the prices of the different ftocks one
with another, it muft be remembered, that the intereft due on them from the time of the laft payment,
is taken into the current price, and the feller never
receives any feparate confideration for it, except in
the cafe of India bonds, where the intereft due is calculated to the day of the fale, and paid by the pur-
chafer over and above the premium agreed for. But
as the intereft on the different ftocks is paid at different times, this, if not rightly underftood, would
lead a perfon not well acquainted with them into
confiderable miftakes in his computation of their value; fome always having a quarter's intereft due on
them more than others, which makes an appearance
of a confiderable difference in the price, when, in
reality, there is none at all. Thus, for inftance,
old South Sea annuities fell at prefent for £. 85 $\frac{1}{4}$ or
£. 85 10 s. while new South Sea annuities fetch only
£. 84 $\frac{1}{4}$, or £. 84 15 s. though each of them produce

the

the fame annual fum of £ 3 per cent. but the old annuities have a quarter's intereft more due on them than
the new annuities, which amounts to 15 s. the exact
difference. There is, however, one or two caufes
that will always make one fpecies of annuities fell
fomewhat lower than another, though of the fame real
value, one of which is, the annuities making but a
fmall capital, and there not being, for that reafon,
fo many people at all times ready to buy into it, as
into others, where the quantity is larger; becaufe
it is apprehended that whenever the government
pays off the national debt, they will begin with that
particular fpecies of annuity, the capital of which is
the fmalleft.,

A ftock may likewife be affected by the court of
Chancery; for if that court fhould order the money
which is under their direction to be laid out in any
particular ftock, that ftock, by having more pur-
chafers, will be raifed to a higher price than any
other of the like value.

By what has been faid, the reader will perceive how
much the credit and intereft of the nation depends
on the fupport of the public funds.—While the annuities, and intereft for money advanced is there regularly paid, and the principal infured by both prince
and people (a fecurity not to be had in other nations)
foreigners will lend us their property, and all Europe be interefted in our welfare; the paper of the
companies will be converted into money and merchandize, and Great Britain can never want cafh to
carry her fchemes into execution.

In other nations, credit is founded on the word of
the prince, if a monarchy; or that of the people, if
a republic; but here it is eftablifhed on the interefts
of both prince and people, which is the ftrongeft fecurity: for however lovely and engaging honefty may
be in other refpects, intereft in money-matters will
always obtain confidence; becaufe many people pay
great regard to their intereft, who have but little veneration for virtue.

A fhort

A short Description of London *.

London, the mettropolis of Great Britain, including Weftminfter and Southwark, is a city of a very furprifing extent, of prodigious wealth, and of the moft extenfive trade; it is at once the largeft and richeft city in Europe. This city is now what ancient Rome once was; the feat of liberty, the encourager of arts, and the admiration of the whole world.

It is fituated on the banks of the Thames, a river, which, though not the largeft in the world, is of the greateft fervice to its commerce. It being continually filled with fleets, failing to or from the moft diftant climates; and its banks being from London-bridge to Blackwall, almoft one continued great magazine of naval ftores, containing three large wet docks, 32 dry docks, and 33 yards for the building of fhips, for the ufe of the merchants, befide the places allotted for the building of boats and lighters; and the king's yards lower down the river for building men of war. As this city is about fixty miles diftant from the fea, it enjoys, by means of this river, all the benefits of navigation, without the danger of being furprifed by foreign fleets, or of being annoyed by the moift vapours of the fea. It rifes regularly from the water-fide, and extending itfelf on both fides along its banks, reaches a prodigious length from eaft to weft; furrounded on both fides by a number of large and populous villages, adorned with handfome commodious buildings, the country-feats of gentlemen and tradefmen; whither the latter retire for the benefit of the frefh air, and to relax their minds from the hurry of bufinefs.

* London is fituated in 51° 30′ north latitude, 400 miles fouth of Edinburgh, and 270 fouth-eaft of Dublin; 200 north-weft of Paris, 180 miles weft of Amfterdam, 500 fouth-weft of Copenhagen, 600 north-weft of Vienna, 1360 north-weft of Conftantinople, 800 north-eaft of Madrid, 850 north-eaft of Lifbon, and 820 north-weft of Rome.

The

6

Road
pike

Marybone
Gardens

Mary le bo

Gray Inn Lane

Holborn

Hatton Street

Leather Lane

Holb

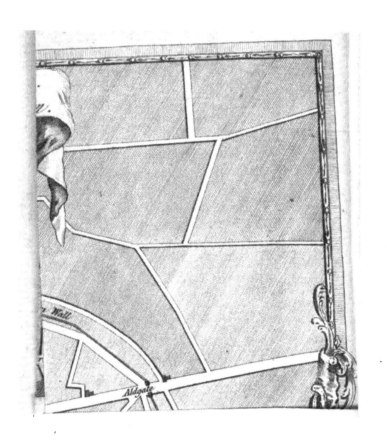

west of Vienna, 1360 north-west of &
orth-east of Madrid, 850 north-east of Li
t of Rome.

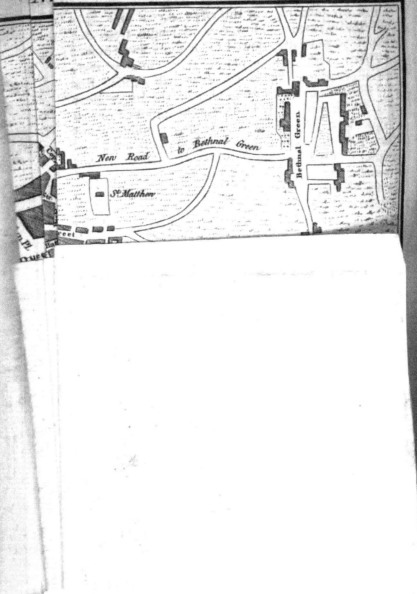

New Road   to Bethnal Green

Bethnal Green

St Matthew

The irregular form of this city makes it difficult to afcertain its extent. However, its length from eaft to weft, is generally allowed to be above feven miles; and its breadth, in fome places, three, in other two; and in other again not much above half a mile. But it is much eafier to form an idea of the large extent of a city fo irregularly built, by the number of the people, who are computed to be near a million; and from the number of edifices devoted to the fervice of religion. Of thefe, befide St. Paul's cathedral, and the collegiate church at Weftminfter, there are 102 parifh-churches, and 69 chapels of the eftablifhed religion; 21 French proteftant chapels; 8 chapels belonging to the Germans, Dutch, Danes, &c. 33 baptift meetings; 26 independent meetings; 28 pref- byterian meetings; 14 popifh chapels, and meeting- houfes for the ufe of foreign ambaffadors, and people of various fects; and 3 Jews fynagogues. So that there are 318 places devoted to religious worfhip, in the compafs of this vaft pile of buildings, without reckoning the 21 out-parifhes, ufually included with- in the bills of mortality.

Of thefe churches the moft famous is St. Paul's cathedral, which is the nobleft of all the proteftant churches in the world. This is an edifice equally re- markable for its beauty and magnificence, containing as few faults as the nature and extent of fo large a building will admit. It is built according to the Greek and Roman orders, under the direction of that celebrated architect Sir Chriftopher Wren, after the model of St. Peter's at Rome. The length within is 500 feet; and its height, from the marble pavement to the crofs on the top of the cupola is 340. The ex- pence of rebuilding this cathedral after the fire of London, is computed at about 800,000 l.

Weftminfter-Abbey, or the collegiate church of Weftminfter, is a venerable pile of building, in the Gothic tafte. It was firft built by Edward the Con- feffor; king Henry III. rebuilt it from the ground, and Henry VII. added a fine chapel to the eaft end of it ; this is the repofitory of the deceafed Britifh-kings and nobility ; and here are alfo monuments erected to the memory of many great and illuftrious perfonages.

Among the other churches, the moft remarkable are St. Paul's Covent-Garden, the churches of St. Mary le Bow, and St. Bride's ; the two latter for having the fineft fteeples in the world. The infide of the church of St. Stephen, Walbroke, is admired all over Europe. And, in fhort, the contrivance and beauty of many other churches, confidering how they were obliged to be thruft up in corners, is furprifingly fine. It is a great misfortune, that though this city abounds with the moft elegant ftructures, and the moft magnificent public and private buildings, yet they are placed in fuch a manner as muft tempt every foreigner to believe that they were defigned to be concealed.

There are here alfo two royal palaces, St. James's and Somerfet-houfe, both of them, efpecially the firft, greatly beneath the dignity of a king of Great Britain ; as to the latter, it has been generally the refidence of the queen-dowagers of England.

There are alfo in and near this city 100 alms-houfes, about 20 hofpitals and infirmaries, 3 colleges, 10 public prifons, 15 flefh-markets ; 1 market for live cattle, 2 other markets more particularly for herbs ; and 23 other markets for corn, coals, hay, &c. 15 inns of court, 27 public fquares, befide thofe within any fingle buildings, as the Temple, &c. 49 halls for companies, 8 public fchools, called free-fchools ; and 131 charity-fchools, which provide education for 5034 poor children ; 7000 ftreets, lanes, courts, and alleys, and 130,000 dwelling-houfes.

The bridges of London and Weftminfter are beheld with admiration by all foreigners ; that of London confifts of 19 ftone arches, 20 feet between each ; it is 900 feet long, 30 wide, and 60 feet high ; and has a draw-bridge in the middle. The Thames in this part is 915 feet broad.

Weftminfte-

Weftminfter-bridge is reckoned one of the moft compleat and elegant ftructures of the kind in the known world. It is built entirely of ftone, and extended over the river at a place where it is 1,223 feet broad; which is above 300 feet broader than at London-bridge. On each fide is a fine balluftrade of ftone, with places of fhelter from the rain. The width of the bridge is 44 feet, having on each fide a fine footway for paffengers. It confifts of 14 piers, and 13 large, and two fmall arches, that in the center being 76 feet wide, and the reft decreafing four feet each from the other; fo that the two leaft arches of the 13 great ones, are each 52 feet. It is computed that the value of 40,000 l. in ftone and other materials is always under water. This magnificent ftructure was built in 11 years and nine months, and coft about 389,500 l.

Another elegant bridge is building at Black Friars, at the expence of the city of London; which, being fituated near the center of this metropolis, will be of the utmoft convenience to town and country.

Weftminfter-hall, though on the outfide it makes a mean, and no very advantageous appearance, is a noble Gothick building, and is faid to be the largeft room in the world, it being 220 feet long, and 70 broad. Its roof is the fineft of its kind that can be feen. Here is held the coronation feafts of our kings and queens; alfo the courts of chancery, king's-bench, and common-pleas, and above ftairs, that of the exchequer.

That beautiful column, called the Monument, erected at the charge of the city, to perpetuate the memory of its being deftroyed by fire, is juftly worthy of notice. This column exceeds all the obelifks and pillars of the ancients, it being 202 feet high, with a ftair-cafe in the middle to afcend to the balcony, which is about 50 feet fhort of the top, from whence there are other fteps, made for perfons to look out at the top of all, which is fafhioned like an urn, with a flame iffuing from it. On the bafe of

the

the Monument, next the street, the destruction of the city is emblematically represented in bas relief. The north and south sides of the base have each a Latin inscription, the one describing its dreadful desolation, and the other its splendid resurrection ; and on the east side is an inscription, shewing when the pillar was begun and finished. The charge of erecting this monument amounted to upward of 13,000 l.

The Royal Exchange is a large noble building, and is said to have cost above 80,000 l.

We might here give a description of the Tower *, Bank of England, the New-treasury, the Admiralty-office,

* In examining the curiosities of the Tower of London, it will be proper to begin with those on the outside the principal gate ; the first thing a stranger usually goes to visit is the wild beasts ; which, from their situation, first present themselves : for having entered the outer gate, and passed what is called the spur-guard, the keeper's house presents itself before you, which is known by a painted lion on the wall, and another over the door which leads to their dens. By ringing a bell, and paying six-pence each person, you may easily gain admittance.

The next place worthy of observation is the Mint, which comprehends near one third of the Tower, and contains houses for all the officers belonging to the coinage. On passing the principal gate you see the White Tower, built by William the Conqueror. This is a large, square, irregular stone building, situated almost in the center, no one side answering to another, nor are any of its watch towers, of which there are four at the top, built alike. One of these towers is now converted into an observatory. In the first story are two noble rooms, one of which is a small armoury for the sea service, it having various sorts of arms, very curiously laid up, for above 10,000 seamen. In the other room are many closets and presses, all filled with warlike engines and instruments of death. Over this are two other floors, one principally filled with arms ; the other with arms and other warlike instruments, as spades, shovels, pick-axes, and cheveaux de frize. In the upper story are kept match, sheep-skins, tanned hides, &c. and in a little room, called Julius Cæsar's chapel, are deposited some records, containing perhaps the ancient usages and customs of the place. In this building are also preserved models of the new invented engines of destruction, that have from time to time been presented to the government. Near the south-west angle of the White Tower is the Spanish armoury, in which are deposited the spoils of what was vainly called the Invincible Armada ; in order to perpetuate to latest posterity, the

office, the Banqueting-houfe at Whitehall, the
Mews, where the king's horfes are kept; the Man-
fion-houfe

the memory of that fignal victory, obtained by the Englifh over
the whole naval power of Spain, in the reign of Philip II.

The trophies preferved here of this memorable victory, with
fome other curiofities, are, 1. A Spanifh battle-ax, fo contrived
as to ftrike four holes in a man's fkull at once; it has befide, a
piftol in its handle, with a match lock. 2. The Spanifh general's halbert, covered with velvet. All the nails are double gilt,
and on the top is the pope's head, curioufly engraven. 3. The
Spanifh morning ftar; a deftructive engine in the form of a
ftar; of which there were many thoufands on board, and all
of them with poifoned points; defigned to ftrike at the Englifh,
in cafe they boarded them. 4. Thumb-fcrews, of which there
were feveral chefts full on board the Spanifh fleet. The ufe
they were intended for is faid to have been, to extort confeffion
from the Englifh where their money was hid, had they prevailed.——Certain it is, that, after the defeat, the whole con-
verfation of the court and country turned upon the difcoveries
made by the Spanifh prifoners, of the racks, the wheels, and
the whips of wire, with which they were to fcourge the Englifh
of every rank, age, and fex. The moft noted heretics were to
be put to death; thofe who furvived were to be branded on the
forehead with a hot iron; and the whole form of government,
both in church and ftate, was to be overturned. 5. A Spanifh
poll-ax, ufed in boarding of fhips. 6. Spanifh halberts, or
fpears, fome of them curioufly engraved, and inlaid with gold.
7. Spanifh Spadas, or long fwords, poifoned at the points, fo
that if a man received but ever fo flight a wound, it would
prove certain death. 8. Spanifh cravats, as they are called;
thefe are engines of torture, made of iron, and put on board
to lock the feet, arms, and heads of Englifh heretics together.
9. Spanifh bilboes, alfo made of iron, to yoke the Englifh prifoners two and two. 10. Spanifh fhot, which are of four forts;
fpike-fhot, ftar-fhot, chain-fhot, and link-fhot; all admirably
contrived, as well for the deftruction of the mafts and rigging
of fhips, as for fweeping the men off the decks. 11. The ban-
ner, with a crucifix upon it, which was to have been carried
before the Spanifh general. Upon it is the pope's benediction
before the Spanifh fleet failed; for the pope, it is faid, came to
the water-fide, and feeing the fleet, bleffed it, and ftiled it Invincible. 12. An uncommon piece of arms, being a piftol
in a fhield, fo contrived that the piftol might be fired, and the
body covered at the fame time. It is to be fired by a match-lock,
and the fight of the enemy taken through a little grate in the
fhield, which is piftol-proof. 13. The Spanifh ran cur, made

in

fion-houfe of the lord mayor, the Cuftom-houfe, India-
houfe, and a vaft number of other public buildings;
                                                    befide

in different forms, and intended either to kill the men on horfeback, or to pull them off their horfes. At the back is a fpike,
which, your attendants fay, was to pick the roaft beef out of
the Englifhman's teeth. And on one of them is a piece of
filver coin, which they intended to make current in England.
On this coin are three heads, fuppofed to be the Pope's, Philip II's, and queen Mary's.——This is a curiofity which moft
Spaniards who arrive in London come to fee, 14. The Spanifh officers lances, finely engraved. Thefe were formerly gilt,
but the gilding is now almoft worn off with cleaning. It is
faid, that when Don Pedro de Valdez, a captain of one of the
Spanifh fhips that was taken, paffed his examination before
lord Burleigh, he told his lordfhip, that thofe fine polifhed
lances were put on board to bleed the Englifh with; to which
that nobleman merrily replied, that, if he were not miftaken,
the Englifh had performed that operation better on their good
friends the Spaniards, with worfe inftruments. 15. The common foldiers pikes, 18 feet in length, pointed with long fharp
fpikes, and fhod with iron; defigned to keep off the horfe, to
facilitate the landing of their foot. 16. The laft thing fhewn
of thefe memorable fpoils, is the Spanifh general's fhield, not
worn by him; but carried before him as an enfign of honour.
Upon it are depicted, in moft curious workmanfhip, fome of
the labours of Hercules, and other allegories, which feem to
throw a fhade upon the boafted fkill of modern artifts. This
was made near an hundred years before the art of printing
was known in England; and upon it is the following infcrip-
tion, in Roman characters. ADVLTERIO DEIANIRA CON-
SPVRCANS OCCIDITVR CACVS AB HERCVL. OPPRIMI-
TVR 13 c. 17. The other curiofities depofited here, are Danifh and Saxon clubs, weapons which each of thofe people are
faid to have ufed in their conqueft of England. Thefe are,
perhaps, curiofities of the greateft antiquity of any in the Tower,
they having lain there above 850 years. The warders call them
the womens weapons, becaufe, fay they, " the Britifh women
made prize of them, when, in one night, they all confpired together, and cut the throats of 35,000 Danes; the greateft piece
of fecrecy the Englifh women ever kept, for which they have
ever fince been honoured with the right-hand of the man, the
upper end of the table, and the firft cut of every difh of victuals
they happen to like beft." The maffacre of the Danes was
not, however, performed by the women alone, but by the private orders of Ethelred II. who in 1012, privately commanded
his officers to extirpate thofe cruel and tyrannical invaders. 18.
                                                        King

·befide the magnificent edifices raifed by our nobility;
as

King Henry VI'I's walking ftaff, which has three match-lock
piftols in it, with coverings to keep the charges dry. " With
this ftaff, the warders tell you, the king fometimes walked
round the city, to fee that the conftables did their duty; and
one night, as he was walking near the bridge-foot, the conftable
ftopt him, to know what he did with fuch an unlucky weapon,
at that time of the night. Upon which the king ftruck him;
but the conftable calling the watchmen to his affiftance, his
majefty was apprehended, and carried to the Poultry Compter,
where he lay till morning, without either fire or candle. When
the keeper was informed of the rank of his prifoner, he difpatched a meffenger to the conftable, who came trembling with fear,
expecting nothing lefs than to be hanged, drawn and quartered:
but inftead of that, the king applauded him for his refolution
in doing his duty, and made him a handfome prefent. At the
fame time he fettled upon St. Magnus's parifh, an annual grant
of 23 l. and a mark, and made a provifion for furnifhing 30
chaldron of coals, and a large allowance of bread annually for
ever, toward the comfortable relief of his fellow-prifoners and
their fucceffors, which, the warders fay, is paid them to this
day." 19. A large wooden cannon, called Policy, becaufe, as
we are informed, when king Henry VIII. befieged Bouloigne, the
roads being impaffable for heavy cannon, he caufed a number of
thefe wooden ones to be made, and mounted on proper batteries before the town, as if real cannon; which fo terrified the
French commandant, that he gave up the place without firing a
fhot.——The truth is, the duke of Suffolk, who commanded at
this fiege under the king, foon made himfelf mafter of the lower
town; but it was not till feven weeks afterward that the upper
town capitulated, in which time the Englifh fuftained great lofs
in poffeffing themfelves of the bray. The warders muft therefore
be greatly miftaken in their account of this piece. 20. The
ax with which queen Anne Bullen, the mother of queen Elizabeth, was beheaded, on the 19th of May 1536. The earl of
Effex, queen Elizabeth's favourite, was alfo beheaded with the
fame ax. 21. A fmall train of ten pieces of pretty little cannon,
neatly mounted on proper carriages, being a prefent from the
foundery of London to king Charles I. when a child, to affift him
in learning the art of gunnery. 22. Weapons made with the
blades of fcythes fixed ftrait to the ends of poles. Thefe were
taken from the duke of Monmouth's party, at the battle of
Sedgemoore, in the reign of James II. 23. The partizans that
were carried at the funeral of king William III. 24. The perfect model of the admirable machine, the idea of which was
brought from Italy by Sir Thomas Lombe, and firft erected at

Derby,

as Charlton-houfe, Marlborough-houfe, and Bucking-
ham-

Derby, at his own expence, for making orgazine or thrown filk.
This model is well worth the obfervation of the curious.

    You now come to the grand ftore-houfe, a noble building,
to the northward of the White Tower, that extends 245 feet in
length, and 60 in breadth. It was begun by king James II.
who built it to the firft floor; but it was finifhed by king William III. who erected that magnificent room called the New, or
Small Armoury, in which that prince, with queen Mary, his
confort, dined in great form, having all the warrant workmen
and labourers to attend them, dreffed in white gloves and
aprons, the ufual badges of the order of mafonry. To this
noble room you are led by a folding door, adjoining to the eaft
end of the Tower chapel, which leads to a grand ftaircafe of
50 eafy fteps. On the left-fide of the uppermoft landing-place
is the work-fhop, in which are conftantly employed about fourteen furbifhers, in cleaning, repairing, and new placing the
arms. On entering the armoury, you fee what they call a
wildernefs of arms, fo artfully difpofed, that at one view you
behold arms for near 80,000 men, all bright, and fit for
fervice: a fight which it is impoffible to behold without
aftonifhment; and befide thofe expofed to view, there were,
before the late war, fixteen chefts fhut up, each cheft holding about 1,200 mufkets. The arms were originally difpofed
by Mr. Harris, who contrived to place them in this beautiful
order, both here and in the guard-chamber of Hampton-court.
He was a common gun-fmith; but after he had performed
this work, which is the admiration of people of all nations, he
was allowed a penfion from the crown for his ingenuity. The
north and fouth walls are each adorned with eight pilafters,
formed of pikes 16 feet long, with capitals of the Corinthian
order, compofed of piftols. At the weft end, on the left-hand,
as you enter, are two curious pyramids of piftols, ftanding upon
crowns, globes, and fcepters, finely carved and placed upon
pedeftals five feet high. At the eaft, or farther end, in the
oppofite corner, are two fuits of armour, one made for that
warlike prince Henry V. and the other for his fon Henry VI.
over each of which is a femicircle of piftols; between thefe is
reprefented an organ, the large pipes compofed of brafs blunderbuffes, the fmall of piftols. On one fide of the organ is the reprefentation of a fiery ferpent, the head and tail of carved work,
and the body of piftols winding round, in the form of a fnake;
and on the other an hydra, whofe feven heads are artfully combined by links of piftols. The inner columns that compofe the
wildernefs, round which you are conducted by your guides,
are, 1. Some arms taken at Bath in the year 1715, diftinguifhed
from

ham-houfe, in St. James's-park ; the duke of Montague's,

from all others in the Tower, by having what is called dog-
locks; that is, a kind of locks with a catch, to prevent their
going off at half-cock. 2. Bayonets and piftols put up in the
forms of half moons and fans, with the imitation of a target
in the center, made of bayonet blades. Thefe bayonets, of
which feveral other fans are compofed, are of the firft invention,
they having plug handles which go into the muzzle of the gun,
inftead of over it, and thereby prevent the firing of the piece,
without fhooting away the bayonet. Thefe were invented at
Bayonne in Spain, and from that place take their name. 3.
Brafs blunderbuffes for fea-fervice, with capitols of piftols over
them. The waves of the fea are here reprefented in old-fafhioned
bayonets. 4. Bayonets and fword-bayonets, in the form of half
moons and fans, and fet in carved fcollop-fhells. The fword-
bayonet is made like the old bayonet, with a plug handle, and
differs from it only in being longer. 5. The rifing fun irra-
diated with piftols, fet in a chequered frame of marine hangers,
of a peculiar make, having brafs handles, and a dog's head on
their pomels. 6. Four beautiful twifted pillars, formed of piftols up to the top, which is about 22 feet high, and placed at
right angles; with the reprefentation of a falling ftar on the
cieling, exactly in the middle of them, being the center of this
magnificent room. Into this place opens the grand ftair-cafe
door, for the admiffion of the royal family, or any of the nobility, whofe curiofity leads them to view the armoury; oppofite
to which opens another door into the balcony, that affords a
fine profpect of the parade, the governor's houfe, the furveyor-
general's, the ftore-keeper's, and other general officers in the
Tower. 7. The form of a large pair of folding gates, made of
ferjeant's halberts, of an antique make. 8. Horfemen's carbines,
hanging very artificially in furbeloes and flounces. 9. Medufa's
head, vulgarly called the Witch of Endor, within three regular
ellipfes of piftols, with fnakes. The features are finely carved,
and the whole figure contrived with the utmoft art. This figure
terminates the north fide. 10. Facing the eaft wall, as you turn
round, is a grand figure of a lofty organ, 10 ranges high, in
which are contained upward of 2,000 pairs of piftols. 11. On
the fouth-fide, as you return, the firft figure that attracts attention, is Jupiter riding in a fiery chariot, drawn by eagles, as
if in the clouds, holding a thunder-bolt in his left-hand; and
over his head is a rainbow : this figure is finely carved, and de-
corated with bayonets. The figures on this fide anfwer pretty
nearly to thofe on the other, and therefore need no farther defcription, till you come again to the center; where, on each
fide the door leading to the balcony, you fee, 12. A fine reprefentation in carved work, of the ftar and garter, thiftle, rofe
and

tague's, and the duke of Richmond's, in the Privy garden;

and crown, ornamented with piftols, &c. and very elegantly enriched with birds, &c. 13. The arms taken from Sir William Perkins, Sir John Friend, Charnock, and others concerned in the affaffination-plot in 1696; among which they fhew the very blunderbufs with which they intended to fhoot king William near Turnham Green, in his way to Hampton Court: alfo the carbine with which Charnock undertook to fhoot that monarch, as he rode a hunting. 14. Laftly, the Highlanders arms, taken in 1715, particularly the earl of Mar's fine piece, exquifitely wrought, and inlaid with mother of pearl: alfo a Highland broad-fword, with which a Highlander ftruck general Evans, and at one blow ftruck him through the hat, wig, and iron fkullcap; on which that general is faid to have fhot him dead; others fay, he was taken prifoner, and generoufly forgiven for his bravery. Here is alfo the fword of juftice, with a fharp point, and the fword of mercy, with a blunt point, carried before the pretender on his being proclaimed king of Scotland, in 1715. Here are likewife fome of the Highlanders piftols, the barrels and ftocks being all iron; alfo a Highlander's Lochabor ax, with which it is faid that colonel Gardner was killed at the battle of Prefton Pans. A difcerning eye will difcover a thoufand peculiarities in the difpofition of fo vaft a variety of arms, which no defcription can reach; and therefore it is fit that every one who has a tafte for the admirable combinations of art, fhould gratify it with the fight of the nobleft curiofities of this kind in the whole world.

Upon the ground floor under the fmall armoury, is a large room of equal dimenfions with that, fupported by 20 pillars, all hung round with implements of war. This room, which is 24 feet high, has a paffage in the middle 16 feet wide. At the fight of fuch a variety of the moft dreadful engines of deftruction, before whofe thunder the moft fuperb edifices, the nobleft works of art, and numbers of the human fpecies, fall together in one common and undiftinguifhed ruin; one cannot help wifhing that thefe horrible inventions had ftill lain, like a falfe conception, in the womb of nature, never to have been ripened into birth. But when, on the other hand, we confider, that with us they are not ufed to anfwer the purpofes of ambition, but for felf defence, and in the protection of our juft rights, our terror fubfides, and we view thefe engines of devaftation with a kind of folemn complacency, as the means Providence has put into our hands for our prefervation. 1. You are fhewn two large pieces of cannon, employed by admiral Vernon before Carthagena; each of which has a large fcale driven out of their muzzles by balls from the caftle of Bocca Chica. 2. Two pieces of excellent workmanfhip, prefented by the city of London to

.the

garden; the earl of Chesterfield's house, near Hyde-
park;

the young duke of Gloucester, son to queen Anne, to assist him
in learning the art of war. 3. Four mortars in miniature, for
throwing hand granadoes, invented by colonel Brown. They
are fired with a lock like a common gun, but have not yet been
introduced into practice. 4. Two fine brass cannon taken from
the walls of Vigo in 1704, by the late lord Cobham. Their
breeches represent lions couchant, with the effigy of St. Barbara,
to whom they were dedicated. 5. A petard for bursting open
the gates of a city or castle. 6. A large train of fine brass battering cannon, 24 pounders. 7. Some cannon of a new invention, from 6 to 24 pounders. Their superior excellence consists, first, in their lightness, the 24 pounders not weighing quite
1,700 weight, whereas formerly they weighed 5,000; the rest
are in proportion; and secondly, in the contrivance for level-
ling them, which is by a screw, instead of beds and coins. This
new method is more expeditious, and saves two men to a gun,
and is said to be the contrivance of his royal highness the duke
of Cumberland. 8. Brass mortars of 13 inches diameter, which
throw a shell of 300 weight; with a number of smaller mortars,
and shells in proportion. 9. A carcase, which they fill at
sieges with pitch, tar, and other combustibles to set towns
on fire. It is thrown out of an 18 inch mortar, and will burn
two hours where it happens to fall. 10. A Spanish mortar
of 12 inches diameter, taken on board a ship in the West Indies.
11. Six French pieces of cannon, 6 pounders, taken from the
rebels at the battle of Culloden, April 16, 1745. 12. A beautiful piece of ordnance, made for king Charles I. when prince
of Wales. It is finely ornamented with emblematical devices;
among which is an eagle throwing a thunderbolt in the clouds.
13. A train of field-pieces, called the galloping train, carrying
a ball of a pound and a half each. 14. A destroying engine,
that throws 30 hand-granadoes at once, and is fired by a train.
15. A most curious brass cannon, made for prince Henry, the
eldest son of king James I. the ornamenting of which is said to
have cost 200 l. 16. A piece with seven bores, for throwing so
many balls at once, and another with three, made as early as
Henry VIII's time. 17. The drum-major's chariot of state, with
kettle-drums placed. It is drawn by four white horses at the
head of the train, when upon a march. 18. Two French field-
pieces taken at the battle of Hochstadt in 1704. 19. An iron
cannon of the first invention, being bars of iron hammered together, and hooped from top to bottom with iron hoops, to
prevent its bursting. It has no carriage, but was to be moved
from place to place by means of six rings, fixed to it at proper
distances. 20. A very large mortar, weighing upward of 6,000
weight, and throwing a shell of 500 weight two miles. This
mortar

park; the duke of Devonſhire's, and the earl of
Bath's,

mortar was fired ſo often at the ſiege of Namur by king William, that the very touch-hole is melted, for want of giving it
time to cool. 21. A fine twiſted braſs cannon, 12 feet long,
made in Edward VI's time, called queen Elizabeth's pocket-
piſtol; which the warders, by way of joke, tell you ſhe uſed
to wear on her right-ſide when ſhe rode a hunting. 22. Two
braſs cannon, three bores each, carrying ſix pounders, taken by
the duke of Marlborough at the glorious battle of Ramelies.
23. A mortar that throws nine ſhells at a time; out of which
the baloons were caſt at the fire-works, for the laſt peace.

Beſide thoſe above enumerated, there were in the ſtove-room,
before the preſent war, a vaſt number of new braſs cannon; together with ſpunges, ladles, rammers, handſpikes, wadhooks,
&c. with which the walls were lined round; and under the
cieling there hang on poles upward of 4,000 harneſs for horſes,
beſide men's harneſs, drag-ropes, &c. And beſide the trophies
of ſtandards, colours, &c. taken from the enemy, it is now
adorned with the tranſparent pictures brought hither from the
fire-works played off at the concluſion of the peace in 1748.

The horſe-armoury is a plain brick-building, a little to the
eaſtward of the White Tower; and is an edifice rather convenient than elegant, where the ſpectator is entertained with a re-
preſentation of thoſe kings and heroes of our own nation, with
whoſe gallant actions it is to be ſuppoſed he is well acquainted;
ſome of them equipped and ſitting on horſeback, in the ſame
bright and ſhining armour they were uſed to wear when they
performed thoſe glorious actions that give them a diſtinguiſhed
place in the Britiſh annals. In aſcending the ſtair-caſe, juſt as
you come to the landing-place, on caſting your eye into the room,
you ſee the figure of a grenadier in his accoutrements, as if
upon duty, with his piece reſted upon his arm; which is ſo
well done, that at the firſt glance you will be apt to miſtake it
for real life. When you enter the room, your conductor pre-
ſents to your notice, 1. The figures of the horſe and foot on
your left-hand, ſuppoſed to be drawn up in military order, to
attend the kings on the other ſide of the houſe. Theſe figures
are as big as the life, and have been lately new painted. 2. A
large tilting lance of Charles Brandon, duke of Suffolk, king
Henry VIII's general in France; a nobleman who excelled at
the then faſhionable diverſion of tilting. 3. A compleat ſuit of
tilting armour, ſuch as the kings, nobility, and gentlemen at
arms uſed to wear; with the tilting lance, the reſt for the lance,
and grand guard. 4. A compleat ſuit of armour, made for
king Henry VIII. when he was but 18 years of age, rough from
the hammer. It is at leaſt ſix feet high, and the joints in the
hands, arms and thighs, knees and feet, play like the joints of
a rattle-

Bath's, in Piccadilly; Northumberland-house, in
the

a rattle-fnake, and are moved with all the facility imaginable.
The method of learning the exercife of tilting, was upon
wooden horfes fet upon caftors, which by the fway of the body
could be moved every way; fo that by frequent practice, the
rider could fhift, parry, ftrike, unhorfe, and recover with furprifing dexterity. Some of the horfes in this armoury have been
ufed for this purpofe; and it is but lately that the caftors have
been taken from their feet. 5. A little fuit of armour made for
king Charles II. when prince of Wales, and about feven or
eight years of age; with a piece of armour for his horfe's head;
the whole moft curioufly wrought and inlaid with filver. 6. Lord
Courcy's armour. This nobleman, as the warders tell you, was
champion of Ireland, and as a proof, fhew you the very fword
he took from the French champion; for which valiant action,
he and all his fucceffors have the honour to wear their hats in the
king's prefence; which privilege is ftill enjoyed by the lord Kinfale, as head of that ancient and noble family. 7. Real coats
of mail, called brigantine jackets. They confift of fmall bits of
fteel, fo artfully quilted one over another, as to refift the point
of a fword, and perhaps a mufket ball, and yet are fo flexible,
that the wearer might bend his body as well as in his ordinary
cloaths. 8. An Indian fuit of armour, fent by the great mogul
as a prefent to king Charles II. This is very great curiofity;
it is made of iron quills about two inches long, finely japanned
and ranged in rows, one row flipping eafily over another: thefe
are bound very ftrong together with filk twift, and are ufed in
that country as a defence againft darts and arrows. 9. A neat
little fuit of armour, worn by a carved figure, reprefenting
Richard duke of York, the youngeft fon of king Edward IV. who,
with his brother Edward V. were fmothered in the Tower,
by order of their uncle and guardian, Richard III. 10. The
armour of John of Gaunt duke of Lancafter, who was the
fon of a king, the father of a king, and the uncle of a king,
but was never king himfelf: and Dugdale obferves, that
more kings and fovereign princes fprang from his loins, than
from any king of Chriftendom. The armour here fhewn is feven
feet high, and the fword and lance of an enormous fize. 11. The
droll figure of Will Somers, who, as the warders tell you, was
king Henry VIII's jefter. They add, " he was an honeft man
of a woman's making —— he had a handfome woman to his wife,
who made him a cuckold; and he wears his horns on his head,
becaufe they fhould not wear holes in his pockets.—— He would
neither believe king, queen, nor any about the court, that he
was a cuckold, till he put on his fpectacles to fee, being a little
dim-fighted, as all cuckolds fhould be:" in which antic manner
he is here reprefented. 12. What your conductors call a collar of torments, which, fay they, " ufed formerly to be put
about

the Strand; the houfes of the duke's of New-
caftle

about the womens necks that cuckolded their hufbands, or fcolded
at them when they came home late; but that cuftom is left off
now-a-days, to prevent quarrelling for collars, there not being
fmiths enough to make them, as moft married men are fure to
want at one time or other."

You now come to the line of kings, which your conductor
begins by reverfing the order of chronology; fo that in following
them we muft place the laft firft. 1. His late majefty king
George I. in a compleat fuit of armour, fitting with a truncheon
in his hand, on a white horfe richly caparifoned, having a fine
Turky bridle gilt, with a globe, crefcent and ftar; velvet furniture laced with gold, and gold trappings. 2. King William III. dreffed in the fuit of armour worn by Edward the Black
Prince, fon to Edward III. at the glorious battle of Creffey. He
is mounted on a forrel horfe, whofe furniture is green velvet
embroidered with filver, and holds in his right-hand a flaming
fword. 3. King Charles II. dreffed in the armour worn by the
champion of England, at the coronation of his prefent majefty.
He fits with a truncheon in his hand, on a fine horfe richly
caparifoned, with crimfon velvet laced with gold. 4. King
Charles I. in a rich fuit of his own armour gilt, and curioufly
wrought, prefented to him by the city of London when he was
prince of Wales, and is the fame that was laid on the coffin at
the funeral proceffion of the late great duke of Marlborough, on
which occafion a collar of SS was added to it, and is now round
it. 5. James I. who fits on horfeback, in a compleat fuit of
figured armour, with a truncheon in his right-hand. 6. King
Edward VI. dreffed in a curious fuit of fteel armour, whereon
are depicted, in different compartments, a great variety of
fcripture hiftories. He fits like the reft on horfeback, with a
truncheon in his hand. 7. King Henry VIII. in his own armour, which is of polifhed fteel, with the foliages gilt or inlaid with gold. He holds a fword in his right-hand. 8. King
Henry VII. who alfo holds a fword. He fits on horfeback in a
compleat fuit of armour, finely wrought, and wafhed with filver.
9. King Edward V. who with his brother Richard was fmothered
in the Tower, and having been proclaimed king, but never
crowned, a crown is hung over his head. He holds a lance in
his right-hand, and is dreffed in a rich fuit of armour. 10. King
Edward IV. father to the two unhappy princes above-mentioned,
is diftinguifhed by a fuit of bright armour ftudded. He holds a
drawn fword in his hand. 11. King Henry VI. who, though
crowned king of France at Paris, loft that kingdom, and was at
laft murdered in the Tower by the duke of Gloucefter, afterward Richard III. 12. The victorious Henry V. who by his
conquefts in France caufed himfelf to be acknowledged regent,
and

caftle and Queenfberry ; of lord Bateman ; of general
Wade,

and prefumptive heir to that kingdom. 13. Henry IV. the fon
of John of Gaunt. 14. King Edward III. John of Gaunt's father, and father to Edward the Black Prince, is reprefented
here with a venerable beard, and in a fuit of plain bright armour, with two crowns on his fword, alluding to his being
crowned king both of England and France. 15. King Edward I.
dreffed in a very curious fuit of gilt armour, and in fhoes of mail.
He has a battle-axe in his hand. 16. William the Conqueror,
the firft in the line, though laft fhewn, fits in a fuit of plain
armour. 17. Over the door where you go out of the armoury
is a target, on which are engraved, by a mafterly hand, the
figures, as it fhould feem, of Juftice, Fortune, and Fortitude;
and round the room, the walls are every where lined with various uncommon pieces of old armour, for horfes heads and
breafts, targets, and many pieces that now want a name.
   In a dark, ftrong, ftone room, about 20 yards to the eaftward
of the grand ftore-houfe or new armoury, the crown jewels are
depofited. I. The imperial crown, with which it is pretended
that all the Kings of England have been crowned fince Edward
the Confeffor, in 1042. It is of gold, enriched with diamonds,
rubies, emeralds, faphires and pearls: the cap within is of
purple velvet, lined with white taffety, turned up with three
rows of ermine. They are however miftaken in fhewing this as
the ancient imperial diadem of St. Edward ; for that, with the
other moft ancient regalia of this kingdom, was kept in the
arched room in the cloifters in Weftminfter Abbey till the grand
rebellion ; when in 1642, Harry Martin, by order of the parliament, broke open the iron cheft in which it was fecured, took
it thence, and fold it, together with the robes, fword, and fcepter
of St. Edward. However, after the reftoration, king Charles II.
had one made in imitation of it, which is that now fhewn.
II. The golden orb or globe, put into the king's right-hand before he is crowned ; and borne in his left with the fcepter in his
right, upon his return into Weftminfter Hall, after he is crowned.
It is about fix inches in diameter, edged with pearl, and enriched with precious ftones. On the top is an amethyft, of a
violet colour, near an inch and a half in height, fet with a rich
crofs of gold, adorned with diamonds, pearls, and precious
ftones. The whole height of the ball and cup is 11 inches.
III. The golden fcepter, with its crofs fet upon a large amethyft
of great value, garnifhed round with table diamonds. The handle
of the fcepter is plain ; but the pummel is fet round with rubies,
emeralds, and fmall diamonds. The top rifes into a *fleur de lis* of
fix leaves, all enriched with precious ftones, from whence iffues
a mound or ball, made of the amethyft already mentioned.
The crofs is quite covered with precious ftones. IV. The fcepter

Wade, in Saville-row; the earl of Granville's, Mr. Pel-
ham's,

ter with the dove, the emblem of peace, perched on the top of
a small Jerufalem crofs, finely ornamented with table diamonds
and jewels of great value. This emblem was firſt uſed by Edward the Confeffor, as appears by his feal; but the ancient fcepter and dove was fold with the reſt of the regalia, and this now in
the Tower was made after the reſtoration. V. St. Edward's ſtaff,
four feet feven inches and a half in length, and three inches three
quarters in circumference, all of beaten gold, which is carried
before the king at his coronation. VI. The rich crown of ſtate,
worn by his majeſty in parliament; in which is a large emerald
feven inches round; a pearl eſteemed the fineſt in the world,
and a ruby of ineſtimable value. VII. The crown belonging to
his royal highneſs the prince of Wales. The king wears his crown
on his head while he ſits upon the throne; but that of the prince
of Wales is placed before him, to ſhew that he is not yet come
to it. VIII. The late queen Mary's crown, globe and fcepter,
with the diadem ſhe wore at her coronation with her confort
king William III. IX. An ivory fcepter, with a dove on the
top, made for king James II's queen, whoſe garniture is gold,
and the dove on the top gold, enamelled with white. X. The
curiana, or fword of mercy, which has a blade 32 inches long,
and near two broad, is without a point, and is borne naked before the king at his coronation, between the two fwords of juſtice, fpiritual and temporal. XI. The golden fpurs, and the ar-
millas, which are bracelets for the wriſts. Theſe, though very
antique, are worn at the coronation. XII. The *ampulla*, or eagle
of gold, finely engraved, which holds the holy oil the kings and
queens of England are anointed with; and the golden fpoon that
the biſhop pours the oil into. Theſe are two pieces of great antiquity. The golden eagle, including the pedeſtal, is about nine
inches high, and the wings expand about feven inches. The
whole weighs about 10 ounces. The head of the eagle fcrews
off about the middle of the neck, which is made hollow, for
holding the holy oil; and when the king is anointed by the
biſhop, the oil is poured into the fpoon out of the bird's bill.
XIII. A rich falt-feller of ſtate, in form like the fquare White
Tower, and fo exquiſitely wrought, that the workmanſhip of
modern times is in no degree equal to it. It is of gold, and
uſed only on the king's table at the coronation. XIV. A noble
filver font, double gilt, and elegantly wrought, in which the
royal family are chriſtened. XV. A large filver fountain, prefented to king Charles II. by the town of Plymouth, very curi-
ouſly wrought; but much inferior in beauty to the above. Befide theſe, which are commonly ſhewn, there are in the jewel
office, all the crown jewels worn by the prince and princeffes at
coronations, and a great variety of curious old plate.

The

ham's, the duke of Bedford's, and Montague-houfe *,
in Bloomfbury; with a great number of others of
the

The Record Office confifts of three rooms, one above another,
and a large round room, where the rolls are kept. Thefe are
all handfomely wainfcoted, the wainfcot being framed into preffes
round each room, within which are fhelves, and repofitories for
the records; and for the eafier finding of them, the year of each
reign is infcribed on the infide of thefe preffes, and the records
placed accordingly. Within thefe preffes, which amount to 56
in number, are depofited all the rolls, from the firft year of the
reign of king John, to the beginning of the reign of Richard III.
but thofe after this laft period are kept in the rolls chapel. The
records in the Tower, among other things, contain, the foundation of abbies, and other religious houfes; the ancient tenures
of all the lands in England, with a furvey of the manors; the
original of laws and ftatutes; proceedings of the courts of common law and equity; the rights of England to the dominion of
the Britifh feas; leagues and treaties with foreign princes; the
atchievements of England in foreign wars; the fettlement of Ireland, as to law and dominion; the forms of fubmiffion of fome
Scottifh kings; ancient grants of our kings to their fubjects;
privileges and immunities granted to cities and corporations during the period above-mentioned; enrollments of charters and
deeds made before the conqueft; the bounds of all the forefts
in England, with the feveral refpective rights of the inhabitants
to common of pafture, and many other important records, all
regularly difpofed, and referred to in near a thoufand folio in-
dexes. This office is kept open, and attendance conftantly given,
from feven o'clock till one, except in the months of December,
January and February, when it is open only from eight to one,
Sundays and holidays excepted. A fearch here is half a guinea,
for which you may perufe any one fubject a year.

* The Britifh Mufeum is depofited in Montague-houfe. Sir
Hans Sloane, bart. (who died in 1753) may not improperly be
accounted the founder of the Britifh Mufeum: for its being
eftablifhed by parliament, was only in confequence of his leaving by will his noble collection of natural hiftory, his large
library, and his numerous curiofities, which coft him 50,000 l.
to the ufe of the public on condition that the parliament would
pay 20,000 l. to his executors. To this collection were added
the Cottonian library, the Harleian manufcripts, and a collection of books given by the late major Edwards. His late majefty,
in confideration of its great ufefulnefs, was gracioufly pleafed to
add thereto, the royal libraries of books and manufcripts collected by the feveral kings of England.

The Sloanian collection confifts of an amazing number of curiofities; among which are, the library, including books of

Vol. VII.   H   drawings,

the nobility and gentry ; but thefe would be fufficient
to fill a large volume.

London is the center of trade, it has an intimate
connection with all the countries in the kingdom ; it
is the grand mart of the nation, to which every
part fend their commodities, from whence they again
are fent back into every town in the nation, and to
every part in the world. From hence innumerable
carriages, by land and water, are conftantly employed, and from hence arifes that circulation in the
national body, which renders every part healthful,
vigorous, and in a profperous condition ; a circulation that is equally beneficial to the head, and the
moft diftant members. Merchants are here as rich
as noblemen ; and there is no place in the world in
which the fhops of tradefmen make fuch a noble and
elegant appearance.

No expence has been fpared to give this city all
the effential advantages that could be procured by
art and induftry. And in particular, no place in the
world is better fupplied with water from the Thames
and the New River ; which is not only of inconceiv-
able fervice to every family, but, by means of fire-
plugs every where difperfed, the keys of which are

drawings, manufcripts and prints, amounting to about 50,000
volumes. Medals and coins, ancient and modern, 23,000. Ca-
meos and intaglios, about 700. Seals, 268. Veffels, &c. of
agate, jafper, &c. 542. Antiquities, 1,125. Precious ftones,
agates, jafpers, &c. 2,256. Metals, minerals, ores, &c. 2,725.
Cryftals, fpars, &c. 1,864. Foffils, flints, ftones, 1,275. Earths,
fands, falts, 1,035. Bitumens, fulphurs, ambers, &c. 599.
Talcs, micæ, &c. 388. Corals, fpunges, &c. 1,421. Tefta-
cea, or fhells, &c. 5,843. Echini, echinitæ, &c. 659. Afte-
riæ, trochi, entrochi, &c. 241. Cruftaceæ, crabs, lobfters, &c.
363. Stellæ marinæ, ftar-fifhes, &c. 173. Fifh and their
parts, &c. 1,555. Birds and their parts, eggs and nefts, of
different fpecies, 1,172. Quadrupeds, &c. 1, 86. Vipers, fer-
pents, &c. 521. Infects, &c. 5,439. Vegetables, 12,506.
Hortus ficcus, or volumes of dried plants, 334. Humana, as
calculi, anatomical preparations, 756. Mifcellaneous things,
natural, 2,098. Mathematical inftruments, 55. A catalogue
of all the above is written in 38 volumes in folio, and 8 in
quarto.

depofited

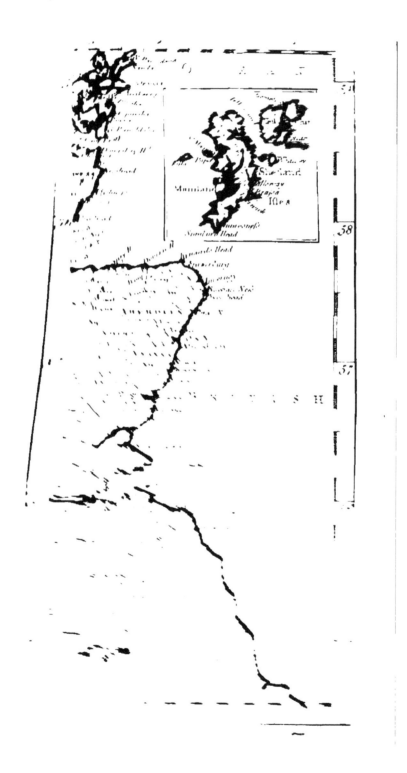

depofited with the parifhes officers, the city is, in a
great meafure, fecured from the fpreading of fire;
for thefe plugs are no fooner opened than there is vaft
quantities of water to fupply the engines.

This plenty of water has been attended with another advantage, it has given rife to feveral companies, who infure houfes and goods, from fire; an advantage, that is not to be met with in any other nation on earth: the premium is fmall, and the recovery, in cafe of lofs, is eafy and certain. Every one
of thefe offices, keep a fet of men in pay, who are
ready at all hours to give their affiftance in cafe of
fire; and who are on all occafions extreamly bold,
dexterous, and diligent; but though all their labours
fhould prove unfuccefsful, the perfon who fuffers by
this devouring element, has the comfort that muft
arife from a certainty of being paid the value of what
he has infured.

O F

N O R T H   B R I T A I N,

OR

S C O T L A N D,

WITH ITS ISLANDS.

THE kingdom of Scotland, or North Britain,
comprehends all the northern part of this ifland
beyond the counties of Cumberland and Northumberland, together with a multitude of iflands, which
amount to about 300; fome of them are very inconfiderable. This country is bounded on all fides by the
ocean, except on the fouth, where it is feparated from
England, beginning at the eaft, by the river Tweed,

Cheviot-

Cheviot-hills, the river Erfk, and Solway Frith. Near Carlifle it is generally reckoned to extend 300 miles in length, from Aldermouth head, near the ifle of Mull, to Buchanefs, and 150 in breadth, where broadeft. The coaft is much indented, and the land in feveral places nearly cut through by bays, gulphs, and rivers, the firft of which form excellent harbours, and the latter abound with frefh water fifh.

North Britain, exclufive of its iflands, lies between the fifty-fourth degree forty minutes, and the fifty-eight degree thirty minutes north latitude, and between the firft degree thirty minutes, and the fixth degree weft longitude. The longeft day is upwards of eighteen hours, and the fhorteft five hours forty-five minutes : but the brightnefs of the northern lights in a great meafure remedy the inconvenience of the fhort days of winter.

The air is very temperate, and not half fo cold as might be imagined from its being feated fo far to the north. This, as in England, is owing to the warm vapours and moderate breezes that continually come from the fea ; which alfo ferve to purify the air, and put it in fuch a conftant agitation, as preferves the inhabitants from any remarkable epidemic difeafes.

Great part of the country, particularly toward the north and weft, is mountainous, and covered with heath ; this is called the Highlands, but thefe in feveral places yield good pafture : between the higher grounds are many rich valleys, which produce corn and cattle. The fouth parts of Scotland are far preferable to the north parts of England, and there are every where all things neceffary for human life ; and not only fufficient for the inhabitants, but alfo to export. They do not want wheat, but the grain moftly cultivated is oats, as it will grow in the mountainous parts. The productions in Scotland are in general much the fame as in England. In the Lowlands there is little timber, but in the more northern parts there are forefts of fir-trees, that might afford

mafts

mafts for the largeft men of war; but it is difficult
to bring them to the fea-fide. There are alfo many.
large woods of oaks, afh, and elms, fit for building, and abundance of fruit-trees in their gardens and
orchards. The foil likewife in many places produces
great plenty of hemp and flax.

Befide the frefh-water fifh found in the lakes and
rivers, feveral of the iflands are frequented by whales;
and cod, ling, haddock, fturgeon, turbot, mackrel,
fcate, fea-urchins, cat-fifh, &c. are caught in great
plenty on all their coafts. Lobfters, crabs, and oyfters, are found in vaft quantities on the Weftern
Iflands; and cockles, muffels, limpets, wilks, fcal-
lops, and fpouts, are caft by the tide in fuch numbers on the ifles, that the people cannot confume
them.

In this country fprings of clear and wholefome water are every where in plenty, not only on the fides,
but on the tops of many of the mountains. Thefe in
their defcent fwell into pleafant rills, and augment-
ing their ftreams become rivers. Many of thefe
meeting with hollow places in their paffage, expand
themfelves into lakes, till finding a proper channel
they refume their form of rivers, and, as the nature
of the foil directs, fometimes expand themfelves again
and again, or continue their progrefs in the fame
form to the fea.

The moft remarkable lochs or lakes in Scotland
are Lochtay, Lochnefs, and Lochlevin, which fend
forth rivers of the fame name with themfelves; Loch-
lomond, which fends forth the river Lomond; and
Lochiern, from which flows the river Iern. There
is a lake in Straitherrach, which never freezes, however fevere the froft, till February, and then in one
night it freezes all over, and if it continues two
nights, the ice grows very thick. Another lake at a
place called Glencanich, is feated on a high ground
between the tops of two mountains, and it is remarkable that the middle of this lake is always frozen

through-

throughout the fummer, notwithftanding the ftrong reflection of the fun-beams from the mountains, which melts the ice at the fides of the lake. Round the lake the ground has a conftant verdure, as if it enjoyed a perpetual fpring; and by feeding on that grafs, cattle grow fooner fat than any where elfe.

In Linlithgowfhire is a lake called Lochoat, from whence a ftream runs under a neighbouring mountain, and after it has purfued its courfe about two hundred paces, iffues with great force from a fpring about three feet broad, when it forms a ftream that turns a mill.

The capital rivers, particularly the Forth, Clyde, Tay, and Nefs, &c. divide the country into peninfulas; thefe running fo far within land as to be intercepted only by a fmall ifthmus, or neck of land.

The kingdom of Scotland, notwithftanding the union of the crowns on the acceffion of their king James VI. to that of England, continued an entirely feparate and diftinct kingdom for above a century, though an union had been long projected: this was judged to be the more eafy to be done, as both kingdoms were antiently under the fame government, and ftill retained a very great refemblance, though far from an identity, in their laws. By an act of parliament 1 Jac. I. c. 1. it is declared, that thefe two, mighty, famous, and antient kingdoms were formerly one. And Sir Edward Coke obferves, how marvellous a conformity there was, not only in the religion and language of the two nations, but alfo in their antient laws. the defcent of the crown, their parliaments, their titles of nobility, their officers of ftate and of juftice, their writs, their cuftoms, and even the language of their laws. Upon which account he fuppofes the common law of each to have been originally the fame, efpecially as their moft antient and authentic book, called *Regiam Majeftatem*, and containing the rules of their antient common law, is extreamly fimilar to that of Glanvil, which contains

the

the principles of ours, as it ftood in the reign of Henry II. The many diverfities, fubfifting between the two laws at prefent, may be well enough accounted for, from a diverfity of practice in two large and uncommunicating jurifdictions, and from the acts of two diftinct and independent parliaments, which have in many points altered and abrogated the old common law of both kingdoms.

However, Sir Edward Coke, and the politicians of that time, conceived great difficulties in carrying on the projected union : but thefe were at length overcome, and the great work was happily effected in 1707, in the fifth of queen Anne; when twenty-five articles of union were agreed to by the parliaments of both nations : the purport of the moft confiderable being as follows :

1. That on the firft of May 1707, and for ever after, the kingdoms of England and Scotland fhall be united into one kingdom, by the name of Great Britain.

2. The fucceffion to the monarchy of Great Britain fhall be the fame as was before fettled with regard to that of England.

3. The united kingdom fhall be reprefented by one parliament.

4. There fhall be a communication of all rights and privileges between the fubjects of both kingdoms, except where it is otherwife agreed.

9. When England raifes 2,000,000 L by a land tax, Scotland fhall raife 48,000 l.

16, 17. The ftandards of the coin, of weights, and of meafures, fhall be reduced to thofe of England, throughout the united kingdoms.

18. The laws relating to trade, cuftoms, and the excife, fhall be the fame in Scotland as in England. But all the other laws of Scotland fhall remain in force; but alterable by the parliament of Great Britain. Yet with this caution : that laws relating to public policy are alterable at the difcretion of the

parlia-

parliament; laws relating to private right are not to be altered but for the evident utility of the people of Scotland.

22. Sixteen peers are to be chosen to represent the peerage of Scotland in parliament, and forty-five members to sit in the house of commons.

23. The sixteen peers of Scotland shall have all privileges of parliament: and all peers of Scotland shall be peers of Great Britain, and rank next after those of the same degree at the time of the union, and shall have all privileges of peers, except sitting in the house of lords and voting on the trial of a peer.

These are the principal of the twenty-five articles of union, which are ratified and confirmed by statute 5 Ann. c. 8. in which statute there are also two acts of parliament recited; the one of Scotland, whereby the church of Scotland, and also the four universities of that kingdom, are established for ever, and all succeeding sovereigns are to take an oath inviolably to maintain the same; the other of England, 5 Ann. c. 6. whereby the acts of uniformity of 13 Eliz. and 13 Car. II. (except as the same had been altered by parliament at that time) and all other acts then in force for the preservation of the church of England, are declared perpetual; and it is stipulated, that every subsequent king and queen shall take an oath inviolably to maintain the same within England, Ireland, Wales, and the town of Berwick upon Tweed. And it is enacted, that these two acts " shall for ever be " observed as fundamental and essential conditions of " the union."

Upon these articles, and act of union, it is to be observed, 1. That the two kingdoms are now so inseparably united, that nothing can ever disunite them again; unless perhaps an infringement of those points which, when they were separate and independent nations, it was mutually stipulated should be " funda- " mental and essential conditions of the union." 2. That whatever else may be deemed " fundamental

" and

" and effential conditions," the prefervation of the two churches, of England and Scotland, in the fame ftate that they were in at the time of the union, and the maintenance of the acts of uniformity which eftablish our common prayer, are exprefsly declared fo to be. 3. That therefore any alteration in the conftitutions of either of thofe churches, or in the liturgy of the church of England, would be an infringement of thefe " fundamental and effential con- " ditions," and greatly endanger the union. 4. That the municipal laws of Scotland are ordained to be ftill obferved in that part of the ifland, unlefs altered by parliament; and, as the parliament has not yet thought proper, except in a few inftances, to alter them, they ftill (with regard to the particulars unaltered) continue in full force. Wherefore the municipal or common laws of England are, generally fpeaking, of no force or validity in Scotland.

The courts of civil judicature in Scotland are,

The college of juftice, commonly called the feffion, which confifts of a prefident, and fourteen fixed fenators or judges, called ordinary lords of feffion, with two extraordinary lords. Under thefe are feven clerks of feffion, and fix inferior officers. Before this court are tried at ftated times, all civil caufes, which they determine by acts of parliament, and the cuftom of the nation; and where thefe are defective, they decide according to the civil law, and the rules of equity. There lies no appeal from this court but to the parliament; and the prefence of nine judges is required to make their decrees valid.

The jufticiary, ufually called the juftice or criminal court, confifts of five lords of the feffion, the juftice-general, and juftice-clerk. Thefe are joined by a pannel of fifteen out of forty-five, cited like juries in England, by whom all caufes of a criminal nature are tried. They hold affizes all over the kingdom twice every year, and from thence are called lords of the circuit.

The

The court of exchequer, which is like that of England, and confifts of a chief and four other barons, &c.

The court of chancery. The officers of ftate are, the keeper of the feal, and lord privy-feal, the lord clerk-regifter, and the lord advocate.

Befide the above national judges, every county or fhire has a chief magiftrate or his deputy, who is ordinary judge in all civil and criminal caufes; but, in moft cafes, an appeal lies from this magiftrate to the feffion and court of jufticiary. The fheriff is in effect the fupream juftice of peace, to whom the law principally intrufts the fecuring the quiet and tranquillity of that part of the kingdom of which he is fheriff. Bailiffs, ftewards, and conftables, in their refpective diftricts, have the fame liberty as fheriffs in their fhires.

The court of admiralty is a fupream court, in which all maritime caufes, crimes, trefpaffes, quarrels, &c. may be tried before the lord high admiral's judge, for he himfelf never judges; he forms his decifions on the civil law, and the cuftoms of Scotland.

There are alfo in Scotland what are called commiffary courts, which are a kind of ecclefiaftical courts, in which caufes are tried by commiffaries. The principal of thefe is at Edinburgh. The four commiffaries of that metropolis particularly try caufes of matrimony and adultery, in order to a plenary divorce, fo that the innocent perfon may marry, as if the offending party were naturally dead.

The Scots nation in general is of the reformed religion, except a fmall part ftill adhering to the church of Rome. The government of their church is denominated prefbyterian, becaufe they allow of no higher office than a preaching prefbyter, who with the elders of the people perform the whole government. The Scots writers declare this to be their primitive form, when the nation firft turned chriftian in the fecond century, and was never altered by the

popifh

popifh prelates till the fourteenth century : and that the church of Scotland was reformed from popery by prefbyters, without fettling any prelacy inftead thereof, is evident from the acts of parliament and general affemblies. The ecclefiaftical courts are the four following.

1. The general affembly, which meets at Edinburg annually in May, and confifts of minifters and elders deputed from every prefbytery in the nation. Thefe determine all appeals from inferior church judicatures, and make laws and regulations for the government of the kirk. A lord commiffioner, who is always a nobleman of the firft quality, prefides here as a reprefentative of the king's perfon. The power of this court is very great, and from it there is no appeal.

2. The provincial fynod, which is compofed of the members of feveral adjacent prefbyteries, meeting twice a year, at a principal place within the bounds, and like the general affembly is opened by a fermon. Their bufinefs is to receive correfpondents from the neighbouring fynods, who are a check upon one another; to determine appeals from the prefbyteries within their diftrict; and to enquire into and cenfure the behaviour of the prefbyteries themfelves. They have likewife power to remove a minifter from one place to another: but appeals lie from the fynod to the general affembly.

3. The prefbytery, which confifts of a minifter and one elder from five to ten or more neighbouring parifhes, who, being affembled, chufe one of the minifters to be præfes, or moderator. Here are tried appeals from the kirk-feffion; and here they infpect into the behaviour of the minifters and elders within their refpective bounds. They fupply vacant parifhes, ordain paftors, examine and licenfe fchool-mafters and young ftudents for probationary preachers.

4. The kirk feffion confifts of the minifter and elders in each parifh, who confider the affairs of the parifh
as

as a religious fociety. They judge in all leffer matters efteemed fcandalous, can fufpend from the communion, and regulate every thing relating to public worfhip and the poor.

The number of kirks or churches in Scotland amounts to about nine hundred and fifty, befide a few chapels, which make up fixty-eight prefbyteries, included in thirteen provincial fynods.

There are here however feveral fects of diffenters from the eftablifhed worfhip, the principal of which are the epifcopalians, who ufe the form of prayer of the church of England: but the nonjurers among thefe are not permitted to have public meeting-houfes, but are only fuffered to preach and read the divine fervice to very fmall congregations; while thofe who take the oaths, and pray for his majefty in exprefs terms, have meeting-houfes. There are alfo the Erfkinites and Gibbonites, fo called from the minifters of thofe names, who have broke off from the church of Scotland, and upon that account they are alfo called feceders. There are likewife mountaineers, thus named from their preaching in the open fields, and on the mountains; thefe are alfo called covenanters.

The law of Scotland has provided againft pluralities, and throughout the whole country there are no benefices worth lefs than fifty pounds fterling per annum; which in that county is a good maintenance, nor any that exceed a hundred and fifty pounds a year.

The members of this ecclefiaftical republic (who are all upon an equality in point of dignity and power) are efteemed to be very fincere in their principles, indefatigable in their minifterial labours, and are greatly refpected by their parifhioners. Befide difcharging their fpiritual duties, thefe gentlemen frequently act in the capacity of arbitrators in matters of difpute between man and man; their healing advice is generally attended with fuccefs, and both

parties

parties return to their families fully reconciled to each other. Where such pastors preside there are few instances of irregularity among the lower classes of the people : adultery, swearing, and fighting, are so very uncommon, that the persons guilty of such practices are considered as the most incorrigible miscreants, despised and shunned by the whole neighbourhood.

The union with England was strongly opposed by the people of Scotland in general, and occasioned such tumults, that the nation was threatned with a civil war. One of the nobles declared in parliament, that his degenerate countrymen were about to give up in half an hour what their warlike predecessors had so bravely defended, and so hardly earned during a contest of many centuries. But the chief grounds of opposition proceeded from a consideration of the heavy taxes that must be levied upon them to pay the interest of debts they never had contracted. Before this time, taxes were almost unknown in that kingdom, provisions were cheap, and by means of their fisheries, mines, and manufactures, they carried on a beneficial trade with Holland and France : but in consequence of the union they were to renounce this trade, and drink port at 2 s. per bottle, in preference to claret at 10 d. because the English carried on a lucrative trade with Portugal. By this treaty the parliament of Scotland, which was annually held at Edinburgh, was to be dissolved, and a limited number of their nobility, together with 45 commoners, were to represent Scotland in the British parliament. It was easy to foresee that so many of their nobility and gentry residing at London would spend one third of the rents of the kingdom in that metropolis.

Such were the objections made by the people of Scotland against this famous treaty, but upon the other hand, the advantages resulting therefrom, though at first they seemed remote and precarious, are many and substantial. An increase of trade has, in the course of 60 years, given a new face to the whole

whole kingdom, but more particularly in the western parts, where the inhabitants soon availed themselves of a free commerce with America. Instead of dark Gothick castles inhabited by a nobility more distinguished for their valour than by wealth, and under whose protection existed a poor, oppressed commonalty, we now behold an incredible number of villas, surrounded with inclosures, and laid out in a manner that does honour to the taste of a trading people. Instead of a few inconsiderable boroughs, remarkable only for the antiquity of their charters, or some ruinous abbey, we meet large and populous towns, well known in the mercantile world for the variety and beauty of their manufactures.

Scotland produces most of the necessaries of life, and supplies other nations with black cattle, sheep, pork, salmon, herrings, and other kinds of fish, corn, barley, salt, tallow, hides, butter, eggs, lead, coals, and freestone; it likewise exports linen cloth, hollands, cambrics, gauzes, silk and worsted stockings, printed cloths, carpets, books, hats, plaid, and coarse woollen cloth, &c. These and many other commodities are chiefly manufactured at Glasgow, a large and beautiful city, situated upon the river Clyde; in point of commerce the first in Scotland. This city likewise carries on a very extensive foreign trade, particularly to America, by means of which, and her own natural productions, Scotland is enabled to remit incredible sums to England, where the fruits of her industry chiefly centers; so that in reality the people of South Britain owe a considerable part of their riches to the very people whose power they are so apt to despise. The difficulty of procuring bills upon London, and the high premiums they bear, are convincing proofs that the balance of trade is greatly in favour of England. It may not be improper in this place to observe also, how grossly this country has been misrepresented by late writers, some wilfully, and others through igno-
                                        rance,

rance, by literally copying from Camden and other old authors, without making proper allowances for the changes and improvements which have taken place, from a gradual increase of trade, and an uncommon attention to agriculture during a period of near two centuries. These compilers of geographical systems would do well to convince us of their extensive knowlege of foreign countries, by giving a more just account of our own. The best modern description of this island seems to be that written by Mr. S. Richardson, intitled, *A Tour through Great Britain.*

The Scots are in general well shaped, strongly made, hardy and robust. They live well, though not grosly, and are wholly unacquainted with some diseases, as well as some vices too common in many other countries. They are, for the most part, an active, industrious, and religious people; and having a great share of natural good sense and sagacity, they generally succeed in their undertakings. The women of inferior rank, and some in higher life, are so remarkable for their industry, that their whole families are generally clothed with their own manufacture. The fidelity of this people is such, that the kings of France, for near 300 years, committed the immediate care of their royal persons to a regiment of Scottish guards. And in 1746, the young pretender wandered several months from place to place, during which time there was not one attempt made toward a discovery, though he was known to many persons, and a reward of 30000 l. offered for his head. The Scotch, however, are not without their faults, and the inferior gentlemen among them have often a greater share of pride than the first English peers; this, however, wears off soon after they have crossed the Tweed, or have visited other countries. Many of them likewise too much affect to imitate their more wealthy neighbours in luxury, and in the other prevailing vices of the times.

Scotland has produced many persons eminent for genius and learning, but no period was ever so dis-

tinguifhed as the prefent, which, if we may ufe the expreffion, may be confidered as the golden age of lite-
rature in that kingdom.

The Scots mufic is univerfally admired; love is generally the fubject, and many of the airs have been
brought upon the Englifh ftage, under new names,
but with this difadvantage, that they are moftly altered for the worle; being ftrip'd of that original
fimplicity which is their effential characteriftic, which
is fo agreeable to the ear, and has fuch powers over
the human breaft.

With regard to the original inhabitants of Scotland, we have no certain accounts; it is probable that
they came in colonies from the neighbouring continent. The Picts feem to be no other than fuch of
the braveft Britons as would not fubmit to the Roman
yoke, and were driven northward by their invaders.
The hiftory of Scotland, fays Dr. Robertfon, may
be properly divided into four periods. The firft
reaches from the origin of that monarchy to the
reign of Kenneth II. who fubdued the Picts in the
year 838, and united under one monarchy all that
country now called Scotland. The fecond, from
Kenneth's conqueft of the Picts to the death of
Alexander III. when the competitors for the crown
put themfelves under the arbitration of Edward I. of
England. The third extends to the death of James V.
The laft, from thence to the acceffion of James VI.
to the crown of England. It has been much re-
gretted, that this celebrated writer confined his hiftory to this laft period, containing only two reigns.
It is obfervable, that Innes, and other Scottifh writers
fince his time, have affected to doubt the very exift-
ence of no lefs than forty of their firft kings. But it
is not very probable that 30000 Caledonians, who oppofed Agricola, could be brought together in thefe
barbarous ages without a leader invefted with fovereign authority; and that thefe people fhould, during
feveral centuries, fuftain the hoftile attacks of united
armies, and at laft oblige the Romans to bound their
empire

empire northward by a wall, which neither their legions, nor the trembling Britons could guard.

This might lead us to a review of the Scots in their military capacity, in which light they are truly great. Their brave defence when attacked by superior arms; their noble struggles in support of the independency and liberties of their country, when reduced to the most distressful circumstances, have gained them a reputation in the annals of Europe, that reflects honour upon their country and their name.

Such were the people whom the wisest of the English monarchs, from various motives of policy, laboured to unite with their own subjects. The Scots, as early as the reign of Charlemagne, had engaged in a league with France, and their inflexible adherence to that nation proved the source of their greatest misery; agriculture, manufactures, and commerce, were sacrificed to their darling profession of arms. Nor did England escape the unhappy consequences of this foreign alliance. At length the wisdom of Henry VII. effected by a marriage, what his predecessors had in vain endeavoured to accomplish by force of arms; and the memorable 1707 united more firmly both nations in one great kingdom. The happy effects of this great event were more easily perceived from a consideration that both nations inhabited the same island, professed the reformed religion, spoke one language, were equally distinguished for bravery, love of liberty, and a similitude in capacity and manners. Since this period, the inhabitants of both nations have mutually exerted themselves in support of the liberties of Europe and of Britain.

I 2

AN

12   7   6   5

55

IRE

Fron

Auth

R

54

53

52

ATLANTIC OCEAN

rants Causway
Rathlin I.
Fair Hd
Head
B. Castle
Coleraine
DON
derry
RRY
Antrim
Carrickfr
Randal
Tyer
Belfast
Newtown
Lisburn
Hilsboro
Dromore
Down
Armagh
Newry
Blany
Peterboro
Dundalk
Atherdees
Drogheda
Navan
Boyne R.
E. MEATH
Kilboy
Trim
Rateth
KILD
Harristown
Naas
Blessington
ARE
Athy
WICKLOW
Ballinglass
Arklow
Caterlogh
CATER
LOON
Tim chany
Ferns
Kylvin
Enniscorthy
WEXFORD
Rosse
Raven Pt.
Wexford
Carnsore Pt.
Bla
Bird Hart

Fair Hd
Maidens
Ailsa
SCOTLAND
Port Patrick
Mull of Galloway
ISLE of
MAN
Calf of Man
IRISH
SEA
Holy Head
Carnarvan
Brachipull Pt.
WALES
Davids
St Brides Bay
Pembroke
Milford Hav
St GEORGES CHANNEL

ANTRIM
ARMAGH
NAHAN
Blarny
N.
LOUTH
DUBLIN
Meath Hd.
DUBLIN
965

British Statute Miles

10   20   30   40   50   60   70

XX

T. Kitchin Sculp.

AN ACCOUNT
OF
IRELAND.

IRELAND is bounded by the Deucaledonian Sea, on the north; and on the weſt and ſouth by the great Atlantic Ocean, which ſeparates it from America; and on the eaſt, by St. George's Channel, which divides it from Britain; and is diſtant from Scotland not full 30 miles, and from Wales, about 60 miles. The whole area, or ſuperficial content of this iſland, is computed to take up about 11,067,712 Iriſh acres, plantation meaſure; the difference between Engliſh and Iriſh acres, being as 16 and an half is to 21; and it is held to bear proportion to England and Wales, as 18 is to 30.

The air is much the ſame with thoſe parts of England that lie under the ſame parallel; only in ſome parts it is more groſs and unhealthy, eſpecially to ſtrangers, on account of its many lakes, bogs, and marſhes. It is remarkable, that no venomous creatures can live in this country, as appears from repeated experiments.

There are ſome bogs in this country ſo deep, as entirely to ſwallow up a man and horſe, who ſink an unknown depth, though they are covered with turf, which ſeems to promiſe ſolid ground; however, roads have been made for horſes and carriages over theſe dreadful bogs, by ranging rows of faggots faſtened together, and covered with earth, which forms a kind of bridge that ſhakes under the feet of the paſſenger. There are other bogs that have too ſtrong a cruſt of turf to be eaſily broken, and are conſtantly paſſed in ſafety, though they ſhake and quiver at every ſtep of the foot.

Ireland is in general a fine level country, abounding in navigable rivers, numerous bays and harbours.

The

The inhabitants, aided by parliament, have of late years applied in good earnest to sundry improvements, as draining of bogs, making canals, building market-towns, inclosing the country, and enriching the soil; so that this kingdom bids fair to rival England in point of beauty and fertility. Its pastures feed prodigious numbers of cattle, whence Ireland is enabled to supply the ships of all European nations with beef and butter: but however advantageous this trade may be in one respect, it is carried on to an excess that is very prejudicial to that kingdom in general, as it causes agriculture to be neglected, which would employ many more hands, and prevent the necessity of importing corn from England, from whence Ireland is likewise supplied with potatoes, in considerable quantities.

The roads in this country are excellent; but there are few or no good inns in the kingdom.

Dublin, whether we consider it in point of extent, beauty, or the wealth of its inhabitants, claims a place among the first cities in Europe. The Liffey, which divides it, is generally covered with the ships of various nations, and the streets that run along both sides of this river, afford a very agreeable prospect.

The Irish were first converted to Christianity in the fifth century, by a zealous and devout person from * North Britain, whom his new disciples distinguished by the name of St. Patrick. The established religion is the same as in England; but the inhabitants of the northern counties still adhere to the church of Scotland. However, the most numerous body are the Papists, who will not submit to the king's supremacy even in temporals, but place the same in a foreign jurisdiction. They have their bishops and other dignitaries, like the established church: but neither they, nor the inferior clergy of that communion, have any other revenues than the voluntary contributions of their poor disciples. It is supposed, that throughout Ire-

* According to his own account, he was born at Kilpatric, a village on the river Clyde, near Dunbarton.

5   land,

land, there are eight Papiſts to one Proteſtant. From
ſuch a diſproportion, the latter, ever ſince the memorable 1641, have placed their ſecurity in the military and a Proteſtant militia.

The preſent inhabitants of Ireland may be divided
into three different claſſes; Firſt, The original natives,
who, from a ſimilitude of language and cuſtoms, are
ſuppoſed to be deſcended from the Britains and Caledonians; particularly the latter, who antiently inhabited the moſt barren parts of Scotland, and being in all ages deſirous of poſſeſſing better countries than their own, it is natural to ſuppoſe that
many of them might quit the bleak mountains of
Argyleſhire, for the more fertile plains of Ulſter,
being within the view of theſe parts. This opinion, of being anciently the ſame people, ſtill pre-
vails among the Highlanders and the Iriſh; and it
is ſaid, that, during the maſſacre of Engliſh Pro-
teſtants in 1641, ſome propoſals were made to except
the Scots from this dreadful butchery. The old
Iriſh are generally repreſented as an ignorant, unci-
vilized people. We may, at leaſt, with equal juſtice
repreſent them as the moſt oppreſſed ſubjects under
the Britiſh government, and the only people who do
not enjoy the benefits of our excellent conſtitution.
This, however, partly proceeds from their adherence
to Popery, but more eſpecially from the inhumanity
and tyranny of their more immediate landlords or
leaſeholders.

Human invention could not contrive a more effectual method for the inſtruction of theſe people in
the real principles of Chriſtianity, and for the inuring
them to induſtry, labour and obedience to their ſovereign, than the inſtitution of Engliſh Proteſtant
working-ſchools over the whole kingdom.

The next claſs of people are the deſcendants of
the Engliſh, who, ſince the conqueſt, gradually extended themſelves over the country, and to whoſe
arts and induſtry Ireland is infinitely indebted; of
theſe are moſt of the nobility, gentry, and merchants.

The third clafs are defcended from a colony of Scots, who were fent thither by king James I. and inhabit Belfaft, Londonderry, and a great part of the province of Ulfter. Thefe people firft introduced the linen manufactory into Ireland, which has been fo very beneficial to that kingdom. They are the people who fo bravely defended Londonderry and Innifkillen againft the Popifh army under James II.

Notwithftanding thefe fupplies from Great Britain, Ireland is in general but thinly inhabited, and according to the lateft computations, does not contain above one million of people.

The inhabitants of Ireland are by no means deficient in genius and bravery. To the Irifh brigades the French were indebted for their boafted victory at Fontenoy; and it cannot be yet forgot that generals of this nation led on the Auftrian troops and boldly faced the greateft warrior of modern times.

Ireland is ftill a diftinct, though a dependent, fubordinate kingdom. It was only entitled the dominion or lordfhip of Ireland, and the king's ftile was no other than *dominus Hilerpiæ*, lord of Ireland, till the 33d year of king Henry VIII. when he affumed the title of King, which is recognized by act of parliament, 35 Hen. VIII. But, as Scotland and England are now one and the fame kingdom, and yet differ in their municipal laws; fo England and Ireland are, on the other hand, diftinct kingdoms, and yet in general agree in their laws. After the conqueft of Ireland by king Henry II. the laws of England were received and fworn to by the Irifh nation, affembled at the council of Lifmore. And as Ireland, thus conquered, planted, and governed, ftill continues in a ftate of dependence, it muft neceffarily conform to, and be obliged by, fuch laws as the fuperior ftate thinks proper to prefcribe.

But this ftate of dependence being almoft forgotten, and ready to be difputed by the Irifh nation, it
became

became necessary, some years ago, to declare how that matter really stood: and therefore by statute 6 Geo. I. it is declared, that the kingdom of Ireland ought to be subordinate to, and dependent upon, the imperial crown of Great Britain, as being inseparably united thereto; and that the king's majesty, with the consent of the lords and commons of Great Britain in parliament, hath power to make laws to bind the people of Ireland.

The constitution of the Irish government is nearly the same with that of England. The power of the lord-lieutenant, who represents the king, is in some measure restrained, and in others enlarged, according to the king's pleasure, or the exigencies of the times. On his entering upon this honourable office, his letters patent are publicly read in the council chamber, and having taken the usual oath before the lord chancellor, the sword, which is to be carried before him, is delivered into his hands, and he is seated in the chair of state, attended by the lord chancellor, the members of the privy council, the peers and nobles, the king at arms, a serjeant at mace, and other officers of state; and he never appears publicly without being attended by a body of horse-guards. Hence, with respect to his authority, his train and splendor, there is no viceroy in Christendom that comes nearer the grandeur and majesty of a king. He has a council composed of the great officers of the crown; namely the chancellor, treasurer, and such of the archbishops, earls, bishops, barons, judges, and gentlemen, as his majesty is pleased to appoint.

The parliament here as well as in England, is the supream court, which is convened by the king's writ; but the representatives of the people enjoy their seat in the house during life, or till the death of the king. The laws are made in Ireland by the house of lords and commons, after which they are sent to England for the royal approbation; when, if approved by his majesty

majesty and council, they pass the great seal of England, and are returned. Thus the two houses of parliament make laws which bind the kingdom, raise taxes for the support of government, and for the maintenance of an army of 16,000 men, who are placed in barracks in several parts of the kingdom.

For the regular distribution of justice, there are also in Ireland, as well as in England, four terms held annually for the decision of causes; and four courts of justice, the chancery, king's-bench, common-pleas, and exchequer.

With respect to the trade of Ireland, the discouragements laid upon it by the act of navigation, and other laws made in England, are so numerous, that it cannot be expected it should flourish to such a degree as its natural situation, extended coasts, commodious harbours, bays and rivers seem to promise. The chief exports of Ireland consist of linen cloth and yarn, lawns and cambricks, which are manufactured to great perfection, and exported to considerable advantage; the English laws giving great encouragements to this branch of trade, which, with a few exceptions, may be said to be the source of all the wealth in Ireland. To these may be added, wool and woollen yarn exported to England only; beef, pork, green hides, some tanned leather, calf-skins dried, great quantities of butter, tallow, candles, ox and cow horns, ox hair, a small quantity of lead, copper-ore, herrings, dried fish, rabbit-skins, and fur; otter-skins, goat-skins, salmon, and a few other particulars. Wool and yarn are allowed to be exported only to England; but from the thirst of gain, many ship-loads are sent by stealth to France, to the great detriment of the woollen trade; and perhaps the best method of preventing it for the future, would be to restore the woollen manufacture to Ireland, at least in the coarse branches of it, and to make it the interest of the Irish to employ their wool at home.

The

The Irish, however, enjoy many advantages un-known to Britons. If they are denied some privi-leges in trade, they are not saddled with our taxes and heavy duties. The productions of their country are cheap; in the metropolis of the kingdom beef sells at two-pence per pound, turkies at one shilling and six-pence, and a variety of fish, at a trifling rate. French claret is landed at little more than one shilling per bottle, and all other foreign commodi-ties (that have not been blessed with a British excise) may be had in the same proportion.

With regard to the other adjacent islands which are subject to the crown of Great Britain, some of them (as the isle of Wight, of Portland, of Thanet, &c.) are comprized within some neighbouring county, and are therefore to be looked upon as annexed to the mother island, and part of the kingdom of Eng-land. Likewise the Orkneys, and many more that belong to Scotland. But there are others which re-quire a more particular confideration.

And, first, the Isle of Man is a distinct territory from England, and is not governed by our laws; neither doth any act of parliament extend to it, un-less it be particularly named therein; and then an act of parliament is binding there. It was formerly a subordinate feudatory kingdom, subject to the kings of Norway; then to king John and Henry III. of England; afterward to the kings of Scotland; and after various grants, it fell at last into the hands of the duke of Athol. But the distinct juris-diction of this little subordinate royalty being found inconvenient for the purposes of public justice, and for the revenue (it affording a commodious asylum for debtors, outlaws, and smugglers) authority was given to the treasury by statute 12 Geo. I. c. 28. to purchase the interest of the then proprietors for the use of the crown: which purchase was at length compleated in the year 1765, and confirmed by statute 5 Geo. III. c. 26 and 39. whereby the whole island and all its dependencies, so granted as aforesaid (except the landed property of the Athol family, their manerial rights and emoluments, and the patronage of the bishopric, and other ecclefiaftical benefices) are unalienably vefted in the crown, and subjected to the regulations of the British excise and cuftoms.

The iflands of Jerfey, Guernfey, Sark, Alderney, and their appendages, were parcel of the dutchy of Normandy, and were united to the crown of England by the firft princes of the Norman line. They are governed by their own laws, which are, for the moft part, the ducal cuftoms of Normandy, being collected in an ancient book of very great authority, intitled, *le Grand Couftumier.* The king's writ, or procefs from the courts of Weftminfter, is there of no force; but his commiffion is. They are not bound by common acts of our parliaments, unlefs particularly named. All caufes are originally determined by their own officers, the bailiffs and jurats of the iflands; but an appeal lies from them to the king in council, in the laft refort.

Befide thefe adjacent iflands, our more diftant plantations in America and elfewhere, are alfo in fome refpects fubject to the Englifh laws. Plantations, or colonies in diftant countries, are either fuch where the lands are claimed by right of occupancy only, by finding them defart and uncultivated, and peopling them from the mother country; or where, when already cultivated, they have been either gained by conqueft, or ceded to us by treaties. And both thefe rights are founded upon the law of nature, or at leaft upon that of nations. But there is a difference between thefe two fpecies of colonies, with refpect to the laws by which they are bound. For it hath been held, that if an uninhabited country be difcovered and planted by Englifh fubjects, all the Englifh laws then in being, which are the birthright of every fubject, are immediately there in force. But this muft be underftood with many and very great reftrictions. Such colonifts carry with them only fo

much

much of the Englifh law, as is applicable to their
own fituation, and the condition of an infant colony;
fuch, for inftance, as the general rules of inheritance, and of protection from perfonal injuries. The
artificial refinements and diftinctions incident to the
property of a great and commercial people, the laws
of police and revenue (fuch efpecially as are inforced
by penalties) the mode of maintenance for the eftablifhed clergy, the jurifdiction of fpiritual courts, and
a multitude of other provifions, are neither neceffary
nor convenient for them, and therefore are not in
force.   What fhall be admitted and what rejected,
at what times, and under what reftrictions, muft,
in cafe of difpute, be decided in the firft inftance,
by their own provincial judicature, fubject to the re-
vifion and control of the king in council; the whole
of their conftitution being alfo liable to be new-
modelled and reformed, by the general fuperintend-
ing power of the legiflature in the mother country.
But in conquered or ceded countries, that have already laws of their own, the king may indeed alter
and change thofe laws; but, till he does actually
change them, the ancient laws of the country remain,
unlefs fuch as are againft the law of God, as in the
cafe of an infidel country. Our American plantations are principally of this latter fort, being obtained
in the laft century, either by right of conqueft, and
driving out the natives (with what natural juftice fhall
not at prefent be decided) or by treaties. And therefore the common law of England, as fuch, has
no allowance or authority there; they being no part
of the mother country, but diftinct (though dependent) dominions. They are fubject, however, to
the control of the parliament; though (like Ireland,
Man, and the reft) not bound by any acts of parliament, unlefs particularly named.
   With refpect to their interior polity, our colonies
are properly of three forts.   1. Provincial eftablifh-
ments, the conftitutions of which depend on the refpective commiffions iffued by the crown to the go-
                                               vernors,

vernors, and the instructions which usually accompany those commissions; under the authority of which, provincial assemblies are constituted, with the power of making local ordinances, not repugnant to the laws of England. 2. Proprietary governments, granted out by the crown to individuals, in the nature of feudatory principalities, with all the interior regalities, and subordinate powers of legislation, which formerly belonged to the owners of counties palatine: yet still with these express conditions, that the ends for which the grant was made, be substantially pursued, and that nothing be attempted, which may derogate from the sovereignty of the mother country. 3. Charter governments, in the nature of civil corporations, with the power of making bye-laws for their own interior regulation, not contrary to the laws of England; and with such rights and authorities as are specially given them in their several charters of incorporation. The form of government in most of them is borrowed from that of England. They have a governor named by the king (or in some proprietary colonies by the proprietor) who is his representative or deputy. They have courts of justice of their own, from whose decisions an appeal lies to the king in council here in England. Their general assemblies, which are their houses of commons, together with their councils of state, being their upper houses, with the concurrence of the king or his representative the governor, make laws suited to their own emergencies. But it is particularly declared by statute 7 and 8 W. III. c. 22. that all laws, bye-laws, usages, and customs, which shall be in practice in any of the plantations, repugnant to any law, made or to be made in this kingdom relative to the said plantations, shall be utterly void and of none effect. And, because several of the colonies had claimed the sole and exclusive right of imposing taxes upon themselves, the statute 6 Geo. III. c. 12. expressly declares, that all his majesty's colonies and plantations

tations in America have been, are, and of right ought to be, fubordinate to and dependent upon the imperial crown and parliament of Great Britain; who have full power and authority to make laws and ftatutes of fufficient validity to bind the colonies and people of America, fubjects of the crown of Great Britain, in all cafes whatfoever.

Thefe are the feveral parts of the dominions of the crown of Great Britain, in which the municipal laws of England are not of force or authority, merely as the municipal laws of England. Moft of them have probably copied the fpirit of their own law from this original; but then it receives its obligation, and authoritative force, from being the law of the country.

As to any foreign dominions which may belong to the perfon of the king by hereditary defcent, by purchafe, or other acquifition, as the territory of Hanover, and his majefty's other property in Germany; as thefe do not in any wife appertain to the crown of thefe kingdoms, they are entirely unconnected with the laws of England, and do not communicate with this nation in any refpect whatfoever. The Englifh legiflature had wifely remarked the inconveniencies that had formerly refulted from dominions on the continent of Europe; from the Norman territory which William the Conqueror brought with him, and held in conjunction with the Englifh throne; and from Anjou, and its appendages, which feil to Henry II. by hereditary defcent. They had feen the nation engaged for near four hundred years together in ruinous wars for defence of thefe foreign dominions; till, happily for this country, they were loft under the reign of Henry VI. They obferved, that, from that time, the maritime interefts of England were better underftood, and more clofely purfued: that, in confequence of this attention, the nation, as foon as fhe had refted from her civil wars, began at this

period

period to flourish all at once; and became much more confiderable in Europe, than when her princes were poffeffed of a larger territory, and her councils diftracted by foreign interefts. This experience, and thefe confiderations, gave birth to a conditional claufe in the act of fettlement, which vefted the crown in his prefent majefty's illuftrious houfe, " That in cafe the crown and imperial dignity of " this realm fhall hereafter come to any perfon " not being a native of this kingdom of England, " this nation fhall not be obliged to engage in any " war for the defence of any dominions or terri- " tories which do not belong to the crown of Eng- " land, without confent of parliament."

[AFTER this review of the Britifh empire, we have, though not introduced by any hiftorical narrative, given a view of the Englifh drefs at two remarkable periods, which when compared with that of our own times, may amufe fome of our readers.]

A SHORT

Dress of a Wealthy Merchant of London in 1588.

bit of the Lady Mayoress of London as 16..

Hall sc.

...bit of the Lady Mayoress of London in 1640.

f an Oliverián an English Partisan in 1650 .

Hall sculp.

A

SHORT VIEW

OF THE

NAVAL TRANSACTIONS

OF

BRITAIN:

Beginning with the Reign of Queen ELIZABETH, and
ending with the PEACE of VERSAILLES in 1762.

THE extenfive commerce of Great Britain having increafed her riches and power, and thence
enabled her to acquire a very refpectable influence
among the European ftates; fome of them much her
fuperiors in extent of territory and numbers of people: it is a very natural fubject of inquiry to afk what
peculiar circumftances operated fo happily in her favour? In this inveftigation, it will not be long before
it is difcovered, that whatever caufes befide might co-
operate; the profperity of Britain is primarily owing
to its infular fituation; and to its being an ifland of
fuch a fize, as to poffefs fufficient internal ftrength
to make proper improvement of its exterior advantages.

Thefe advantages were indeed enjoyed but in part,
before the two kingdoms underftood their mutual intereft fo well as to unite together in one empire.
England, it is true, was always formidable before;
but it is fince that happy period that Great Britain
has fhone with fuperior luftre; and fhewn, what a

VOL. VII. Q brave

brave and a free people, fo fortunately fituated, can perform, under prudent conduct, for their common intereft.

After a general collection of voyages and travels, in which we have ranged the globe at large, and informed ourfelves concerning diftant nations; as we find our own ifland fo peculiarly calculated for a maritime power, and fo eminently diftinguifhed as one; it will certainly be a very interefting amufement to a Britifh reader, to trace, in a hiftorical view, thofe fignal naval tranfactions, from which our mariners have derived fo much glory, and our country fuch capital emoluments, and fuch afcendancy on the ocean.

England from the earlieft ages was diftinguifhed as a maritime nation, compared with her cotemporaries at the feveral periods. But it was not until the time of Queen Elizabeth, that the conftitution began to fettle; and a commercial intereft to take place of the old feudal fyftem. This infpired the government with a vigour heretofore little known; the effects of which were fhewn to great advantage under the refolute princefs with whom we fhall commence a review of the Britifh marine.

Perhaps there never was a kingdom in a more diftreffed condition than England, at the acceffion of Queen Elizabeth. It was engaged in a war abroad for the intereft of a foreign prince; at home the people were divided and diftracted about their religious and civil concerns. Thofe of the reformed religion had been lately expofed to the flames, and thofe of the Roman community found themfelves now in a declining ftate. On the continent we had no allies; in this very ifland the Scots were enemies, and their queen claimed the Englifh crown. The exchequer was exhaufted; moft of the forts and caftles throughout the kingdom mouldering into ruins; at fea we had loft much of our ancient reputation; and a too

fharp

sharp sense of their misfortunes, had dejected the whole nation to the last degree.

Elizabeth was about twenty-five years of age, had quick parts, an excellent education, much prudence, and withal, what she inherited from her father, a high and haughty spirit, qualified by a warm and tender affection for her people, and an absolute contempt of those pleasures, by the indulging which, princes are too commonly misled. She received the compliments on her accession, with majesty; and she supported her dignity even in her dying moments.

The first act of the queen's government was asserting her independency. She made an order in council, in the preamble of which it was recited, that the distresses of the kingdom were chiefly owing to the influence of foreign counsels in the late reign; and therefore the queen thought fit to declare, that she was a free princess, and meant so to act, without any farther applications to Spain, than the concerns of her people absolutely required. On the twenty-first of November, when she had worn the crown but three days, she sent orders to vice-admiral Malyn, to draw together as many ships as he could for the defence of the narrow seas, and for preventing likewise all persons from entering into, or passing out of the kingdom without licence; which he performed so strictly, that in a short time the council were forced to relax their orders, and to signify to the warden of the Cinque-ports, that the queen meant not to imprison her subjects, but that persons might pass and repass about their lawful concerns.

With like diligence, provision was made for the security of Dover, Portsmouth, and the Isle of Wight, so that by the end of the year, the kingdom was out of all danger from any sudden insult, and the queen at leisure to consider how she might farther strengthen it, so as to render all the projects of her enemies abortive. Her entrance on government had the same appearance of wisdom as if she had been years upon the

throne,

throne, and the hopes raiſed by her firſt actions were ſupported and even exceeded by the ſteadineſs of her conduct; ſo that by a firm and uniform behaviour ſhe ſecured the reverence and affection of her ſubjects at home, and eſtabliſhed a character abroad that prevented any immediate enterprizes upon her dominions in that feeble and fluctuating condition in which ſhe found them.

In the month of April 1559, peace was concluded with France; and therein, amongſt other things, it was provided, that, after the term of eight years, the French ſhould render to the queen the town of Calais, or pay her fifty thouſand crowns by way of penalty. In this treaty, the Dauphin and the queen of Scots were alſo included: but this was very indifferently performed; for the French immediately began to ſend over great forces into Scotland, where they intended, firſt to root out the proteſtant religion, and then to have made themſelves entirely maſters of the kingdom. This proceeding ſo alarmed the nobility of Scotland, that they applied for protection to Queen Elizabeth; who foreſeeing the conſequence of ſuffering the French to eſtabliſh an intereſt in Scotland, determined to ſend thither aſſiſtance both by land and ſea.

In the mean time a ſtrict but legal inquiry was made into the loſs of Calais in the late reign. The Lord Wentworth, on whom many aſperſions had fallen, was very fairly tried and honourably acquitted by his peers; but the captains Chamberlain and Harleſton, were condemned, though the queen thought fit to pardon them. As for Lord Grey, his gallant defence of the fortreſs, wherein he was governor, exempted him from any proſecution; inſtead of which, he was appointed commander in chief of the forces that were to march into Scotland. The fleet was commanded by Admiral Winter, which ſailed up the Frith of Forth, blocked up Leith by ſea, while the army of the Scots lords, and the Engliſh auxiliaries under

Lord

Lord Grey, befieged it by land, and in a very fhort fpace forced the French garrifon to capitulate. Thus all the defigns of France on that fide, were entirely broken, and the queen left to look to her own concerns, which fhe did with fuch diligence, that in two years fpace, religion was reftored, the principal grievances felt under the former government redreffed; bafe money taken away, the forts throughout the kingdom repaired, and trade brought into a flourifhing condition.

But above all, the navy was the queen's peculiar care; fhe directed a moft exact furvey of it to be made, a very ftrict enquiry into the caufes of its decay, and the fureft means by which it might be recovered. She iffued orders for preferving timber fit for building, directed many pieces of brafs cannon to be caft, and encouraged the making gunpowder here at home, which had been hitherto brought from abroad at a vaft expence. For the fecurity of her fleet, which generally lay in the river Medway, fhe built a ftrong fortrefs, called Upnore-Caftle. The wages of the feamen fhe raifed, enlarged the number, and augmented the falaries of her naval officers; drew over foreigners fkilled in the arts relating to navigation, to inftruct her people, and by the pains fhe took in thefe affairs, excited a fpirit of emulation among her fubjects, who began every where to exert themfelves in like manner, by repairing of ports, and building veffels of all fizes, efpecially large and ftout fhips, fit for war, as well as commerce. From all which, as Mr. Camden tells us, the queen juftly acquired the glorious title of the RESTORER of NAVAL POWER, and SOVEREIGN of the NORTHERN SEAS; infomuch, that foreign nations were ftruck with awe at the queen's proceedings, and were now willing refpectfully to court a power, which had been fo lately the object of their contempt.

The civil diffentions in the kingdom of France, which gave the court a pretence for oppreffing thofe

of

of the reformed religion, whom they called Hugue-
nots, produced in the year 1562, very deftructive
confequences to their neighbours. The French proteftants had long fued to Elizabeth for protection,
and offered to put the port of Havre de Grace, then
called Newhaven, into her hands; which fhe at length
accepted, and fent over Ambrofe Dudley, earl of
Warwick, in the month of September 1562, with a
confiderable fleet, and a good body of troops on
board, who entered into the town, and kept poffeffion
of it till the twenty-ninth of July following.

The taking into our hands this place, proved of
infinite detriment to the French; for the court having
declared all Englifh fhips good prize, fo long as the
queen held that port, fhe found herfelf obliged to
iffue a like proclamation; whereupon, fuch numbers
of privateers were fitted out from Englifh ports, and
from Newhaven, that the fpoil they made is almoft
incredible. A maritime power injured, inftead of
expoftulating, immediately makes reprifals, and thereby extorts apologies from the aggreffors made fenfible
of their paft miftake. But by degrees this fpirit of
privateering grew to fuch a height, that the queen for
her own fafety, and the honour of the nation, was
obliged to reftrain it.

Philip II. of Spain, from the time of Queen Elizabeth's acceffion to the throne, had dealt with her
very deceitfully, fometimes pretending to be her firm
friend, at others, feeking every occafion to injure and
moleft her fubjects, which he had more frequent opportunities of doing, from the great commerce they
carried on in Flanders. Yet, while thefe things dif-
turbed the nation's tranquillity in a certain degree,
France and the Low Countries, were much more
grievoufly torn through religious difputes, which by
degrees kindled a civil war. The proteftants being
the weakeft, and withal the moft injured party, the
queen was inclined to favour them, and to afford them
affiftance, though fhe was not willing abfolutely
to

to break either with the moſt Chriſtian, or with the Catholic king.

In the midſt of theſe difficulties, the queen took every opportunity to encourage her people, in proſecuting new ſchemes of trade abroad, or purſuing what might be an improvement of their lands at home. With this view ſhe ſometimes contributed ſhips, ſometimes gave money, at others, entered into partnerſhip: in ſhort, ſhe neglected nothing which might ſhew her maternal tenderneſs for all her ſubjects.

The provinces of Zealand and Holland had now delivered themſelves from the Spaniſh bondage, and were growing conſiderable in the world by their maritime power. This however, had a bad effect on the diſpoſition of the common people, who became inſufferably inſolent to all their neighbours, and particularly to us who had been their principal benefactors. Their pretence for this was, our correſponding with the inhabitants of Dunkirk, who were their enemies. At firſt, therefore, they took only ſuch ſhips as were bound to that port; but by degrees they went farther, and committed ſuch notorious piracies, that the queen was again forced to ſend the comptroller of the navy, Mr. Holſtock, with a ſmall ſquadron to ſea, who quickly drove the Dutch frigates into their harbours, and ſent two hundred of their ſeamen to priſon. The queen, not ſatisfied with this puniſhment, ſent Sir William Winter, and Robert Beale, Eſq; to demand reſtitution of the goods taken from her ſubjects; which, however, they did not obtain; and on this account the Dutch factors here ſuffered ſeverely.

But as for ſuch refugees of all nations, as fled hither for the ſake of religion, ſhe not only received them kindly, but granted them various privileges, in order to induce them to ſtay, and fix here the manufactures in which they had laboured in their own countries. This policy ſucceeded ſo well, that Colcheſter, Norwich, Yarmouth, Canterbury, and many other places were filled with those industrious foreigners, who taught us to weave variety of silk and worsted stuffs; while many also from Germany were sent into the North, where they employed themselves in mining, making salt-petre, forging all sorts of tools made of iron, which were arts absolutely unknown to us before their arrival.

The growth of this kingdom's power and commerce, being so conspicuous, left King Philip of Spain, the most penetrating prince of his time, no room to doubt, that his projects for assuming the supream dominion of Europe, or at least the absolute direction of it, would be rendered entirely abortive, unless some method could be contrived for ruining England at once. The catholic king had three points in view, not for distressing only, but for destroying Queen Elizabeth, and utterly subverting the English state. The first of these was, uniting against her, under colour of religion, most of the princes and states abroad; which, by the assistance of the pope, joined to his own extensive influence, he, in a good measure, effected. His second point was, perplexing the queen at home, by countenancing the popish faction, and by maintaining, at a vast expence, such fugitives as fled from hence, in which he was likewise for some time successful. The last thing King Philip had at heart was the providing, as secretly as might be, such a force as, with the assistance of his other schemes, might enable him to make himself entirely master of England at once: to which end he with great diligence sought to increase his maritime power, and upon the pretence of his wars in the Netherlands, to keep under the command of the prince of Parma, one of the ablest generals that, or perhaps any age ever produced, such an army in constant readiness there, as might be sufficient to atchieve this conquest, when he should have a fleet strong enough to protect them in their passage. In the prosecution fecution of thefe deep laid projects, Philip met with many favourable circumftances, which might, and very probably did, ftrongly flatter his hopes : particularly, the death of the queen of Scots, which ftained the character of Elizabeth in foreign courts ; and his own acquifition of the kingdom of Portugal, by which he gained a vaft acceffion of naval ftrength.

Queen Elizabeth and her minifters, were too penetrating, and had too quick, as well as certain intelligence, to be at all in the dark, as to the purpofe of the king of Spain ; and their prudence was fuch, that by every method poffible, they prepared to difappoint him, without difclofing their apprehenfions to the world. With this intent they laboured to convince foreign ftates, that King Philip was a common enemy, and that he aimed alike at fubduing all his neighbours ; which being alfo ftrictly true, had, undoubtedly, a proper weight. In the next place, pains were taken to cultivate a clofer correfpondence with his difcontented fubjects in the Netherlands, and to furnifh them with money, and fecretly with other aids, whereby they were enabled to give fome check to his power, both by fea and land. Our own privateers were allowed to pafs into the Weft Indies, where they carried on an illicit trade, not more to their own profit than the public benefit : for, by this means, they gained a perfect acquaintance with the ports, rivers, and fortreffes in the Weft Indies, with the nature of the commerce tranfacted there, the method of fharing it by fair means, or of deftroying it by force. Thus, notwithftanding their immenfe wealth, and extenfive dominions, the Englifh were in fome meafure a match for the Spaniards, in all places and at all points.

But ftill, the great fecret by which the queen defeated all King Philip's political inventions, feems to have been fcarcely known, to moft of the writers, who have undertaken to acquaint us with the tranfactions of her reign. It was in reality this ; fhe difcovered
the

the principal inftruments he intended to make ufe of for her deftruction; but inftead of expofing or deftroying them, fhe contrived fo to manage them by her creatures, as to make them actually fulfill her purpofes, though they remained all the time tools and penfioners to Spain.

The queen's apprehenfions of the Spaniard's defigns, were certainly conceived much earlier than moft of our hiftorians imagine, as appears from the ftate-papers in her reign; among which, from the year 1574, we meet with nothing more frequent, than inftructions for viewing fortifications, examining the condition of our forts, enquiring into the ftrength, and pofture of our militia, taking frequent mufters; and, in fine, forming upon all thefe enquiries, a brief ftate of the military and naval power of her dominions: whereby it appears, that the able men throughout England, were computed to be one hundred, eighty-two thoufand, nine hundred, twenty-nine, by which were intended ferviceable men; and of fuch as were armed, and in a continual capacity of acting, there were fixty-two thoufand, four hundred, and fixty-two; and of light horfe two thoufand five hundred fixty-fix. In an account of the royal navy in 1578, it alfo appears, that it confifted of no more than twenty-four fhips of all fizes. The largeft was called the Triumph, of the burthen of a thoufand tons; the fmalleft was the George, which was under fixty tons. At the fame time, all the fhips throughout England, of an hundred tons and upward, were but one hundred thirty-five; and all under an hundred, and upward of forty tons, were fix hundred and fixty fix.

It muft give every candid and attentive reader a very high idea of the wifdom and fortitude of Queen Elizabeth, and her minifters, when he is told, that during the whole time Spain was providing fo formidable an invafion, they were affiduoufly employed in cherifhing the commerce and naval power of England;

land; without suffering themselves to be at all intimidated, either by the enemy's boasts, or by the intelligence they had of their great strength and vast preparations. To distress King Philip in bringing home his treasures from the West Indies, many adventurers were licensed to cruise in those seas, and the queen herself lent some ships for this purpose. To delay the invasion as much as possible, or if it had been practicable, to defeat it, the queen sent a stout fleet under Sir Francis Drake, in 1587, to Cadiz; where that admiral performed rather more than could be expected: for he forced six gallies which were designed to have guarded the port, to shelter themselves under the cannon of their castles, and then burnt a hundred ships and upward in the bay, all of which were laden with ammunition and provisions. From thence he sailed to Cape St. Vincent, where he surprized some forts, and entirely destroyed the fishing craft in the neighbourhood.

Arriving at the mouth of the Tayo, and understanding that the Marquis de Santa Cruz lay hard by, with a squadron of good ships, he challenged him to come out and fight; but the marquis, who was one of the best seamen in Spain, adhering closely to his master's orders, chose rather to let Drake burn and destroy every thing on the coast than hazard an engagement. Sir Francis, having done this, steered for the Azores, where he took a large ship homeward bound from the East Indies, which added as much to his profit, as his former glorious exploits had done to his reputation; and so returned home in triumph. This expedition delayed the Spaniards for some months; but in the spring of the next year, his enormous fleet being almost ready, King Philip gave orders that it should rendezvous at Lisbon, in order to pass from thence to England.

His catholic majesty presumed so much on the force of this extraordinary fleet, superior certainly to any thing that had been fitted out for ages before, that

instead

inftead of concealing its ftrength, he caufed a very accurate account of it to be publifhed in Latin, and moft of the languages fpoken in Europe, except Englifh. This piece was dated May 20th, 1588; and according to it, the moft happy Armada, as it was therein ftiled, (afterward chriftened by the pope the Invincible Armada) confifted of 130 fhips, in all 57,868 tons; on board which were 8450 mariners, 19,295 foldiers, 2088 flaves, and 2630 pieces of cannon. Befide, there was a large fleet of tenders, with a prodigious quantity of arms on board, intended for fuch as fhould join them. There were alfo on board this fleet 124 volunteers of quality, and about 180 monks of feveral orders.

The command of the whole was originally defigned to have been vefted in the abovementioned marquis de Santa Cruz, a nobleman of known valour, and great experience, of which he had given high proofs in the famous battle of Lepanto: but he dying, the duke of Medina Sidonia, Don Alphonfo de Gufman, was appointed in his ftead, rather on account of his fuperior quality than his diftinguifhed merit. Under him ferved Don Martinez de Ricalde, an old experienced Bifcaneer, who had the direction of all things, and by whofe advice the general was entirely led.

In the firft place, the queen took care to give proper information to all foreign ftates, of the nature and intent of this project of the king of Spain's, pointing out to them, not her own, but their danger, in cafe that monarch fhould prevail; which method being as prudently carried into practice, as it was wifely contrived, the king of Denmark, at the requeft of her ambaffador, laid an embargo on a very ftrong fquadron of fhips hired for the ufe of King Philip in his dominions. The Hanfe-Towns, determined enemies at that time to England, retarded, however, the fhips they were to have fent to Spain, which, though a very feafonable act of prudence then, proved fatal to them afterward. King James VI. of Scotland
buried

buried all his refentments for his mother's death, and
fteadily adhered to his own, by following the queen's
interefts.   The French were too wife to afford the
Spaniards any help ; and the Dutch fitted out a confiderable navy, for the fervice of the queen, under the
command of Count Juftin of Naffau.

A Lift of the Englifh Fleet, under the Command of
   Charles Lord Howard of Effingham, Lord High
   Admiral.

Men of war belonging to her majefty,	17
Other fhips hired by her majefty for this fervice,	12
Tenders and ftore-fhips,	6
Furnifhed by the city of London, being double the number the queen demanded, all well-manned, and throughly provided with ammunition and provifion,	16
Tenders and ftore-fhips,	4
Furnifhed by the city of Briftol, large and ftrong fhips, and which did excellent fervice,	3
A tender,	1
From Barnftaple, merchant-fhips converted into frigates,	3
From Exeter,	2
A ftout pinnace,	1
From Plymouth, ftout fhips, every way equal to the queen's men of war,	7
A fly-boat,	1
Under the command of Lord Henry Seymour, in the narrow feas, of the queen's fhips and veffels in her fervice,	16
Ships fitted out at the expence of the nobility, gentry, and commons of England,	43
By the merchant-adventurers, prime fhips, and excellently well furnifhed,	10
Sir William Winter's pinnace,	1

In all   143
The

The lift at large given by Mr. Entick, makes them amount to 197 fhips. The quantity of guns carried by the Englifh fleet is not to be found; but though we outnumbered the Spaniards in veffels, the Englifh fleet was greatly inferior both in tonnage, and in the number of men.

The Englifh fleet was commanded by Charles Lord Howard of Effingham, then high-admiral, who had under him for his vice-admiral, Sir Francis Drake; for his rear-admiral, Sir John Hawkins, and abundance of experienced officers, who had fignalized their courage and conduct: their orders were to lie on the weftern coaft, that they might be ready to receive the enemy. Lord Henry Seymour, in conjunction with Count Naffau, cruized on the coaft of Flanders, the better to prevent the prince of Parma from making any defcent, as it was expected he would attempt to do with the army under his command.

In regard to a land-force, the queen had three armies; the firft confifted of 20,000 men, cantoned along the fouthern coaft; another of 22,000 foot and 1000 horfe, which was encamped near Tilbury, under the command of the earl of Leicefter; the third, which was made up of 34,000 foot, and 2000 horfe, all chofen men, was for the guard of the queen's perfon, their commander being the Lord Hunfdon, a brave, active, and refolute nobleman, the queen's near relation.

The Spanifh fleet failed from the river of Lifbon, on the firft of June, N. S. with as great pomp, and as fanguine hopes, as any fleet ever did. The king's inftructions to the duke of Medina Sidonia, were to repair to the road of Calais, in order to be joined there by the prince of Parma, and then to purfue fuch further orders as he fhould find in a fealed letter delivered to the general with his inftructions. It was further recommended to him, to keep as clofe as poffible to the French fhore, in order to prevent the Englifh from having any intelligence of his approach;

and in case he met our fleet, he was to avoid fighting
to the utmost of his power, and to endeavour only to
defend himself. But in doubling the North-cape, the
fleet was separated by foul weather, which obliged
the general to sail to the Groyne, where he re-
assembled his ships, and had intelligence, that the
English fleet, believing their expedition laid aside, was
put into Plymouth.

Upon this he held a council of war, to consider
whether they should adhere strictly to the king's order,
or embrace this favourable opportunity of burning
the English fleet in their harbour; an attempt certainly not impracticable. After a long debate, wherein many were of a contrary opinion, it was resolved
to attempt the English fleet; and this chiefly at the
instigation of Don Diego Flores de Valdes, admiral
of the Andalusian squadron. The pretence, indeed,
was very plausible; and, but for an unforeseen accident, they had certainly carried their point. The
first land they fell in with was the Lizard, which they
mistook for the Ram's-head near Plymouth; and being toward night, stood off to sea, till the next morning. In this space of time they were descried by a
Scots pirate, one Captain Fleming, who bore away
immediately for Plymouth, and gave the lord admiral
notice; which proved the utter ruin of their design,
as well as the sole cause of the preservation of the English fleet.

The season was so far advanced, and the English
had so little intelligence of the Spaniard's departure,
that their fleet was not only returned into port, but
several of their ships also were already laid up, and
their seamen discharged. The admiral, however,
failed on the first notice, and though the wind blew
hard into Plymouth Sound, got out to sea, with great
difficulty. The next day, being the 20th of July,
they saw the Spanish navy drawn up in a half-moon,
sailing slowly through the channel, its wings being
near seven miles asunder. The admiral suffered them

to

to pafs by quietly, that, having the advantage of the wind, he might the better attack them in the rear; which he performed with equal courage and fuccefs: and though Don Martinez de Ricalde, did all that it was poffible for a brave officer to do, yet they were put into the utmoft diforder, and many of them received confiderable damage. More had been done, but that a great part of the Englifh fleet lay at too great a diftance, fo that the admiral was forced to wait for them.

The night following, a Dutch gunner, who had been ill treated by fome Spanifh officers, fet fire to the fhip on board which was their treafure; nor was it without great difficulty, that the flames were extinguifhed. The greateft part of the money was put on board a galleon commanded by Don Pedro de Valdez, which foon after fprung her foremaft; and being thus difabled, and the night very dark, fell into the hands of Sir Francis Drake. He fent her captain to Dartmouth, and left the money on board to be plundered by his men. The next day was fpent by the Spanifh general in difpofing his fleet, iffuing orders to his officers, and difpatching an advice-boat to haften the duke of Parma; by giving him an account of the great lofs he had already fuffered, and the extream danger he was in. On the twenty-third they fought again, with variety of fuccefs, which however demonftrated to the Spaniards, that the mighty bulk of their fhips was a difadvantage to them, their fhot flying over the heads of the Englifh, while every bullet of theirs took place.

On the twenty-fourth, the Englifh were able to do little for want of ammunition; but a fupply arriving in the evening, the admiral made all neceffary difpofitions for attacking the Spaniards in the midft of the night; dividing his fleet into four fquadrons, the firft commanded by himfelf, the fecond by Sir Francis Drake, the third by Admiral Hawkins, and the fourth by Captain Martin Frobifher; but a dead calm prevented

vented the execution of his defign. On the twenty-
fifth, one of the Spanifh fhips was taken; and on the
twenty-fixth, the admiral refolved to make no further
attempts upon them, till they fhould enter the
ftreights of Dover, where he knew Lord Henry Seymour, and Sir William Winter, waited for them with
a frefh fquadron. He alfo took this opportunity of
knighting Lord Thomas Howard, Lord Sheffield,
Roger Townfend, Admiral Hawkins, and Captain
Frobifher, for their gallant behaviour throughout the
engagement.

The wind favouring the Spanifh fleet, they continued their courfe up the channel, with the Englifh
fhips clofe in their rear. The ftrength of the Spaniards had not only alarmed, but excited the courage
of the whole nation; infomuch, that every man of
quality and fortune was ambitious of diftinguifhing
himfelf, by appearing upon this occafion, againft the
common enemy. With this public fpirited view, the
earls of Oxford, Northumberland, and Cumberland,
Sir Thomas Cecil, Sir Robert Cecil, Sir Walter Raleigh, Sir Thomas Vavafor, and many others, fitted
out fhips at their own expence, and went, moft of
them in perfon, to attend the admiral. Men of lower
rank fhewed their zeal and loyalty by fending ammunition and provifions; and fo unanimous were all
men againft thefe foreigners, that even the papifts,
whom the Spaniards expected to have found in arms,
were glad to wipe away the afperfions which had been
thrown upon them, by ferving as common foldiers.

When, therefore, the Spanifh fleet anchored on the
twenty-feventh of July before Calais, the Englifh admiral had with him near a hundred and forty fhips,
which enabled him to gall the enemy extreamly.
But, perceiving on the twenty-eighth, that the Spaniards had fo difpofed their larger fhips, that it would
be a very difficult matter to put them again into diforder, he refolved to practife an expedient long before in contemplation in cafe the enemy fhould have

come up the river Thames; which was converting
some of their worst vessels into fire-ships. This method he accordingly pursued, filling eight large barks
with all sorts of combustible matter, and sending
them under the command of the Captains Young and
Prowse, about midnight, into the thickest part of the
Spanish fleet, where they speedily began to blaze;
and, as the admiral had foreseen, obliged the navy
to separate, and each ship, by steering a different
course, to seek its own safety. This is the first account we meet with of fire-ships being used in sea-
engagements.

The next day a large galeass ran ashore on the sands
of Calais, where she was plundered by the English.
Desirous, however, of attempting somewhat, the
Spaniards again rendezvoused near Graveling; where
they waited some time, in hopes the prince of Parma
would have come out: but in this they were disappointed, whether through the want of power, or of
will, in that great general, is uncertain. At last,
finding themselves hard pressed by the English fleet,
which continued to make a terrible fire upon them,
they made a bold attempt, to have retreated through
the streights of Dover: but the wind, coming about
with hard gales at north-west, drove them on the
coast of Zealand; but soon after steering to the south-
west, they tacked and got out of danger. The duke
de Medina Sidonia took this opportunity of calling a
council of war; wherein, after mature deliberation, it
was resolved, that there were now no hopes left of
succeeding, and therefore, the most prudent thing
they could do, was to drop their design and to save
as many ships as possible.

This resolution being once fixed, was immediately
carried into execution, and the whole Spanish navy
made all the sail they could for their own coast, going
north about, which exposed them to variety of unforeseen dangers. The English admiral very prudently sent Lord Henry Seymour with a strong squa-

dron to cruize on the coaſt of Zealand, to prevent any danger from their joining with the prince of Parma, and afterward left them to purſue their courſe. When the Spaniſh fleet arrived on the Scots coaſt, and found that care was every where taken they ſhould meet with no ſupply, they threw their horſes and mules overboard; and ſuch of them as had a proper ſtore of water, bore away directly for the bay of Biſcay, with the duke of Medina Sidonia, making in all about twenty-five ſhips. The reſt, about forty ſail, under the command of the vice-admiral, ſtood over for the coaſt of Ireland, intending to have watered at Cape Clare. On the ſecond of September, however, a tempeſt aroſe, and drove moſt of them aſhore, ſo that upward of thirty ſhips, and many thouſand men, periſhed on the Iriſh coaſt.

Some likewiſe were forced a ſecond time into the Engliſh channel, where they were taken, ſome by the Engliſh, and ſome by the Rochellers. Several very large veſſels were loſt among the weſtern iſles, and upon the coaſt of Argyleſhire. Out of theſe, about five hundred perſons were ſaved; who came into Edinburgh, in a manner naked; and, out of mere charity, were cloathed by the inhabitants of that city; who alſo attempted to ſend them home to Spain. But, as if misfortunes were always to attend them, they were forced in their paſſage upon the coaſt of Norfolk, and obliged to put into Yarmouth; where they ſtayed, till advice was given to the queen and council: who conſidering the miſeries they had already felt, and not willing to appear leſs compaſſionate than the Scots, ſuffered them to continue their voyage.

Thus, in the ſhort ſpace of a month, this mighty fleet, which had been no leſs than three years preparing, was deſtroyed and brought to nothing. Of one hundred and thirty ſhips, there returned but fifty-three or four; and of the people embarked there periſhed twenty thouſand men at leaſt. We may beſt

form

form an idea of their lofs, from the precaution taken by King Philip to hide it, which was publifhing a proclamation to prohibit mourning. As to the cou-rage and conftancy he exprefled upon this occafion, it is certain, that the lord treafurer Burleigh received intelligence " That the king fhould fay, after mafs, " that he would fpend the wealth of Spain, to one of " thofe candlefticks upon the altar, rather than not " revenge himfelf upon the Englifh." His future conduct agreed fo exactly with this threatning, that we may well conclude, if he did not fay, he thought fo, and was therefore far from being fo unmoved at this difafter as is commonly reported. What might in fome meafure juftify his refentment, was, the fall-ing out of this mifchief, through the breach of his orders, which is well remarked by a writer of our own: for, if the king's inftructions had been pur-fued, it is more than probable, that Queen Elizabeth's government had run the utmoft hazard of being over-turned.

The duke of Medina Sidonia efcaped punifhment, through the intereft of his wife; but as for Don Diego Flores de Valdez, whofe perfuafions induced the general to take that rafh ftep, he was arrefted as foon as he fet foot on fhore, and conducted to the caftle of St. Andero; after which, he was never heard of more. The fame writer, from whom we have this particular, remarks alfo an error in the con-duct of the Englifh; viz. that they did not attack the Spanifh fleet after it arrived before Graveling; which, however, he affures us, was not through any fault in the admiral, but was occafioned through the negli-gence of fome under-officers, who had the direction of the military ftores, and had been too fparing of powder and ammunition. Otherwife, he tells us, it was thought, the duke de Medina Sidonia, at the perfuafion of his confeffor, would have yielded both himfelf and his fhips, which, it feems, were, in that particular, not at all better provided. This would

have

have been a conquest indeed, a conquest equally glorious and important, the loss of which, ought to teach posterity, not to be too hasty in censuring great officers, or too remiss in punishing little ones.

The queen having intelligence that the Spaniards meditated a second attempt upon her dominions, resolved, like a wise princess, to find them work at home; in order to which, in the spring of the year 1589, she expressed her royal intention of assisting Don Antonio to recover his kingdom of Portugal. The expedition was undertaken partly at the queen's charge, and partly at the expence of private persons. Sir Francis Drake, and Sir John Norris, were joint commanders; and the whole navy consisted of 146 sail. To which also the Dutch, as much interested as we, joined a small squadron.

This armament landed near Corunna, commonly called the Groyne, which place they attacked, burnt the adjacent country, together with many magazines of naval stores: they then reimbarked their forces, and sailed, as they had at first designed, for the river of Lisbon. On their arrival before Peniche, the troops were landed; the place quickly surrendered to Don Antonio; and from thence the whole army marched by land toward Lisbon; where they expected to have met the fleet under the command of Sir Francis Drake: but he finding it impossible to proceed up the river with safety to her majesty's ships, staid at the castle of Cascais, which place he took, and also seized sixty sail of ships belonging to the Hanse-Towns, laden with corn and ammunition; which, with about 150 pieces of cannon, were the principal fruits of this voyage. It was indeed, intended, to have gone to the Canaries; but by this time the soldiers and sailors were so weakened with sickness, that it was thought more expedient to return. In their passage home they landed at Vigo, took and plundered it; and having made some addition to their booty, reached England; after having been about ten weeks abroad.

P 3

This

This expedition was inexpreffibly deftructive to the Spaniards, difappointed all their defigns, weakened their naval force, and fpread a mighty terror of the Englifh arms through their whole dominions. But as to any advantages which the proprietors reaped, they were but very inconfiderable; and the generals met with a cold reception in England. The chief grounds of their mifcarriage were in thofe days, when men could beft judge, held to be thefe. Firft, They were but indifferently manned and victualled. Secondly, Their landing at the Groyne was contrary to their in-ftructions; gave the men an opportunity of drinking new wines, and expofed them to a great and unne-ceffary lofs. Thirdly, The difagreement of the ge-nerals before Lifbon, defeated the remaining part of their defign; whereas, if in purfuance of their inftruc-tions, they had failed directly to the coafts of Portugal, and landed their forces there, it is more than probable, they had effectually placed Don Antonio upon the throne of Portugal, which would have given a deadly ftroke to the power of Spain.

The difappointments which happened in this voy-age, did not difcourage either the queen or her fub-jects from purfuing the war by fea. In order to this, her majefty fettled a part of her revenue for the ordi-nary fupply of the navy, amounting to about nine thoufand pounds a year: and by expreffing a very high efteem for fuch young lords, and other perfons of diftinction, as had fhewn an inclination to the fea-fervice, fhe encouraged others to undertake yet greater things. Amongft thefe, the earl of Cumberland par-ticularly diftinguifhed himfelf by fitting out a ftout fquadron, in the fummer of the year 1589, with which he failed to the Tercera iflands, where he did the Spaniards incredible mifchief, and obtained con-fiderable advantages for himfelf, and for his friends.

In 1590, Sir John Hawkins and Sir Martin Fro-bifher were at fea with two fquadrons; and by im-peding the return of the Spanifh plate-fleets from

America,

America, and other fervices, kept King Philip entirely employed at home, though his thoughts were ftill bufy in contriving another expedition againft England.   The fucceeding year, Lord Thomas Howard, fecond fon to the duke of Norfolk, failed with a fquadron to the iflands, in hopes of intercepting the Spanifh fleet from the Weft Indies, which now was forced to return home.   In this he had probably fucceeded, if his force had been greater; but having no more than feven of the queen's fhips, and about as many fitted out by private adventurers, he very narrowly efcaped being totally deftroyed by the Spaniards.

In 1591, the earl of Cumberland made another expedition: and in 1592, Sir Martin Frobifher, and Sir John Boroughs, infefted the Spanifh coaft, and did much mifchief.   In 1594, the queen fent a fmall fquadron to fea, under the command of Sir Martin Frobifher, to reduce the port of Breft in Bretagne, which the king of Spain had taken, by the affiftance of the Leaguers in France, from King Henry IV. A place that if it had been long kept, muft have been very troublefome to that monarch, and would have given the Spaniards great advantages againft us.   It was ftrong, as well by fituation, as by the art and expence employed in fortifying it; and had, befide, a numerous garrifon of Spanifh troops.   Sir John Norris, with a fmall Englifh army, formed the fiege by land; Sir Martin Frobifher, with only four men of war, forced an entrance into the harbour; and having thus blocked up the place by fea, landed his failors, and in conjunction with Sir John Norris, ftormed the fort; which, though gallantly defended, was taken; with the lofs of abundance of brave men; and amongft them, may be reckoned Sir Martin himfelf, who died in the wounds he received in that fervice.   The fame year Sir Francis Drake, and Sir John Hawkins failed on their laft expedition into the Weft Indies.

The

The Spaniards, who feldom abandon any defign they once undertake, were all this time employed in affembling and equipping another fleet for England; and as an earneft of their intentions, in the year 1595, Don Diego Brochero, with four gallies, arrived in Mount's-Bay, in Cornwall, and landing with all his men, burnt three little places; but without killing or taking fo much as a fingle man. This, however, alarmed the nation, and engaged the queen to undertake an invafion of the Spanifh dominions, to prevent any fuch future vifits to her own; in order to which, a ftout fleet and a numerous army were provided, under the moft experienced officers of thofe times.

The true defign of this expedition, was, to deftroy the Spanifh fleet in the port of Cadiz, and to make themfelves mafters of that rich city. The force employed was very great, not lefs in all than 150 fail; of which, 126 were men of war; but of thefe, only feventeen were the queen's fhips, the reft were hired from traders and fitted for this voyage. On board this mighty fleet, were embarked upward of 7000 men. The joint commanders of the expedition were, the earl of Effex, and the lord high-admiral (Howard) affifted by a council of war. There was befide, a Dutch fquadron, under the command of Admiral Van Davenvoord, confifting of twenty-four fhips, well manned and victualled. This navy lay for fome time at Plymouth, till all things could be got ready; and then, on the firft of June 1596, failed for the coaft of Spain with a fair wind, and the good wifhes of all their countrymen.

They were fo happy as to arrive in fight of Cadiz on the twentieth of the fame month, before they were either looked for, or fo much as apprehended. They found the town indifferently well fortified, and defended by a ftrong caftle. In the port were fifty-nine Spanifh fhips; amongft them, many laden with treafure, and nineteen or twenty gallies. Some time was loft before their coming to a refolution how to act,

owing

owing to the joint command : for the earl of Effex, who was young and warm, affected to dictate ; while the admiral, who had as much courage, and more experience, could not brook being controuled. At laft, it was determined to attack the fhips in the haven, before any attempt was made upon the town ; whereupon a new difficulty arofe, which was, who fhould command this attack. In the execution, fome errors were committed, through the too great heat and emulation of the commanders; but others much more grofs and fatal by the Spaniards; who, when they found themfelves compelled to fly, did it without any of thofe precautions whereby they might have provided for their fafety : for inftead of running their fhips afhore under the town, where they would have been covered by their own artillery, and where at leaft their men might have gone afhore in fafety, they ran them up the bay, as far from the enemy as poffible ; by which means, part fell into the hands of the Englifh, and the reft were burnt.

In the mean time, the earl of Effex landed his men quietly, the enemy deferting a ftrong fort, from which they might have done him much mifchief : three regiments alfo were fent to make themfelves mafters of the caufeway which unites the ifland to the main. This they performed with very fmall lofs; but afterward quitted it again, which gave the gallies an opportunity of efcaping ; another overfight, for which no account can be given. The lord admiral, hearing the earl was landed, landed alfo with the remainder of the forces, doubting much whether his lordfhip could have kept the place : and while the two generals were employed in reducing the city, Sir Walter Raleigh was fent to feize the fhips in the harbour of Port-Real; to prevent which, the duke of Medina Sidonia caufed them to be fet on fire, and burnt, whereby twenty millions were buried in the fea. The city and its forts they poffeffed for a fortnight ; and the earl of Effex was very defirous of being

ing left there with a garrifon, however fmall; which was, notwithftanding, over-ruled by the council of war. It was then agreed to fail to Faro, in the kingdom of Algarve, where they found the place deferted by its inhabitants, and void of any thing that could be made plunder. To repair this difappointment, the earl of Effex was for failing to the Azores, there to wait for the Eaft India fhips; but in this too he was over-ruled, becaufe there was a great complaint of the want of provifion and ammunition on board the fleet. In their return, they looked into the ports of Groyne, St. Andero, and St. Sebaftian, where they expected to find fhips, but met with none; and after this, nothing remarkable happened till their arrival in England, which was on the eighth of Auguft the fame year. They brought with them two galleons, one hundred brafs guns, and an immenfe booty; the defire of keeping which, is conceived to have hindered them from performing more.

In the fpring of the year 1597, the king of Spain fitted out a frefh armada from Lifbon, compofed not only of his own fhips and gallies, but alfo of all that he could take up, and hire in Italy, or elfewhere. On board of thefe, he embarked a great body of troops, efpecially of the Irifh, intending to have invaded both England and Ireland; but the winds difappointed him, fcattered his fleet, and thirty-fix fail were caft away. In the mean time the queen fitted out another fleet of 40 men of war under the command of the earl of Effex, with an intent to intercept the plate-fleet near the Azores, after burning fuch veffels as were in the harbours of the Groyne and Ferrol. They failed from Plymouth the 9th of July; but a ftorm arifing, they were forced back thither again, and did not fail the fecond time till the 7th of Auguft. They ufed their beft endeavours to perform the firft part of their inftructions, but finding it impracticable, they thought it expedient to fteer for the iflands. In this voyage Sir Walter Raleigh's

fhip

ship sprung her mast, which, however, did not hinder him, when he had repaired his loss, from proceeding to the place of rendezvous. He had scarce begun to wood and water there, before the earl of Essex sent him orders to follow him to Fayal, which island the general himself intended to attempt. Raleigh obeyed him; but not finding Essex on his arrival, and perceiving that the people were securing their goods, throwing up retrenchments, and making every other preparation necessary for their defence, he with the advice of his officers resolved, in case Essex did not arrive in four days, to attempt the reduction of the island, which accordingly he performed: but though he got reputation by this exploit, yet he lost the general's friendship, so that a coldness thenceforth prevailed, which afterward encreased to open opposition and the most rancorous hatred.

After Essex's arrival they sailed together to Graciosa, which immediately submitted. Here the general intended to have staid; and if he had done so, undoubtedly it had answered his purpose, and he had taken the whole Spanish fleet: but being too easily brought to alter his purposes, he took another method, which gave the Spaniards, who arrived the next day, an opportunity of proceeding for Tercera, with the loss of no more than three ships, which were taken by Sir William Monson. The rest of the fleet, consisting of about thirty-seven sail, arrived safely in the port of Angra, which was well defended by several forts; so that on mature deliberation, it was judged impracticable to attempt any thing there with reasonable hopes of success.

The earl of Essex, vexed at this disappointment, resolved to do somewhat of consequence before he returned; and therefore landing, surprised the town of Villa Franca and plundered it: after which he reimbarked his forces, and prepared for his return home. In his passage he had the good luck to take a very rich Spanish ship, which fell into his fleet,
mistaking

miftaking it for their own. In the mean time, the Spaniards were meditating great defigns. The abfence of the Englifh fleet gave them an opportunity of fending out their fquadrons from the Groyne and Ferrol. With thefe they intended to have made a defcent in Cornwall, and to have poffeffed themfelves of the port of Falmouth. The Spanifh admiral proceeded to the iflands of Scilly, almoft within fight of our fhore: but it fo happened, that a very high ftorm arofe, which entirely feparated their fleet. In this ftorm eighteen capital fhips were loft, feveral forced into Englifh ports were taken, and the Spanifh admiral's fchemes thereby entirely difconcerted. Nor did our fleet efcape the fury of this tempeft; but with much difficulty reached the weftern coaft in the latter end of the month of October.

In 1598, the earl of Cumberland fitted out a fquadron of eleven fail at his own expence; with which he firft attempted to intercept the Lifbon fleet in its paffage to the Eaft Indies. Being difappointed in that, he failed to the Canaries, where he made a defcent on the ifland of Lancerota, plundered it, and then proceeded to America, where he promifed himfelf great things. The place he fixed upon was the ifland of Puerto Rico, where he landed, and took the capital with fmall lofs. This city he determined to keep, with an intent to have cruifed from thence upon the Spanifh coafts; but he was quickly convinced that the defign was impracticable, difeafes fpreading amongft his foldiers and feamen to fuch a degree, that he was obliged to abandon his conqueft.

In 1599, there was a great fleet fitted out by the queen's command: but it feems rather with an intent to watch the Spaniards, than to undertake any other enterprize of importance; fince after remaining about three weeks in the Downs, it was again laid up. Yet the equipping this fleet had a great effect upon Spain, and all the powers of Europe; for it was drawn together in twelve days time, well victualled, and

throughly

throughly manned, which shewed the strength of our maritime power, and how much it was improved since 1588. The next year, being 1600, Sir Richard Levison was sent to intercept the plate-fleet; which design, though it was well contrived and wisely executed, yet failed. In 1601, the same admiral was employed in Ireland, where he did good service, in obliging the Spaniards, who had landed a considerable body of forces, to relinquish their design, and withdraw out of that island.

In 1602, the same admiral, in conjunction with Sir William Monson, was employed in an expedition for intercepting the galleons, which had infallibly taken effect, if the Dutch had sent their squadron, agreeable to their engagements with the queen. Notwithstanding this disappointment, they continued on the coast of Portugal, and at length resolved to attack a galleon which lay with eleven gallies in the road of Cerimbra; which was one of the most gallant exploits performed in the whole war. The town of Cerimbra was large and well built with free-stone, defended by a good citadel well furnished with artillery. Above the town, on the top of a mountain, stood the abbey, so fortified as to command the place, the citadel, and the road. The galleon was moored close to the shore, so as to defend by its fire, part of the citadel and part of the town : the gallies had so flanked and fortified themselves, that they were able to make a great fire upon the English fleet, without receiving any damage themselves, till such time as our ships were just before the town. Yet, in spite of these and many other disadvantages, the English admirals resolved to attack them; which they did on the 3d of June. A gale of wind blowing fresh about two in the morning, the admiral weighed, and made the signal for an attack. The vice-admiral did the like, and soon after they fell upon the enemy with great fury; and though the Spaniards defended themselves with much resolution, yet in the end several

of

of the gallies were burnt, the garrison driven from
the caftle, and the rich galleon, for which all
this ftruggle was made, taken, with about a million
of pieces of eight on board. Frederic Spinola, in
the St. Lewis, failed from Cerimbra, with the reft of
the gallies that had efcaped, viz. The St. John Baptift, the Lucera, the Padilla, the Philip, and the St.
John, for the coaft of Flanders; and on the 23d of
September entered the Britifh channel. Here they fell
in with fome Englifh and Dutch fhips;. by whom three
of them were funk: the reft with great difficulty reached Dunkirk in fafety.

This was the laft great exploit performed by fea in
this reign; for the queen, now far in years, and worn
out with the cares and fatigues of government, died
on the 24th of March following, in the forty-fifth
year of her reign, and in the feventieth of her life:
when fhe had fettled the proteftant religion throughout her kingdom, had reftored the crown to its ancient reputation, fupported her allies with the greateft
firmnefs, and humbled her enemies, fo as to compel
them to think of foliciting for peace.

Her attention to trade appears in many inftances,
of fome of which it may not be amifs to treat more
particularly. The merchants of the Hanfe-towns
complained loudly in the beginning of her reign, of
the ill-treatment they had received in the days of Edward and queen Mary; to which fhe very prudently
anfwered, "That as fhe would not innovate any
" thing, fo fhe would protect them ftill in the im-
" munities and condition fhe found them:" which
not contenting them, their commerce was foon after
fufpended for a time, to the great advantage of the
English merchants. At laft the Hanfe-towns prevailed fo far in virtue of their German connections as
to gain an imperial edict, whereby the Englifh merchants were prohibited all commerce in the empire;
this was anfwered by a proclamation, in confequence
of which, fixty fail of their fhips were taken in the
river of Lifbon, laden with contraband goods for the

uſe

ufe of the Spaniards. Thefe fhips the queen intended to have reftored, as fincerely defiring to have com-
promifed all differences with thofe trading cities : but
when fhe was informed that a general affembly was
held at the city of Lubeck, in order to concert meafures for diftreffing the Englifh trade, fhe caufed the
fhips and their cargoes to be confifcated ; only two of
them were releafed to carry home this news, and that
the queen had the greateft contempt imaginable for
all their proceedings.

After this, Sigifmond king of Poland interpofed in
their behalf, fending hither an ambaffador, who talk-
ing in a very high ftile ; the queen, in her anfwers told
him plainly, that the king his mafter made no right
eftimate of his own power, and that himfelf was very
little fit for the employment in which fhe found him.
Thus were we ridded for ever of thefe incorporated
foreign factors, and our own merchants eftablifhed in
the right of managing our commerce. In the latter
end of her reign, fome difputes happening with the
king of Denmark, and he moft unadvifedly feizing
the Englifh fhips that were in his ports, the queen
fent one Dr. Parkins to demand immediate and adequate fatisfaction : which he did in fo peremptory a
ftile, that the Dane was glad to compound the matter
for forty thoufand dollars, which he paid her majefty,
and which fhe caufed to be proportionably divided
among the merchants who were injured.

Thefe are inftances of her noble fpirit in obtaining
redrefs of grievances in foreign countries, even in the
moft perillous times, and when her affairs were in
the utmoft embarraffment. As to her care of trade
and navigation within her own dominions, we have
already mentioned many particulars ; however, it may
not be amifs to obferve, that in 1563, an act was
made for the better regulation, maintenance, and increafe of the navy ; and in 1566, there was a law to
enable the mafter, wardens, and the affiftants of the
Trinity-houfe, to fet up beacons and fea-marks. The
fame year there paffed an act for incorporating, and
more

more effectually establishing the company of merchant
adventurers. In 1581, there likewise passed an act
for the increase of mariners, and for the maintenance
of navigation, and more especially for recovering the
trade to Iceland, which began then to decay, and in
which there had been employed annually upward of
two hundred sail of stout ships. In 1585, the queen
erected by her letters patent, a new company for the
management of the trade to Barbary; and in the
year 1600, she incorporated a society of merchants
trading to the East Indies, whence the present East
India company is derived *.

Beside these numerous marks of her royal favour,
and the strict attention to the commerce of her subjects, the queen afforded others continually, by sending envoys and agents to the Czar, to the Shah of
Persia, to several great princes in the East Indies:
and in short, wherever her interposition could be of
any use to open, to promote, or to recover any branch
of traffic; as appears by all the histories that are ex-
tant of her reign. It may be said, and which is more,
may be said with truth and justice, that in the midst
of these great things done for industry and trade, the
prerogative was carried very high : many monopolies
erected, and several exclusive privileges granted,
which have been found injurious to trade. But the
discussing these points belong to general history.

This disposition of the queen, excited a like spirit
throughout the whole nation. Not only persons bred
to trade, and some of the middle gentry of the kingdom, launched out into expeditions for discoveries,
and planting new-found countries; but even persons
of the first distinction, became encouragers and adventurers in those designs : such as the lord-treasurer
Burleigh, the earl of Warwick, the earl of Leicester,
&c. and some of them actually engaged in the exe-

* See the first voyage on account of the English East India company, under Sir James Lancaster ; in the second volume of this
Collection.

5   cution

cution of such projects, amongst whom were the earls of Cumberland, Essex, and Southampton, Sir Walter Raleigh, Sir Richard Grenville, Sir Humphry Gilbert, Sir Robert Dudley, &c. And therefore we need not wonder at the surprising increase of our maritime power, or the number of remarkable undertakings of this sort, within so short a period of time. Let us mention only a few. In 1575, Sir Humphry Gilbert attempted the discovery of a north-west passage; in 1577, Sir Martin Frobisher sought one the same way; Pet and Jackman sailed on a like design in 1580, by the direction of the governor and company of merchant-adventurers: an expedition was undertaken at a great expence by Sir Humphry Gilbert, in order to settle Florida; nor did it miscarry through any error of the undertaker. The great Sir Walter Raleigh would have settled Virginia in 1584, if prudence, industry, and public spirit could have effected it; but though he failed in the extent, yet he was not totally defeated in his hopes, since he laid the foundation of that settlement, which hath since so happily succeeded.

It may in this place contribute not a little to our satisfaction, if we enquire what quantity of coin, both gold and silver, there might be in the nation, toward the close of her reign; that is, at the beginning of the last century, because it is of very great consequence to have a just notion of what was the nation's stock in ready money at that period, when our great foreign commerce began. We have indeed an authentic account of her entire coinage in silver, amounting to above four millions and a half; but then if we consider that she recoined almost all the silver specie of the kingdom, and that there was a small alteration in the standard in the latter end of her reign, which raised silver from five shillings, to five and two-pence an ounce, which occasioned a new fabrication; so that much of the former coin came into the mint again as bullion: we may, with the judicious Dr. Davenant, estimate the filver coin at that time in this kingdom, at two millions and a half; to which, if we add the gold of her own and her predecessors coin, and estimate this at a million and a half, we may be pretty sure that we are not much wide of the truth; and that one hundred and fifty years ago, the current coin of England amounted in the whole, to four millions or thereabout.

King James, at his accession to the English throne, was about thirty-six years of age; and, if he had been a private person, would not have rendered himself very remarkable either by his virtues or his vices. The greatest of his failings were timidity, diffimulation, and a high opinion of his own wifdom : thefe, however, were more excufable than modern writers are willing to allow, if we confider the accident that happened to his mother before his birth, the strange treatment he met with in Scotland, from the feveral factions prevailing in that kingdom during his junior years, and the exceffive flatteries that were heaped on him after he came hither, by all ranks of people. It was impoffible for him to have made himfelf much acquainted with maritime affairs while he continued in Scotland, yet it does not at all appear, that he was negligent of naval concerns, after he was feated on the English throne ; unlefs his hafty conclufion of a peace with Spain fhould be thought liable to the like cenfure.

The accession of king James gave a fair opportunity to the houfe of Auftria, to make an end of the long quarrel which had fubfifted with England ; becaufe, during all that time, they had been in peace and amity with king James as king of Scots. Immediately on his arrival at London, the arch-duke fent over a minifter to the English court, and in confequence of his negotiations, a peace was foon after concluded with Spain. Some of the writers of thofe ---- tell us, that it was chiefly brought about by the ---- es given to all the king's minifters and favourites.

vourites. It seems, however, more reasonable to conclude, that this peace was in reality the effect of the king's inclination, supported by the advice of his most eminent statesmen; some of whom were known to have been for this measure in the queen's time. There were two treaties, one of peace and alliance, the other of commerce, both signed at London, the 18th of August, 1604; the constable of Castile, the greatest subject in Spain, being sent for that purpose. All the trading part of the nation were very well pleased with this proceeding, and would have been much more so, if the king had not taken a very strange step upon its conclusion. He erected a company of merchants, who were to carry on the Spanish commerce exclusively; which gave both an universal and very just offence; for as the whole nation had borne the expence of the war, and trade in general had suffered thereby, it was but reasonable, that the benefits of peace should be as diffusive. This evil, however, was of no long continuance. But if this treaty gave some dissatisfaction at home, it raised no less discontent abroad. The Hollanders, who were left to shift for themselves, and who had reaped so great advantages from the favour of queen Elizabeth, were exceedingly exasperated at a step so much to their immediate disadvantage. But as they found themselves still strong enough, not only to cope with the Spaniards, but also to make a greater figure than most other nations at sea; they lost that respect which was due to the English flag; and began to assume to themselves a kind of equality even in the narrow seas. This was quickly represented to the king as an indignity not to be borne; and thereupon he directed a fleet to be fitted out, the command of which was given to Sir William Monson, with instructions to maintain the honour of the English flag, and that superiority which was derived to him from his ancestors in the British seas. This fleet put to sea in the spring of 1604, and was continued annually under the same

admiral,

admiral, who appears to have been a man of great spirit and much experience; for, as he tells us in his own memoirs, he served in the first ship of war fitted out in the reign of queen Elizabeth, and was an admiral in the last fleet she ever sent to sea. Yet he found it a very difficult matter to execute his commission; the Dutch, whenever he conferred with any of their chief officers, gave him fine language, and fair promises: but they minded them very little, taking our ships on very frivolous pretences, and treating those they found on board them with great severity, till such time as it appeared the admiral would not bear such usage, and began to make reprisals, threatening to hang, as pirates, people who shewed themselves very little better in their actions. There were also high contests about the flag, which began through some accidental civilities shewn to the Hollanders, in the late reign, when they sailed under the command of English admirals, upon joint expeditions, and were on that account treated as if they had been her majesty's own subjects; which favours they now pretended to claim as prerogatives due to them in quality of an independent state.

These disputes continued for many years; and though, through the vigilance of admiral Monson, the Dutch were defeated in all their pretensions, and the prerogatives of the British sovereignty at sea were thoroughly maintained; yet the republic of Holland still kept up a spirit of resentment, which broke out in such acts of violence, as would not have been past by in the days of queen Elizabeth. Nevertheless our admiral does not seem to charge the king, or his ministry in general, with want of inclination to do themselves justice; but lays it expresly at the door of secretary Cecil, afterward earl of Salisbury; who thought it, says he, good policy, to pass by such kind of offences: but he does not report any reasons upon which that kind of policy was grounded. However it did not absolutely or constantly prevail, even in the councils
cils

cils of king James; for upon some surmises that foreigners took unreasonable liberties in fishing in our seas, a proclamation was published in the year 1608, asserting the king's sovereignty in that point, and prohibiting all foreign nations to fish on the British coast. This, though general in appearance, had yet a more particular relation to the Dutch, who found themselves greatly affected thereby, especially when the king appointed commissioners at London, for granting licences to such foreigners as would fish on the English coast; and at Edinburgh, for granting licences of the like nature to such as would fish in the northern sea. To these regulations, though with great reluctance, they submitted for the present; the reason of which seems to be, their having affairs of great moment to manage with the court of Great Britain. In these important concerns, notwithstanding all that had passed, they succeeded; and two treaties were concluded on the 26th of June, 1608, between the crown of Great Britain and the States-General: the one of peace and alliance, the other for stating and settling the debt due to king James. One would have imagined, that the advantages obtained by these treaties, should have brought the republic to a better temper, in respect to other matters; but they did not: for within a short time after, they disputed paying the assize-herring in Scotland, and the licence-money in England; and to protect their subjects from the penalties which might attend such a refusal, they sent ships of force to escort their herring-busses. These facts, as they are incontestable, are related, though without the least prejudice against the Dutch; who are a people certainly to be commended for all instances of public spirit, when they are not inconsistent with the rights of their neighbours, and the law of nations.

But at this time of day, ministers were too much afraid of parliaments to run the hazard of losing any of the nation's rights, for want of insisting upon them; and therefore they prevailed upon the king to republish his proclamation, that a parliament, whenever they met, might see they had done their duty, and advise the king thereupon as they should think fit.

There were also some struggles in this reign with the French, about the same rights of fishery, and the sovereignty of the sea; in which, through the vigorous measures taken by Sir William Monson, the nation prevailed, and the French were obliged to desist from their practices of disturbing our fishermen, and otherwise injuring our navigation. In 1614, the same admiral was sent to scour the Scotch and Irish seas, which were much infested with pirates. The noise, however, of their depredations far exceeded the damage; for when, on the first of June, Sir William Monson made the coast of Cathness, the most northern part of Scotland, he found that, instead of twenty pirates, of whom he expected to have intelligence in those parts, there were in fact but two; one of whom immediately surrendered, and the other was afterward taken by the admiral on the coast of Ireland : where, by a proper mixture of clemency and severity, he extirpated these rovers, and reclaimed the inhabitants of the sea-coast from affording shelter and protection to pirates, furnishing them with provisions, and taking their plunder in exchange.

In 1617, Sir Walter Raleigh was released from his imprisonment in the Tower, and had a commission from the king, to discover and take possession of any countries in the south of America, which were inhabited by heathen nations, for the enlargement of commerce, and the propagation of religion; in the undertaking which expedition, his expences were borne by himself, his friends, and such merchants as entertained a good opinion of the voyage. His design has been variously represented; but it is sufficiently evident, that the complaints of the Spanish minister, don Diego Sarmiento d'Acuna, so well known afterward

ward by the title of Count Gondemar, were not so
much grounded on any notions of the injustice of this
design, as on a piece of Spanish policy, by raising a
clamour on false pretences, to discover the true scope
and intent of Sir Walter's voyage. In this he was
but too successful; for upon his representations, that
excellent person was obliged to give a distinct account, as well of his preparations for executing, as of
the design he was to execute: and this (by what
means is not clear) was communicated to the Spaniards, who thereby gained an opportunity, first of
disappointing him in America, and then of taking
off his head upon his return, to the lasting dishonour
of this reign, as well as the great detriment of the
nation: for, without all doubt, this project of Sir
Walter Raleigh's, for settling in Guiana, was not
only well contrived, but well founded; and, if it
had been followed, might have been as beneficial to
Britain, as Brazil is to Portugal.

The disputes with the states of Holland, in reference to the right of fishing, broke out again, in the
year 1618, from the old causes; which were plainly
a very high presumption of their own maritime force,
and an opinion they had entertained of the king's being much addicted to peace. Mr. Camden, in his
annals of the reign of this prince, says, that the deputies of the states, at their audience of the king,
on the 1st of December, 1618, intreated that nothing might be done in respect to the herring-fishing;
as it was the great support of their commonwealth,
and the only succour and relief of the common people, in regard to the troubles then amongst them.

King James however asserted his rights through
the course of this negotiation, and brought the states
themselves to acknowledge, that these rights had a
just foundation. If it should be enquired how it came
to pass, that after carrying things so far, and to such
a seeming height, they should fall again into silence
and oblivion, the best answer that can be given to

Q 4

this

this queftion is, that in the midft of this difpute, the
prince of Orange afked Sir Dudley Carleton a very
fhrewd queftion, viz. Whether this claim about the
fifhery might not be quieted for a fum of money?
That gentleman, who was afterward created Vifcount
Dorcheftes, was certainly a man of honour; but
whether fome men in power might not find a method
by agents of their own, to convey an anfwer to fo
plain a demand, is more than at this diftance of time
can be determined. Sir William Monfon tells us,
that in reference to the difputes about the flag, the
Dutch found a kind of protector in the great earl of
Salifbury; nor is it at all impoffible, that they might
alfo find an advocate in this important bufinefs of the
fifhery: but if they did, this muft have been a minifterial and not a national bargain, fince we fhall
find, that in the next reign, this claim was infifted
upon as warmly, and with fomewhat better effect.

We come now to the only naval expedition of confequence, undertaken during the time this king fat
upon the throne, which was the attempt upon Algiers. What the real grounds were of this romantic
undertaking, feem not eafy to be difcovered. The
common ftory is, that count Gondemar, having gained
an afcendancy over his majefty's underftanding, perfuaded him, contrary to his natural inclination, which
feldom permitted him to act vigoroufly againft his
own enemies, to fit out a formidable fleet, in order
to humble the foes of the king of Spain. But we
have it from other hands, that this was a project of
much older ftanding: that the earl of Nottingham
had follicited the king to fuch an expedition, before
he laid down his charge of lord high admiral; and
that Sir Robert Maniel infufed it into the head of his
fucceffor Buckingham, that it would give a great reputation to his management of naval affairs, if fuch
a thing was entered upon in the dawn of his adminiftration. As Buckingham eafily brought the king to
confent to whatever himfelf approved, there is the
utmoft

utmost probability, that it was by his influence this design was carried into execution.

In the month of October, 1620, this fleet sailed from Plymouth. It consisted of six men of war, and twelve stout ships hired from the merchants. Of these Sir Robert Mansel, then vice-admiral of England, had the command in chief: Sir Richard Hawkins was vice, and Sir Thomas Button, rear-admiral. On the 27th of November, they came to an anchor in Algier-road, and saluted the town; but without receiving a single gun in answer. On the 28th, the admiral sent a gentleman with a white flag to let the Turkish viceroy know the cause of his coming; who returned him an answer by four commissioners, that he had orders from the Grand Seignior to use the English with the utmost respect, to suffer their men to come on shore, and to furnish them with what provisions they wanted. Upon this, a negotiation ensued; in which it is hard to say, whether the Turks or the admiral acted with greater chicanery. The former refused to dismiss the gentleman first sent, unless an English consul was left at Algiers; and the latter, to rid himself of this difficulty, prevailed upon a seaman to put on a suit of good cloaths, and to pass for a consul: this cheat not being discovered by the Turks, they sent forty English slaves on board the admiral, and promised to give him satisfaction as to his other demands; upon which, he sailed again for the Spanish coast, attended by six French men of war, the admiral of which squadron had struck to the English fleet on his first joining it, which seems to have been the greatest honour, and perhaps the greatest advantage too that attended this whole expedition.

It had been well if this enterprize had ended thus; but after receiving a supply of provisions from England, it was resolved to make another attempt upon Algiers in the spring, and, if possible, to burn the ships in the mole. Accordingly in the month of May the fleet left the coast of Majorca, and upon the 21st

of

of the fame month, anchored before Algiers, and began to prepare for the execution of this defign. Two fhips taken from the Turks, one of an hundred, the other of fixty tons, were fitted up for this purpofe. Seven armed boats followed to fuftain thofe of the fire-fhips, in cafe they were purfued at their coming off. Thefe were likewife furnifhed with fireworks to deftroy the fhips without the mole.

The wind not being favourable, the attempt was put off till the 24th, and blowing then at S. S. W. the fhips advanced with a brifk gale toward the mole; but when they were within lefs than a mufket-fhot of the mole's head, the wind died away, and it grew fo calm they could not enter. However, the boats and brigantines finding they were difcovered, by the brightnefs of the moon, which was then at full, and being informed by a chriftian flave, who fwam from the town, that the Turks had left their fhips unguarded, with only a man or two, in each of them, they refolved to proceed; which they did, but performed little or nothing, and then retired with the lofs of fix men. After a day or two's ftay they put to fea, and in the month of June returned to England. This ill-concerted enterprize had no other effect, than that of expofing our own commerce to the infults of the Algerines, who did us a great deal of mifchief, while we did them little or none. Two other fleets were afterward fent againft them, one under the command of the lord Willoughby, and the other under that of the earl of Denbigh; but both did fo fmall fervice, that very few of our hiftories take any notice of them. Sir William Monfon has made fome fevere, but juft obfervations, upon thefe undertakings; and particularly remarks, that notwithftanding the whole nation was grievoufly offended, as they will always be at fuch mifcarriages, yet they never had any fatisfaction given them; which irritated them exceedingly, and contributed not a little to raife that fpirit, which vented itfelf afterward in a civil war.

In

In 1623, happened the bloody affair of Amboyna; of which we have given a detail in vol. 2. p. 421.

It is indeed strange, that, considering the strength of the nation at sea at the time we received this insult, and the quick sense the English always have of any national affront; no proper satisfaction was obtained, nor any vigorous measures entered into, in order to exact it. But the wonder will in a great measure cease, when we consider the state of the crown, and of the people at that period. Therefore, though it made a great noise, and occasioned much expostulation with that republic, yet the attention of the crown to the proposed war with Spain, and its concern for the recovery of the Palatinate, joined to the necessity there was of managing the Dutch at so critical a juncture, hindered our proceeding any farther than remonstrances, while our competitors kept exclusively so very considerable a branch of trade.

Nothing of importance relating to naval affairs in this reign remains unmentioned, except the sending a fleet to bring home prince Charles from Spain, may be reckoned in that number. It consisted, however, of a few ships only, but in good order, and well manned; so that the Spaniards are said to have expressed great satisfaction at the sight of it: which, however, true or false, is a matter of no great consequence. This voyage, though a short one, gave prince Charles some idea of maritime affairs; which proved afterward of benefit to the nation. The breaking the Spanish match made way for a war with that kingdom, much to the satisfaction of the English; but in the midst of the preparations that were making for it, the king ended his days at Theobald's, on the 27th of March, 1625, in the 59th year of his age, and in the 23d of his reign. His pacific temper occasioned our having but little to say at this period; but it will be proper to give the reader a concise view of the improvement of trade and navigation,

gation, as well as a brief account of the colonies
settled, while this prince sat upon the throne.

It has been already shewn, that under the public-
spirited administration of queen Elizabeth, this nation first came to have any thing like a competent
notion of the benefits of an extensive commerce; and
began to think of managing their own trade themselves, which down to that period had been almost
entirely in the hands of foreigners. So long as the
war continued with Spain, our merchants went on in
a right way; they prosecuted their private advantage
in such a manner, as that it proved likewise of public utility, by increasing the number of seamen, and
of stout ships belonging to this kingdom: but after
king James's accession, and the taking place of that
peace which they had so long and so earnestly expected, things took a strange turn. Our traders saw the
manifest advantage of using large and stout ships;
but instead of building them, were contented to
freight those of their neighbours, because a little
money was to be saved by this method. In consequence of this notion, our shipping decayed in proportion as our trade encreased; till in the year 1615,
things were come to so strange a pass, that there were
not ten ships of 200 tons belonging to the port of
London. Upon this, the Trinity-house petitioned the
king, setting forth the matter of fact, and the dreadful consequences it would have, with respect to our
naval power, through the decay of seamen; and
praying, that the king would put in execution some
good old laws, which were calculated for the redress
of this evil: suggesting also the example of the state
of Venice, which, on a like occasion, had prohibited
their subjects to transport any goods in foreign bottoms. The merchants unanimously opposed the mariners in this dispute, and, having at this juncture
better interest at court, prevailed. Yet, in a year's
time, the tables were turned, and the merchants convinced

vinced of their own mistake, joined with the mariners in a like application. An extraordinary accident produced this happy effect. Two ships, each of the burden of three hundred tons, came into the river Thames, laden with currants and cotton, the property of some Dutch merchants residing here. This immediately opened the eyes of all our traders: they saw now, that, through their own error, they were come back to the very point from which they set out; and if some bold and effectual remedy was not immediately applied, our commerce would be gradually driven again by foreigners on foreign bottoms. They instantly drew up a representation of this, and laid it before the king and his council; upon which a proclamation was issued, forbidding any English subject to export or import goods in any but English bottoms.

When a people have once entered into a course of industry, the benefits accruing from it, will generally keep them in that road; and even the difficulties they meet with, turn to their advantage. Thus, after the English merchants had built a few large ships in their own ports, and furnished them with artillery and other necessaries, they found themselves in a condition to launch into many trades, that were unthought of before. For some time, indeed, they suffered not a little by the pirates of Barbary; yet, in the end, it put them upon building still larger ships, as well as taking more care in providing and manning small ones. This had such an effect in the space of seven years, that whereas ships of a hundred tons had been before esteemed very large vessels, and were generally built and brought from beyond the seas; there were now many merchantmen of three, four, and five hundred tons belonging to several ports. So that before the death of king James, our trade was so far increased, that, in the opinion of Sir William Monson, we were little, if at all inferior in maritime force to the Dutch.

In

In refpect to the encouragements given by the crown, for promoting commerce and plantations in the Eaft Indies, and America, they were as great under this reign, as under any fucceeding one. Several voyages were made on account of the Eaft India company, and the king did not fpare fending an ambaffador into thofe parts for their fervice *. Virginia and New England were in a great meafure planted; Barbadoes poffeffed and fettled, and Bermudas difcovered in his time. Even the attempts made for fixing colonies in Newfoundland, and Acadia, or New Scotland, though ineffectual, occafioned building a great many good fhips, increafed the Newfoundland fifhery, added to the number of our failors, and kept alive that fpirit of difcovering, which is effential to a beneficial commerce. Befide, they engaged abundance of knowing and experienced perfons to write upon all branches of traffic; and their books, which yet remain, fufficiently prove, that there were numbers in thofe days, who thoroughly underftood all the arts neceffary to promote manufactures, navigation and ufeful commerce.

As to the navy, which was more particularly the care of the crown, we find it frequently engaged the attention of the king himfelf, as well as of his minifters. In moft of our naval hiftories, we have a lift of nine fhips added to the royal navy of England by this prince. But of the greateft fhip built in this king's reign, we have fo exact, and at the fame time fo authentic an account, in Stow's Annals, that it may not be amifs to tranfcribe it.

" This year, 1610, the king built a moft goodly fhip for war; the keel whereof was one hundred and fourteen feet long, and the crofs-beam was forty-four feet in length: fhe will carry fixty-four pieces of great ordinance, and is of the burthen of fourteen hundred tons. This royal fhip is double built, and is moft fumptuoufly adorned, within and without, with all
man-

manner of curious carving, painting, and rich gilding, being in all respects the greatest and goodliest ship that ever was built in England ; and this glorious ship the king gave unto his son Henry prince of Wales. The 24th of September, the king, the queen, the prince of Wales, the duke of York, and the lady Elizabeth, with many other lords, went unto Woolwich, to see it launched ; but because of the narrowness of the dock, it could not then be launched : whereupon the prince came the next morning by three o'clock, and then, at the launching thereof, the prince named it after his own dignity, and called it The Prince. The great workmaster in building this ship, was master Phineas Pet, gentleman, sometime master of arts of Emanuel College in Cambridge."

In the same author, we have an account of the king's going on board the great East India ship of twelve hundred tons, which was built here, and seems to have been the first of that size launched in this kingdom. The king called it, The Trade's Increase; and a pinnace of two hundred and fifty tons, which was built at the same time, he called, The Pepper-Corn. This shews that he was a favourer of navigation. The king also granted a commission of enquiry, for reforming the abuses in the navy; the proceedings upon which are still preserved in the Cotton-library. He was liberal also to seamen, and naturally inclined to do them honour ; but as in other things, so in this, he was too much governed by his favourites.

Upon the demise of king James, his only son Charles prince of Wales succeeded him ; not only quietly, and without disturbance, but with the general approbation of his subjects. He was then in the flower of his age, had shewn himself possessed of great abilities ; and after the breaking off the Spanish match, he rendered himself for a time very popular by his conduct. His father left him in a situation much in-
cumbered

cumbered at the time of his decease ; for the government was deeply in debt, a war with Spain was just begun, and his prime minister, the duke of Buckingham, who had been likewise his father's, was generally hated. In this sad state of public affairs, every thing was subject to wrong constructions. Eight thousand men, raised for the service of the Palatinate, were ordered to rendezvous at Plymouth ; and in their passage thither, coat and conduct-money were demanded of the country, to be repaid out of the Exchequer. The behaviour of these troops was very licentious ; and the long continuance of peace, made it appear still a greater grievance. The clamour thereupon grew high ; and the king, to remedy this evil, granted a commission for executing martial-law; which, instead of being considered as a remedy, was taken for a new grievance, more heavy than any of the rest.

During the time that Buckingham remained in the king's council, all things were attributed to him ; and the nation was so prejudiced against him, that whatever was reputed to be done by him, was thought a grievance: and though no man saw this more clearly than the king, yet by an infatuation, not easily to be accounted for, he trusted him as much, and loved him much more than his father had ever done.

The marriage of Charles with the princess Henrietta-Maria, daughter to Henry IV. of France, had been concluded in the life-time of king James ; and after his decease, the king was married to her by proxy. In the month of June, 1625, Buckingham went to attend her with the royal navy, and brought her to Dover ; from thence she came to Canterbury, where the marriage was consummated : and on the 16th of the same month, their majesties entered London privately, the plague daily increasing in the suburbs. It was not long before an unfortunate transaction rendered this marriage disagreeable to the people, and as this related to the navy, it falls particularly under our cognizance; which we shall therefore handle more at large, because in most of our general histories it is treated very confusedly.

The marquis d'Effiat, ambassador from France to king James, had represented to his majesty, that the power of the catholic king in Italy was dangerous to all Europe; that his master was equally inclined with his Britannic majesty to curtail it: but wanting a sufficient maritime force, was desirous of borrowing from his majesty a few ships, to enable him to execute the design he had formed against Genoa. To this the king condescended; and it was agreed, that the Great Neptune, a man of war, commanded by Sir Ferdinando Gorges, and six merchant ships, each of between three and four hundred tons burden, should be lent to the French: but soon after this agreement, the Rochellers made an application here, signifying, that they had just grounds to apprehend, that this English squadron would be employed for destroying the protestant interest in France, instead of diminishing the king of Spain's power in Italy.

The duke of Buckingham, knowing that this would be little relished by captain Pennington, who was to go admiral of the fleet, and the owners of the ships; he gave them private instructions, contrary to the public contract with France, whereby they were directed not to serve against Rochelle: but upon their coming into a French port, in the month of May, they were told by the duke of Montmorency, that they were intended to serve, and should serve against Rochelle; upon which, the sailors on board the fleet signed, what is called by them, a round Robin, that is, a paper containing their resolution not to engage in that service, with their names subscribed in a circle, that it might not be discerned who signed first.

Upon this, Pennington fairly sailed away with the whole squadron, and returned into the Downs in the beginning of July; from whence he fent a letter to the duke of Buckingham, defiring to be excufed from that fervice. The duke, without acquainting the king, or confulting the council, directed lord Conway, then fecretary of ftate, to write a letter to captain Pennington, commanding him to put all the fhips into the hands of the French. This, however, not taking effect, the duke fuperftitioufly, and without the king's knowing any thing of the defign upon Rochelle, procured his letter to captain Pennington, to the fame effect. Upon this, in the month of Auguft, he failed a fecond time to Dieppe, where, according to his inftructions, the merchant fhips were delivered to the French; but Sir Ferdinando Gorges, who commanded the king's fhip, weighed anchor and put to fea: and fo honeft were all the feamen on board thefe fhips, that, except one gunner, they all quitted them, and returned to England: but as for the fhips, they remained with the French, and were actually employed againft Rochelle, contrary to the king's intention, and to the very high difhonour of the nation. This affair made a great noife, and came at laft to form an article in an impeachment againft the duke of Buckingham.

In the mean time the defign ftill went on of attacking and invading Spain, and a ftout fleet was provided for that purpofe; but as Buckingham, in quality of lord high-admiral, had the fupream direction of that affair, the nation looked upon it with an evil eye, and were not fo much difpleafed at its mifcarriage, as glad of an opportunity of railing at the duke, and thofe who, by his influence, were entrufted with the command of the fleet, and forces on board it. The whole of this tranfaction has been very differently related, according to the humours of thofe who penned the accounts; however, there are very authentic memoirs remaining, which inform us that this war with Spain was chiefly of the duke of

Buck-

Buckingham's procuring, and seems to have proceeded more from his personal distaste to count Olivarez, than any solid or honourable motive.

While the clamour subsisted on the want of success attending this fleet abroad, the duke of Buckingham fell into another error, in the execution of his office as lord high-admiral at home. He was vexed at the noise that had been made about the merchant ships put into the hands of the French, and employed against Rochelle ; and therefore took occasion in the latter end of the year 1626, to cause a French ship, called the St. Peter, of Havre de Grace, to be arrested. The pretence was, that it was laden with Spanish effects ; which, however, the French denied, and asserted, that all the goods in the ship belonged to French merchants, or to English and Dutch. Upon this a commission was granted to hear evidence as to that point ; and it appearing plainly, there was no just ground of seizure, the ship was ordered to be released, but not before the French king made some reprisals : which so irritated the nation, that this also was made an article in the duke's impeachment. The matter, however, was compromised between the two kings, and the good correspondence between their subjects for a time restored ; but at the bottom, there was no cordial reconciliation : and so this quarrel, like a wound ill cured, broke quickly out again with worse symptoms than before.

The war in which the king was engaged, in order to have procured the restitution of the Palatinate to his brother-in-law, had drawn him into a league with Denmark, which obliged him to send a squadron of ships to that king's assistance ; and this being attended with small success, he was called upon for farther supplies. His parliaments all this time were little inclined to assist him, because he would not part with Buckingham ; and this obliged him to have recourse to such methods for supply, as his lawyers assured him were justifiable. Amongst the rest, he obliged all

R 2

the

the fea-ports to furnifh him with fhips: of the city of London he demanded twenty, and of other places in proportion.

The inhabitants thought this fo hard, that many, who had no immediate dependence on trade, were for quitting their refidence in maritime places, and retiring up into the country. This conduct of theirs made the burden ftill more intolerable upon thofe who ftaid behind; and the confequence of their remonftrances was a proclamation, requiring fuch as had quitted the fea-coaft, to return immediately to their former dwellings: and this it was gave rife to the firft difturbances in this unfortunate reign. They were quickly increafed by the rafh management of Buckingham; who, though he faw his mafter fo deeply embarraffed with the wars in which he was already engaged, yet plunged him into another with France, very precipitately, and againft all the rules of true policy.

The queen's foreign fervants, who were all bigotted papifts, had not only acted indifcreetly in matters relating to their religion, but had likewife drawn the queen to take fome very wrong, to fay the truth, fome ridiculous and extravagant fteps; upon which Buckingham engaged his majefty to difmifs her French fervants, which he did the firft of July, 1626, and then fent the lord Carleton to reprefent his reafons, for taking fo quick a meafure, to the French king. That monarch refufed him audience, and to fhew his fenfe of the action, immediately feized one hundred and twenty of our fhips which were in his ports, and undertook the fiege of Rochelle; though our king had acted but a little before, as a mediator between him and his proteftant fubjects. Upon this, the latter applied themfelves to king Charles, who ordered a fleet of thirty fail to be equipped for their relief, and fent it under the command of the earl of Denbigh: but this being fo late in the year as the month of October, his lordfhip found it impracticable

I

cable to execute his commiſſion; and ſo, after continuing ſome time at ſea in hard weather, returned into port; which not only diſappointed the king's intention, but alſo blemiſhed his reputation, as the Rochellers began to ſuſpect the ſincerity of this deſign.

The duke of Buckingham, to put the thing out of diſpute, cauſed a great fleet to be drawn together the next year, and an army of ſeven thouſand men to be put on board it; reſolving to go himſelf as admiral and commander in chief. He ſailed from Portſmouth the 27th of June, and landed on the iſland of Rhe; though at firſt he intended to have made a deſcent on Oleron, and actually promiſed ſo much to the duke of Soubiſe, whom he ſent to Rochelle, to acquaint the inhabitants of his coming to their relief. They received this meſſage coldly; for the French king having corrupted ſome by his gold, and terrifying many more by his power, the Rochellers were now afraid to receive the very ſuccours they had demanded.

The town of St. Martin's however was ſpeedily taken by the Engliſh, and his grace then inveſted the citadel; but gave evident proofs of his want of military ſkill in managing the ſiege. By this time the Rochellers had declared for the Engliſh; and this declaration of theirs, and the expectation he had of ſuccours from England, engaged Buckingham to remain ſo long in his camp, that his troops were much diminiſhed. At length, on the 6th of November, he made a general aſſault; when it appeared, that the place was impregnable to forces under ſuch circumſtances as his were. Two days after, he reſolved upon a retreat; which was as ill conducted as the reſt of the expedition. With equal ſhame and loſs therefore, the duke concluded this unlucky expedition, embarking all his forces on the 9th of the ſame month, and ſending the Rochellers a ſolemn promiſe, that he would come back again to their relief; which, however, he did not live to perform. To compleat his misfortune, as he entered Plymouth, he met the

earl

earl of Holland with the promifed fuccours failing out, who now returned with him.

To remedy thofe evils, a parliament was called in the beginning of 1628, wherein there paffed nothing but difputes between the king and the commons; fo that at laft it was prorogued without granting fupplies. The king, however, exerted himfelf to the utmoft, in preparing a naval force to make good what the duke of Buckingham had promifed to the inhabitants of Rochelle. With this view a fleet of fifty fail was affembled at Plymouth in the fpring, and a large body of marines embarked; the command of it was given to the earl of Denbigh, who was brother-in-law to Buckingham, and who failed from that port on the 17th of April, coming to anchor in the road of Rochelle on the 1ft of May. On his arrival, he found twenty fail of the French king's fhips riding before the harbour; and being much fuperior in number and ftrength, he fent advice into the town, that he would fink the French fhips as foon as the wind came weft, and made a higher flood. About the 8th of May, the wind and tide ferved accordingly, and the Rochellers expected and follicited that deliverance: but the earl, without remembering his promife, or embracing the opportunity, weighed anchor and failed away, fuffering four of the French fhips to purfue, as it were, the Englifh fleet, which arrived at Plymouth on the 26th of May.

This fecond inglorious expedition was ftill a greater difcouragement to the poor Rochellers; and increafed the fears and jealoufies of a popifh intereft at home. One Le Brun, a Frenchman, but captain in the Englifh fleet, gave in depofitions before the mayor of Plymouth, on the 6th of May, which argued treachery, or apparent cowardice, in the management of this late expedition. This account was certified by the mayor of Plymouth, and the two burgeffes of that town in parliament, by whom it was communicated to the council-table; from whence a letter was

directed

directed to the duke of Buckingham, as lord high-admiral, dated the 30th of May, 1628, to fignify his majefty's pleafure, that the earl of Denbigh fhould return back to relieve the town of Rochelle, with the fleet under his charge, and with other fhips prepared at Portfmouth and Plymouth. But, notwithftanding this order of council, no fuch return was made; nor any enquiry into the difobedience of the king's order for it.

Notwithftanding thefe repeated defeats, the cries of the Rochellers, and the clamours of the people were fo loud, that a third fleet was prepared for the relief of that city, now, by a clofe fiege, reduced to the laft extremity. The duke of Buckingham chofe to command in perfon, and to that end came to Portfmouth; where, on the 23d of Auguft, he was affaffinated by one Felton, an enthufiaftic officer of the army.

This accident did not prevent the king's profecuting his defign; the very next day his majefty made the earl of Lindfey admiral, Monfon and Mountjoy, vice and rear admirals: and, as an illuftrious foreign writer affures us, his care and prefence had fuch an effect in the preparing for this voyage, that more was difpatched now, in ten or twelve days, than in many weeks before. This expedition, however, was not more fortunate than the former. The fleet failed the 8th of September, 1628, and arriving before Rochelle, found the boom raifed to block up the entrance of the port, fo ftrong, that though many attempts were made to break through it, yet they proved vain; fo that the Rochellers were glad to accept of terms from their own prince, and actually furrendered the place on the 18th of October, the Englifh fleet looking on, without being able to help them. With this expedition ended the operations of the war with France.

From this time, the French began to be ambitious of raifing a maritime power, and to be extreamly uneafy at the growth of the Englifh fhipping. This

R 4   was

was the effect of Richlieu's politics, who best understood the different interests of the feveral European
powers, of any minifter that nation ever had, or, it
is to be hoped, for the peace of Chriftendom, will
ever have.   He revived the difpute between the
Dutch and us, refpecting the fifhery; and the famous
Hugo Grotius was induced to write a treatife, under
the title of *Mare Liberum*, wherein, with great elo-
quence, he endeavoured to fhew the weaknefs of our
title to dominion over the fea : which, according to
his notion, was a gift from God, common to all nations.
This was anfwered by Selden, in his famous treatife,
entitled, *Mare Claufum*; wherein he has effectually
demonftrated, from the principles of the law of
nature and nations, and from hiftory, that a dominion over the fea may be, and has been, acquired.
This book of Mr. Selden's was publifhed in 1634,
and by the countenance then, and afterward, fhewn
by king Charles toward this extraordinary perfor-
mance, we may fairly conclude, that he had very juft
and generous notions of his own, and his people's
rights in this refpect, though he was very unfortunate
in taking fuch methods as he did to fupport them.

The French minifter perfifted fteadily in his Ma-
chiavellian fcheme, of ufing the power and induftry
of the Dutch, to interrupt the trade, and leffen the
maritime force of Britain.   With this view alfo, a
negotiation was begun between that crown and the
ftates of Holland, for dividing the Spanifh Netherlands between them; and under colour of thus affift-
ing them, in fupport of their pretenfions to an equal
right over the fea, and in promoting their trade, to
the prejudice of ours, Richlieu carried on fecretly
and fecurely his darling object of raifing a naval force
in France : to promote which, he fpared not either
for pains or expence, procuring from all parts the
ableft perfons in all arts and fciences, any way relating to navigation, and fixing them in the French fervice, by giving them great encouragement.

The

The apprehensions which the king had entertained of this new league between the French and Dutch, were so heightened in the year 1635, by the junction of the fleets of those two powers, and the intelligence he had, that France was shortly to declare war against Spain, and from thence to derive that occasion they had been so long seeking to divide the Netherlands between themselves and their new allies; all whose pretensions, in respect to the right of fishing in, and using an unrestrained navigation in the seas, they had undertaken to support, that he resolved to be no longer passive. In order to defeat this design, and maintain the sovereignty annexed to the English crown, as well as the nation's credit, as a maritime power; the king saw, that it was necessary to equip and put to sea a superior naval force.

This it seemed exceeding hard to do, without the assistance of a parliament; and yet the delays in granting aids had been so great in former parliaments, that his majesty was very doubtful of succeeding, if for this he trusted to a parliamentary supply. His lawyers, knowing both the nature of the case, and his deep distress, suggested to him, that upon this occasion, he might have recourse to his prerogative; which opinion having been approved by the judges, he thereupon directed writs to be issued, for the levying of ship-money. These writs were, for the present, directed only to sea-ports, and such places as were near the coast; requiring them to furnish a certain number of ships, or to grant the king an equivalent thereto. The city of London was directed to provide seven ships for twenty-six days, and other places in proportion. To make the nation more easy under this tax, the king directed, that the money raised thereby, should be kept apart in the exchequer; and that a distinct account should be given of the services to which it was applied. Yet, in spite of these precautions, the people murmured grievously;
which,

which, however, did not hinder this project from being carried into execution.

With the help of this money, the king, in the month of May, 1635, fitted out a fleet of forty sail, under the command of Robert earl of Lindsey, who was admiral; Sir William Monson, vice-admiral, Sir John Pennington, rear-admiral: as also another of twenty sail, under the earl of Essex. The first of these fleets sailed from Tilbury-Hope on the 26th of May. Their instructions were, to give no occasion of hostility and to suffer nothing that might prejudice the rights of the king and kingdom. The French and Dutch fleets joined off Portland, the last of this month; and made no scruple of giving out, that they intended to assert their own independency, and to question that prerogative which the English claimed in the narrow seas; but as soon as they were informed that the English fleet was at sea, and in search of them, they quitted our coast, and repaired to their own.

Our admiral sent a bark upon the coast of Britany, to take a view of them; and from the time of the return of this bark, to the 1st of October, this fleet protected our own seas and shores, gave laws to the neighbouring nations, and effectually asserted that sovereignty which the monarchs of this kingdom have ever claimed. The good effect of this armament, and the reputation we gained thereby abroad, in some measure quieted the minds of the people; as it convinced them, that this was not an invention to bring money into the exchequer, without respect had to the end for which it was raised.

The king, perfectly satisfied with what had been done this year, and yet well knowing that it would signify little if another, and that at least as good a fleet, was not set out the next; to raise the money necessary for equipping such a force, had recourse again to his writs for levying of ship-money: but now the aid was made more extensive. The burden, indeed,

in

in itfelf, was far from being preffing : at the utmoft it did not amount to above 236,000 l. per annum, which was not quite 20,000 l. a month throughout the whole kingdom ; yet the making it an univerfal aid, and the affeffing and collecting it in the parliamentary methods, without parliamentary authority, gave it an air of oppreffion, and made it extreamly odious.

In order to prevent all doubts from his own fubjects, and alfo to prevent any falfe furmifes gaining ground in foreign nations, as to the defign of this potent armament ; the king thought fit to exprefs his royal intentions to the world, in the moft public, and in the moft authentic manner : that, at one and the fame time, it might appear what himfelf demanded, and what had been paid in acknowledgment of the right of his anceftors in regard to thofe things, as to which thefe demands were made.

In 1636, the king fent a fleet of fixty fail to fea, under the command of the earl of Northumberland, admiral ; Sir John Pennington, vice-admiral, and Sir Henry Marom, rear-admiral. They failed firft to the Downs, and from hence to the north, where the Dutch buffes were fifhing upon our coaft. The admiral required them to forbear ; which they not feeming difpofed to do, he fired upon them : this put them into great confufion, and obliged them to have recourfe to other methods. The Dutch, therefore, applied themfelves to the earl of Northumberland ; defired him to mediate with the king, that they might have leave to go on with their fifhing this year, for which they were content to pay 30,000 l. and exprefled alfo a willingnefs to obtain a grant from the king, for his permiffion for their veffels to fifh there for the time to come, paying an annual tribute.

Such is the beft account that can be collected of the caufes and confequences of this expedition, from our beft hiftorians. But the earl of Northumberland delivered a journal of his whole proceedings, figned

with

with his own hand; which is, or at leaft was preferved in the paper-office. In that journal, there are
feveral memorable particulars. The Dutch fifhing-
buffes, upon the appearance of his lordfhip's fleet,
did take licences, to the number of two hundred,
though he arrived amongft them pretty late in the
year. He exacted from them twelve pence per ton,
as an acknowledgment; and affirms that they went
away well fatisfied., It was pretended by the Dutch
in king Charles the fecond's time, that this was an
act of violence; and that nothing could be concluded
as to the right of this crown, from that tranfaction:
fince the Dutch did not pay, becaufe they thought
what was infifted upon to be due, but, becaufe they
were defencelefs. His lordfhip's journal fets this pretence entirely afide; fince it appeared from thence,
that they had a fquadron of ten men of war for their
protection; as alfo, that Auguft the 20th, 1636,
the Dutch vice-admiral Dorp, came with a fleet of
twenty men of war: but inftead of interrupting the
earl in his proceedings, he faluted him by lowering
his topfails, ftriking his flag and firing his guns; after
which he came on board, and was well entertained by
the earl of Northumberland. It is farther mentioned
in that journal, that upon his lordfhip's return from
the north, and anchoring in the Downs, he had notice of a Spanifh fleet of twenty-fix fail, bound for
Dunkirk; to reconnoitre which he fent one of the fhips
of his fquadron, called the Happy Entrance; to
which fingle fhip, that fleet paid the marks of refpect, which were due to the Englifh flag whenever
it appeared.

The king meant to have continued both this method of raifing money, and of fitting out fleets annually; and by giving feveral young noblemen commands at fea, to have rendered them the more capable of ferving their country in times of greater
danger: but he quickly found this impracticable.
The nation grew fo exceedingly diffatisfied with this

method of raising money, and the great case of Mr. Hampden made it so clear, that a constant and regular levying of this tax was dangerous to the constitution, and to the freedom of the subject ; that the king was obliged to lay aside this scheme, and to content himself with using all the methods that could be thought of, to awaken the people's attention in regard to the sovereignty of the sea. With this view, his majesty made an order in council, that a copy of Mr. Selden's book upon that subject, should be kept in the council-chest, that another copy should be kept in the court of exchequer, and a third in the court of admiralty ; there to remain as perpetual evidence of our just claim to the dominion of the seas.

Nothing of consequence occurs in regard to naval affairs till the year 1639, when the Spaniards fitted out a powerful fleet, consisting of sixty-seven sail of large ships, manned with 25,000 seamen, and having on board 12,000 land forces, designed for the relief of Flanders. The Dutch had two or three squadrons at sea ; the Spanish fleet coming up the channel, was met in the streights by one of them, consisting of seventeen sail, under the command of Martin, the son of Herbert Van Tromp, who, notwithstanding the enemy's great superiority, attacked them : but finding himself too weak, was obliged to sheer off towards Dunkirk ; where, being joined by the other squadrons, he so roughly handled the Spanish fleet, under the command of Don Antonio de Oquendo, that at last he forced them on the English coast near Dover.

Admiral Van Tromp finding himself in want of powder and ball, stood away for Calais ; where he was liberally supplied by the governor, and then returned to attack the enemy. Upon his approach, the Spaniards got within the South-Foreland, and put themselves under the protection of our castles. Things being in this situation, the Spanish resident importuned king Charles, that he would oblige the

Dutch

Dutch to forbear hostilities for two tides, that the Spaniards might have an opportunity of bearing away for their own coast; but the king being in amity with both powers, was resolved to stand neuter: and whereas the Spaniards had hired some English ships to transport their soldiers to Dunkirk, upon complaint made thereof by the Dutch ambassadors, strict orders were given, that no ships or vessels belonging to his majesty's subjects, should take any Spaniard on board, or pass below Gravesend without licence.

However, after much plotting and counterplotting on both sides, the Spaniard at length outwitted his enemy; and found means, by a stratagem in the night, to convey away through the Downs, round by the North-Sand-Head, and the back of the Godwin, twelve large ships to Dunkirk, and in them four thousand men. In excuse of this gross neglect of the Dutch admirals, in leaving that avenue from the Downs unguarded; they affirmed they were assured by the English, that no ships of any considerable burden could venture by night to sail that way. The two fleets had now continued in their stations near three weeks, when king Charles sent the earl of Arundel to the admiral of Spain, to desire him to retreat upon the first fair wind: but by this time the Dutch fleet was, by continual reinforcements from Zealand and Holland, increased to an hundred sail; and seeming disposed to attack their enemies, Sir John Pennington, admiral of his majesty's fleet, who lay in the Downs with thirty-four men of war, acquainted the Dutch admiral, that he had received orders to act in defence of either of the two parties, which should be first attacked.

The Spaniards, however, growing too presumptuous on the protection they enjoyed, a day or two after, fired some shot at Van Tromp's barge, when himself was in her; and killed a man with a cannon-ball on board of a Dutch ship, whose dead body was presently sent on

board

board Sir John Pennington, as a proof that the Spaniards were the first aggressors, and had violated the neutrality of the king of England's harbour.   Soon after this the Dutch admiral, on receiving fresh orders from the states, came to a resolution of attacking the Spaniards; but before he put it in execution, he thought fit to write to admiral Pennington, telling him, that the Spaniards having infringed the liberties of the king of England's harbours, and being clearly become the aggressors, he found himself obliged to repel force by force, and attack them; in which, pursuant to the declaration he had made to him, he not only hoped for, but depended on his assistance: which, however, if he should not please to grant, he requested the favour, that he would at least give him leave to engage the enemy; otherwise he should have just cause of complaint to all the world, of so manifest an injury.

This letter being delivered to the English admiral, Van Tromp immediately weighed and stood to the Spaniards in six divisions, cannonading them furiously, and vigorously pressing them at the same time with his fire-ships; so that he quickly forced them all to cut their cables, and of fifty-three, which the Spaniards were in number, twenty-three ran ashore and stranded in the Downs: of these, three were burnt, two sunk, and two perished on the shore.   The remainder of the twenty-three, which were stranded and deserted by the Spaniards, were manned by the English, to save them from falling into the hands of the Dutch.   The other Spanish ships, with Don Antonio de Oquendo, the commander in chief, and Lopez, admiral of Portugal, got out to sea, and kept in good order, till a thick fog arising, the Dutch took advantage thereof, interposed between the admirals and their fleet, and fought them valiantly till the fog cleared up, when only ten escaped.   The first hostility having been indisputably committed by the Spaniards, was a plea of which the Dutch made use in

their

their juftification to us ; and at the fame time became a fufficient argument to defend the conduct of
the Englifh government, in fuffering one friend to deftroy another within its harbours.

It may not be amifs to obferve, that in reality the
people of England were not forry for this misfortune
that befel the Spaniards, though the court took all
the care imaginable to prevent it : and the reafon of
this was, that fome furmifed this to be a new Spanifh Armada, fitted out nominally againft the Dutch;
but in truth, intended to act againft heretics in general.

The expedition of the marquis of Hamilton againft
the Scots, was undertaken this year; in which there
is very little worth mentioning. He arrived in the
Frith of Forth the firft of May : there he continued for fome time, treating with the Scots to little
or no purpofe, till the feafon being loft, he returned
without effecting any thing.

The fleet was from this time forward fo entirely
out of the king's power, that the naval hiftory of
this reign ends properly here : and therefore having
already related, the feveral expeditions undertaken by
his authority, we come now to mention the progrefs
of trade, the increafe of fhipping, and the encouragement of our plantations, during the fame fpace.

This prince, before the rebellion broke out, among
others, added one fhip to the royal navy of England ;
which on account of its fize, and other remarkable
particulars, deferves to be mentioned in this place,
more efpecially as it has efcaped the notice of all our
naval writers. This famous veffel was built at Woolwich in 1637. She was in length by the keel 128
feet; in breadth 48 feet; in length, from the fore-
end of the beak-head, to the after-end of the ftern, 232
feet : and in height, from the bottom of the keel to
the top of her lanthorn, 76 feet. Bore five lanthorns,
the biggeft of which would hold ten perfons upright:
had three flufh-decks, a forecaftle, half-deck, quarter-deck and round-houfe. Her lower tier had thirty
ports,

ports, middle tier thirty ports, third tier twenty-fix ports, forecaftle twelve ports, half-deck fourteen ports; thirteen or fourteen ports more within board, befide ten pieces of chace-ordnance forward, and ten right aft, with many loop-holes in the cabins for muf-ket-fhot. She had eleven anchors, one of four thou-fand four hundred pounds weight. She was of the burthen of one thoufand fix hundred and thirty-feven tons; and was built by Peter Pett, Efq; under the in-fpection of Captain Phineas Pett, one of the principal officers of the navy.

It appears from Sir William Monfon, and indeed from all the unprejudiced writers of thofe times, who were competent judges of thefe matters, that the commerce of this ifland increafed exceedingly during the firft fifteen years of this king's reign; infomuch that the port of London only could have fupplied a hundred fail, capable of being eafily converted into men of war, and well furnifhed with ordnance. The trade to the Eaft Indies, which was but beginning in his father's time, became now very lucrative; and our fhips gave law in thofe parts to almoft all foreign nations. The trade to Guinea grew likewife to be of confiderable benefit to the Englifh fubjects; and our intercourfe with Spain, after the ending of the war, proved of infinite advantage likewife. It is true, there happened fome confiderable difputes between the government and the merchants, about cuftoms, which fome of the minifters of the crown thought de-pended immediately thereupon, and might be taken by virtue of the prerogative only; whereas others conceived, as moft of the merchants themfelves did, that nothing of this kind could be levied but by the confent of parliament: But thefe very difputes fhew that trade was in a flourifhing condition; for if the cuftoms had not rifen to a confiderable height, beyond what they did in former times, no miniftry would have run the hazard of fuch a conteft.

But the principal fource of our naval ftrength then, (as it has been ever fince) was our plantations, to the encouragement and augmentation of which, even thofe accidents highly contributed, which might have been otherwife fatal to fofiety; fuch as our civil and ecclefiaftical divifions, which inclined numbers of fober, induftrious, and thinking people, to prefer liberty, and whatever they could raife in diftant and hitherto uncultivated lands, to the uneafy fituation in which they found themfelves at home.

The colony of Virginia had ftruggled under great difficulties, from the time it fell under the direction of a company, till the king was pleafed to take it into his own hands; which he did very foon after his coming to the crown, and then directed the conftitution of that colony to be a governor, council, and affembly, conformable to that of this kingdom, and under which the colony quickly began to flourifh. That of New England had its name beftowed by his majefty when prince, and was better fettled in King James's time, than any other of our colonies; and throughout the whole reign of King Charles I. was conftantly fupplied with large draughts of people; fo that by degrees it was divided into four governments.

The papifts in England, finding themfelves liable to many feverities, were defirous of having an afylum in the new world, as well as other nonconformifts; and this gave rife to the planting of Maryland, a country which had been hitherto accounted part of Virginia, between 37" and 40º of N. L. It was granted by King Charles, the 20th of June, 1632, to the anceftor of the prefent Lord Baltimore, and derived its name of Maryland, from his queen Henrietta-Maria.

The Summer Iflands which were planted in the laft reign, and fettled under a regular government in the year 1619, flourifhed exceedingly, the country being extreamly pleafant and fruitful, and the air much

much more wholefome than in any other part of America. As for the ifland of Barbadoes, which had been regularly planted about the beginning of the king's reign, it was granted to the earl of Carlifle, who gave fuch encouragement to all who were inclined to go thither, and moft of thofe who went became fo fpeedily rich, that it was quickly well peopled, and even within this period, was efteemed the moft populous of all our plantations. The ifland of St. Chriftopher and Nevis were alfo fettled about this time.

Upon the commencement of violence between Charles and his parliament; it was natural for each party to be folicitous about the fleet, for many reafons; and for this particularly, that whoever was mafter of that, would be confidered as the fupreain power by foreign princes. The earl of Northumberland was at this time lord high-admiral: the king had given him that commiffion, to fatisfy the houfe of commons, who had a confidence in him; and granted it during pleafure only, becaufe his intention was to confer that office on his fon the duke of York, as foon as he became of age. Sir Robert Manfel was vice-admiral of England; a gentleman very loyal, but withal very infirm and far in years. Sir John Pennington was vice-admiral of the fleet, then in the Downs, and Sir John Mennes was rear admiral; both well affected to his majefty.

The parliament having formed a project of difpoffeffing the king of his fleet, executed it fuccefsfully; notwithftanding thefe circumftances fo favourable for his majefty, and though he had the affections of the feamen, whofe wages he had raifed, and for whom he had always fhewn a very particular regard. In the fpring of the year, 1641, the parliament defired, that is, in effect directed, the earl of Northumberland to provide a ftrong fleet for the nation's fecurity by fea, and appropriated a proper fund for this fervice. They next defired, that he would appoint the earl of

S 2   Warwick

Warwick admiral of that fleet, on account of his own indifpofition, which rendered it impoffible for him to command in perfon. The king took this ill, and infifted on Sir John Pennington's keeping his command; but the earl had fo much refpect to the parliament's recommendation, that he ordered the fleet to be delivered up to the earl of Warwick, and granted him a commiffion to command it, as by his own he had power to do. This was one great point gained. The parliament then would have made Captain Cartwright comptroller of the navy, vice-admiral in the room of Sir John Pennington; but he refufing to undertake this fervice without the king's permiffion, his majefty was pleafed to fignify his pleafure, that he fhould decline it; which he did, and the parliament thereupon appointed one Batten, vice-admiral, who was remarkably difaffected toward the king: and their orders being complied with, the fleet in the fpring 1642, fell into their hands; though the king was perfuaded in his own mind that he could at any time recover it, which was the true reafon of his not removing at that time, as he afterward did, the earl of Northumberland from his high office. It was not long before he had good reafon to change his opinion; for the queen, fending his majefty a fmall fupply from Holland, in the Providence, the only fhip the king had left, the fhips from the Downs chafed the veffel into the Humber, and there forced the captain to run her afhore. Upon this the king refolved to attempt feizing the fleet; and the defign, had it been executed as well as it was laid, might very probably have taken effect; but through the mifmanagement of Sir John Pennington it mifcarried, and ferved only to defeat the king's hopes for the future, by affording the earl of Warwick an opportunity of removing all the king's friends, which he had long wanted.

The parliament, as they had difcovered great care and induftry in fecuring, fo they fhewed no lefs wif-

dom

dom in the conduct of the fleet, which they always kept in good order and well paid. In 1643, vice-admiral Batten having intelligence, that the queen intended to go by sea from Holland into the north of England, he did his utmost to intercept her, though on board a Dutch man of war. This proving ineffectual, he chafed the ship into Burlington-Bay; and when the queen was landed, having intelligence that she lodged in a house upon the key, he fired upon it, so that many of the shot went through her chamber; and she was obliged, though very much indisposed, to retire for safety into the open fields. This service, which was performed in the month of February, was very grateful to the parliament, because it shewed how much the officers of the fleet were in their interest.

While the presbyterian party remained uppermost, all affairs relating to the navy went on smoothly. The earl of Warwick was entirely devoted to them, and so were all the officers by him appointed. Every summer a stout squadron was fitted out to serve as occasion required, and by this means the trade of the nation was tolerably protected. But in the year 1648, when the independents came by their intrigues to prevail, things took a new turn, and it was resolved to remove the earl of Warwick from his command, notwithstanding the services he had performed, and to make Colonel Rainsborough admiral. This gentleman had been bred a seaman, and was the son of a commander of distinction; but had for some time served as an officer in the parliament-army, and was then a colonel of foot. When this news came to the fleet in the Downs, it put the seamen into great confusion; and their officers, the earl of Warwick, and vice-admiral Batten, were so little pleased with the usage they had met with, that instead of softening, they augmented their discontents: insomuch, that they seized upon Rainsborough, and such officers as adhered to him, set them on shore, and resolved to

sail

fail over to Holland, in order to take on board the duke of York, whom they called their admiral; because the king's intention of making him so, was a thing generally known.

Though the king was then a prisoner, and his affairs reduced to a very low ebb, yet, if this revolt of the fleet had been properly managed, it might have had very happy effects : but as it was conducted, it is scarcely possible to conceive how little advantage was drawn from an incident which promised so much. The great misfortune was, that this strange turn was entirely concerted by the seamen ; so that when they declared for the king, they had very few officers among them ; and as they were little inclined to use the advice of any who were not of their own profession, there was a good deal of time lost before they positively resolved what to do. This gave the parliament an opportunity of recovering themselves from the consternation into which this unexpected event had thrown them ; and the first resolution they took was a very wise one, viz. the restoring the earl of Warwick to his title and command, sending him orders to draw together a fleet as soon as possible.

It was about this time that the parliament, if the assembly which then met as one, could be considered as the national body, brought the king to a public trial ; in consequence of which he was executed at Whitehall, January 30th 1649 : a transaction so singular in its nature, and so much being to be said on both sides ; that it is not easy to decide on ; nor can we pretend to enter on the merits of it in our brief narrative. Thus much however may be observed ; that Charles did not suffer so extraordinary a fate, so much for violating the old constitution, as to make way for the introduction of a new one : one, which after the commotions so naturally to be expected, in such an undertaking, has happily settled in that moderate frame of government, under which we now live. But to proceed in our detail.

The

The parliament recovered their fovereignty at fea; where they kept fuch ftrong fquadrons continually cruifing, that it was not thought advifeable for King Charles II. to venture his perfon on that element, in order to go to Ireland, where his prefence was neceffary. Yet the earl of Warwick, who had ferved them fo faithfully, and with fuch fuccefs, was removed from the command of the fleet, which was put into the hands of land-officers, fuch as Blake, Deane, and Popham; who, notwithftanding, behaved well, quickly gained the love of the failors, and grew in a fhort time very knowing feamen themfelves.

Blake was a man of heroic courage and a generous difpofition, the fame perfon who had defended Lyme and Taunton with fuch unfhaken obftinacy againft the king; and though he had hitherto been accuftomed only to land fervice, into which too he had not entered till paft fifty years of age, he foon raifed the naval glory of the nation to a higher pitch than it had ever attained in any former period. A fleet was committed to him; and he received orders to purfue Prince Rupert, to whom the king had given the command of that fquadron, which had deferted to him. Rupert took fhelter in Kinfale; and efcaping thence, fled toward the coaft of Portugal. Blake purfued, and chafed him into the Tagus; where he intended to attack that prince: but the king of Portugal, moved by the favour, which, throughout all Europe, attended the royal caufe, refufed Blake admittance, and aided Prince Rupert in making his efcape. To be revenged of this partiality, the Englifh admiral made prize of twenty Portuguefe fhips richly laden, and threatened ftill farther vengeance. The king of Portugal, dreading fo dangerous a foe to his new acquired dominion, and fenfible of the unequal conteft, in which he was engaged, made all poffible fubmiffions to the haughty republic, and was at laft admitted to negotiate the renewal of his alliance with England. Prince Rupert, having loft a great part of his fqua-

S 4

dra

dron on the coaft of Spain, made fail toward the Weft
Indies.   His brother, Prince Maurice, was there
fhip-wrecked· in a hurricane.   Every where, this
fquadron fubfifted by privateering, fometimes on
Englifh, fometimes on Spanifh veffels.   And Rupert
at laft returned to France; where he difpofed of the
remnants of his fleet, together with all his prizes.

All the fettlements in America, except New England, which had been planted entirely by the puritans,
adhered to the royal party, even after the fettlement
of the republic; and Sir George Ayfcue was fent
with a fquadron to reduce them to obedience.   Bermudas, Antigua, Virginia, were foon fubdued.
Barbadoes, commanded by Lord Willoughby of
Parham, made fome refiftance; but was at laft obliged to fubmit.

With equal eafe were Jerfey, Guernfey, Scilly,
and the ifle of Man, brought under fubjection to the
republic; and the fea, which had been much infefted
by privateers from thefe iflands, was rendered entirely
fafe to the Englifh commerce.   The countefs of
Derby defended the ifle of Man; and with great reluctance yielded to the neceffity of furrendring to the
enemy.   This lady, a daughter of the illuftrious
houfe of Trimoüille in France, had, during the civil
wars, difplayed a manly courage by her obftinate defence of Latham Houfe againft the parliamentary
forces; and fhe retained the glory of being the laft
perfon in the three kingdoms, and in all their depen-
dant dominions, who fubmitted to the victorious commonwealth.

The movements of great ftates are often directed
by as flender fprings as thofe of individuals.   Though
war with fo confiderable a naval power as the Dutch,
who were in peace with all their other neighbours,
might feem dangerous to the yet unfettled commonwealth, there were feveral motives, which at this time
induced the Englifh parliament to embrace hoftile
meafures.

The

The caufes of this war are differently related, according to the humours and opinions of different writers: the truth, however, feems to be, that the old commonwealth grew quickly jealous of the new one, and began to apprehend, that, whatever the reft of the world might be, Holland was like to be no gainer by this change of government in England. The parliament, on the other fide, was no lefs jealous of its new acquired fovereignty, and expected, therefore, extraordinary marks of regard from all the powers with which it correfponded. To divert the attention of the public from domeftic quarrels toward foreign tranfactions, feemed alfo in the prefent difpofition of mens minds to be good policy. The fuperior power of the English commonwealth, together with the advantages of fituation, promifed it fuccefs; and the parliamentary leaders hoped to gain many rich prizes from the Dutch; to diftrefs and fink their flourifhing commerce, and by victories to throw a luftre on their eftablifhment, which was fo new and unpopular.

To cover thefe hoftile intentions, the parliament, under pretence of providing for the interefts of commerce, embraced fuch meafures as they knew would give difguft to the States. They framed the famous act of navigation; which prohibited all nations to import into England in their bottoms any commodity, which was not the growth and manufacture of their own country. By this law, though the terms, in which it was conceived, were general, the Dutch were principally hurt; becaufe their country produces few commodities, and they fubfift chiefly by being the general carriers and factors of the world. Letters of reprizal were granted to feveral merchants, who complained of injuries, which, as they pretended, they had received from the States; and above eighty Dutch fhips fell into their hands, and were made prize of. The cruelties practifed on the English at Amboyna, which were certainly enormous, but which

seemed

feemed to be buried in oblivion by a thirty years fi-
lence, were again, with fome other matters, made
the grounds of complaint. The minds of men, in
both ftates, were every day more and more irritated
againft each other; and it was not long before thefe
malignant humours broke forth into action.

Tromp, an admiral of great renown, received from
the States the command of a fleet of forty-two fail, in
order to protect the Dutch navigation againft the privateers of the Englifh. He was forced by ftrefs of
weather, as he alleged, to take fhelter in the road of
Dover; where he met with Blake, who commanded
an Englifh fleet much inferior in number. Who was
the aggreffor in the action, which enfued between
thefe two admirals, both of them men of fuch prompt
and fiery difpofitions, it is not eafy to determine;
fince each of them fent to his own ftate a relation
totally oppofite in all its circumftances to that of the
other, and yet fupported by the teftimony of every
captain in his fleet. Blake pretended, that, having
given a fignal to the Dutch admiral to ftrike, Tromp,
inftead of complying, fired a broad-fide at him.
Tromp afferted, that he was preparing to ftrike,
and that the Englifh admiral, neverthelefs, began
hoftilities. It is certain, that the admiralty of Holland, who are diftinct from the council of ftate, had
given Tromp no orders to ftrike, but had left him to
his own difcretion with regard to that vain, but much
contefted ceremonial. They feemed willing to intro-
duce the claim of an equality with the new commonwealth, and to interpret the former refpect, which
they had ever payed the Englifh flag, as a deference
due only to the monarchy. This circumftance forms
a ftrong prefumption againft the narrative of the
Dutch admiral. The whole Orange party, it muft be
remarked, to which Tromp was fufpected to adhere,
were defirous of a war with England.

Blake, though his fquadron confifted only of fifteen
veffels, re-inforced, after the battle began, by eight
under

under Captain Bourne, maintained the fight with great bravery for five hours, and funk one ſhip of the enemy, and took another. Night parted the combatants, and the Dutch fleet retired toward the coaſt of Holland. The populace of London were enraged, and would have inſulted the Dutch ambaſſadors, who lived at Chelſea, had not the council of ſtate ſent guards to protect them.

When the States heard of this action, of which the fatal conſequences were eaſily foreſeen, they were in the utmoſt conſternation. They immediately diſpatched Paw, penſionary of Holland, as their ambaſſador extraordinary to London; and ordered him to lay before the parliament the narrative which Tromp had ſent of the late rencounter. They entreated them, by all the bands of their common religion, and common liberties, not to precipitate themſelves into hoſtile meaſures, but to appoint commiſſioners, who ſhould examine every circumſtance of the action, and clear up the truth, which lay in obſcurity. And they pretended, that they had given no orders to their admiral to offer any violence to the Engliſh, but would ſeverely puniſh him, if they found upon enquiry, that he had been guilty of an action, which they ſo much diſapproved. The parliament would hearken to none of theſe reaſons or remonſtrances. Elated with the numerous ſucceſſes, which they had obtained over their domeſtic enemies, they thought, that every thing muſt yield to their fortunate arms; and they gladly ſeized the opportunity, which they ſought, of making war upon the States. They demanded, that, without any farther delay or enquiry, reparation ſhould be made for all the damages which the Engliſh had ſuſtained. And when this demand was not complied with, they diſpatched orders for commencing war againſt the United Provinces.

Blake ſailed northward with a numerous fleet, and fell upon the herring buſſes, which were eſcorted by twelve men of war. All theſe he either took or diſperſed.

perfed. Tromp followed him with a fleet of above a hundred fail. When thefe two admirals were within fight of each other, and preparing for battle, a furious ftorm attacked them. Blake took fhelter in the Englifh harbours. The Dutch fleet was difperfed and received great damage.

Sir George Ayfcue, though he commanded only forty fhips according to the Englifh accounts, engaged near Plymouth the famous de Ruyter, who had under him fifty fhips of war, with thirty merchant-men. The Dutch fhips were indeed of inferior force to the Englifh. De Ruyter, the only admiral in Europe, who has attained a renown equal to that of the greateft general, defended himfelf fo well, that Ayfcue gained no advantage over him. Night parted them in the greateft heat of the action. De Ruyter next day failed off with his convoy. The Englifh had been fo fhattered in the fight, that they were not able to purfue.

Near the coaft of Kent, Blake, feconded by Bourne and Pen, met the Dutch fleet, nearly equal in number, commanded by de Witte and de Ruyter. A battle was fought much to the difadvantage of the Dutch. Their rear-admiral was boarded and taken. Two other veffels were funk, and one blown up. The Dutch fleet next day made fail toward Holland.

The Englifh were not fo fuccefsful in the Mediterranean. Van Galen with much fuperior force attacked Captain Badily, and defeated him. He bought, however, his victory with the lofs of his life.

Sea-fights are feldom fo decifive as to difable the vanquifhed from making head in a little time againft the victors. Tromp, feconded by de Ruyter, met near the Goodwins; with Blake, whofe fleet was inferior to the Dutch; but who was refolved not to decline the combat. A furious battle commenced, where the admirals on both fides, as well as the inferior officers and feamen, exerted extraordinary bravery. In this action, the Dutch had the advantage. Blake
himfelf

himself was wounded. The Garland and Bonaventure
were taken. Two ships were burned, and one funk ;
and night came very opportunely to fave the Englifh
fleet. After this victory, Tromp, in a bravado, fixed
a broom to his main-maft ; as if he were refolved to
fweep the fea entirely of all Englifh veffels.

Great preparations were made in England, in order
to wipe off this difgrace. A gallant fleet of eighty
fail was fitted out. Blake commanded, and Dean
under him, together with Monk, who had been fent
for from Scotland. When the Englifh lay off Portland, they defcried near break of day the Dutch fleet
of feventy-fix veffels, failing up the channel, along
with a convoy of 300 merchant-men, who had received orders to wait at the ifle of Rhé, till the fleet
fhould arrive to efcort them. Tromp and de Ruyter
commanded the Dutch. This battle was the moft
furious which had yet been fought, between thefe
warlike and rival nations. Three days was the battle
continued with the utmoft rage and obftinacy : and
Blake, who was victor, gained not more honour than
Tromp, who was vanquifhed. The Dutch admiral
made a fkilful retreat, and faved all the merchant
fhips, except thirty. He loft however eleven fhips of
war, had 2000 men flain, and 1500 taken prifoners.
The Englifh, though many of their fhips were extreamly fhattered, had but one funk. Their flain
were not much inferior in number to thofe of the
enemy.

All thefe fucceffes of the Englifh were chiefly owing
to the fuperior fize of their veffels; an advantage
which all the fkill and bravery of the Dutch admirals
could not compenfate. By means of fhip-money, an
impofition, which had been fo much complained of,
and in fome refpects with reafon, the late king had
put the navy into a fituation, which it had never attained in any former reign : and he ventured to build
fhips of a fize which was then unufual. But the mif-
fortunes which the Dutch met with in battle, were
small

fmall in comparifon of thofe which their trade fuftained from the Englifh. Their whole commerce by the
Channel was cut off. Even that to the Baltic was
much infefted by the Englifh privateers. Their
fifheries were totally fufpended. A great number of
their fhips, above 1600, had fallen into the enemy's
hands. And all this diftrefs they fuffered, not for
any national intereft or neceffity; but from vain points
of honour and perfonal refentments, of which it was
difficult to give a fatisfactory account to the public.
They refolved therefore to gratify the pride of the
parliament, and to make fome advances toward a
peace. Their reception, however, was not favourable; and it was not without pleafure, that they
learned the diffolution of that haughty affembly by
the violence of Cromwel; an event from which they
expected a more profperous turn to their affairs.

The Dutch, however, did not inftantly receive any
great benefit from this fudden revolution; but then
it muft be confidered, that the chief officers of the
fleet concurred in this meafure. The government of
the parliament, was a government of order and laws,
(however they came by their authority) the government of the general, afterward protector, was entirely
military: no wonder, therefore, that both the navy
and the army were pleafed with him. Some advantage, however, the enemy certainly reaped from this
change in Englifh affairs; for Van Tromp conveyed
a great fleet of merchant-men to the north, (for they
were now forced to try that rout rather than the channel) and though our navy followed him to the height
of Aberdeen, yet it was to no purpofe: he efcaped
them both going and coming back, which gave him
an opportunity of coming into the Downs, making
fome prizes, and battering Dover caftle. This fcene
of triumph lafted but a bare week; for Tromp came
thither on the 26th of May, and on the laft of that
month he had intelligence, that Monk and Deane,
who commanded the Englifh fleet, were approaching,

5   and

and that their whole fleet confifted of ninety-five fail of men of war, and five fire-fhips. The Dutch had ninety-eight men of war, and fix fire-fhips; and both fleets were commanded by men the moft remarkable for courage and conduct in either nation.

On the 2d of June in the morning, the Englifh fleet difcovered the enemy, whom they immediately attacked with great vigour. The action began about 11 o'clock; and the firft broadfide from the enemy, carried off the brave admiral Deane, whofe body was almoft cut in two by a chain-fhot. Monk, with much prefence of mind, covered his body with his cloak: and here appeared the wifdom of having both admirals on board the fame fhip; for as no flag was taken in, the fleet had no notice of this accident, but the fight continued with the fame warmth as if it had not happened. The fight continued very hot till three o'clock, when the Dutch fell into great confufion, and Tromp faw himfelf obliged to make a kind of running fight till nine in the evening, when a ftout fhip, commanded by Cornelius van Velfen, blew up. This increafed the confternation in which they were before; and though Tromp ufed every method in his power to oblige the officers to do their duty, and even fired upon fuch fhips as drew out of the line; yet it was to no purpofe, but rather ferved to increafe their misfortune. In the night, Blake arrived in the Englifh fleet, with a fquadron of eighteen fhips, and fo had his fhare in the fecond day's engagement.

Admiral Tromp did all that was confiftent with his honour, to avoid fighting the next day; but the Englifh fleet came up with him again by eight in the morning, and engaged with the utmoft fury for about four hours; and vice-admiral Penn boarded Tromp twice, and had taken him, if he had not been feafonably relieved by de Witte and de Ruyter. At laft the Dutch fell again into confufion, which was fo great, that a plain flight quickly followed; and they efcaped to Zealand. Our writers agree, that the Dutch had fix of their beſt ſhips ſunk, two blown up, and eleven taken; ſix of their principal captains were made priſoners, and upward of fifteen hundred men. Among the ſhips before mentioned, one was a vice, and two were rear-admirals. We need not wonder then, that the Dutch, whilſt in ſuch circumſtances, ſent ambaſſadors into England, to negotiate a peace almoſt on any terms. Theſe Cromwell received with haughtineſs enough, talked high, and aſſumed to himſelf the credit of former victories, in which he could have little ſhare, but of which he very ably availed himſelf now. The States, however, were far from truſting entirely to negotiations; but at the time they treated, laboured with the utmoſt diligence to repair their paſt loſſes, and to fit out a new fleet. This was a very difficult taſk; and in order to effect it, they were forced to raiſe the ſeamens wages, though their trade was at a full ſtop: they came down in perſon to their ports, and ſaw their men embarked, and advanced them wages beforehand; and promiſed them, if they would fight once again, they would never aſk them to fight more. The ſcheme laid down by the States was this, that to force the Engliſh fleet to leave their ports, this navy of theirs ſhould come and block up ours. But firſt it was reſolved, Van Tromp ſhould ſail to the mouth of the Texel, where de Ruyter, with twenty-five ſail of ſtout ſhips, was kept in by the Engliſh fleet, in order to try if they might not be provoked to leave their ſtation, and give the Dutch ſquadron thereby an opportunity of coming out.

On the 29th of July 1653, the Dutch fleet appeared in ſight of the Engliſh, upon which the latter did their utmoſt to engage them: but Van Tromp, having in view the releaſe of de Witte, rather than fighting, kept off; ſo that it was ſeven at night before General Monk in the Reſolution, with about thirty ſhips, great and ſmall, came up with them, and charged through their fleet. It growing dark ſoon after, there paſſed nothing more that night, Monk

ſailing

failing to the fouth, and Van Tromp to the north-ward; and this not being fufpected by the Englifh, he both joined de Witte's fquadron, and gained the weather-gage. The next day proving very foul and windy, the fea ran fo high, that it was impoffible for the fleets to engage, the Englifh particularly, finding it hard enough to avoid running upon the enemy's coafts.

On Sunday July 31, the weather being become fa-vourable, both fleets engaged with terrible fury. The battle lafted at leaft eight hours, and was the moft hard-fought of any that had happened throughout the war. The Dutch fire-fhips were managed with great dexterity; many of the large veffels in the Englifh fleet were in the utmoft danger of perifhing by them; and the Triumph was fo effectually fired, that moft of her crew threw themfelves into the fea, and yet thofe few who ftaid behind, were fo lucky as to put it out. Lawfon engaged de Ruyter brifkly, killed and wound-ed above half his men, and fo difabled his fhip, that it was towed out of the fleet: yet the admiral did not leave the battle fo, but returned in a galliot, and went on board another fhip. About noon, Van Tromp was fhot through the body with a mufket-ball, as he was giving orders. This miferably difcouraged his countrymen; fo that by two, they began to fly in great confufion, having but one flag ftanding amongft them. The lighteft frigates in the Englifh fleet pur-fued them clofely, till the Dutch admiral, perceiving they were but fmall, and of no great ftrength, turned his helm, and refolved to engage them; but fome bigger fhips coming into their affiftance, the Dutch-man was taken. It was night by that time their fcat-tered fleet recovered the Texel.

This was a terrible blow to the Dutch, of whom, according to Monk's letter, no lefs than thirty fhips were loft; but, from better intelligence, it appeared, that four of thefe had efcaped, two into a port of Ze-land, and two into Hamburgh. Their lofs, however,

was very great: between four and five thousand men
killed, twenty-six ships of war either burnt or sunk.
On the side of the English, there were two ships only,
viz. the Oak and the Hunter frigate burnt, and upward of five hundred seamen.

Some very singular circumstances attended this extraordinary victory, and deserve therefore to be mentioned.   There were several merchant-men in the
fleet, and Monk, finding occasion to employ them,
thought proper to send their captains to each other's
ships, in order to take off their concern for their owners vessels and cargoes; a scheme which answered his
purpose perfectly well, no ships in the fleet behaving
better.   He had likewise issued his orders in the beginning of the fight, that they should not either give
or take quarter; which, however, were not so strictly
observed, but that twelve hundred Dutchmen were
taken out of the sea, while their ships were sinking.

The parliament then sitting, who were of Cromwell's appointment, upon the eighth of August 1653,
ordered gold chains to be sent to the generals Blake
and Monk, and likewise to vice-admiral Penn, and
rear-admiral Lawson; they sent also chains to the rest
of the flag-officers, and medals to the captains.   The
25th of August was appointed for a day of solemn
thanksgiving, and Monk being then in town, Cromwell, at a great feast in the city, put the gold chain
about his neck, and obliged him to wear it all dinner-
time.   As for the States, they supported their loss
with inexpressible courage and constancy: they buried
Tromp very magnificently at the public expence.

From the rigorous terms prescribed by the parliament, the negotiation carried on by the Dutch ministers at London, met at first with many difficulties:
but an accident (if indeed the effect of Cromwell's
intrigues ought to be called so) delivered them out of
their distress.   The parliament, on the 12th of December 1653, took a sudden resolution of delivering
up their power to him from whom it came, viz. the

lord

lord general Cromwell; who soon after took upon
him the supreme magiftracy, under the title of protector. He quickly admitted the Dutch to a treaty
upon fofter conditions, though he affected to make
use of high terms ; and this treaty ended in a peace,
which was made the fourth of April 1654. In this
negotiation it was in the firft place ftipulated, that
fuch as could be found of the perfons concerned in
the maffacre at Amboyna, fhould be delivered up to
juftice. This was very fpecious, and calculated to
give the people a high idea of the protector's patrio-
tifm, who thus compelled the Dutch to make fatisfaction for an offence, which the two former kings could
never bring them to acknowlege. But as this article
was never executed, fo we may reafonably conclude,
that the Dutch knew the protector's mind before they
made him this boafted conceffion. They acknowleged the dominion of the Englifh at fea, by confent-
ing to ftrike the flag, fubmitted to the act of navigation, undertook to give the Eaft India company fatisfaction for the loffes they had fuftained ; and by a
private article bound themfelves, never to elect any
of the houfe of Orange to the dignity of Stadtholder.

The war between England and Holland had not
continued quite two years; and yet, in that time, the
Englifh took no lefs than one thoufand feven hundred
prizes, valued by the Dutch themfelves at fixty-two
millions of guilders, or near fix millions fterling.
On the contrary, thofe taken by the Dutch could not
amount to the fourth part, either in number or value.
Within that fpace the Englifh were victorious in no
lefs than five general battles, whereas the Hollanders
cannot juftly boaft of having gained one. For the
action between de Ruyter and Ayfcue, in which they
pretended fome advantage, was no general fight ; and
the advantage gained by Tromp in the Downs, is
owned to have been gained over a part only of the
Englifh fleet. As fhort as this quarrel was, it brought

T 2   the

the Dutch to greater extremities, than their fourscore
years war with Spain.

Hostilities between France and England still continued; our ships of war taking, sinking, or burning
theirs wherever they met them; and the French privateers disturbing our commerce as much as they
were able. An attempt was made by the French ministry, to have got France, as well as Denmark, included in the peace made with the states: but Cromwell would not hear of this, because he knew how
to make his advantage of the difficulties the French
then laboured under another way; in which he succeeded perfectly well, obliging them in 1655, to
submit to his own terms, and to give up the interests
of the royal family, notwithstanding their near relation to the house of Bourbon. He likewise obtained
a very advantageous treaty of commerce; and without question his conduct with regard to France would
have deserved commendation, if, for the sake of securing his own government, he had not entered too
readily into the views of cardinal Mazarine, and
thereby contributed to the aggrandizing of a power
which has been troublesome to Europe ever since. It
is generally supposed, that the primary as well as principal instigation to the Spanish war came from him;
who gave the protector to understand, that the English maritime force could not be better employed,
than in conquering part of the Spanish West Indies,
while France attacked the same crown in Europe;
and to purchase his assistance, would readily relinquish the royal family, and so rid him from all fears
of an invasion.

No sooner was the Dutch war ended, than the protector ordered his navy to be repaired, augmented,
and put into good condition; whence it was evident
enough, that he intended not to be idle, though no
body knew against whom this new force was to be
exerted. In the summer of the year 1654, he ordered two great fleets to be provided: and while he

was

was making thefe preparations, all the neighbouring nations, ignorant of his intentions, remained in fufpence, and looked with anxious expectation on what fide the ftorm would difcharge itfelf. One of the fquadrons, confifting of thirty capital fhips, was fent into the Mediterranean under Blake; whofe fame was now fpread over all Europe. No Englifh fleet, except during the Croifades, had ever before failed thofe feas; and from one extremity to the other, there was no naval force, Chriftian or Mahometan, able to refift them. The Roman pontiff, whofe weaknefs and whofe pride, equally provoke attacks, dreaded invafion from a power, which profeffed the moft inveterate enmity againft him; and which fo little regulated its movements by the common motives of intereft and prudence. Blake, cafting anchor before Leghorn, demanded and obtained of the duke of Tufcany fatisfaction for fome loffes, which the Englifh commerce had formerly fuftained from him. He next failed to Algiers, and compelled the Dey to make peace; and to reftrain his pyratical fubjects from all farther violences on the Englifh. He prefented himfelf before Tunis, and having made the fame demands, the Dey of that republic bade him look to the caftles of Porto-Farino and Goletta, and do his utmoft. Blake needed not to be rouzed by fuch a bravado: he drew his fhips clofe up to the caftles, and tore them in pieces with his artillery. He fent a numerous detachment of feamen in their long-boats into the harbour, and burned every fhip which lay there. This bold action, which its very temerity, perhaps, rendered fafe, was executed with very little lofs; and filled that part of the world with the renown of Englifh valour.

The other fquadron was not equally fuccefsful. It was commanded by Pen; and carried on board 4000 men, under the command of Venables. About 5000 more joined them from Barbadoes and St. Chriftophers. Both thefe officers were inclined to the king's

T 3   fervice;

service; and it is pretended, that Cromwel was obliged
to hurry the soldiers on board, in order to prevent
the execution of a conspiracy, which had been formed among them, in favour of the exiled family. The
ill success of this enterprize, may justly be ascribed,
as much to the injudicious contrivance of the protector, who planned it, as to the bad execution of the
officers, by whom it was conducted.

It was agreed by the admiral and general to attempt
St. Domingo, the only place of strength in the island
of Hispaniola. On the approach of the English, the
Spaniards in a fright deserted their houses, and fled
into the woods. Contrary to the opinion of Venables,
the soldiers were disembarked without guides ten
leagues distant from the town. They wandered four
days through the woods without provisions; and what
was still more intolerable in that sultry climate, without water. The Spaniards gathered courage, and
attacked them. The English, discouraged with the
bad conduct of their officers, and scarce alive from
hunger, thirst, and fatigue, had no spirit to resist.
A very inconsiderable number of the enemy put the
whole army to rout; killed 6co of them, and chaced
the rest on board their vessels.

The English commanders, in order to atone, if possible, for this unprosperous attempt, bent their course
to Jamaica, which was surrendered to them without a
blow. Pen and Venables returned to England, and
were both of them sent to the Tower by the protector, who, though commonly master of his fiery temper, was thrown into a violent passion at this disappointment. He had made a conquest of much greater
importance, than he was himself at that time aware
of; yet was it much inferior to the vast projects,
which he had formed. He gave orders, however, to
support it by men and money; and that island has
ever since remained in the hands of the English: the
chief acquisition which they owe to the enterprising
spirit of Cromwel.

As

As soon as the news of this enterprize, which was a most unwarrantable violation of treaty, arrived in Europe, the Spaniards declared war against England; and seized all the ships and goods of English merchants, of which they could make themselves masters. The Spanish commerce, so profitable to the nation, was cut off; and near 1500 vessels, it is computed, fell in a few years into the hands of the enemy. Blake, to whom Montague was now joined in command, after receiving new orders, prepared himself for hostilities against the Spaniards.

Blake lay some time off Cadiz, in expectation of intercepting the plate-fleet; but was obliged, for want of water, to make sail toward Portugal. Captain Steyner, whom he had left on the coast with a squadron of seven vessels, came in sight of the galleons, and immediately set sail to pursue them. The Spanish admiral ran his ship ashore; two others followed his example: the English took two ships, valued at near two millions of pieces of eight: two galleons were set on fire; and the marquis of Bajadox, viceroy of Peru, with his wife and his daughter, betrothed to the young duke of Medina Celi, were destroyed in them. The marquis himself might have escaped; but seeing these unfortunate women, astonished with the danger, fall in a swoon, and perish in the flames, he chose rather to die with them, than drag out a life, embittered with the remembrance of these dismal scenes. When the treasures, gained by this enterprize, arrived at Portsmouth, the protector, from a spirit of ostentation, ordered them to be transported by land to London.

The next action against the Spaniards was more glorious, though less profitable to the nation. Blake, having heard that a Spanish fleet of sixteen ships, much richer than the former, had taken shelter in the Canaries, immediately made sail toward them. He found them in the bay of Santa Cruz, disposed in a most formidable posture. The bay was secured

T 4

with

with a ftrong caftle, well fortified with cannon; befide feven forts in feveral parts of it, all united by a
line of communication, manned with mufqueteers.
Don Diego Diagues, the Spanifh admiral, ordered all
his fmaller veffels to moor clofe to the fhore; and
pofted the larger galleons farther off, at anchor, with
their broadfides to the fea.

Blake was rather animated, than daunted with this
appearance. The wind feconded his courage; and
blowing full into the bay, in a moment brought him
among the thiekeft of his enemies. After a refiftance
of four hours, the Spaniards yielded to the Englifh
valour; and abandoned their fhips, which were fet on
fire, and confumed with all their treafures. The
greateft danger ftill remained to the Englifh. They
lay under the fire of the caftles and all the forts, which
muft, in a little time, have torn them in pieces. But
the wind fuddenly fhifting, carried them out of the
bay; where they left the Spaniards in aftonifhment at
the happy temerity of their audacious victors.

This was the laft and greateft action of the gallant
Blake. He was confumed with a dropfy and fcurvy,
and haftened home, that he might yield up his laft
breath in his native country; which he fo paffionately
loved, and which he had fo much adorned by his valour. As he came within fight of land, he expired.
Never man, fo zealous for a faction, was fo much refpected and efteemed even by the oppofite factions.
He was by principle an inflexible republican; and
the late ufurpations, amidft all the truft and careffes
which he received from the ruling powers, were
thought to be very little grateful to him. " It is ftill
our duty (he faid to the feamen) to fight for our
country, into whatever hands the government may
fall." Difinterefted, generous, liberal; ambitious
only of true glory; dreadful only to his avowed enemies: he forms one of the moft perfect characters of
that age, and the leaft ftained with thofe errors and
violences, which were then fo predominant. The
pro-

protector ordered him a pompous funeral at the public charge: but the tears of his countrymen were the moft honourable panegyric on his memory.

When the confufions of a diftracted ftate, rendered the reftoration of the king, the moft eligible alternative; the feamen fhewed greater readinefs than any other fort of men to execute this falutary defign: and without waiting for any farther orders, than thofe which came from their own officers, chearfully carried the fleet over to the Dutch coaft; where, after giving new names to the fhips, they received his majefty, the duke of York, and other perfons of principal quality, who had attended him, on board, the 23d of May, 1660, and fafely landed them in Kent. For this fervice, Mr. Montague, who commanded that fleet, was created earl of Sandwich; had a garter, and was appointed vice-admiral of England, under his royal highnefs the duke of York. Sir John Lawfon, Sir Richard Stayner, and other officers, received the honour of knighthood; and the king was pleafed to promife the feamen in general, a particular fhare in his favour. In September, 1660, the earl of Sandwich went, with a fquadron of nine men of war, to Helvoetfluys, to bring over the king's fifter, the princefs of Orange; who not long after died.

A treaty of marriage having been concluded between his majefty and the infanta of Portugal, with whom he was to receive a portion of three hundred thoufand pounds, the ifland of Bombay in the Eaft Indies, and the city of Tangier in Africa; it became neceffary to fend a fleet to bring over the queen, and to fecure the laft mentioned city againft any attempt from the Moors. For this purpofe, the earl of Sandwich was again fent with a numerous fleet, which failed on the 19th of June, 1661, from the Downs. His lordfhip failed firft to Lifbon, and from thence to Tangier; which place was put into the hands of the Englifh on the 30th of January, 1662, when the earl of Peterborough marched into it with an Englifh garrifon,

garrifon, and had the keys delivered to him by the Portuguefe governor. The admiral then returned to Lifbon, where he received the queen's portion ; confifting in money, jewels, fugars, and other commodities, in bills of exchange, and then failed with her majefty for England, and arrived at Spithead the 14th of May, 1662.

It is apparent that there was no occafion for fo large a fleet, merely to bring over the queen ; but as it afforded a fair pretence for fending fuch a force into the Mediterranean, this opportunity was feized to execute things of greater moment. The Algerines, and other pyratical ftates of Barbary, taking advantage of our inteftine confufions, had broke the peace they made with admiral Blake. To put an end to their depredations, the earl of Sandwich, with his fleet, came before Algiers the 29th of July, 1661, and fent captain Spragge with the king's letter to the principal perfon in the government, and a letter of his own, with orders alfo to bring off Mr. Brown, the conful ; which was accordingly done. Anfwer was returned, that the government of Algiers would confent to no peace, whereby they were deprived of the right of fearching our fhips. This infolence of thefe fea-robbers fprung out of the jealoufy of the chriftian powers, who would never unite to crufh this neft of pirates, and give the beautiful and rich country they inhabit to fome prince of their own faith ; which would be a common benefit to all commercial nations.

In the mean time, to fhew they were in earneft, they wrought very hard at a boom, which, with much ado, they brought over from the mole-head, to the oppofite corner of the port ; that, by the help of this, and many other new works which they had raifed, they might be able to defend themfelves from any attempts that could be made by fea. The earl of Sandwich, however, refolved to make a bold trial to burn the fhips in the harbour ; but the wind prevented him ;

him : fo that after a good deal of firing on both fides, wherein more hurt was done to the city than the fhips, the admiral thought fit to fail for Lifbon on the firft of Auguft, leaving Sir John Lawfon, with a ftrong fquadron to protect the Englifh trade, and harrafs the enemy. This he performed with fuch fuccefs, that, after taking many of their fhips, he, by degrees, forced all thefe pyratical ftates to conclude a peace with Great Britain, without any refervation as to their favourite article of fearching our fhips.

On his firft return to the throne of his anceftors, king Charles and his minifters had certainly fhewn a great concern for the true intereft of the nation ; as will appear to any attentive reader of our hiftory, who obferves the advantages we gained by the treaties of commerce which he concluded with Spain and Holland. He alfo reftored to the nation the advantages they drew from the Spanifh trade : and the affection of this people to the Englifh, preferable to any other nation, appeared in this, that they immediately fell out with the Dutch, and even forbade their fhips of war to enter their ports, as the Dutch writers themfelves tell us. The treaty with Holland not only fecured the refpect due to the Englifh flag, but likewife procured fome other conceffions very honourable for the nation, and the ifland of Poleron, more correctly Pulo-Ron, i. e. the ifle of Ron, for the Eaft India company. His majefty had alfo an intention to have fecured abfolutely and for ever the fifhery on the Britifh coaft to his own fubjects : but, before that could be effectually done, the war broke out; for the true grounds of which, it is not eafy to account.

The Dutch quickly began to conceive jealous prejudices againft the king's government ; and in reality to apprehend our becoming their fuperiors in commerce, in which we were every day vifibly increafing. Thefe fentiments engaged them, and efpecially their Eaft and Weft India companies, to take various fteps in thofe parts of the world to the prejudice of the Englifh,

Englifh. The Eaft India company particularly delayed the liquidation of the damages the Englifh were
to receive; peremptorily refufed to deliver up the
ifland before mentioned: and pretended to prefcribe
the places where, and the terms on which the Englifh fhould trade in the reft of the ports of India.
The other company trod exactly in their fteps; and
proceeded fo far as to get Cape Corfe-caftle into their
hands, which belonged to the Englifh African company.

Charles confined not himfelf to memorials and remonftrances. Sir Robert Holmes was fecretly difpatched with a fquadron of twenty-two fhips to the
coaft of Africa. He not only expelled the Dutch
from Cape Corfe, but he likewife feized the Dutch
fettlements of Cape Verde and the ifle of Goree, together with feveral fhips trading on that coaft. And
having failed to America, he poffeffed himfelf of Nova Belgia, fince called New York; a territory which
James the firft had given by patent to the earl of Sterling, but which had never been planted but by the
Hollanders. When the ftates complained of thefe
hoftile meafures, the king pretended to be totally ignorant of Holmes's enterprize. He likewife confined
Holmes to the Tower; but fome time after reftored
him to his liberty.

The Dutch, finding that their applications for redrefs were likely to be eluded, and that a ground of
quarrel was induftrioufly fought for by the Englifh,
began to arm with diligence. They even exerted,
with fome precipitation, an act of vigour, which haftened on the rupture. Sir John Lawfon and de
Ruyter had been fent with combined fquadrons into
the Mediterranean, in order to chaftife the pyratical
ftates on the coaft of Barbary; and the time of their
feparation and return was now approaching. The
ftates fecretly difpatched orders to de Ruyter, that he
fhould take in provifions at Cadiz; and failing toward the coaft of Guinea, fhould retaliate on the Englifh,

lifh, and put the Dutch in poffeffion of thofe fettlements whence Holmes had expelled them. De Ruyter, having a confiderable force on board, met with
no oppofition in Guinea. All the new acquifitions of
the Englifh, except Cape Corfe, were recovered from
them : they were even difpoffeffed of fome old fettlements. Such of their fhips as fell into his hands,
were feized by de Ruyter. That admiral failed next
to America: he attacked Barbadoes, but was repulfed: he afterward committed hoftilities on Long
Ifland.

Meanwhile, the Englifh preparations for war were
advancing with vigour and induftry. The king had
received no fupplies from parliament; but by his own
funds and credit, he was enabled to equip a fleet:
the city of London lent him 100,000 pounds: the
fpirit of the nation feconded his armaments: he himfelf went from port to port, infpecting with great diligence, and encouraging the work: and in a little
time the Englifh navy was put in a very formidable
condition. Eight hundred thoufand pounds are faid
to have been expended on this armament. When
Lawfon arrived, and communicated his fufpicion of
de Ruyter's enterprife, orders were iffued for feizing
all Dutch fhips; and 135 fell into the hands of the
Englifh. Thefe were not confifcated, nor declared
prizes, till afterward, when war was proclaimed.

The Dutch faw, with the utmoft regret, a war approaching, whence they might dread the moft fatal
confequences, 'but which afforded no profpect of advantage. They tried every art of negotiation, before
they would come to extremity. Their meafures were
at that time directed by John de Wit; a minifter
equally eminent for greatnefs of mind, for capacity,
and for integrity. By his management, a fpirit of
union was preferved in all the provinces; great fums
were levied; and a navy was equipped, compofed of
larger fhips than the Dutch had ever built before, and
able to cope with the fleet of England.

5   As

When certain intelligence arrived of de Ruyter's enterprizes, Charles declared war againſt the ſtates, 22d Feb. 1665. His fleet, conſiſting of 114 ſail, beſide fire-ſhips and ketches, was commanded by the duke of York, and under him prince Rupert and the earl of Sandwich. It had about 22,000 men on board. Opdam, who was admiral of the Dutch navy, of nearly equal force, declined not the combat. In the heat of action, when engaged in cloſe fight with the duke of York, Opdam's ſhip blew up. This accident much diſcouraged the Dutch, who fled toward their own coaſt. Tromp alone, ſon of the famous admiral, killed during the protectorſhip, bravely ſuſtained with his ſquadron the efforts of the Engliſh, and protected the rear of his countrymen. The vanquiſhed had nineteen ſhips ſunk and taken : the victors loſt only one. Sir John Lawſon died ſoon after of his wounds.

It is affirmed, and with great appearance of reaſon, that this victory might have been rendered much more compleat ; had not orders been iſſued to ſlacken ſail by Brounker, one of the duke's bedchamber, who pretended authority from his maſter. The duke diſclaimed the orders; but Brounker never was ſufficiently puniſhed for his temerity. It is allowed, however, that the duke behaved with great bravery during the action : he was long in the thickeſt of the fire. The earl of Falmouth, lord Muſkerry, and Mr. Boyle, were killed by one ſhot at his ſide, and covered him all over with their brains and gore. And it is not likely, that in a purſuit, where even perſons of inferior ſtation, and of the moſt cowardly diſpoſition acquire courage ; a commander ſhould feel his ſpirits to flag, and ſhould turn from the back of an enemy, whoſe face he had not been afraid to encounter.

This diſaſter threw the Dutch into conſternation, and determined dé Wit, who was the ſoul of all their councils, to exert his military capacity, in order to

ſupport

support the declining courage of his countrymen. He went on board the fleet, which he took under his command; and he soon remedied all those diforders which had been occafioned by the late misfortune. The genius of this man was of the moft extenfive nature. He quickly became as much mafter of naval affairs, as if he had from his infancy been educated in them; and he even improved fome parts of pilotage and failing, beyond what men expert in those arts had ever been able to attain.

The misfortunes of the Dutch determined their allies to act for their affiftance and fupport. The king of France was engaged in a defenfive alliance with the States; but as his naval force was yet in its infancy, he was extremely averfe, at that time, from entering into a war with fo formidable a power as England. He tried long to mediate a peace between the two parties; and for that purpofe fent an embaffy to London, which returned without effecting any thing.

The king of France, though he was refolved to fupport the Hollanders in that unequal conteft, in which they were engaged; yet protracted his declaration, and employed the time in naval preparations, both in the ocean and in the Mediterranean. The king of Denmark mean while was refolved not to remain an idle fpectator of the conteft between the maritime powers. The part which he acted was extraordinary: he made a fecret agreement with Charles to feize all the Dutch fhips in his harbours, and to fhare the fpoils with the Englifh; provided they would affift him in executing this meafure. In order to increafe his prey, he perfidioufly invited the Dutch fhips to take fhelter in his ports; and accordingly the Eaft India fleet, very richly laden, had put into Bergen. Sandwich, who now commanded the Englifh navy (the duke having gone afhore) difpatched Sir Thomas Tiddiman with a fquadron to attack them; but whether from the king of Denmark's delay in fending orders to the governor, or what

what is more probable, from his avidity in endeavouring to engrofs the whole booty, the Englifh admiral, though he behaved with great bravery, failed of his purpofe. The Danifh governor fired upon him; and the Dutch, having had leifure to fortify themfelves, made a very gallant refiftance.

The king of Denmark, feemingly afhamed of his conduct, concluded with Sir Gilbert Talbot, the Englifh envoy, an offenfive alliance againft the States; and at the very fame time, his refident at the Hague, by his orders, concluded an offenfive alliance againft England. To this laft alliance he adhered, probably from jealoufy of the increafing naval power of England; and he feized and confifcated all the Englifh fhips in his harbours. This was a very fenfible check to the advantages which Charles had obtained over the Dutch; a great blow was given to the Englifh commerce: the king of Denmark's naval force was alfo confiderable, and threatened every moment a conjunction with the Hollanders. That prince ftipulated to affift his allies with a fleet of thirty fail; and he received in return a yearly fubfidy of 1,500,000 crowns, of which 300,000 were paid by France.

The king endeavoured to counterbalance thefe confederacies, by acquiring new friends and allies. He had difpatched Sir Richard Fanfhaw into Spain, who met with a very cold reception. That monarchy was funk into a great degree of weaknefs, and was menaced with an invafion from France; yet could not any motive prevail with Philip to enter into a cordial friendfhip with England. Charles's alliance with Portugal, the detention of Jamaica and Tangiers, the fale of Dunkirk to the French; all thefe offences funk fo deep into the mind of the Spanifh monarch, that no motive of intereft was fufficient to outweigh them. The bifhop of Munfter was the only ally that Charles could acquire.

The Dutch, encouraged by all thefe favourable circumftances, continued refolute to exert themfelves

to

to the utmoft in their own defence. De Ruyter, their great admiral, was arrived from his expedition to Guinea; their India fleet was come home in fafety; their harbours were crowded with merchant fhips; faction at home was appeafed; the young prince of Orange had put himfelf under the tuition of the ftates of Holland, and of de Wit, their penfionary, who executed his truft with great honour and fidelity: and the animofity which the Hollanders entertained againft the attack of the Englifh fo unprovoked, as they thought it, made them thirft for revenge, and hope for better fuccefs in their next enterprize. Such vigour was exerted in the common caufe, that, in order the better to man the fleet; all merchant fhips were prohibited to fail, and even the fifheries were totally fufpended.

The Englifh likewife continued in the fame difpofition, though another more grievous calamity had joined itfelf to that of war. The plague had broke out in London; and that with fuch violence as to cut off, in lefs than a year, near 100,000 inhabitants. The king was obliged to fummon the parliament at Oxford.

After France had declared war, England was evidently over-matched in force. Yet fhe poffeffed this advantage by her fituation, that fhe lay between the fleets of her enemies; and might be able, by fpeedy and well-concerted operations, to prevent their junction. But fuch was the unhappy conduct of her commanders, or fuch the want of intelligence in her minifters, that this circumftance turned rather to her prejudice. Lewis had given orders to the duke of Beaufort, his admiral, to fail from Toulon; and the French fquadron, under his command, confifting of above forty fail, was now commonly fuppofed to be entering the channel. The Dutch fleet, to the number of feventy-fix fail, was at fea, under the command of de Ruyter and Tromp, in order to join him. The Duke of Albemarle and prince Rupert commanded the English fleet, which exceeded not seventy-four sail. Albemarle, who, from his successes under the protectorship, had too much learned to despise the enemy, proposed to detach prince Rupert with twenty ships, in order to oppose the duke of Beaufort. Sir George Ayscue, well acquainted with the bravery and conduct of de Ruyter, protested against the temerity of this resolution: but Albemarle's authority prevailed. The remainder of the English set sail to give battle to the Dutch; who, seeing the enemy advance quickly upon them, cut their cables, and prepared for the combat. The battle, which ensued, is one of the most memorable which we read of in history; whether we consider its duration, or the desperate courage with which it was fought. Albemarle made here some atonement by his valour for the rashness of the attempt. No youth, animated by glory and ambitious hopes, could exert himself more than did this man; who was now in the decline of life, and who had reached the summit of honours. We cannot enter minutely into particulars. It will be sufficient to mention the chief events of each day's engagement.

In the first day, Sir William Berkeley, vice-admiral, leading the van, fell into the thickest of the enemy, was over-powered, and his ship taken. He himself was found dead in his cabin, all covered with blood. The English had the weather-gage of the enemy; but as the wind blew so high, that they could not use their lower tire, they received small advantage from this circumstance. The Dutch shot, however, fell chiefly on their sails and rigging; and few ships were sunk or much damaged. Chain shot was at that time a new invention; which is commonly attributed to de Wit. Sir John Harman exerted himself extreamly this day. The Dutch admiral, Evertz, was killed in engaging him. Darkness parted the combatants.

The

The second day, the wind was somewhat fallen, and the combat became more steady and more terrible. The English now found, that the most heroic valour cannot compensate the superiority of numbers, against an enemy who is well conducted, and who is not defective in courage. De Ruyter and Van Tromp, rivals in glory, and enemies from faction, exerted themselves in emulation of each other; and de Ruyter had the advantage of disengaging and saving his antagonist, who had been surrounded by the English, and was in the most imminent danger. Sixteen fresh ships joined the Dutch fleet during the action: and the English were so shattered, that their fighting ships were reduced to twenty-eight, and they found themselves obliged to retreat toward their own coast. The Dutch followed them, and were just on the point of renewing the combat; when a calm, which came a little before night, prevented the engagement.

Next morning, the English were necessitated to continue their retreat; and a proper disposition was made for that purpose. The shattered ships were ordered to stretch a-head; and sixteen of the most entire followed them in good order, and kept the enemy in awe. Albemarle himself closed the rear, and presented an undaunted countenance to his victorious foes. The earl of Ossory, son to Ormond, a gallant youth, who sought honour and danger in every action throughout Europe, was then on board the admiral. Albemarle confessed to him his intention rather to blow up his ship and perish gloriously, than yield to the enemy. Ossory applauded this desperate resolution.

About two o'clock, the Dutch had come up with their enemy, and were ready to renew the fight; when a new fleet was descried from the south, crowding all their sails to reach the scene of action. The Dutch flattered themselves that Beaufort was arrived, to cut off the retreat of the vanquished: the English hoped, that prince Rupert had come to turn the scale of ac-

tion.

tion. Albemarle, who had received intelligence of the prince's approach, bent his course toward him. Unhappily, Sir George Ayscue, in a ship of a hundred guns, the largest in the fleet, struck on the Galloper sands, and could receive no assistance from his friends, who were hastening to join the reinforcement. He could not even reap the consolation of perishing gloriously, and revenging his death on his enemies. They were preparing fireships to attack him, and he was obliged to strike. The English sailors, seeing the necessity, with the utmost indignation surrendered themselves prisoners.

Albemarle and prince Rupert were now determined to face the enemy; and next morning, the battle began afresh, with more equal force, and with equal valour. After long cannonading, the fleets came to a more close combat; which was continued with great violence, till parted by a mist. The English retired first into their harbours.

Though the English, by their obstinate courage, reaped the chief honour in this engagement, it is somewhat uncertain, who obtained the victory. The Hollanders took a few ships; and having some appearances of advantage, expressed their satisfaction by all the signs of triumph and rejoicing. But as the English fleet was repaired in a little time, and put to sea more formidable than ever, together with many of those ships which the Dutch had boasted to have burned or destroyed; all Europe saw, that those two brave nations were engaged in a contest, which was not likely to prove decisive.

It was the conjunction of the French alone, which could give the superiority to the Dutch. In order to facilitate this junction, de Ruyter, having repaired the fleet, posted himself at the mouth of the Thames. The English, under prince Rupert and Albemarle, were not long in coming to the attack. The numbers of each fleet amounted to about eighty sail; and the valour and experience of the commanders, as
well

well as of the feamen, rendered the engagement fierce and obftinate.   Sir Thomas Allen, who commanded the white fquadron of the Englifh, attacked the Dutch van, whom he entirely routed; and he killed the three admirals who commanded it.   Van Tromp engaged Sir Jeremy Smith; and during the heat of action, he was feparated from de Ruyter and the main body, whether by accident or defign was never certainly known.   De Ruyter, with great conduct and valour, maintained the combat againft the main body of the Englifh; and though over-powered by numbers, kept his ftation, till night ended the engagement.   Next day, finding the Dutch fleet fcattered and difcouraged, his high fpirit was obliged to fubmit to a retreat; which yet he conducted with fuch fkill, as to render it equally honourable to himfelf as the greateft victory.   Full of indignation however for yielding the fuperiority to the enemy, he frequently exclaimed, " My God! what a wretch am I? among " fo many thoufand bullets, there is not one to put " an end to my miferable life!"   One de Witte, his fon-in-law, who ftood near, exhorted him, fince he fought death, to turn upon the Englifh, and render his life a dear purchafe to the victors.   But de Ruyter efteemed it more worthy a brave man to perfevere to the uttermoft, and, as long as poffible, to render fervice to his country.   All that night and next day, the Englifh preffed upon the rear of the Dutch; and it was chiefly by the redoubled efforts of de Ruyter, that the latter faved themfelves in their harbours.

The lofs of the Hollanders in this action was not very confiderable; but as violent animofities had broke out between the two admirals, who engaged all the officers on one fide or other, the confternation which took place, was very great among the provinces. Tromp's commiffion was at laft taken from him; but though feveral captains had mifbehaved, they were fo well protected by their friends in the magiftracy of the towns, that moſt of them eſcaped puniſhment: many were ſtill continued in their commands.

The Engliſh now rode inconteſtible maſters of the ſea, and inſulted the Dutch in their harbours. A detachment under Holmes was ſent into the road of Vlie, and burned a hundred and forty merchantmen, two men of war, together with Bandaris, a large and rich village on the coaſt. The merchants, who loſt by this enterprize, uniting themſelves to the Orange faction, exclaimed againſt an adminiſtration, which, they pretended, had brought ſuch diſgrace and ruin on their country. None, but the firm and intrepid mind of de Wit, cou'd have ſupported itſelf under ſuch a complication of calamities.

The deſtroying the Dutch ſhips, and the burning the town of Bandaris, though done by Engliſhmen, was no Engliſh project. One captain Heemſkerk, a Dutchman, who fled hither, for fear of his being called to an account for miſbehaviour under Opdam, was the author of that diſmal ſcene. After the return of the fleet, he was one day at court, and boaſting, in the hearing of king Charles the ſecond, of the bloody revenge he had taken upon his country: that monarch, with a ſtern countenance, bid him withdraw, and never preſume to appear again in his preſence. He ſent him, however, a very conſiderable ſum of money for the ſervice; with which he retired to Venice. This inſtance of magnanimity, in that generous prince, has been long and highly applauded by the Dutch.

As ſoon as the fleet was ready, the command was beſtowed on Michael de Ruyter; Tromp having at that time, in conſequence of his diſpute with de Ruyter, laid down his commiſſion. This navy conſiſted of ſeventy-nine men of war and frigates, and twentyſeven fire-ſhips. The firſt deſign they had, was to join the French ſquadron, which Louis XIV. had promiſed to fit out for their aſſiſtance; in this they were moſt egregiouſly diſappointed, and after a dan

gerous

gerous navigation, in which they were more than once chafed by a fuperior Englifh fleet, they were glad to return, though fired with indignation at fuch ufage: which, it is faid, wrought fo powerfully on the mind of the gallant de Ruyter, as to throw him into a fit of ficknefs.

When the French thought the coaft was become pretty clear, they ventured out with their fleet; but Sir Thomas Allen attacking them with his fquadron, boarded the Ruby, a fine fhip of a thoufand tons, and fifty-four guns, and carrying her in a fhort time, it fo difcouraged the French miniftry, that they fcarcely trufted their navy afterward out of fight of their own fhores.

Charles began to be fenfible, that all the ends for which the war had been undertaken, were likely to prove entirely ineffectual. The Dutch, even when alone, had defended themfelves with great vigour, and were every day improving their military fkill and preparations. Though their trade had fuffered extreamly, their extenfive credit enabled them to levy prodigious fums; and while the feamen of England loudly complained for want of pay, the Dutch navy was regularly fupplied with every thing requifite for its fubfiftence. As two powerful kings now fupported them, every place, from the extremity of Norway to the coafts of Bayonne, was become hoftile to the Englifh. And Charles, neither fond of action, nor ftimulated by any violent ambition, gladly fought for means of reftoring tranquillity to his people; heartily difgufted with a war, which, being joined with the plague and fire of London, had proved fo fruitlefs and deftructive.

The firft advances toward an accommodation were made by England. When the king fent for the body of Sir William Berkeley, he infinuated to the ftates his defire of peace on reafonable terms; and their anfwer correfponded in the fame amicable intentions. Charles, however, to maintain the appearance of fuperiority,

U 4   ftill

ftill infifted, that the ftates fhould treat at London; and they agreed to make him this compliment fo far as concerned themfelves: but being engaged in an alliance with two crowned heads, they could not, they faid, prevail with thefe to depart in that refpect from their dignity. It was in the end agreed to treat at fome other place; and Charles made choice of Breda.

Whatever projects might have been formed by Charles for fecreting the money granted him by parliament, he had hitherto failed in his intention. The expences of fuch vaft armaments had exhaufted all the fupplies; and even a great debt was contracted to the feamen. The king therefore was refolved to fave, as far as poffible, the laft fupply of 1,800,000 pounds; and to employ it for payment of his debts, as well thofe occafioned by the war, as thofe which either neceffity, pleafure, or generofity,' had formerly engaged him to contract. In this fituation, Charles rafhly remitted his preparations, and expofed England to one of the greateft affronts, which it has ever received. Two fmall fquadrons alone were equipped; and during a war with fuch potent and martial enemies, every thing was left almoft in the fame fituation as in times of the moft profound tranquillity.

De Wit protracted the negotiations at Breda, and haftened the naval preparations. The Dutch fleet appeared in the Thames under the command of de Ruyter, and threw the Englifh into the utmoft confternation! A chain had been drawn crofs the river Medway; fome fortifications had been added to Sheernefs and Upnore caftle: but all thefe preparations were unequal to the prefent neceffity. Sheernefs was foon taken; nor could it be faved by the valour of Sir Edward Spragge, who defended it. Having the advantage of a fpring-tide, and an eafterly wind, the Dutch preffed on, and broke the chain, though fortified by fome fhips, which had been there funk by order of the duke of Albemarle. They burned the

three

three ships, which lay to guard the chain, the Matthias, the Unity, and the Charles the Fifth. After damaging several vessels, and possessing themselves of the hull of the Royal Charles, which the English had burned, they advanced with six men of war and five fire-ships, as far as Upnore-castle, where they burned the Royal Oak, the Loyal London, and the Great James. Captain Douglas, who commanded on board the Royal Oak, perished in the flames, though he had an easy opportunity of escaping. " Never was it known," he said, " that a Douglas " had left his post without orders." The Hollanders fell down the Medway without receiving any considerable damage; and it was apprehended, that they might next tide sail up the Thames, and extend their hostilities even to the bridge of London. Nine ships were sunk at Woolwich, four at Blackwall: platforms were raised in many places, furnished with artillery; the train-bands were called out; and every place was in the utmost disorder. The Dutch sailed next to Portsmouth, where they made a fruitless attempt; they met with no better success at Plymouth: they insulted Harwich: they sailed again up the Thames as far as Tilbury, where they were repulsed by Sir Edward Spragge, who had with him five frigates, and seventeen fire-ships. This proved a very sharp action, at least between the fire-ships; of which the Dutch writers themselves confess, they spent eleven to our eight.

The next day the English attacked the Dutch in their turn; and, notwithstanding their superiority, forced them to retire, and to burn the only fire-ship they had left, to prevent her being taken. On the twenty-fifth they bore out of the river, with all the sail they could make, followed at a distance by Sir Edward Spragge, and his remaining fire-ships. On the twenty-sixth, in the mouth of the river, they were met by another English squadron from Harwich, consisting of five men of war, and fourteen fire-ships.

They

They boldly attacked the Dutch, and grappled the vice-admiral of Zealand, and another large ſhip ; but were not able to fire them, though they frightened a hundred of their men into the ſea. The rear-admiral of Zealand was forced on ſhore, and ſo much damaged thereby, as to be obliged to return home.

The Dutch fleets, notwithſtanding theſe diſappointments, and though it was now very evident that no impreſſion could be made, as had been expected, on the Engliſh coaſts, continued ſtill hovering about, even after they were informed that the peace was actually ſigned, and ratifications exchanged at Breda. Our writers are pretty much at a loſs to account for this conduct ; but a Dutch hiſtorian has told us very plainly, that Cornelius de Wit ordered all our ports, on that ſide, to be ſounded, and took incredible pains to be informed of the ſtrength of our maritime forts, and the proviſion made for protecting the mouths of our rivers : This ſhewed plainly, that though this was the firſt viſit, it was not intended to be the laſt. The whole coaſt was in alarm ; and had the French thought proper at this time to join the Dutch fleet, and to invade England, conſequences the moſt fatal might juſtly have been apprehended. But Lewis had no intention to puſh the victory to ſuch extremities. His intereſt required, that a ballance ſhould be kept between the two maritime powers ; not that an uncontrouled ſuperiority ſhould be given to either.

Great indignation prevailed amongſt the Engliſh, to ſee an enemy, whom they regarded as inferior, whom they had expected totally to ſubdue, and over whom they had gained many honourable advantages ; now of a ſudden ride undiſputed maſters of the ocean, burn their ſhips in their very harbours, fill every place with confuſion, and ſtrike a terror into the capital itſelf. But tho' the cauſe of all theſe diſaſters could be aſcribed neither to bad fortune, to the miſconduct of admirals, nor the miſbehaviour of ſeamen, but ſolely to the avarice, at leaſt to the improvidence

of

of the government; no dangerous symptoms of discontent appeared, and no attempt for an insurrection was made by any of those numerous sectaries, who had been so openly branded for their rebellious principles, and who upon that supposition had been treated with such severity.

But the signing the treaty at Breda, extricated the king from his present difficulties. The English ambassadors received orders to recede from those demands, which, however frivolous in themselves, could not now be relinquished, without acknowledging a superiority in the enemy. Polerone remained with the Dutch; satisfaction for the ships, Bonaventure and Good Hope, the pretended grounds of the quarrel, was no longer insisted on: Acadie was yielded to the French. The acquisition of New York, a settlement so important by its situation, was the chief advantage which the English reaped from a war, in which the national character of bravery shone out with great lustre; but where the misconduct of the government, especially in the conclusion, had been no less apparent.

The Dutch war being over, his majesty sent Sir Thomas Allen with a stout squadron into the Mediterranean, to repress the insults of the Algerines, who taking advantage of our differences, had disturbed both the English commerce and the Dutch. The latter sent admiral Van Ghendt with a squadron to secure their trade. These squadrons having engaged six corsairs, forced them to fly to their own coasts, where they were attacked by the English and the Dutch in their boats; and being abandoned by their respective crews, were all taken, and a great number of christian slaves of different nations released. The same year some of our frigates attacked seven of the enemies best ships near cape Gaeta. The admiral and vice-admiral of the Algerines carried fifty-six guns each; their rear-admiral, the biggest ship in the squadron, carried sixty, and the least forty. Yet,

after

after a sharp engagement, the vice-admiral was sunk, and the rest forced to retire, most of them miserably disabled.

At last, Sir Edward Spragge was sent, in 1670, with a strong squadron of men of war and frigates, to put an end to the war. He cruised for some days before their capital, without receiving any satisfactory answer to his demands. Upon this, he sailed from thence, with six frigates and three fire-ships, to make an attempt upon a considerable number of those corsairs, which lay in the haven of Bugia. By the way, he lost the company of two of his fire-ships; yet not discouraged by this accident, he persisted in his resolution. Being come before the place, he broke the boom at the entrance of the haven, forced the Algerines a-ground, and (notwithstanding the fire of the castle) burnt seven of their ships, which mounted from twenty-four to thirty-four guns, together with three prizes: after which he destroyed another of their ships of war near Teddeller. These and other misfortunes caused such a tumult among the Algerines, that they murdered their dey, and chose another, by whom the peace was concluded to the satisfaction of the English, on the ninth of December in the same year: and as they were now sufficiently humbled, and saw plainly enough that the continuance of a war with England must end in their destruction, they kept this peace better than any they had made in former times.

We are now come to the third Dutch war (more frequently called the second, because it was so in respect to this reign) and to account for the beginning of it, will be no easy matter. The last treaty of peace was made by king Charles against his will, and on terms, to which force only made him consent. We need not wonder, therefore, that he still retained a dislike to the Dutch. Beside, there had been many other things done, sufficient to give distaste to any crowned head. For instance, their factory at Gambron

bron in Perfia, after the peace, burnt the king in effigy ; having firft dreffed up the image in an old fecond-hand fuit, to exprefs the diftrefs in which they knew him in his exile : for this, as the king thought it beneath him to demand, fo the ftates-general looked upon themfelves as above giving him, any fatisfaction.

They likewife fuffered fome medals to be ftruck, in which their vanity was very apparent. Amongft others, becaufe the triple alliance had given a check to the power of France, and their mediation had been accepted in the treaty of Aix-la-Chapelle, they were pleafed to arrogate to themfelves the fole honour of giving peace to Europe, and of being arbiters among contending princes. Here, however, it muft be owned that, in making war upon them, at this juncture, king Charles acted too much under the direction of French counfels. He had about him the worft fet of minifters that ever curfed this, or perhaps any other nation. Men of different faiths, (if bad ftatefmen have any) and who agreed only in promoting thofe arbitrary acts, which, while they feemed to make their mafter great, in reality ruined his, and, if they could have been fupported, would have exalted their power.

This infamous crew (for however decked with titles by their mafter, no Englifhman will tranfmit their names to pofterity with honour) were then called, the CABAL; and thefe engaged the king to liften to the propofitions of his moft chriftian majefty, who, as he had before deceived him to ferve the Dutch, fo he now offered to deceive the Dutch, to gratify our king. That Charles might not hefitate at this ftep, Louis le Grand betrayed his creature de Wit, and difcovered a project he had fent him for entering into an offenfive alliance againft England ; which, with other articles for his private advantage, moft unhappily determined our monarch to take a ftep prejudicial to the proteftant intereft, repugnant to that of

the

the nation, and dangerous to the balance of power in Europe.

By virtue of secret engagements with France, this war was to end in the total destruction of the republic of Holland. Part of her dominions was to be added to those of France, and the rest to fall to the share of England. In order to have a pretence for breaking with them, the captain of the Merlin-yatcht, with Sir William Temple's lady on board, had directions to pass through the Dutch fleet in the channel; and, on their not striking to his flag, was commanded to fire; which he did: yet this not being thought enough, he was blamed instead of being rewarded for it; and for not sufficiently asserting the king's right, he was, on his arrival in England, committed to the Tower. The pretence, however, thus secured, the French next undertook to lull the Dutch asleep, as they had done us, when our ships were burnt at Chatham; and this too they performed, by offering their mediation to accommodate that difference which they had procured, and upon which the execution of all their schemes depended. Yet de Wit trusted to this; till, as the dupe of France, and the scourge of his own nation, he fell a sacrifice to the fury of an enraged people. The war once resolved on, Sir Robert Holmes, who began the former by his reprisals in Guinea, had orders to open this too, though as he did that, without any previous declaration, by attacking the Smyrna fleet.

That fleet consisted of seventy sail, valued at a million and a half; and the hopes of seizing so rich a prey had been a great motive for engaging Charles in the present war, and he had considered that capture as a principal resource for supporting his military enterprizes. Holmes, with nine frigates and three yatchts, had orders to go in search of this fleet; and he passed Spragge in the channel, who was returning home with a squadron from a cruize in the Mediterranean. Spragge informed him of the near approach

of

of the Hollanders; and had not Holmes, from a defire of engroffing all the honour and profit of the enterprize, kept the fecret of his orders, the conjunction of thefe fquadrons had rendered the fuccefs in-
fallible. When Holmes approached the Dutch, he
put on an amicable appearance, and invited the admiral, Van Nefs, who commanded the convoy, on
board of him: one of his captains' gave a like infidi-
ous invitation to the rear-admiral. But thefe officers
were on their guard. They had received an intimation of the hoftile intentions of the Englifh, and had
already put all the fhips of war and merchantmen
in an excellent pofture of defence. Three times were
they valiantly affailed by the Englifh; and as often
did they as valiantly defend themfelves. In the third
attack one of the Dutch fhips of war was taken; and
three or four of their moft inconfiderable merchantmen fell into the enemies hands. The reft,
fighting with great fkill and courage, continued their
courfe; and, favoured by a mift, got fafe into their
own harbours. This attempt is denominated perfi-
dious and piratical by the Dutch writers, and even
by many of the Englifh. It merits at leaft the appellation of irregular; and as it had been attended
with bad fuccefs, it brought double fhame upon the
contrivers. The Englifh miniftry endeavoured to
cover the action, by pretending that it was a cafual
rencounter, arifing from the obftinacy of the Dutch,
who refufed the honours of the flag: but the contrary
was fo well known, that even Holmes himfelf had
not the affurance to perfift in this affeveration.

War againft the Dutch was declared on the 28th
of March, 1672, in the cities of London and Weftminfter; and great pains were taken to impofe upon
the world a grofs and groundlefs notion, that it was
undertaken at the inftance, or, at leaft, with the concurrence, of the people in general: whereas they
knew their intereft too well, not to difcern how little
this might agreed with it. And therefore, though
the

the king had then a parliament much to his mind; yet he found it extreamly difficult to obtain supplies; while the Dutch, in the midst of all their miseries, went on receiving sixty millions of their money (which is between five and six millions of ours) annually from their subjects. So great difference there is between taxes levied by authority, and money chearfully paid to preserve the common-wealth. The French king's declaration of war contained more dignity, if undisguised violence and injustice could merit that appellation. He pretended only, that the behaviour of the Hollanders had been such, that it did not consist with his glory any longer to bear it.

In the mean time de Ruyter put to sea with a formidable fleet, consisting of ninety-one ships of war and forty-four fire-ships. Cornelius de Wit was on board, as deputy from the states. They sailed in quest of the English, consisting of sixty-five ships; who were under the command of the duke of York, and who had already joined the French squadron of thirty-six sail, under marefchal d'Etrées. The combined fleets lay at Solebay in a very negligent posture; and Sandwich, being an experienced officer, had given the duke warning of the danger; but received, it is said, such an answer as intimated, that there was more of caution than of courage in his apprehensions. Upon the appearance of the enemy, every one ran to his post with precipitation; and many ships were obliged to cut their cables, in order to be in readiness. Sandwich commanded the van; and though determined to conquer or perish, he so tempered his courage with prudence, that the whole fleet was visibly indebted to him for its safety. He hastened out of the bay, where it had been easy for de Ruyter with his fire-ships to have destroyed the combined fleets, which were crowded together; and by this wise measure he gave time to the duke of York, who commanded the main body, and to marefchal d'Etrées, admiral of the rear, to disengage themselves.

felves. He himfelf meanwhile was engaged in clofe fight with the Hollanders ; and by prefenting himfelf to every danger, had drawn upon him all the braveft of the enemy. He killed Van Ghendt, the Dutch admiral, and beat off his fhip : he funk another fhip, which ventured to lay him aboard : he funk three fire-fhips, which endeavoured to grapple with him : and though his veffel was torne in pieces with fhot, and of a thoufand men fhe contained, near fix hundred lay dead upon the deck ; he continued ftill to thunder with all his artillery in the midft of the enemy. But another fire-fhip, more fortunate than the preceding, having laid hold of his veffel, her deftruction was now inevitable. Warned by Sir Edward Haddock, his captain, he refufed to make his efcape ; and bravely embraced death as a fhelter from that ignominy, which a rafh expreffion of the duke, he thought, had thrown upon him.

During this fierce engagement with Sandwich, de Ruyter remained not inactive. He attacked the duke of York, and fought him with fuch fury for above two hours, that of two and thirty actions, in which he had been engaged, he declared this combat to be the moft obftinately difputed. The duke's fhip was fo fhattered, that he was obliged to leave her, and remove his flag to another. His fquadron was overpowered with numbers, till Sir Jofeph Jordan, who had fucceeded to Sandwich's command, came to his affiftance ; and the fight, being more equally balanced, was continued till night, when the Dutch retired, and were not followed by the Englifh. The lofs fuftained by the fleets of the two maritime powers was nearly equal, if it did not rather fall more heavy on the Englifh. The French fuffered very little, becaufe they had fcarce been engaged in the action ; and as this backwardnefs is not their national character, it was concluded, that they had received orders to fpare their fhips, while the Dutch and Englifh fhould weaken themfelves by their mutual animofity.

Vol. VII.   X   Almoft

Almoſt all the other actions during the preſent war tended to confirm this ſuſpicion.

It brought great honour to the Dutch to have fought with ſome advantage the combined fleets of two ſuch powerful nations; but nothing leſs than a compleat victory could ſerve the purpoſe of de Wit, or ſave his country from thoſe calamities, which from every quarter threatened to overwhelm her. Lewis invaded the Dutch territories by land, and took their towns as faſt as he appeared before them. A general aſtoniſhment ſeized the Hollanders, from the combination of ſuch powerful princes againſt the republic; and no where was reſiſtance made, ſuitable to the antient glory or preſent greatneſs of the ſtate. Governors without experience commanded troops without diſcipline; and deſpair had univerſally extinguiſhed that ſenſe of honour, by which alone, men in ſuch dangerous extremities can be animated to a valorous defence. Every hour brought to the ſtates news of the rapid progreſs of the French, and of the cowardly defence of their own garriſons.

The Prince of Orange, with his ſmall and diſcouraged army, retired into the province of Holland; where he expected, from the natural ſtrength of the country, ſince all human art and courage failed, to be able to make ſome reſiſtance. Three provinces were already in the hands of the French; Guelderland, Overyſſel, and Utrecht; Groninghen was threatened; Frieźland lay expoſed: The only difficulty lay in Holland and Zealand; and the monarch deliberated concerning the proper meaſures for reducing them.

The town of Amſterdam alone ſeemed to retain ſome courage; and by forming a regular plan of defence, endeavoured to infuſe ſpirit into the other cities: and the ſluices being opened, the neighbouring country, without regard to the great damage ſuſtained, was laid under water. All the province followed this example; and ſcrupled not, in this

extre-

extremity, to reſtore to the ſea thoſe fertile fields, which with infinite art and expence had been won from it.

The ſtates of Holland met to conſider, whether any means were left to ſave the remains of their lately flouriſhing, and now diſtreſſed commonwealth. The nobles gave their vote, that, provided their religion, liberty, and ſovereignty could be ſaved, every thing elſe ſhould without ſcruple be ſacrificed to the conqueror: eleven towns concurred in the ſame ſentiments. Amſterdam ſingly declared againſt all treaty with inſolent and triumphant enemies: but notwithſtanding that oppoſition, they reſolved once more to try the force of intreaties; with which view they ſent four deputies to England, and as many to the French king. The buſineſs of the former, was to ſhew the danger of the proteſtant religion, the apparent and near approaching ruin of the balance of Europe, and the diſmal conſequences which muſt follow, even to England, from the further proſecution of the war. As to the latter, they were charged to offer any ſatisfaction to his moſt chriſtian majeſty, that he ſhould require.

The terms inſiſted on by Lewis were ſuch as totally deſtroyed, not only the exiſtence, but the very appearance, of independence in the ſtates: and the ambaſſadors, who came to London, met with ſtill worſe reception. No miniſter was allowed to treat with them; and they were retained in a kind of confinement. But notwithſtanding this rigorous conduct of the court, the preſence of the Dutch deputies excited the ſentiments of tender compaſſion, and even indignation among the people in general, but eſpecially among thoſe who could foreſee the aim and reſult of thoſe dangerous councils. The two moſt powerful monarchs, they ſaid, in Europe, the one by land, the other by ſea, have, contrary to the faith of ſolemn treaties, combined to exterminate an illuſ-

trious

trious republic : what a difmal profpect does their fuccefs afford to the neighbours of the one, and to the fubjects of the other? Charles had formed the triple league, in order to reftrain the exorbitant power of France : a fure proof, that he does not now err from ignorance.

But though the fear of giving offence to his confederate had engaged Charles to treat the Dutch ambaffadors with fuch rigour, he was not altogether without uneafinefs, on account of the rapid and unexpected progrefs of the French arms. Were Holland entirely conquered, its whole commerce and naval force, he faw, muft become an acceffion to France; the Spanifh Low Countries muft foon follow; and Lewis, now independent of his ally, would no longer think it his intereft to fupport him againft his difcontented fubjects. Charles, though he never ftretched his attention to very diftant confequences, could not but forefee thefe obvious events; and though incapable of envy or jealoufy, he was touched with anxiety, when he found every thing yield to the French arms, while fuch vigorous refiftance was made to his own. He foon difmiffed the Dutch ambaffadors, left they fhould cabal among his fubjects, who bore them great favour : but he fent over Buckingham and Arlington, and foon after lord Halifax, to negotiate anew with the French king, in the prefent profperous fituation of that monarch's affairs.

Thefe minifters paffed through Holland; and as they were fuppofed to bring peace to the diftreft republic, they were received every where with the loudeft acclamations. " God blefs the king of England ! God blefs the prince of Orange ! Confufion to the States !" This was every where the cry of the populace. The ambaffadors had feveral conferences with the States and the prince of Orange ; but made no reafonable advances toward an accommodation. They went to Utrecht, where they renewed the

league

league with Lewis; and agreed, that neither of the kings fhould ever make peace with HoHand, but by common confent.

The terms propofed by Lewis bereaved the repu-blic of all fecurity againft any land invafion from France: thofe demanded by Charles expofed them equally to an invafion by fea from England: and when both were joined, they appeared abfolutely in-tolerable; and reduced the Hollanders, who faw no means of defence, to the utmoft defpair. What extreamly augmented their diftrefs, were the violent factions with which they continued to be every where agitated. Their rage at laft broke all bounds, and bore every thing before it. They rofe in an infurrec-tion at Dort; and this proved a fignal of general re-volt throughout all the provinces. The two brothers of de Wit were affaffinated, and the prince of Orange invefted with the ftadtholderfhip.

In the mean time the French and Englifh fleets failed again for the Dutch coafts, with a defign to make a defcent on Zealand, the only province into which the French had not carried their arms by land. Here they found the Dutch fleet; but not thinking proper to attack them among the fands, they defer-red the execution of their defign, and blocked up the Maefe and Texel; which de Ruyter (having ftrict orders from the States not to hazard a battle) faw with concern, yet wanted power to prevent. The duke of York was refolved to debark on the ifle of Texel, the body of troops on board his fleet. The occafion was favourable in all refpects; the French and the bifhop of Munfter were in the heart of the Dutch territories, fo that no great force could be drawn together to refift them on fhore.

It was upon the 3d of July this refolution was taken; and it was intended, that their forces fhould have landed the next flood. But providence inter-pofed in favour of a free people, and faved them from a yoke, which feemed already to prefs upon

X 3   their

their necks. The ebb, inftead of fix, continued twelve hours, which defeated the intended defcent for that time; and the ftorm, that rofe the night following, forced the fleet out to fea, where they ftruggled for fome time with very foul weather, and, the opportunity being quite loft. returned, without performing any thing of confequence, to the Englifh fhore. The Dutch clergy magnified this accident into a miracle; and, though fome of our writers have thereupon arraigned them of fuperftition, yet their excefs of piety was, in this refpect, very pardonable; efpecially, if we confider, there could not be a higher ftroke of policy, at that time, than to perfuade a nation, ftruggling againft fuperior enemies, that they were particularly favoured by heaven.

After this difappointment, there was no other action thought of at fea for this year, except the fending Sir Edward Spragge, with a fquadron, to difturb the Dutch herring-fifhery; which he performed with a degree of moderation that became fo great a man: contenting himfelf with taking one of their veffels, when he faw that was fufficient to difperfe the reft. But while the war feemed to flumber in Europe, it raged fufficiently in the Weft and Eaft Indies. All this time commerce in general fuffered exceedingly on both fides: noble plantations were ruined; and the French, who, before this war, had very little fkill in navigation, and fcarcely at all underftood the art of fighting at fea, as their own writers confefs, improved wonderfully in both, at the joint expence of Britain and Holland. Thus their felf-interefted political end was plainly anfwered, while the maritime powers were fighting with, and weakening each other; and this too as much againft their inclinations, as their interefts.

The money, granted by parliament, fufficed to equip a fleet, 1673, of which prince Rupert was declared admiral: for the duke was fet afide by the teft. Sir Edward Spragge and the earl of Offory

com-

commanded under the prince. A French squadron joined them, commanded by d'Etrées. The combined fleets set sail toward the coast of Holland, and found the enemy, lying at anchor, within the sands of Schonvelt. There is a natural confusion attending sea-fights, even beyond other military transactions; derived from the precarious operations of winds and tides, as well as from the smoke and darkness, in which every thing is there involved. No wonder, therefore, that relations of these battles are apt to contain uncertainties and contradictions; especially when composed by writers of the hostile nations, who take pleasure in exalting their own advantages, and suppressing those of the enemy. All we can say with certainty of this battle, is, that both sides boasted of the victory; and we may thence infer, that the action was not decisive. The Dutch, being near home, retired into their own harbours. In a week, they were refitted, and presented themselves again to the combined fleets. A new action ensued, not more decisive than the foregoing. It was not fought with great obstinacy on either side; but whether the Dutch or the allies first retired, seems to be a matter of uncertainty. The loss in the former of these actions fell chiefly on the French, whom the English, diffident of their intentions, took care to place under their own squadrons; and they thereby exposed them to all the fire of the enemy. There seems not to have been a ship lost on either side in the second engagement.

It was sufficient glory to de Ruyter, that with a fleet much inferior to the combined squadrons of France and England, he could fight without any notable disadvantage; and it was sufficient victory, that he could defeat the project of another descent in Zealand; which, had it taken place, had endangered, in the present circumstances, the total overthrow of the Dutch commonwealth. Prince Rupert also was suspected not to favour the king's project of

subduing

subduing Holland, or enlarging his authority at home; and from these motives, he was thought not to have pressed so hard on the enemy, as his well-known valour gave reason to expect. It is indeed remarkable, that, during this war, though the English with their allies much over-matched the Hollanders, they were not able to gain any advantage over them; while in the former war, though often over-borne by numbers, they still exerted themselves with the most heroic courage, and always acquired great renown, sometimes even signal victories. But they were disgusted with the present measures, which they esteemed pernicious to their country; they were not satisfied in the justice of the quarrel; and they entertained a perpetual jealousy of their confederates, whom, had they been permitted, they would with much more pleasure have destroyed than even the enemies themselves.

If prince Rupert was not favourable to the designs of the court, he enjoyed as little favour from the court, at least from the duke, who, though he could no longer command the fleet, still possessed the chief authority in the admiralty. The prince complained of a total want of every thing, powder, shot, provisions, beer, and even water; and he went into harbour, that he might refit the fleet, and supply its numerous necessities. After some weeks he was refitted; and he again put to sea. The hostile fleets met at the mouth of the Texel, and fought the last battle, which, during a course of so many years, these neighbouring maritime powers have disputed with each other. De Ruyter, and under him Tromp, commanded the Dutch in this action, as in the two former: for the prince of Orange had reconciled these two gallant rivals; and they retained nothing of their former animosity, except that emulation, which made them exert themselves with more distinguishing bravery against the enemies of their country. Brankert was opposed to d'Etrées, de Ruyter to prince
Rupert,

Rupert, Tromp to Spragge. It is remarkable, that in all actions these brave admirals last mentioned had still selected each other, as the only antagonists worthy each others valour; and no decisive advantage had as yet been gained by either of them. They fought in this battle, as if there were no mean between death and victory.

D'Etrées and all the French squadron, except rear-admiral Martel, kept at a distance; and Brankert, instead of pressing on them, bore down to the assistance of de Ruyter, who was engaged in furious combat with prince Rupert. On no occasion did the prince acquire more deserved honour: his conduct, as well as valour, shone out with signal lustre. Having disengaged his squadron from the numerous enemies, with which he was every where surrounded, and having joined Sir John Chichely, his rear-admiral, who had been separated from him, he made haste to the relief of Spragge, who was very hard pressed by Tromp's squadron. The Royal Prince, in which Spragge first engaged, was so disabled, that he was obliged to hoist his flag on board the St. George; while Tromp was, for a like reason, obliged to quit his ship, the Golden Lion, and to go on board the Comet. The fight was renewed with the utmost fury by these valorous rivals, and by the rear-admirals, their seconds. Ossory, rear-admiral to Spragge, was preparing to board Tromp, when he saw the St. George terribly torn, and in a manner disabled. Spragge was leaving her, in order to hoist his flag on board a third ship, and return to the charge; when a shot, which had passed through the St. George, took his boat, and sunk her. The admiral was drowned, to the great regret of Tromp himself, who bestowed on his valour the deserved praises.

Prince Rupert found affairs in this dangerous situation, and saw most of the ships in Spragge's squadron disabled from fight. The engagement was renewed,

newed, and became very clofe and bloody. The prince threw the enemy into great diforder: to increafe it, he fent among them two fire-fhips; and at the fame time made a fignal to the French to bear down, which if they had done, a total victory muft have enfued. But the prince, when he faw that they neglected his fignal, and obferved that moft of his fhips were in no condition to keep the fea long, wifely provided for their fafety, by making eafy fail toward the Englifh coaft. The victory in this battle was as doubtful, as in all the actions fought during the prefent war.

The turn, which the affairs of the Hollanders took by land, was more favourable. The prince of Orange, by his conduct and fuccefs, obliged Lewis to recal his forces, and to abandon all his conquefts, with greater rapidity than he had at firft made them.

The king plainly faw, that he could expect no fupply from the commons for carrying on a war, which was fo odious to them. He refolved therefore to make a feparate peace with the Dutch, on the terms which they had propofed through the canal of the Spanifh ambaffador. With a cordiality, which, in the prefent difpofition on both fides, was probably but affected, but which was obliging, he afked advice of parliament. The parliament unanimoufly concurred, both in thanks for this gracious condefcenfion, and in their advice for peace. Peace was accordingly concluded at London, February 9th, 1674. The honour of the flag was yielded by the Dutch in the moft extenfive terms: a regulation of trade was agreed to: all poffeffions were reftored to the fame condition as before the war: the Englifh planters in Surinam were allowed to remove at pleafure: and the States agreed to pay to the king the fum of eight hundred thoufand patacoons, near three hundred thoufand pounds. Thus ended the laft of our Dutch wars, which, though made againft the intereft and will of the people, terminated highly to

their

their advantage; whereas the former war, though it was begun at the instance of the nation, ended but indifferently: so little correspondence there is between the grounds and issues of things.

The corsairs of Tripoli having for some time committed great outrages on the English trade, Sir John Narborough was sent, in the latter end of the year 1675, to reduce them to reason. The 14th of January following, Sir John came before the place, and having blocked up the port in the night, so that no ship could go in, or come out, he manned all his boats, and sent them under the command of lieutenant Shovel (afterward Sir Cloudesly, the famous admiral) into the harbour; where he seized the guard-ship, and afterward burnt the vessels, which lay at that time in the harbour: after which, he safely returned to the fleet without the loss of a single man. This extraordinary action struck the Tripolines with amazement, and made them instantly sue for peace; which, however, did not immediately take place, because they absolutely refused to make good the losses sustained by the English. Sir John, thereupon, cannonaded the town; and, finding that ineffectual, landed a body of men about twenty leagues from thence, and burnt a vast magazine of timber, which was to have served for the building of ships. When all this failed of reducing these people, Sir John sailed to Malta; and, after remaining there for some time, returned suddenly upon the enemy, and distressed them so much, that they were glad to submit to a peace, on the terms prescribed.

However, soon after the conclusion of this treaty, some of their corsairs, returning into port, not only expressed a great dislike thereto, but actually deposed the dey for making it; and, without any regard to it, began to take all English ships, as before. Sir John remaining still in the Mediterranean, and having immediate notice of what passed, suddenly appeared with eight frigates before Tripoli, and began

with

with such violence to batter the place, that the inhabitants were glad once more to renew the peace, and
deliver up the authors of the late disturbance to con-
dign punishment.

In 1679, we had some differences with the Algerines; upon which Sir John Narborough was sent
with a squadron to demand satisfaction: this he
procured, as it must always be procured, by dint of
force. This peace, however, did not last long; but
commodore Herbert, afterward so well known to the
world by the title of earl of Torrington, went thither
with a few ships, and compelled them to make satisfaction for the breach of it, and to give the strongest
assurances of their future conduct. That expedition,
which was performed in 1682, proved the last in this
reign.

There is yet one transaction more which calls for
our notice, and that is, the demolition of the strong
and expensive fortress of Tangier. In the space of
twenty years it cost the nation an immense sum of
money; and yet many doubted, all things considered, whether, after all, it was of any real use to
us, or not. When we first had it, the harbour was
very dangerous; to remedy which, there was a fine
mole run out at a vast charge. Several societies, or
copartnerships, which undertook to perfect this work,
raised great sums for that purpose; and, after wast-
ing them, miscarried. At last, however, all difficulties were, in a manner, overcome; and this work
finished in such a manner, that it might be said to
vie with those of the Romans. But the house of
commons, in 1680, having expressed a dislike to the
management of the garrison kept there, which they
suspected to be no better than a nursery for a popish
army; and discovering, withal, no thoughts of providing for it any longer; the king began, likewise,
to entertain thoughts of quitting, destroying, and
bringing home his forces from thence. In 1683, the
lord Dartmouth was constituted captain-general of

          his

his majefty's forces in Africa, and governor of Tangier, and fent, as admiral of an Englifh fleet, to de-
molifh the works, blow up the mole, and bring home
the garrifon from thence; all which he very effectually performed : fo that the harbour is, at this time,
entirely fpoiled; and, though now in the hands of
the Moors, is a very inconfiderable place.   One circumftance, attending its demolition, deferves to be
remarked, becaufe it fhews the temper and fpirit of
the king. He directed a confiderable number of new-
coined crown-pieces to be buried in the ruins, that
if (through the viciffitudes of fortune, to which all
fublunary things are liable) this city fhould ever be
reftored, there might remain fome memorial of its
having had once the honour of depending on the
crown of Britain.   Thus, through difputes between
the king and parliament, whatever party-fufpicions
might fuggeft, the Britifh nation loft a place and port
of great importance.

It is on all hands confeffed, that never any Englifh, perhaps it might, without diftinction of countries, be faid, any prince, underftood maritime concerns
fo well as Charles the fecond.   He piqued himfelf
very much on making, as occafion offered, minute
enquiries into whatever regarded naval affairs : he
underftood fhip-building perfectly, and made draughts
of veffels with his own hands : he was no ftranger
to the conveniencies and inconveniencies of every
port in his dominions.   But he was fo expenfive in
his pleafures, the jealoufies raifed againft him were
fo ftrong, he was fo much in the hands of favourites
and miftreffes, he was fo frequently and fo egregi-
oufly betrayed by both, and his finances, through his
whole reign, were fo cramped, and in fuch diforder;
that he was not able to accomplifh any great defigns.

How intent he was, for the firft ten years of his
reign, in promoting whatever had a tendency to increafe the naval power of his kingdom, appears, from
all the candid hiftories of thofe times, and from the
collections

collections of orders, and other public papers relating to the direction of the navy, while the duke of York was admiral, publifhed of late years, and in every body's hands. The lord keeper Bridgman affirmed, that, from 1660 to 1670, the charge of the navy had never amounted to lefs than half a million a year. But after the fecond Dutch war, the king grew more faving in this article; and yet, in 1678, when the nation in general expected a war with France, his navy was in excellent order. The judicious Mr. Pepys, fecretary to the admiralty, has left us a particular account of its ftate in the month of Auguft that year; which as it is very fhort, it may not be amifs to infert.

ABSTRACT of the FLEET.

	Rates.	Number.	Men.
	1	5	3135
	2	4	1555
	3	16	5010
	4	33	6460
	5	12	1400
	6	7	423
Fire-fhips		6	340
Total		83	18323

Of thefe, feventy-fix were in fea-pay, the ftore-houfes and magazines in compleat order; and, which is ftill more to the purpofe, thirty capital fhips were then actually on the ftocks.

The Eaft India company were exceedingly favoured and protected, efpecially in the beginning of this reign: the African company was in the zenith of its glory, and brought in vaft profits to the proprietors, and the nation. Many of our plantations were fettled by his majefty's favour; fuch as Penfilvania, Caro-

lina,

lina, &c. Others were reftored to this nation by his
arms; fuch as New York and the Jerfeys: and all
had fuch encouragement, that they made quite another
figure than in former times, as we may guefs from
what a modern writer (no way partial to this prince)
fays of Barbadoes; that, during his reign, it maintained four hundred fail of fhips, produced two hundred thoufand pounds a year clear profit to this nation, and maintained one hundred thoufand people
there and here.

These are high calculations : Sir William Petty calculated our exports at ten millions per annum. This
agrees very well with the ftate of our cuftoms, which
fell then little fhort of a million ; though in 1660,
they were farmed out for four hundred thoufand
pounds, as they were once let by queen Elizabeth
at thirty-fix thoufand. Dr. Davenant, an excellent
judge in thefe matters, having duly weighed thefe
calculations, and compared them with all the lights.
he had received from long experience; pronounces
the balance of trade to have been in our favour, in
this reign, two millions a year. The bounds pre-
fcribed to this work, will not allow more to be faid
on this fubject.

Few princes have ftruggled with greater difficulties, before they afcended their thrones, than king
James II. and few ever fuftained a greater load of
trouble afterward. He fucceeded his brother the 6th
of February, 1685, with the general acclamations
of his fubjects, who expected great things from a
king who came to the throne with fuch advantages.
He was then turned of fifty-one, had good natural
parts, improved and ftrengthened both by education
and experience; inclined to, and very diligent in
bufinefs; an able œconomift: in fine, a prince, who,
if he had conducted public affairs with the fame eafe
and dexterity which he fhewed in the management of
his private concerns, his reign might have been as

happy

happy and glorious; as it proved troublesome and unfortunate.

It was his great foible, that he was constantly influenced by foreign councils, which is what the English nation cannot endure ; and, indeed, it is impossible they should : for, as our constitution differs from the constitution of all the states upon the continent, it is simply impracticable to govern us well, by any other system of politics than our own. King James knew this well enough ; and yet his fondness for the popish religion, threw him into the arms of France, and engaged him, while a subject, to act as a tool ; when a king, to rule as a viceroy to Lewis XIV. and this at a juncture, when, if he had been of the religion of his fathers, and had complied with the delires of his people, he might have given law to that haughty monarch, and been esteemed the deliverer of Europe.

Nevertheless, wrong as his conduct was, in almost every other particular, the care he took of naval affairs deserves to be mentioned. He had long exercised the office of lord high-admiral, in the reign of his brother, and understood it thoroughly : he knew, too, the disorders which had crept into the whole œconomy of the fleet, in the six years immediately preceding his accession ; and was well acquainted, beside, with the difficulties the late king had found, in applying remedies to these mischiefs.

As soon, therefore, as he was seated on the throne, he began to consider how a total reformation might be wrought, and the affairs of the navy be not only set right for the present, but also be put into such a settled course, as that they might not suddenly go wrong again. With this view, he consulted Mr. Pepys, and some other persons, on whose abilities and integrity he could depend ; and having learned from them what was necessary to be done to bring about the ends at which he aimed, he first assigned stated ftated fund of four hundred thoufand pounds a year, payable quarterly out of the treafury, for the fervice of the navy; and then iffued a fpecial commiffion for fettling all things relating to it, and for putting the management thereof into fuch a method, as might need few or no alterations in fucceeding times.

This was the wifeft act of his whole reign, and anfwered very effectually all that could be expected from it; and was grounded, as to form, on a commiffion which had iffued, for the fame purpofe, in the reign of his grandfather. This commiffion was dated the 17th of April, 1686, and by it the commiffioners were directed to enquire into, and remedy all the diforders that were then in the navy, to reftore it, in every refpect, to good order, and from time to time to report the proceedings to his majefty and the privy council.

The commiffioners vefted with thefe powers loft no time; but fell immediately on a diligent infpection into the ftate of the navy, enquired ftrictly into the caufes of paft mifcarriages, with refpect rather to things than men; and taking fuch meafures for the immediate remedy of the mifchiefs they difcovered, that the old fhips were perfectly repaired; the new ones altered and mended; the yards properly fupplied with the ableft workmen; all the ftorehoufes filled with whatever was requifite, bought at the beft hand, and, in all refpects, the beft in their kind: the eftimates brought into proper order, and the whole oeconomy of the navy reduced into fo clear a method, that it was impoffible any officer could miftake in his duty, the public fervice fuffer in any of its various branches; or the king run any hazard of being cheated.

While this commiffion fubfifted, the king iffued new inftructions to the officers commanding his fhips of war; thefe are dated the 15th of July, 1686, and are extreamly well calculated for promoting the public fervice, fecuring difcipline, and preferving proper memorials of every man's particular merit, by obliging all captains, and superior officers, to deposit a perfect copy of their journals with the secretary of the admiralty. As many things, in these regulations, might seem to bear hard upon commanders, and to deprive them of those emoluments which their predecessors had long enjoyed; his majesty was pleased to grant them very considerable favours: such as a settled allowance for their tables, several advantages in respect to prizes, &c. and, in the close, promised to reward every instance of courage, care, or diligence, in any of his officers, upon proper attestations deposited with the secretary of the admiralty.

We need not wonder, that, in consequence of so unwearied an attention, the British fleet was in very good order when king James had the first notice of the prince of Orange's intended invasion; but we may be justly surprised at the strange management of maritime affairs from that time. A squadron of ships was, indeed, immediately ordered to sea, under the command of Sir Roger Strickland, then rear-admiral of England; who was, perhaps, the most improper man in the world to command them, on account of his being obnoxious to the seamen, by the readiness he had shewn in bringing priests on board the fleet. His squadron was ordered to the Downs very indifferently manned; and when he complained of it, and desired to have soldiers at least sent on board, even this was very slowly complied with.

When the danger appeared more clearly, this fleet was directed to retire to the Buoy in the Nore; and lord Dartmouth was ordered to sea, with such a reinforcement as made the whole fleet, under his command, consist of forty men of war: of which, thirty-eight were of the line of battle, and eighteen fire-ships. A council of war was called, wherein Sir William Jenings, who commanded a third rate, proposed to put to sea, and stand over to the Dutch coasts, as the shortest and surest way to prevent an

inva-

invasion. This propofition, however, was rejected, by a great majority; and fo it was refolved to continue there. The true ground of this, as Mr. fecretary Burchet fairly tells us, was, the fecret refolution of the greateft part of the captains to hinder the admiral, in cafe he had come up with the Dutch fleet, from doing them much damage : and thus it appears, how ineffectual fleets and armies are, when princes have loft the confidence of their fubjects.

In the mean time, the prince of Orange had about his perfon abundance of Englifh noblemen and gentlemen. The fleet that was to carry thefe, confifted of about fifty fail, moft of them third or fourth rates, and the tranfports were about five hundred. Thefe, with twenty-five fire-fhips, made up the whole navy : the land forces embarked, were four thoufand horfe and dragoons, and ten thoufand foot. It was very remarkable, that though all the captains of thefe veffels were Dutch, yet the chief command was given to admiral Herbert, who very lately commanded the Englifh fleet, and this with a view, either to engage fhips to come over, or, at leaft, to encourage the feamen to defert.

In order to do this more effectually, Herbert firft addreffed a letter to his countrymen in the fea-fervice, and then ftood with the Dutch fleet over to the Downs, in order to look at the Englifh fquadron, and try what effects his exhortation had produced. At that time his fuccefs did not promife much; and, after a fortnight's cruizing, he returned to the Dutch coafts, with a better opinion of the king's fleet, and a worfe of his own, than when he failed. But, for all this, his epiftle did almoft as much fervice as the force he commanded: for though the defertion was inconfiderable; yet, by degrees, the failors loft their fpirits, and their officers began to cabal.

On the firft of November the fleet failed. The prince intended to have gone northward, and to have landed his forces in the mouth of the Humber; but a ftrong eaft wind rendered this impracticable, and feemed to direct them to a better courfe. His high-nefs then failed weftward, the fame wind which brought him to the Englifh coaft keeping in the king's fhips. They paffed the Englifh navy, during a fog, undifcerned, except a few tranfports which failed in fight, while the Englifh fleet rode with their yards and top-mafts down, and could not, by reafon of the extraordinary violence of the wind, purchafe their anchors. The prince and his army landed fafely in Torbay, on the fifth of November, the anniverfary of the gun-powder plot.

The conduct of the king, after the arrival of the Dutch fleet, was unaccountable: fince, if we except the care he took in fending away his family, it does not appear that he iffued any orders relating to the fleet, which will feem ftill the more extraordinary, if we confider, that his admiral was not only a man of quality, and one on whofe fidelity he could abfolutely depend; but alfo an experienced officer, and a man extreamly beloved by the failors. In all probability, he was deterred from taking any meafures of this fort, by what happened at the docks, where the work-men employed in the fervice of the royal navy, rofe on a fudden, and, without any other arms than the tools belonging to their trades, drove out the regi-ment of regular troops quartered at Rochefter, and Chatham, and declared for the proteftant religion, and the prince of Orange. To fay the truth, the fea-faring people declared unanimoufly againft his meafures, and did all in their power to prevent the moft obnoxious of his minifters, fuch as chancellor Jefferies, and father Petre, from making their efcape: which can be attributed to nothing but the juft fenfe they had of the iniquitous meafures thefe people had purfued: for, as to themfelves, they had no particu-lar grievances.

The miftakes committed on this fide, were heigh-tened, in their appearance, by the great caution and

wife

wife management on the other, as well as by the fore-
feen and unforefeen consequences of the whole tranfaction. The embarkation was made with eafe; the
paffage better regulated by the winds, than it could
have been by their prudence; the defcent in the fit-
teft place in England for landing of horfe; fo that
it was performed without difficulty, as well as without danger.

In Holland, they triumphed on the exact execution of the plan laid down by the ftates; and the moft
eminent news-writer they then had, made this obfervation on the fuccefs of the prince's enterprize, in
his reflections on the hiftory of Europe, for November, 1688. " The expence beftowed on the fleet
" and army fet out from Holland, is a fign they are
" morally affured of the fuccefs of the expedition,
" which, I am apt to think, has been a long time
" in agitation, though it was carried with that pru-
" dence and fecrecy, as not to be difcovered, till it
" could be no longer concealed." When fkill, induftry, and zeal, were vifibly on the part of the
prince; and weaknefs, irrefolution, and diffidence
apparent in all the king's meafures; it was impoffible
things fhould continue long in difpute, or that his
highnefs, who knew fo well how to ufe all the advantages that were in his hands, fhould not prevail.

When lord Dartmouth faw the difpofition of his
officers, and how little it was in his power to ferve
his mafter; he wifely yielded to neceffity: and, failing once again into the Downs, held a council of war,
in which it was refolved, firft, to difmifs from their
commands, all fuch officers as were known to be
papifts, or fufpected fo to be; and then to fend up
an addrefs to his highnefs, fetting forth their fteady
affection to the proteftant religion, and their fincere
concern for the fafety, freedom, and honour of their
country. Not long after this, the fhips were difperfed, fome to the dock-yards, to be difmantled and
laid up; others to be cleaned and repaired; and fuch

as were in the beft condition for the fea, were appointed for neceffary fervices.

These were all the exploits performed by the Englifh navy, during the reign of a prince, who, while a
fubject, had ferved and acquired a reputation at fea;
who underftood maritime affairs perfectly well, and
who attended to them with extraordinary diligence.
But it ought to be remembered, that though this
fleet was ufelefs to him, yet it was of the higheft advantage to the nation. If he had been lefs careful in
this refpect; if he had left the navy in a low condition; nay, if he had left it as he found it at his brother's deceafe, it would have been impoffible for us
to have withftood the naval power of France, which
had been for feveral years growing: and about the
time of the revolution, or a little before, it had attained to its greateft height.

An abftract of the lift of the royal navy of England,
  upon the 18th of December, 1688, with the force
  of the whole.

Ships and veffels.		Force.	
Rates.	Number.	Men.	Guns.
1	9	6705	878
2	11	7010	974
3	39	16545	2640
4	41	9480	1908
5	2	260	69
6	6	420	90
Bombers,	3	120	34
Fire-fhips,	26	905	218
Hoys,	6	22	00
Hulks,	8	50	00
Ketches,	3	115	24
Smacks,	5	18	00
Yatchts,	14	353	104
Total.	173	42003	6930

No sooner was the crown placed on the head of the prince of Orange, than he began to feel the weight of it, and found himself obliged to embark in a war, as soon as he was seated on the throne. A war in which all Europe was engaged; for the ambitious designs of Lewis XIV. were now so evident, that even the powers, least inclined to action, saw themselves obliged to provide for their own safety, by entering into a confederacy for effectually opposing the encroachments of that aspiring prince.

The French king, on the other hand, instead of discovering any dread of this formidable alliance, began first by falling upon the empire, and declaring war against Spain, at the same time that he provided for his ally, king James, whom he sent over into Ireland, with a considerable force, escorted by a fleet of thirty sail of men of war, and seven frigates. On the 12th of March, 1688-9, that monarch landed at Kingsale, from whence he went to Cork.

Admiral Herbert, who commanded the English fleet, in the beginning of the month of April, 1689, sailed for Cork, with a squadron which consisted of no more than twelve ships of war, one fire-ship, two yatchts, and two smacks. Here he received information, that king James had landed at Kingsale, about two months before. He then thought it proper to attempt the cutting off the convoy that had attended him from France: with this view he sailed for Brest, and cruised off that port for some time; but hearing nothing of the French men of war from the advice-boats he daily received, and having increased his force to nineteen sail, he again steered for the Irish coast, and toward the latter end of April, appeared off Kingsale.

On the 29th of that month, he discovered a fleet of forty-four sail, which he judged were going into Kingsale, and therefore did his utmost to prevent it. The French shipped the stores and money they had brought for James's army, on board six fire-ships,

and

and some merchantmen they had with them, to land at
a place in the bay, seven leagues distant, while they
engaged the English squadron, that at all events they
might be safe.

Authors vary not a little as to the strength of both
fleets; but bishop Kennet reckons the English ships
twenty-two, wherein he agrees with the French relations. The enemy's fleet consisted, according to our
accounts, of twenty-eight; according to their own,
of no more than twenty-four sail. The English had
certainly the wind, and might therefore have avoided
fighting, if they had so pleased; but this was by no
means agreeable to admiral Herbert's temper: he
therefore endeavoured all he could to get into the
bay, that he might come to a close engagement; but
the French saved him the labour, by bearing down
upon him in three divisions, about ten in the morning on the first of May. The fight was pretty warm
for about two hours; but then slackened, because a
great part of the English fleet could not come up;
but they continued firing on both sides till about five
in the afternoon, when the French fleet stood into the
bay, which put an end to the fight. The English
writers ascribe this either to want of courage, or to
the admiral's being restrained by his orders; but the
French inform us, that he retired in order to take
care of the ships under his convoy; and that after
they had entirely debarked the supply they had
brought, he disposed every thing in order to put to
sea the next morning, which he did. This is the
battle in Bantry Bay, which though inconsiderable
enough in itself, (since the English, who had certainly
the worst of it, lost only one captain, one lieutenant,
and ninety-four men) is yet magnified by some writers into a mighty action.

After the action, admiral Herbert bore away for
the Scilly islands, and having cruised there for some
time, returned to Spithead; upon which occasion,
king William went down in person to Portsmouth,
where,

where, to shew he would distinguish and reward merit, though not pointed out to him by success, he declared admiral Herbert earl of Torrington, and knighted captain John Ashby of the Defiance, and captain Cloudesly Shovel of the Edgar; giving, at the same time, a bounty of ten shillings to each seaman, and making a provision for Mrs. Ailmer, relict of captain Ailmer, and for the rest of the widows of such as had been killed in the action. This was perfectly well judged by that prince, and was indeed an act of his own, flowing from the thorough knowlege he had of mankind, and the necessity there is of keeping up the spirits of the seamen, if we expect they should perform great things.

When king James landed in Ireland, his affairs had certainly a very promising aspect on that side. He brought with him a very considerable supply, and he found there an army of 40,000 men compleat. There were but two places in the north that held out against him, viz. London-Derry and Inniskilling, Of these he determined to make himself master; and might have easily done it, if he had been well advised: but, as bishop Burnet justly observes, there was a kind of fatality that hung on his councils.

Commodore Rooke, who had been sent with a squadron in the month of May to the coast of Ireland, performed all that could be expected from him there, by keeping king James and his army from having any intercourse with the Scots; and on the eighth of June, he sailed in with the Bonaventure, Swallow, Dartmouth, and a fleet of transport-ships, under the command of major-general Kirke, who was come with his force to relieve London-Derry. When they came to examine the method taken by the enemy to prevent their relieving the place, they found they had laid a boom cross the river, composed of chains and cables, and floated with timber, there being strong redoubts at each end, well provided with cannon. Major-general Kirke having properly disposed

the

the men of war, on the 30th of July, fent the Mountjoy of Derry, captain Browning, and the Phœnix of
Colrain, captain Douglas, both deeply laden with
provifions, under the convoy of the Dartmouth frigate, to attempt breaking the boom. The Irifh army
made a prodigious fire upon thefe fhips as they paffed,
which was very brifkly returned, 'till the Mountjoy
ftruck againft the boom, and broke it, and was by
the rebound run afhore; upon this, the Irifh gave a
loud huzza, made a terrible fire upon her, and with
their boats attempted to board her : but the failors
firing a broadfide, the fhock loofened her fo, that
they floated again, and paffed the boom, as did the
Phœnix alfo, under cover of the Dartmouth's fire.
This feafonable fupply faved the remains of that brave
garrifon, which, after a hundred and five days clofe
fiege, and being reduced from feven thoufand five
hundred, to four thoufand three hundred, had fubfiftence for only two days left, the enemy raifing the
fiege on the laft of July.

The naval tranfactions of 1690, will commence
properly with an account of admiral Ruffel's failing
into the Mediterranean, though this is, generally
fpeaking, accounted a tranfaction of the former year;
but the reafon for placing it here, is the fleet's not
putting to fea 'till the fpring, though orders were
given for it in the preceding winter. His catholic
majefty, Charles II. having efpoufed a princefs of
the houfe of Neubourg, fifter to the reigning emprefs,
and to the queen of Portugal, demanded an Englifh
fleet to conduct her fafely to his dominions, which
was readily granted; and indeed fuch a compliment
never had been refufed even to the ftates in war with
us, becaufe it was always taken as a tacit confeffion
of our dominion at fea. On the 24th of November,
admiral Ruffel failed with feven large men of war,
and two yatchts, to Flufhing, in order to receive her
catholic majefty, and her attendants; and had orders,
as foon as the queen came on board, to hoift the
union

union flag at the main-top-maft head, and to wear it there as long as her majefty was on board. The admiral had orders to put to fea with the firft fair wind, and was inftructed to block up the harbour of Toulon, in order to prevent the French fquadron there from coming out. He failed, after fome delays for want of a fair wind, on the 7th of February, with a ftout fquadron of thirty men of war, under his command, and a fleet of four hundred merchantmen, bound for the Streights ; and after a very tempeftuous paffage, landed her catholic majefty, on the 16th, at the Groyne. From thence he failed to execute his other commiffion ; which having effected, and having left vice-admiral Killegrew, with the Mediterranean fquadron, behind him ; bore away with the firft fair wind for England.

Vice-admiral Killegrew arrived at Cadiz on the 8th of April, where having, according to his inftructions, taken all poffible care of the trade, and having been joined by two Dutch men of war, the Guelderland and Zurickzee, he was next to proceed from thence in order to attend the motions of the Toulon fquadron. In this, however, he met with no fmall difficulty, by reafon of the ftormy weather, which injured feveral fhips of his fquadron extreamly ; and the two Dutch fhips, one of 72, and the other of 62 guns, after lofing all their mafts, except a mizen, foundered. In repairing thefe unlucky accidents, a great deal of time was wafted ; and, when he afterward got fight of the French fhips, they ftretched away, and being cleaner fhips, would not let our fquadron come up with them : on which our admiral gave over the chace.

The French had been very induftrious this year, in fending a large fleet to fea, early in the feafon ; for on the 1ft or 2d of March, they embarked a great fupply for Ireland, under the convoy of a fquadron of 36 men of war, attended by four fire-fhips, and five flutes, which were afterward joined by another fquadron from Provence, with feveral tranfports ; fo

that

that in all, they convoyed over 6000 men, befide ammunition and money. On the 8th of April, they left the coafts of that ifland, in order to return into the road of Breft; which they did fafely on the 23d, and then prepared to join their grand fleet, which had orders to affemble under the command of the count de Tourville.

While the French were thus employed, our councils were chiefly bent in fending over a royal army, to be commanded by king William in perfon, to Ireland. This great defign was brought to bear about the beginning of the month of June, when his majefty left London, and embarked his forces on board 288 tranfports on the 11th, efcorted by a fquadron of fix men of war, under Sir Cloudefly Shovel: he failed for Carrickfergus, where he faiely arrived on the 14th of the fame month, and foon after difmiffed rear-admiral Shovel, with the Plymouth fquadron, with orders to join the grand fleet; which he could not do, till it was too late.

There was nothing better underftood in England, than the abfolute neceffity of affembling early in the year, a ftrong fleet in the channel. The nation's fafety depended on this meafure, fince the king, and the greateft part of his forces were abroad. Yet, for all this, our maritime proceedings were very flow, for which, various, and fome fcarcely credible caufes are affigned. On the other hand, it was late before the Dutch fent their fleet to fea; and the Englifh, knowing that nothing of confequence could be done, till after their junction, were the lefs folicitous about putting themfelves in order, till they heard of their being at fea.

The conduct of the French, in the mean time, was of quite another kind; for while the fquadron before mentioned was gone to Ireland, orders were given for equipping a fleet of fixty fail at Breft, which was to put to fea by the end of May: and though they were forced by contrary winds, to put back again, yet on

the

the 12th of June, they put to sea in three squadrons,
each squadron being divided into three divisions : in
all there were 78 men of war, 22 fire-ships, and the
whole fleet carried upward of 4700 pieces of cannon,
under admiral Tourville.   On the 13th of June, they
steered for the English coast, and the 20th found
themselves off the Lizard.   The next day the admiral took some English fishing-boats, and after having
paid the people who were on board for their fish, he
set them at liberty again ; and these were the men,
such was our supineness ! that first brought advice of
the arrival of the French fleet on our coast.

The earl of Torrington was at St. Helen's, when
he received this news, which must have surprized him
very much, since he was so far from expecting any
advice of this kind, that he had no scouts to the westward.   He put to sea, however, with such ships as
he had, and stood to the south-east, on Midsummer-
day, leaving his orders, that all the English and
Dutch ships which could have notice, should follow
him.   His whole strength, when collected, consisted
of about 34 men of war of several sizes ; and the
three Dutch admirals had under their command 22
large ships.   We need not wonder, therefore, that
seeing himself out-numbered by above twenty sail,
he was not willing to risk his own honour, and the
nation's safety, upon such unequal terms.   But the
queen, who was then regent, having been informed,
that her father's adherents intended a general insurrection ; and that if the French fleet continued longer
on the coast, this would certainly take effect ; by advice of the privy-council, sent him orders to fight at
all events, in order to force the French fleet to withdraw.   In obedience to this order, as soon as it was
light, on the 30th of June, the admiral threw out
the signal for drawing into a line, and bore down
upon the enemy, while they were under sail.

The signal for a battle was made about eight, when
the French braced their head sails to their masts, in
order

order to lie by. The action began about nine, when the Dutch squadron, which made the van of the united fleets, fell in with the van of the French, and put them into some disorder. About half an hour after, our Blue squadron engaged their rear very warmly; but the Red, commanded by the earl of Torrington in person, which made the center of our fleet, could not come up till about ten: so that the Dutch were almost surrounded by the enemy. The admiral seeing their distress, drove between them and the enemy; and in that situation, anchored about five in the afternoon, when it grew calm: but discerning how much the Dutch had suffered, and how little probability there was of regaining any thing by renewing the fight, he weighed about nine at night, and retired eastward with the tide of flood.

The next day it was resolved in a council of war, held in the afternoon, to preserve the fleet, by retreating; and rather to destroy the disabled ships, if they should be pressed by the enemy, than to hazard another engagement, by endeavouring to protect them. This resolution was executed with as much success as could be expected; which, however, was chiefly owing to want of experience in the French admirals: for by not anchoring when the English did, they were driven to a great distance, and by continuing to chace in a line of battle, instead of leaving every ship at liberty to do her utmost, they could never recover what they lost by their first mistake.

As soon as the earl of Torrington came to town, he was examined before the council; where he justified himself with great presence of mind. The council, however, thought proper to commit his lordship to the Tower; and that they might lessen the clamours of the crowd, and give some satisfaction to the Dutch, they directed a committee to repair to Sheerness, where they were to make a thorough enquiry into the real causes of this disaster.

After

After raising the siege of Limerick, king William returned into England; where, in a council held on the affairs of Ireland, which were still in a very precarious condition, many of the great cities, and most of the convenient ports being still held for king James, the earl of Marlborough proposed a plan for the immediate reduction of that island. He observed first, that our fleet was now at sea, and that of the French returned to Brest; in which situation, therefore, there was nothing to be feared in relation to descents. He farther remarked, that there were at least 5000 land forces lying idle in England, which might be embarked on board the fleet, even in this late season of the year, and land time enough to perform considerable service. The king readily accepted this offer, gave the command of the troops to the earl of Marlborough, and sent orders to the admirals to send the great ships about to Chatham, and to take on board the remainder of the fleet, the forces ordered for this service.

The admirals hoisted their flag on board the Kent, a third rate; and having embarked the troops with all imaginable expedition, arrived with them before the harbour of Cork, on the 21st of September, in the afternoon. On the 23d, the forces were landed, and joined a body of between 3 and 4000 men, under the command of the duke of Wirtemberg; who, by an ill-timed dispute about the command, had like to have ruined the whole expedition. The city of Cork was very well fortified, and had in it a body of 4000 men: but the earl of Marlborough having observed that the place was commanded by an adjacent hill, he ordered a battery to be erected there on the 24th; and after playing on the town for a few hours, made so considerable a breach, that on the 25th the generals resolved to attack it. The besieged were so terrified at this, that the Irish instantly capitulated. The reduction of Kingsale followed soon after.

The

The fleet arrived in the Downs on the 8th of October, bringing over with them, by the earl of Marlborough's desire, the governor of Cork, and several persons of quality, who were made prisoners when that city was taken. There the admirals received orders to divide their fleet into small squadrons for several services, and leave only a strong squadron in the Downs, under the command of Sir Cloudesly Shovel, who cruised the remaining part of the year in the Soundings, without any success remarkable enough to deserve notice.

The care of the administration to repair all past errors in naval affairs, and to retrieve the honour of the maritime powers, appeared visibly in the measures taken for sending a great fleet early to sea, in the spring of the year 1691. In order to this, after the earl of Torrington was dismissed from his command, Edward Ruffel, Esq; was appointed admiral and commander in chief, and immediately received instructions to use the utmost expedition in drawing together the ships of which his fleet was to be composed; and a lift of them, to the number of 91, of which 57 were of the line of battle, was annexed to his instructions. He executed these directions with the utmost skill and diligence, and by the 7th of May was ready to put to sea. His orders were to proceed in the Soundings, as soon as he should be joined by the Dutch; and he was likewise directed to take care to block up the port of Dunkirk, in order to prevent the French privateers from disturbing our trade. These directions, however, were but indifferently executed; which our writers attribute to the slowness of the Dutch in sending their ships to join the confederate fleet, which they had stipulated to do by the beginning of May. It is certain, that notwithstanding all his skill and care, admiral Ruffel found his fleet but indifferently manned, and scantily victualled; at the same time that he was so perplexed by his

7.　　　　　　　　　　　　　orders,

orders, and with the difficulties ftarted upon every occafion by the Dutch admiral, who very probably was as much cramped by his; that a great part of the months of May and June were fpent to very little purpofe: and though the French fleet was not in fuch forwardnefs this year as it had been the laft, yet it was at fea fome time before ours had any intelligence of it.

Lewis XIV. feemed at this time to fhew a fingular vanity in maintaining a prodigious naval force, to make all Europe fee how foon, and how effectually, his councils had been able to create a maritime power. He had at this time to deal with the Englifh, Spaniards, and Dutch; and as he was now in the zenith of his glory, he exhaufted his treafures, in order, had it been poffible, to render himfelf mafter at fea. He appointed the count d'Eftrees, vice-admiral of France, to command in the Mediterranean a fleet confifting of four large men of war, 5 frigates, 26 gallies, and three bomb-veffels: and, on the other hand, count Tourville was directed to affemble the grand fleet intended for the ocean. This fleet, though very confiderable, and excellently provided with every thing neceffary, yet was inferior in force to that of the confederates; and therefore count Tourville was inftructed to avoid an engagement as much as poffible, and to amufe the enemy, by keeping as long as might be in the channel. It muft be obferved alfo, that a fquadron had been fent, under the command of the marquis de Nefmonde, to carry fupplies of all forts for the relief of king James's army in Ireland.

The Smyrna fleet was expected home this fpring; and as the Englifh and Dutch had a joint concern therein, to the amount of upward of four millions fterling, both nations were extreamly apprehenfive of its being attacked by the French. Precife orders were therefore fent to admiral Ruffel, to ufe his utmoft care for its prefervation: this he performed with equal induftry and fuccefs; and then fteered his courfe for the coaft of France.

Arriving in this station, Sir Cloudesley Shovel was sent to look into Brest, where he saw about forty sail coming out of that port; which proved to be a fleet of merchant-ships from Bretagne, escorted by three men of war. Sir Cloudesley, to decoy these ships into his hands, made use of an excellent stratagem: he knew the French had intelligence that a small squadron of their fleet had made prizes of several English merchantmen; laying hold, therefore, of this piece of false news, he ordered part of his squadron to put out French colours, and the rest to take in theirs. By this method he thought to deceive the French, who might naturally suppose it that squadron with their prizes. This succeeded in part; but the enemy discovered the cheat before he was near enough to do much mischief.

About the latter end of July, admiral Russel fell in with a convoy going to the French fleet with fresh provisions; some of these were taken, and from them he learnt that count. Tourville had orders to avoid fighting, which he very punctually obeyed, keeping scouts at a considerable distance on all points of the compass by which he could be approached, and these being chased by ours, they immediately ran, making signals to others, that lay within them; so that it was impossible to come up with the body of their fleet.

Being sensible of the dangers that might attend this situation, the admiral wrote home for fresh orders, which he received; but found them so perplexed, that having intelligence of the French fleet's being gone into Brest, he, in the beginning of August, pursuant to the resolution of a council of war, returned to Torbay, from whence he wrote up to court to have his last orders explained. In return he was directed to put to sea again, which he did; and notwithstanding his frequent representations of the inconvenience of having such large ships exposed to the rough weather, which usually happens about the equinox; he was obliged to continue in the Soundings to the 2d of Sep-

September, when he met with such a violent storm, that after doing all that could be done for the preservation of the fleet, it sustained considerable damage, the Coronation, a second rate, and the Harwich, a third rate, being lost.

The whole nation were now convinced, that with respect to our honour and interest in this war, the management of affairs at sea was chiefly to be regarded; and yet, by an unaccountable series of wrong councils, the management of these affairs was worse conducted than any other. The absolute reduction of Ireland, and the war in Flanders, seemed to occupy the king's thoughts entirely; and the care of the navy was left wholly to the board of admiralty, who, to speak in the softest terms, did not manage it much to the satisfaction of the nation. There were, beside, some other things which contributed to hurt our maritime proceedings. A faction was grown up in the fleet against the admiral, and at the same time the government entertained a great jealousy of many of the officers; though to this hour it remains a secret, whether it was, or was not, well founded. The truth appears to be, that king James was better known to the officers of the fleet, than to any other set of men in England; most of them had served under him when lord high-admiral, and many had been preferred by him; which rendered it highly probable, they might have an esteem for his person: but that any of these officers intended to act in his favour, in conjunction with a French force, against their country, is very unlikely: especially if we consider the unanimity with which they went into the revolution, which had been openly acknowleged, and they solemnly thanked for it by the convention. However it was, this is certain, that in parliament, at court, and in the navy, nothing was heard of but jealousies, ill conduct, and want of sufficient supplies for the service; a kind of discourse that lasted all the winter, and which answered very bad purposes.

In

In the spring of the year 1692, a little before the king went to Holland, he began to communicate his intentions, as to the employment of the fleet, to admiral Ruffel, who, however, was very far from standing in high favour: but his character, as an officer, and his known steadiness in revolution-principles, supported him; and the king resolved to confide the fleet to his care.

When Lewis XIV. perceived, that it was impossible to support the war in Ireland any longer to advantage, he came to a resolution of employing the forces that were still left king James, to serve his purpose another way. With this view he concerted with the malecontents in England, an invasion on the coast of Suffex; and though for this design it was necessary to draw together a great number of transports, as well as a very considerable body of forces, yet he had both in readiness, before it was so much as suspected here. In short, nothing was wanting to the execution of this design in the beginning of April, but the arrival of count d'Estrees's squadron of 12 men of war, which was to escort the embarkation; while the count de Tourville cruized in the channel with the grand fleet, which was also ready to put to sea, but was detained by contrary winds. Things being in this situation, king James sent over some agents to give his friends intelligence of his motions; and some of these people, in hopes of reward, gave the first clear account of the whole design to the government at home: upon which, order after order was sent to admiral Ruffel to hasten out to sea, in whatever condition the fleet might be at this time.

King William, as soon as he arrived in Holland, took care to hasten the naval preparations with unusual diligence; so that the fleet was ready to put to sea much sooner than had been expected. As for our admiral, he went on board in the beginning of May; and observing how great advantage the French might reap by the division of our fleet, his first care was to

write to court to defire, that a certain place might be
fixed for their conjunction. In return to this, he had
orders fent him to cruize between Cape la Hogue and
the Ifle of Wight, till the fquadrons fhould join
with him, though he had propofed the junction fhould
be made off Beachy-head. However, he obeyed his
orders as foon as he received them, and plyed it down
through the fands, with a very fcanty wind, contrary
to the opinion of many of his officers, and all the pilots, who were againft hazarding fo great a fleet in fo
dangerous an attempt ; and yet to this bold ftroke of
the admiral's, was owing all his following fuccefs.

On the 11th day of May, Ruffel failed from Rye
to St. Helen's, where he was joined by the Englifh
fquadrons under Delaval and Carter; and by the
Dutch fquadrons, commanded by Allemonde, Callembergh, and Vandergoes. He fet fail for the coaft
of France on the 18th day of May, with a fleet of
99 fhips of the line, befide frigates and fire-fhips.

Next day, about three o'clock in the morning, he
difcovered the enemy, under the count de Tourville,
and threw out the fignal for the line of battle, which
by eight o'clock was formed in good order, the
Dutch in the van, the blue divifion in the rear, and
the red in the center. The French fleet did not exceed 63 fhips of the line, and as they were to windward, Tourville might have avoided an engagement;
but, he had received a pofitive order to fight, on
the fuppofition that the Dutch and Englifh fquadrons
had not joined. Tourville, therefore, bore down
along-fide of Ruffel's own fhip, which he engaged
at a very fmall diftance. He fought him with great
fury till one o'clock, when his rigging and fails being confiderably damaged, his fhip, the Rifing Sun,
that carried 104 cannon, was towed out of the line
in great diforder. Neverthelefs, the engagement continued till three, when the fleets were parted by a
thick fog. When this abated, the enemy were defcried flying to the northward; and Ruffel made the

fignal

signal for chafing. Part of the blue fquadron came
up with the enemy about eight in the evening, and
engaged them half an hour, during which admiral
Carter was mortally wounded. At length, the French
bore away for Conquet-Road, having loft four fhips
in this day's action. Next day, about eight in the
morning, they were difcovered crowding away to the
weftward, and the combined fleets chafed with all
the fail they could carry, until Ruffel's foretop-maft
came by the board. Though he was retarded by
this accident, they ftill continued the purfuit, and
he anchored near Cape la Hogue. On the 22d of
the month, about feven in the morning, part of the
French fleet was perceived near the Race of Alderney, fome at anchor, and fome driving to the eaftward with the tide of flood. He, and the fhips
neareft him, immediately flipt their cables and chafed.
The Rifing-Sun, having loft her mafts, ran afhore
near Cherbourg, where fhe was burned by Sir Ralph
Delaval, together with the Admirable, another firft
rate, and the Conquerant of eighty guns. Eighteen
other fhips of their fleet ran into La Hogue, where
they were attacked by Sir George Rooke, who deftroyed them, and a great number of tranfports loaded with ammunition, in the midft of a terrible fire
from the enemy, and in fight of the Irifh camp. Sir
John Afhby, with his own fquadron and fome Dutch
fhips, purfued the reft of the French fleet, which
efcaped through the Race of Alderney, by fuch a
dangerous paffage as the Englifh could not attempt,
without expofing their fhips to the moft imminent
hazard.

This was a very mortifying defeat to the French
king, who had been fo long flattered with an unin-
terrupted feries of victories: and reduced James to
the loweft ebb of defpondence, as it fruftrated the
whole fcheme of his embarkation, and overwhelmed
his friends in England with grief and defpair. Some
hiftorians allege, that Ruffel did not improve his
victory

victory with all advantages that might have been obtained before the enemy recovered of their conster-nation. But this is a malicious imputation; and a very ungrateful return for his manifold fervices to the nation. He acted in this whole expedition with the genuine fpirit of a Britifh admiral: and, in a word, obtained fuch a decifive victory, that during the remaining part of the war, the French would not hazard another battle by fea with the Englifh.

Ruffel having ordered Sir John Afhby, and the Dutch admiral Callembergh, to fteer toward Havre de Grace, and endeavour to deftroy the remainder of the French fleet, failed back to St. Helen's, that the damaged fhips might be refitted, and the fleet furnifhed with frefh fupplies of provifion and ammunition: but, his principal motive was to take on board a number of troops provided for a defcent upon France, which had been projected by England and Holland, with a view to alarm and diftract the enemy in their own dominions. In the latter end of July, 7000 men, commanded by the duke of Leinfter, embarked on board of tranfports, to be landed at St. Maloe's, Breft, or Rochfort; and the nation conceived the moft fanguine hopes of this expedition. A council of war, confifting of land and fea-officers, being held on board the Breda, to deliberate upon the fcheme of the miniftry, the members unanimoufly agreed, that the feafon was too far advanced to put it in execution.

Nothing could be more inglorious for the Englifh than their operations by fea in the courfe of the fummer 1693. The king had ordered the admirals to ufe all poffible difpatch in equipping the fleets, that they might block up the enemy in their own ports, and protect the commerce, which had fuffered feverely from the French privateers. They were, however, fo dilatory in their proceedings, that the fquadrons of the enemy failed from their harbours before the Englifh fleet could put to fea. About

the

the middle of May it was affembled at St. Helen's, and took on board five regiments, intended for a defcent on Breft; but this enterprize was never attempted. When the Englifh and Dutch fquadrons joined, fo as to form a very numerous fleet, the public expected they would undertake fome expedition of importance; but the admirals were divided in their opinion, nor did their orders warrant their executing any fcheme of confequence. Killigrew and Delaval did not efcape the fufpicion of being difaffected to the fervice; and France was faid to have maintained a fecret correfpondence with the malecontents in England. Lewis had made furprifing efforts to repair the damage which his navy had fuftained. He had purchafed feveral large veffels, and converted them into fhips of war; he had laid an embargo on all the fhipping of his kingdom, until his fquadrons were manned: he had made a grand naval promotion, to encourage the officers and feamen; and this expedient produced a wonderful fpirit of activity and emulation. In the month of May his fleet failed to the Mediterranean, in three fquadrons, confifting of 71 capital fhips, befide bomb-ketches, fire-fhips, and tenders.

In the beginning of June, the Englifh and Dutch fleets failed down the channel. On the 6th, Sir George Rooke was detached to the Streights, with a fquadron of 23 fhips, as convoy to the Mediterranean trade. The great fleet returned to Torbay, while he purfued his voyage, having under his protection about 400 merchant fhips belonging to England, Holland, Denmark, Sweden, Hamburgh, and Flanders. On the 16th, his fcouts difcovered part of the French fleet under Cape St. Vincent: next day their whole navy appeared, to the amount of 80 fail. Rooke avoided engaging them, which he thought could only tend to their ruin; he directed the veffels neareft land to put into the firft Spanifh ports, while he ftood off with the remainder; however a great number fell into the enemy's hands. The value of the lofs fuftained

on this occasion amounted to one million sterling.
Mean while Rooke stood off with a fresh gale, and
on the 19th sent home the Lark ship of war, with
the news of his misfortune; then he bore away for
the Madeiras, where]having taken in wood and water,
he set sail for Ireland; and in pursuance of orders,
he joined the great fleet then cruising in the chops
of the channel. On the 25th day of August, they
returned to St. Helen's, and the four regiments were
landed.

The French admirals, instead of pursuing Rooke
to Madeira, made an unsuccessful attempt upon Cadiz, and bombarded Gibraltar, where the merchants
sunk their ships, that they might not fall into the
hands of the enemy. Then they sailed along the
coast of Spain, destroyed some English and Dutch
vessels at Malaga, Alicant, and other places; and
returned in triumph to Toulon. About this period,
Sir Francis Wheeler returned to England with his
squadron, from an unfortunate expedition in the West
Indies. In conjunction with colonel Codrington, governor of the Leeward islands, he made unsuccessful
attempts upon the islands of Martinique and Dominique. Then he sailed to Boston in New England,
with a view to concert an expedition against Quebec,
which was judged impracticable. He afterward steered for Placentia in Newfoundland, which he would
have attacked without hesitation; but the design was
rejected by a majority of voices in the council of war.
Thus disappointed, he set sail for England; and
arrived at Portsmouth in a very shattered condition.

In November another effort was made to annoy the
enemy. Commodore Benbow sailed with a squadron
of 12 capital ships, four bomb-ketches, and ten brigantines, to the coast of St. Malo; and anchoring
within half a mile of the town, cannonaded and
bombarded it for three days successively. Then they
landed on an island, where they burnt a convent.
On the 19th, they took the advantage of a dark
night,

night, a frefh gale, and a ftrong tide, to fend in a
fire-fhip, of a particular contrivance, ftiled the In-
fernal, in order to burn the town; but, fhe ftruck
upon a rock before fhe arrived at the place, and the
engineer was obliged to fet her on fire, and retreat.
She continued burning for fome time, and at laft
blew up, with fuch an explofion as fhook the whole
town like an earthquake, unroofed 300 houfes, and
broke all the glafs and earthen ware for three leagues
round. A capitan, that weighed 200 pounds, was
tranfported into the place, and falling upon a houfe,
levelled it to the ground; the greateft part of the wall
toward the fea tumbled down; and the inhabitants
were overwhelmed with confternation: fo that a fmall
number of troops might have taken poffeffion without refiftance; but there was not a foldier on board.
Neverthelefs, the failors did confiderable damage to
the town of St. Malo, which had been a neft of privateers that infefted the Englifh commerce. Though
this attempt was executed with great fpirit, and fome
fuccefs, the clamours of the people became louder
and louder. But if the Englifh were difcontented,
the French were miferable, in fpite of all their victories. That kingdom laboured under a dreadful
famine, occafioned partly from unfavourable feafons,
and partly from the war, which had not left hands
fufficient to cultivate the ground. Notwithftanding
all the diligence and providence of their miniftry, in
bringing fupplies of corn from Sweden and Denmark, their care in regulating the price, and furnifhing the markets, their liberal contributions for the
relief of the indigent; multitudes perifhed of want,
and the whole kingdom was reduced to poverty and
diftrefs. Lewis pined in the midft of his fuccefs.
He faw his fubjects exhaufted by a ruinous war, in
which they had been involved by his ambition. He
tampered with the allies apart, in hope of dividing
and detaching them from the grand confederacy: he
folicited the northern crowns to engage as mediators

S

for

for a general peace. A memorial was actually prefented by the Danifh minifter to king William, by
which it appears, that the French king would have
been contented to purchafe a peace with fome confiderable conceffions. But the terms were rejected by
the king of England, whofe ambition and revenge
were not yet gratified; and whofe fubjects, though
heavy laden, could ftill bear additional burdens.

King William having received intelligence of the
defign of the French upon Barcelona, endeavoured to
prevent the junction of the Breft and Toulon fquadrons, by fending Ruffel to fea as early as the fleet
could be in a condition to fail : but before he arrived
at Portfmouth, the Breft fquadron had quitted that
harbour. And a body of land-forces, intended for a
defcent upon the coaft of France, under the command
of general Tollemache, failed on the 29th of May,
1694, but effected nothing, and loft their general.

After this unfortunate attempt, lord Berkeley,
with the advice of a council of war, failed back for
England; and at St. Helen's received orders from
the queen to call a council, and deliberate in what
manner the fhips and forces might be beft employed.
They agreed to make fome attempt upon the coaft
of Normandy. With this view they fet fail on the
5th day of July. They bombarded Dieppe, and Havre
de Grace; and haraffed the French troops, who
marched after them along-fhore. They alarmed the
whole coaft, and filled every town with fuch confternation, that they would have been abandoned by the
inhabitants, had not they been detained by military
force.

During thefe tranfactions, admiral Ruffel with the
grand fleet failed for the Mediterranean ; and being
joined by rear-admiral Neville from Cadiz, together
with Callembergh and Evertzen, he fteered toward
Barcelona, which was befieged by the French fleet
and army. At his approach, Tourville retired with
precipitation into the harbour of Toulon ; and Noailles
aban-

abandoned his enterprize. The Spanish affairs were in such a deplorable condition, that without this timely assistance, the kingdom must have been undone. While he continued in the Mediterranean, the French admiral durst not venture to appear at sea; and all his projects were disconcerted. After having asserted the honour of the British flag in those seas during the whole summer, he sailed in the beginning of November to Cadiz, where, by an express order of the king, he passed the winter; during which he took such precautions for preventing Tourville from passing the Streights, that he did not think proper to risque the passage.

While admiral Russel asserted the British dominion in the Mediterranean-sea, the French coasts were again insulted in the channel by a separate fleet, under the command of lord Berkeley, of Straton, assisted by the Dutch admiral Allemonde. On the fourth day of July, 1695, they anchored before St. Malos, which they bombarded from nine ketches covered by some frigates, which sustained more damage than was done to the enemy. On the 6th, Granville underwent the same fate; and then the fleet returned to Portsmouth. The bomb-vessels being refitted, the fleet sailed round to the Downs, where 400 soldiers were embarked for an attempt upon Dunkirk, under the direction of Meesters, the famous Dutch engineer: but to no effect, owing to the ill understanding between the Dutch engineer and the English officers.

A squadron had been sent to the West Indies, under the joint command of captain Robert Wilmot and colonel Lilingston, with 1200 land-forces. They had instructions to co-operate with the Spaniards in Hispaniola, against the French settlements on that island, and to destroy their fisheries on the banks of Newfoundland, in their return. They were accordingly joined by 1700 Spaniards, raised by the president of St. Domingo; but, instead of proceeding

7 against

againſt Petit-Guavas, according to the directions they had received, Wilmot took poſſeſſion of Fort-Francois, and plundered the country for his own private advantage, notwithſtanding the remonſtrances of Lilingſton.

Notwithſtanding the great efforts the nation had made to maintain ſuch a number of different ſquadrons for the protection of commerce, as well as to annoy the enemy, the trade ſuffered ſeverely from the French privateers, which ſwarmed in both channels, and made prize of many rich veſſels. The marquis of Carmaerthen being ſtationed with a ſquadron off the Scilly iſlands, miſtook a fleet of merchant-ſhips for the Breſt fleet, and retired with precipitation to Milford-Haven. In conſequence of this retreat, the privateers took a good number of ſhips from Barbadoes, and five from the Eaſt Indies, valued at a million ſterling. The merchants renewed their clamour againſt the commiſſioners of the admiralty, who produced their orders and inſtructions in their own defence. The marquis of Carmaerthen had been guilty of a flagrant miſconduct on this occaſion; but the chief ſource of thoſe national calamities was the circumſtantial intelligence tranſmitted to France from time to time, by the malcontents of England: for, they were actuated by a ſcandalous principle, which they ſtill retain, namely, that of rejoicing in the diſtreſs of their country.

Toward the end of the year 1696, the nation was again alarmed with the report of an invaſion. It was known that the French were fitting out a ſtrong ſquadron at Breſt; and for what ſervice, the intelligence our ſecretaries had, could not inform them. Sir Cloudeſley Shovel, therefore, was ſent with a conſiderable force to block them up, which however the French avoided; and it was then given out at home, that our vigilance had diſappointed the deſigns of the enemy. In this we only deceived ourſelves; for our merchants quickly came at the knowlege of the true
ſcheme,

fcheme, which was the fending a ftrong fquadron into
the Weft Indies, to attack fome of the Spanifh plantations in thofe parts. The Sieur Pointis was the
perfon who formed the plan of this undertaking, and
who had been no lefs than three years in bringing it
to bear.

The Spaniards were not a little inflamed by the
fuccefs of Pointis in America, where he took Carthagene, in which he found a booty amounting to eight
millions of crowns. Having ruined the fortifications
of the place, and received advice that an Englifh
fquadron, under admiral Nevil, had arrived in the
Weft Indies, with a defign to attack him in his return, he bore away for the ftreights of Bahama. On
the 22d day of May, he fell in with the Englifh fleet,
and one of his fly-boats was taken; but, fuch was
his dexterity, or good fortune, that he efcaped, after
having been purfued five days. After fome other difappointments, Neville failed through the gulph of
Florida to Virginia, where he died of chagrin; and the
command of the fleet devolved to captain Dilkes,
who arrived in England on the 24th day of October,
with a fhattered fquadron half manned, to the un-
fpeakable mortification of the people; who flattered
themfelves with the hopes of wealth and glory from
this expedition, Certain it is, the fervice was greatly
obftructed by the faction among the officers, which
with refpect to the nation had all the effects of treachery and mifconduct.

Our limits will not admit our entering into the
detail of any naval tranfactions but thofe which either
in themfelves or in their confequences were of importance: and by this time the commerce and maritime ftrength of the kingdom, were fo far advanced,
as to render our tranfactions at fea very numerous and
of great influence to our proceedings by land. On
fo precarious an element, many fleets are fitted out
which return without effecting any thing; many fuch
we muft occafionally overlook, that we may not omit

others

others that merit fpecial notice. Peace was concluded between England, Spain, and Holland, on the one fide, and the crown of France on the other, at Ryfwick, on September 10th, 1697, by which the French king acknowleged king William's title, and, as the French hiftorians fay, gave up more towns than the confederates could have taken in twenty years: but this was not from any principle either of juftice or moderation, but with views of quite another fort, as was forefeen then, and in the fpace of a few years fully appeared.

We have now brought this long war to a conclufion, and it is but juft that we fhould offer the reader fome reflections on the confequences of it, to the naval power and commerce of England. Firft then, with refpect to our navy, we have feen that the war opened with a very bad profpect; for though we had an excellent fleet, a vaft number of able feamen, and, perhaps, as good officers as any in the world, yet the French got earlier to fea than we did, appeared with a greater force, and managed it better, though we acted then in conjunction with Holland, and according to the general rule of political reafoning, ought to have had it in our power to have driven the French out of the fea.

All this proceeded from the fudden change in our government, which, perhaps, left many of our officers difaffected, and many more without having any proper degree of credit at court. Want of confidence between the adminiftration and the commanders of our fleets, is always deftructive to our maritime power; and therefore, inftead of wondering that things went on fo ill, we may with more juftice be furprifed, that they went no worfe. Our partydivifions not only enervated our own ftrength, but created fuch jealoufies between us and the Dutch, as blafted the fruits that muft have been otherwife produced by this clofe and fortunate union of the maritime powers.

But

But when once the government was thoroughly settled, and we acted cordially in conjunction with the States, it soon became evident, that we were much more than a match for France at sea : and on the whole, the French suffered much more in their maritime power than we : consequently, if we consider the situation of both nations, the ease with which it was in our power to repair our losses, and the almost insuperable difficulties the French had to struggle with in this respect, we must conclude, that not only they, but the whole world had full evidence from thence, of their being no way able to struggle against the Dutch and us in a maritime war. To make this still more apparent, king William, in his speech to both houses of parliament, at the conclusion of the war, asserted our naval force to be near double what it was at his accession.

It will now be necessary to take a retrospective view of some past affairs, in order to preserve a connexion with others to come. The revolution brought back to Scotland several worthy patriots, whom the jealousy of former reigns had driven into other countries. These, from the time of their return, thought of nothing so much as the putting of the trade of Scotland, which had been hitherto in a manner totally neglected, on a proper footing. With this view they procured, in 1693, an act of the Scots parliament, for the encouragement of foreign commerce ; and in consequence of that law, another in 1695, for setting up an East India company. When this was done, it was found requisite to take in subscriptions : and, as it was not easy to find money enough in Scotland, for the carrying on so expensive a design, the company's agents endeavoured to procure subscriptions abroad, particularly at London, Hamburgh, and Amsterdam, in which they were certainly sufficiently supported both by the royal and legislative authority. But this scheme, as might be foreseen, gave great umbrage to the East India companies in England and Holland,

Holland, and they took the beſt meaſures they could to hinder the ſucceſs of theſe applications. This, however, had ſome very untoward conſequences, ſince theſe companies could effect nothing but by the interpoſition of their reſpective governments ; and by this means his majeſty's name, as king of England and ſtadtholder of Holland, came to be made uſe of, to thwart theſe deſigns which actually had his ſanction as king of Scotland.

In the enſuing ſeſſion of parliament in 1698, the government found itſelf not a little embarraſſed with the affairs of the Engliſh. Eaſt India company. A ſcheme had been offered for erecting a new company, which was to advance two millions for the public ſervice at eight per cent. and were to carry on this trade by a joint ſtock. To make way for this, it was propoſed to diſſolve the old company. The pretence for diſſolving it, was a clauſe in that very charter, reſerving ſuch a power to the crown. But as it was not ſo much as aſſerted, that ſince the granting this new charter, they had done any thing that ought to ſubject them to a diſſolution, by moderate and impartial people, who knew nothing of ſtock-jobbing, this was thought not a little hard.

The Eaſt India company in Scotland, finding their deſigns ſo vigorouſly oppoſed, and having, as they conceived, very large powers veſted in them by the late act of parliament, reſolved to turn their endeavours another way for the preſent, and to attempt the ſettlement of a colony in America, on the Iſthmus of Darien. This is that narrow track of country which unites the two continents of North and South America, and conſequently muſt be very advantageouſly ſeated for commerce. As the inhabitants had never been conquered by the Spaniards, and, as the new colony ſent thither, actually purchaſed their lands from the native proprietors, and ſettled there by conſent, it was apprehended, that the Spaniards had no right to diſpute the eſtabliſhment ; and that if they did, the planters might defend themfelves without involving the nation in a war. But it was foon found, that great miftakes had been made in relation to the confequences expected from it. For the Spaniards not only confidered it as an invafion on their rights, and began to take our fhips upon it; but the Englifh alfo grew very uneafy, and made warm reprefentations to his majefty on this fubject: this produced private orders to the governors of Jamaica, and other neighbouring plantations, not only to avoid all commerce with the Scots at Darien, but even to deny them provifions. As it was fore-feen that thefe meafures would naturally occafion great difturbances in that part of the world, it was found requifite to fend a fquadron thither, under admiral Benbow, to protect our trade, to awe the Spaniards, and to hinder the increafe of pirates, which had been very great ever fince the conclufion of the peace; oc-cafioned chiefly by the multitude of privateers that were then thrown out of employment.

In Scotland difputes ran very high on the ruin of the Darien colony. Things were printed on both fides on purpofe to inflame the minds of the people, and many thought that it would at laft have created a breach between the two nations. The coldnefs of the king's temper prevented this; he could not either be heated by the Englifh reprefentations, or blown into a paffion by the hafty refolutions of the Scots parliament. His moderation toward each of them, if it did not bring them both to a good temper, which was indeed never effected in his reign, yet it gave him an opportunity to keep the wifeft people in England and in Scotland, firm to his government, while in the mean time many unforefeen accidents brought about the ruin of the Scots company; fo that the ends of their Englifh adverfaries were anfwered, with-out their having recourfe to any harfh means.

The death of the king of Spain now changed all the affairs of Europe, and forced us, who had fo

lately

lately made a very neceffary peace, upon a new, expenfive, and dangerous war. It is certain that the
king did all he could to avoid it; and that this was
the great, if not the fole foundation of the two famous partition-treaties, which were fo much exclaimed againft b. thofe whofe fteady oppofition to a war,
had firft brought the king and his miniftry to think
of them.

When the refolution was once taken to have recourfe again to arms, in order to preferve the balance
of power, the firft care was for the fleet, which his
majefty refolved fhould be much fuperior to that of
the enemy. Preparatory to this was the new commiffion of the admiralty in the fpring of the year
1701, at the head of which was placed the earl of
Pembroke, a man univerfally beloved and efteemed.

The command of the fleet was very judicioufly beftowed upon Sir George Rooke, who, on the 2d of
July, went on board the Triumph in the Downs,
where he hoifted the flag. He foon after failed to
Spithead, where he was fpeedily joined by the reft of
the fleet, confifting of 48 fhips of the line, befide
frigates, fire-fhips, and fmall veffels. He had under
him fome of the greateft feamen of the age, viz. Sir
Cloudefley Shovel, Sir Thomas Hopfon, John Benbow, Efq; and Sir John Munden: he was not long
after reinforced by 15 Dutch men of war of the line,
befide frigates and fmall veffels, under the command
of lieutenant-admiral Allemonde, vice-admiral Vandergoes, and rear-admiral Waeffenaar.

Toward the latter end of Auguft he failed from
Torbay, and the fecond of September he detached
vice-admiral Benbow with a ftout fquadron for the
Weft Indies; and as this was the principal bufinefs
of the fleet, and indeed a thing in itfelf of the higheft
importance, the admiral detached a ftrong fquadron
of Englifh fhips under the command of Sir John
Munden, and ten fail of Dutch men of war, befide
frigates, under rear-admiral Waeffenaar, to fee the

West India squadron well into the sea. The French expected that this fleet would have actually proceeded to the Mediterranean; and it was to confirm them in this belief, we had demanded the free use of the Spanish harbours: but this was only to conceal things, and to gain an opportunity of sending a squadron early to the West Indies, without putting it in the power of the French to procure any exact account of its strength: the admiral, after performing this, cruised according to his instructions for some time, and then returned with the largest ships into the Downs.

After this fleet was sent to sea, his majesty, on the 18th of January, thought proper to revoke his letters patent to the commissioners of the admiralty, and to appoint Thomas earl of Pembroke and Montgomery, lord high admiral of England and Ireland, and of the foreign plantations. The design of this promotion was, to be rid of the disadvantages attending a board: and this end it answered perfectly.

The war was now the great object of attention, as well here as in France, though hitherto it was not declared; and negotiations were still carried on in Holland, as if both parties had inclined to an amicable determination of these differences; which was, in reality, the intention of neither. In the midst of our preparations, however, care was taken of a point which nearly concerned trade, and that was uniting the two East India companies; which was done under an act of arbitration: and this agreement was the foundation of that company which has subsisted with so great credit to themselves, and benefit to the nation, ever since.

King William's extraordinary attention to business is thought to have hastened his death, which happened on the 8th of March, 1701-2, about eight in the morning. He died, as he lived, with great steadiness of mind; and shewed himself in his last moments, as much a hero as he had ever done in the field. Never any prince better understood the general interest of
Europe,

Europe, or purfued it with greater firmnefs; and whatever unlucky accidents fell out in his reign to the prejudice of our affairs, were not fo much owing to any miftakes in his conduct, as to the circumftances of the times, and our own unfortunate divifions.

Queen Anne afcended the throne on the eighth of March, 1702, in the flower of her age, being then about thirty-eight. She had fhewn a very juft moderation in her conduct from the time of the revolution, and knew how to temper her relation to the ftate, with that which fhe bore to her family; of which fhe gave a remarkable inftance in the latter part of her life, by procuring the ifland of Sicily for her coufin the duke of Savoy: and fhe opened her reign by a very wife and well-confidered fpeech to her privy-council. She expreffed plainly her opinion for carrying on the preparations againft France, and fupporting the allies; and faid, fhe would countenance thofe who concurred with her in maintaining the prefent conftitution and eftablifhment.

The queen, in conformity to this declaration, wrote to the States-general to affure them, that fhe would follow exactly the fteps of her predeceffor, in the fteady maintenance of the common caufe againft the common enemy: and the prudent choice of her fervants, was fufficient to demonftrate the reality of the queen's intentions.

The firft expedition in this reign, was that of Sir John Munden, rear-admiral of the Red, which was intended for intercepting a fquadron of French fhips, that were to fail from the Groyne, in order to carry the new vice-roy of Mexico to the Spanifh Weft Indies. He failed on the 12th of May, 1702, with eight fhips of the third rate, the Salifbury a fourth rate, and two frigates. On the 28th day of the month, he chafed 14 fail of fhips into Corunna. Then he called a council of war, in which it was agreed, that as the place was ftrongly fortified, and by the intelligence they had received, it appeared

A a 3

that

that 17 of the enemy's ships of war rode at anchor in the harbour; it would be expedient for them to follow the latter part of their instructions, by which they were directed to cruise in soundings for the protection of the trade. They returned accordingly; and being distressed by want of provisions, came into port, to the general discontent of the nation. For the satisfaction of the people, Sir John Munden was tried by a court-martial, and acquitted; but as this miscarriage had rendered him very unpopular, prince George, who was now created lord high-admiral, dismissed him from the service.

King William had projected a scheme to reduce Cadiz, with intention to act afterward against the Spanish settlements in the West Indies. This design queen Anne resolved to put in execution. Sir George Rooke commanded the fleet, and the duke of Ormond was appointed general of the land-forces destined for this expedition. The combined squadrons amounted to fifty ships of the line, exclusive of frigates, fireships, and smaller vessels; and the number of soldiers embarked was not far short of 14,000. In the latter end of June the fleet sailed from St. Helen's; and on the 12th of August they anchored at the distance of two leagues from Cadiz: but the attempt miscarried. However, captain Hardy, having been sent to water in Lagos-bay, received intelligence, that the galleons from the West Indies had put into Vigo, under convoy of a French squadron. He sailed immediately in quest of Sir George Rooke, who was now on his voyage back to England; and falling in with him on the 6th day of October, communicated the substance of what he had learned. Rooke immediately called a council of war, in which it was determined to alter their course and attack the enemy at Vigo.

He forthwith detached some small vessels for intelligence, and received a confirmation, that the galleons, and the squadron, commanded by Chateau Renault,

Renault, were actually in the harbour. They failed thither, and appeared before the place on the 11th day of October. The paffage into the harbour was narrow, fecured by batteries, forts, and breaft-works on each fide; by a ftrong boom, confifting of iron chains, topmafts, and cables, moored at each end to a feventy gun fhip, and fortified within by five fhips of the fame ftrength, lying athwart the channel, with their broad-fides to the offing. As the firft and fecond rates of the combined fleets were too large to enter, the admirals fhifted their flags into fmaller fhips; and a divifion of 25 Englifh and Dutch fhips of the line, with their frigates, firefhips and ketches, was deftined for the fervice. In order to facilitate the attack, the duke of Ormond landed with 2500 men, at the diftance of fix miles from Vigo, and took by affault a fort and platform of forty pieces of cannon, at the entrance of the harbour.

The Britifh enfign was no fooner feen flying at the top of this fort, than the fhips advanced to the attack. Vice-admiral Hopfon, in the Torbay, crowding all his fail, ran directly againft the boom, which was broken by the firft fhock; then the whole fquadron entered the harbour, through a prodigious fire from the enemy's fhips and batteries. Thefe laft, however, were foon ftormed and taken by the grenadiers who had been landed. The great fhips lay againft the forts at each fide of the harbour, which in a little time they filenced; though vice-admiral Hopfon narrowly efcaped from a firefhip by which he was boarded. After a very vigorous engagement, the French finding themfelves unable to cope with fuch an adverfary, refolved to deftroy their fhips and galleons, that they might not fall into the hands of the victors. They accordingly burned and ran afhore eight fhips and as many advice-boats; but the ten fhips of war were taken, together with eleven galleons. Though they had fecured the beft part of their plate and merchandize before the Englifh fleet arrived, the

value

value of fourteen million of pieces of eight, in plate
and rich commodities, was deftroyed in fix galleons
that perifhed; but, about half that value was brought
off by the conquerors: fo that this was a dreadful
blow to the enemy, and a noble acquifition to the allies. Immediately after this exploit Sir George Rooke
was joined by Sir Cloudefley Shovel, who had been
fent out with a fquadron to intercept the galleons.
This officer was left to bring home the prizes and dif-
mantle the fortifications, while Rooke returned in
triumph to England.

The glory which the Englifh acquired in this expedition was in fome meafure tarnifhed by the conduct of fome officers in the Weft Indies. Thither
admiral Benbow had been detached with a fquadron
of ten fail, in the courfe of the preceding year. At
Jamaica he received intelligence, that monfieur Du
Caffe was in the neighbourhood of Hifpaniola, and
refolved to beat up to that ifland. At Leogane he
fell in with a French fhip of fifty guns, which her
captain ran afhore and blew up. He took feveral
other veffels, and having alarmed Petit-Guavas, on
the 19th of Auguft, difcovered the enemy's fquadron
near St. Martha, confifting of ten fail, fteering along
fhore. He formed the line; and an engagement enfued, in which he was very ill feconded by fome of
his captains. Neverthelefs, the battle continued till
night, and he determined to renew it next morning,
when he perceived all his fhips at the diftance of three
or four miles aftern, except the Ruby, commanded
by captain George Walton, who joined him in ply-
ing the enemy with chace guns. On the 21ft, thefe
two fhips engaged the French fquadron; and the
Ruby was fo difabled, that the admiral was obliged to
fend her back to Jamaica. Next day the Greenwich,
commanded by Wade, was five leagues aftern; and the
wind changing, the enemy had the advantage of the
weather-gage. On the 23d, the admiral renewed the
battle with his fingle fhip, unfuftained by the reft of

the

the fquadron. On the 24th, his leg was fhattered by
a chain-fhot; notwithftanding which accident, he remained on the quarter-deck in a cradle, and continued the engagement. One of the largeft fhips of
the enemy lying like a wreck upon the water, four
fail of the Englifh fquadron poured their broad-fides
into her, and then ran to leeward, without paying
any regard to the fignal for battle. Then the French,
bearing down upon the admiral with their whole force,
fhot away his maintopfail-yard, and damaged his rigging in fuch a manner, that he was obliged to lie by
and refit, while they took their difabled fhip in tow.
During this interval, he called a council of his captains, and expoftulated with them on their behaviour.
They obferved, that the French were very ftrong, and
advifed him to defift. He plainly perceived that he
was betrayed, and with the utmoft reluctance returned to Jamaica, having not only loft a leg, but alfo
received a large wound in his face, and another in his
arm, while he in perfon boarded the French admiral.

Exafperated at the treachery of his captains, he
granted a commiffion to rear-admiral Whetftone and
other officers to hold a court-martial, and try them
for cowardice. Hudfon, of the Pendennis, died before his trial : Kirby and Wade were convicted, and
fentenced to be fhot : Conftable, of the Windfor, was
cafhiered and imprifoned : Vincent, of the Falmouth,
and Fogg, the admiral's own captain of the Breda,
were convicted of having figned a paper, that they
would not fight under Benbow's command; but, as
they behaved gallantly in the action, the court inflicted upon them no other punifhment than that of
a provifional fufpenfion. Captain Walton had likewife joined in the confpiracy while he was heated with
the fumes of intoxication; but he afterward renounced the engagement, and fought with admirable
courage until his fhip was difabled. The boifterous
manners of Benbow had produced this bafe confederacy. He was a rough feaman; but remarkably
                                        brave,

brave, honeſt, and experienced. He took this miſcarriage ſo much to heart, that he became melancholy; and his grief co-operating with the fever occa-
ſioned by his wounds, put a period to his life. Wade
and Kirby were ſent home in the Briſtol; and, on
their arrival at Plymouth, ſhot on board of the ſhip,
by virtue of a dead-warrant for their immediate execution, which had lain there for ſome time.   The
ſame precaution had been taken in all the weſtern
ports, in order to prevent applications in their favour.
When Du Caſſe arrived at Carthagene, he wrote a
letter to Benbow to this effect:—" Sir, I had little
hope on Monday laſt, but to have ſupped in your
cabin; but it pleaſed God to order it otherwiſe.   I
am thankful for it.   As for thoſe cowardly captains
who deſerted you, hang them up; for, by God, they
deſerve it.   Yours, Du Caſſe."
    The grand fleet was commanded in 1703 by Sir
Cloudeſley Shovel: it conſiſted at firſt of 27 ſhips of
the line, and the admiral had under him rear-admiral
Byng, and Sir Stafford Fairborne; and being afterward reinforced with eight ſhips more, theſe were
commanded by vice-admiral Leake.   His inſtructions were very large; but all of them might be reduced to theſe three heads, viz. annoying the enemy, aſſiſting our allies, and protecting our trade.
He purſued his inſtructions as far as he was able; and
having ſecured the Turkey fleet, he intended to have
ſtaid ſome time upon the coaſt of Italy.   But the
Dutch admiral, who was with him, informed him,
that both his orders and his victuals required his thinking of a ſpeedy return; and it was with much difficulty that Sir Cloudeſley Shovel prevailed upon him
to go to Leghorn.   In the mean time, the inſtructions he had to ſuccour the Cevennois, who were
then in arms againſt the French king, were found
impracticable.   This admiral having renewed the
peace with the piratical ſtates of Barbary, returned
to England, without having been able to execute

                                                        any

any thing that looked like the refult of a concerted scheme. The nation naturally murmured at this fruitlefs expedition, by which it had incurred fuch a confiderable expence. The merchants complained that they were ill fupplied with convoys. The fhips of war were victualled with damaged provifion ; and every article of the marine being mifmanaged, the blame fell upon thofe who acted as council to the lord high-admiral.

Nor were the arms of England by fea much more fuccefsful in the Weft Indies. Sir George Rooke, in the preceding year, had detached from the Mediterranean captain Hovenden Walker, with fix fhips of the line and tranfports, having on board four regiments of foldiers, for the Leeward iflands. Being joined at Antigua by fome troops under colonel Coddrington, they made a defcent upon the ifland Guadaloupe, where they razed the fort, burned the town, ravaged the country, and reimbarked with precipitation, in confequence of a report that the French had landed 900 men on the back of the ifland. They retired to Nevis, where they muft have perifhed by famine, had not they been providentially relieved by vice-admiral Graydon, in his way to Jamaica. This officer had been fent out with three fhips to fucceed Benbow, and was convoyed about 150 leagues by two other fhips of the line. He had not failed many days, when he fell in with part of the French fquadron, commanded by Du Caffe, on their return from the Weft Indies, very foul and richly laden. Captain Cleland of the Montague engaged the fternmoft ; but he was called off by a fignal from the admiral, who proceeded on his voyage without taking farther notice of the enemy.

The only exploit that tended to the diftrefs of the enemy, was performed by rear-admiral Dilkes, who, in the month of July, failed to the coaft of France with a fmall fquadron : and, in the neighbourhood of
Granville,

Granville, took or deſtroyed about 40 ſhips and their convoy. Yet this damage was inconſiderable when compared to that which the Engliſh navy ſuſtained from the dreadful tempeſt that began to blow on the 27th day of November, accompanied with ſuch flaſhes of lightning, and peals of thunder, as overwhelmed the whole kingdom with conſternation. The houſes in London ſhook from their foundations, and ſome of them falling, buried the inhabitants in their ruins: but the chief national damage fell upon the navy. Thirteen ſhips of war were loſt, together with 1500 ſeamen, including rear-admiral Beaumont, who had been employed in obſerving the Dunkirk ſquadron, and was then at anchor in the Downs, where his ſhip foundered. This great loſs, however, was repaired with incredible diligence, to the aſtoniſhment of all Europe. The queen immediately iſſued orders for building a greater number of ſhips than that which had been deſtroyed; and ſhe exerciſed her bounty for the relief of the ſhipwrecked ſeamen, and the widows of thoſe who were drowned, in ſuch a manner as endeared her to all her ſubjects.

The emperor having declared his ſecond ſon Charles, king of Spain, he was conveyed to Portugal by the Engliſh fleet, under Sir George Rooke. The admiral having landed king Charles at Liſbon, ſent a ſquadron to cruiſe off cape Spartell, under the command of rear-admiral Dilkes, who, on the 12th of March, 1704, engaged and took three Spaniſh ſhips of war, bound from St. Sebaſtian to Cadiz. On the 16th day of June, Sir George Rooke, being joined by Sir Cloudeſley Shovel, reſolved to proceed up the Mediterranean in queſt of the French fleet, which had ſailed thither from Breſt, and which Rooke had actually diſcovered in the preceding month, on their voyage to Toulon. On the 17th day of July, the admiral called a council of war in the road of Tetuan, when they reſolved to make an attempt upon Gibraltar, which was but ſlenderly provided with a garriſon.

Thither

Thither they failed, and on the 21st day of the month the prince of Hesse landed on the isthmus with eighteen hundred marines: next day the admiral gave orders for cannonading the town; and perceiving that the enemy were driven from their fortifications at the south molehead, commanded captain Whitaker to arm all the boats, and assault that quarter. The captains Hicks and Jumper, who happened to be nearest the mole, immediately manned their pinnaces, and entered the fortifications sword in hand. The Spaniards sprung a mine, by which two lieutenants and about 100 men were killed or wounded. Nevertheless, the two captains took possession of a platform, and kept their ground until they were sustained by captain Whitaker and the rest of the seamen, who took by storm a redoubt between the mole and the town. Then the governor capitulated; and the prince of Hesse entered the place, amazed at the success of this attempt, considering the strength of the fortifications, which might have been defended by fifty men against a numerous army.

A sufficient garrison being left with his highness, the admiral returned to Tetuan to take in wood and water; and when he sailed, on the 9th day of August, he descried the French fleet, to which he gave chace with all the sail he could spread. On the 13th he came up with it, as it lay in a line off Malaga ready to receive him, to the number of 52 great ships, and 24 gallies, under the command of the count de Tholouse, high-admiral of France, with the inferior flags of the white and blue divisions. The English fleet consisted of 53 ships of the line, exclusive of frigates; but they were inferior to the French in number of guns and men, as well as in weight of metal; and altogether unprovided of gallies, from which the enemy reaped great advantage during the engagement. A little after ten in the morning, the battle began with equal fury on both sides, and continued to rage with doubtful success till two in the

after-

afternoon, when the van of the French gave way: nevertheless the fight was maintained till night, when the enemy bore away to leeward. The wind shifted before morning, the French gained the weather-gage; but they made no use of this advantage: for two successive days, the English admiral endeavoured to renew the engagement, which the count de Tholoufe declined, and at last he disappeared. The loss was pretty equal on both sides, though not a single ship was taken or destroyed by either: but the honour of the day certainly remained with the English.

Philip king of Spain, alarmed at the reduction of Gibraltar, sent the marquis de Villadarias with an army to retake it. The siege lasted four months; during which the prince of Hesse exhibited many shining proofs of courage and ability: but the Spaniards were at length forced to abandon the undertaking. A second attempt succeeded no better.

While these great things were doing in the Mediterranean, Sir George Byng was sent with a small squadron of cruisers into the Soundings. He sailed in the latter end of January, 1705, with a large and rich fleet of outward-bound merchant-ships. As soon as he had seen these safe into the sea, he disposed of his squadron in such a manner, as he thought most proper for securing our own trade, and for meeting with the French privateers. He was so fortunate as to take from the enemy a man of war of 44 guns, 12 privateers, and 7 merchant-ships, most of which were richly laden from the West Indies. The number of men taken on board all these prizes was upward of 2,000, and of guns 334. This gave such a blow to the French privateers, that they scarce ventured into the channel all the year after, but chose rather to sail northward, in hopes of meeting with some of our ships homeward-bound from the Baltic.

The first orders received by the grand fleet, commanded by the famous earl of Peterborough, and Sir Cloudesley Shovel, as joint admirals; were, to

proceed

proceed for the Mediterranean, with the force then ready, which amounted to 29 fail of line of battle ships, befide frigates, firefhips, bombs, and, other fmall craft. On the 11th of June they arrived in the river of Lifbon, where they found Sir John Leake, with a fquadron, in great want of provifions. On the 15th of June, a council of war was held, in which it was determined to put to fea with 48 fhips of the line, Englifh and Dutch, and difpofe them in fuch a ftation between cape Spartell and the bay of Cadiz, as might beft prevent the junction of the French fquadrons from Toulon and Breft.

On the 22d of June, Sir Cloudefley Shovel, with the fleet, failed for Lifbon; from thence he failed to Altea-bay, and there took in his catholic majefty, who preffed the earl of Peterborough to make an immediate attempt on the city of Barcelona, and the province of Catalonia; where he was affured the people were well affected to him. This being agreed to, the fleet failed accordingly to Barcelona, and arrived on the 12th of Auguft. The furrender of this capital of Catalonia fo ftrengthened king Charles's party, that the whole principality, Rofes only excepted, fubmitted foon after.

All the world knows, that the reduction of Barcelona has been confidered as one of the moft extraordinary events that fell out in this, or, perhaps, in any modern war; and though we have already many accounts of it, which feem to attribute it, fome to one thing, fome to another; yet nothing but the affiftance given by our fleet could poffibly have reduced it.

In this year our fucceffes had been fo great both by fea and land, and there appeared fo fair a profpect of humbling the houfe of Bourbon in Flanders, and of driving them out of Spain, that when her majefty thought fit to recommend the Spanifh war in a particular manner to parliament, the houfe of commons immediately voted large fupplies for the year 1706:
fo

4

ſo that the miniſtry had nothing to conſider, but how
to employ them in ſuch a manner, as that thoſe, upon
whom they were raiſed, might be ſatisfied that they
were laid out for their ſervice; and this produced a
reſolution of equipping a numerous fleet, as early as
it was poſſible. This, with the ſettling the terms of
the union, were the matters which principally took
up the attention of this ſeſſion of parliament.

Had the iſſue of the campaign in Catalonia been
ſuch as the beginning ſeemed to prognoſticate, the
French king might have in ſome meaſure conſoled
himſelf for his diſgraces in the Netherlands. On the
6th day of April, king Philip, at the head of a numerous army, undertook the ſiege of Barcelona,
while the count de Thoulouſe blocked it up with a
powerful ſquadron: but the arrival of an Engliſh
fleet, under Sir John Leake, ſaved the city: the
French ſquadron ſailed away for Toulon, and king
Philip abandoned the ſiege. The Engliſh fleet continued all the ſummer in the Mediterranean: they
ſecured Carthagena, which had declared for Charles:
they took the town of Alicant by aſſault, and the
caſtle by capitulation. Then ſailing out of the
Streights, one ſquadron was detached to the Weſt
Indies, another ordered to lie at Liſbon, and the reſt
were ſent home to England. But affairs fell into
ſuch diſtraction in the Weſt Indies, that we were not
either in a condition to hurt the enemy's ſettlements,
or ſo much as able to defend our own. The truth
ſeems to be, that the great fleets we fitted out every
year to the Mediterranean, and the cruiſers that were
neceſſary upon our coaſts, took up ſo many ſhips,
that it was ſcarcely poſſible to ſupply even the reaſonable demands of the Weſt Indies.

A ſcheme being formed to attempt Toulon, and
Sir Cloudeſley Shovel having joined Sir George Byng
near Alicant, the fleet came to an anchor before Final
on the 5th of June, 1707, conſiſting of 43 men of
war and 57 tranſports; where, in a council of war,

at

at which prince Eugene affifted, it was refolved to force a paffage near the van, in which the Englifh admiral promifed to affift. On the laft day of June this enterprife was undertaken, to the great aftonifhment of the French, who believed their works upon that river to be impregnable. Sir John Norris, with fome Britifh, and one Dutch man of war, failed to the mouth of the river, and embarking 600 feamen and marines in open boats, entered it, and advanced within mufket-fhot of the enemy's works, making fuch a terrible fire upon them, that their cavalry and many of their foot began to quit their entrenchments, and could not be prevailed upon by their officers to return. Sir Cloudefly Shovel, who followed Sir John, no fooner faw this confufion, than he ordered the latter to land with the feamen and marines in order to flank the enemy. This was performed with fo much fpirit, and Sir John and his feamen fcampered fo fuddenly over the French works, that the enemy, ftruck with a pannic, threw down their arms and fled with the utmoft precipitation. The duke of Savoy immediately purfued this advantage, and in half an hour paffed that river, which had, without this affiftance, proved the ne plus ultra of his expedition; and marched toward Toulon, with an army of thirty-five thoufand men. The fiege of this place was not formed before the 15th of July, when 100 cannon, with 200 rounds of powder and fhot, and a confiderable number of feamen to ferve as gunners, with all other things wanting for the camp, were fupplied from the fhips: fo that affairs had a very good afpect till the 4th of Auguft, when the enemy, making a vigorous fally, forced the confederate troops out of the works, and drew eight or ten guns into the town. In this action were killed and wounded above 800 men: fo that on the 6th, after embarking the fick and wounded, and withdrawing the cannon, the fiege from that time was turned only to a cannonading and bombardment.

Vol. VII.   B b   The

The very day the army began to march, five bomb veffels, fupported by the lighteft frigates and all the boats of the men of war, under the command of rear-admiral Dilkes, advanced into the creek of fort St. Lewis; and notwithftanding a prodigious fire from the place, bombarded the town and harbour from noon till five next morning with all the fuccefs which could be expected, the land army in the mean time quitting their camp at La Villette, which they did in five columns with great fafety, the duke of Savoy marching back in two days as far as in his approach to the place he had done in fix.

Sir Cloudefly Shovel being not a little chagrined at the mifcarriage of an expedition on which he had fet his heart, bent his courfe homeward. Coming into the Soundings on the 23d of October, he ftruck upon the rocks called the Bifhop and his Clerks, and in two minutes nothing more of him or his fhip was feen, and three or four more of his fleet alfo perifhed with him.

But at the time that our fleets were every where fuperior to thofe of the enemy, our trade fuffered in almoft all parts of the world by their fmall fquadrons of men of war, as well as privateers.

About this time the French played off a project, which they repeated more than once fince. This was, the attempt upon Scotland, in favour of the chevalier de St. George; which was the Nomme de Guerre they were pleafed to give the perfon, whom the queen foon after diftinguifhed by the name of the Pretender.

The troops intended for this attempt, were about eleven or twelve battalions, under the command of the marquis de Gace, afterward ftiled the marfhal de Matignon. The fleet confifted of but eight men of war, which was commanded by the count de Forbin, who is faid to have difliked the defign, becaufe, very probably, he knew the bottom of it: for it is very certain, the French never intended to land, and refufed the chevalier to fet him on fhore, though he
would

would have gone with his own fervants. The true fcheme of the French king was, to create a diverfion to embarrafs the queen and her miniftry at home, that they might have the lefs leifure to profecute their views abroad : and from thefe motives, he ordered his minifters in all foreign courts, to talk in very magnificent terms, of the fuccours he gave to the king of England, as he thought fit to call him; that on the rebound, they might make the louder noife in Britain. Our public fecurities fell furprifingly, and things would have fallen into downright confufion, if the fright had not been quickly over. This was owing to the care of the admiralty, who, with remarkable diligence, fitted out a fleet of 24 men of war, with which, Sir George Byng, and lord Durfley, failed for the French coaft, on the 27th of February, 1708. On Sir George Byng's anchoring before Gravelin, the French officers laid afide their embarkation; but upon exprefs orders from court, were obliged to refume it; and on the 6th of March, actually failed out of Dunkirk; but being taken fhort by contrary winds, came to an anchor till the 8th, and then continued their voyage for Scotland.

Sir George Byng purfued them with a fleet of forty fhips of the line, befide frigates and firefhips. He afterward detached rear-admiral Baker, with a fmall fquadron, to convoy the troops that were fent from Oftend, and profecuted his expedition with the reft.

He failed directly to the frith of Edinburgh, where he arrived almoft as foon as the enemy, who immediately took the advantage of a land-breeze, and bore away with all the fail they could carry. The Englifh admiral gave chace; and the Salifbury, one of their fhips, was boarded and taken. At night monfieur de Fourbin altered his courfe; fo that the next day they were out of reach of the Englifh fquadron. The pretender defired they would proceed to the northward, and land him at Invernefs, and Fourbin feemed willing to gratify this requeft; but the wind changing

and

and blowing in their teeth with great violence, he reprefented the danger of attempting to profecute the
voyage ; and, with the confent of the chevalier de
St. George and his general, returned to Dunkirk,
after having been toffed about a whole month in very
tempeftuous weather. In the mean time, Sir George
Byng failed up to Leith road, where he received the
freedom of the city of Edinburgh in a golden box,
as a teftimony of gratitude for his having delivered
them from the dreadful apprehenfions under which
they laboured.

Certain it is, the pretender could not have chofen
a more favourable opportunity for making a defcent
upon Scotland. The people in general were difaffected to the government on account of the union;
the regular troops under Leven did not exceed 2500
men ; and even great part of thefe would in all probability have joined the invader : the caftle of Edinburgh was deftitute of ammunition, and would in all
appearance have furrendered at the firft fummons;
in which cafe the Jacobites muft have been mafters
of the equivalent money lodged in that fortrefs; a
good number of Dutch fhips loaded with cannon,
fmall arms, ammunition, and a large fum of money,
had been driven on fhore in the fhire of Angus :
where they would have been feized by the friends of
the pretender, had the French troops been landed;
and all the adherents of that houfe were ready to appear in arms.

The campaign in Catalonia, which we cannot enter
into, was productive of a great event. Sir John
Leake, having taken on board a handful of troops,
under the conduct of the marquis D'Alconzel, fet
fail for Cagliari, in Sardinia, and fummoned the viceroy to fubmit to King Charles. As he did not fend
an immediate anfwer, the admiral began to bombard
the city, and the inhabitants compelled him to furrender at difcretion. The greater part of the garrifon
enlifted themfelves in the fervice of Charles. Major-
general

general Stanhope having planned the conqueſt of Minorca, and concerted with the admiral the meaſures
neceſſary to put it in execution, obtained from count
Staremberg a few battalions of Spaniards, Italians,
and Portugueſe, embarked at Barcelona, with a fine
train of Britiſh artillery, accompanied by brigadier
Wade and colonel Petit, an engineer of great reputa-
tation. They landed on the iſland about two miles
from St. Philip's fort, on the twenty-ſixth of Auguſt,
with about eight hundred marines, which augmented
their number to about three thouſand. Next day
they erected batteries; and general Stanhope ordered
a number of arrows to be ſhot into the place, to which
papers were affixed, written in the Spaniſh and French
languages, containing threats, that all the garriſon
ſhould be ſent to the mines, if they would not ſur-
render before the batteries were finiſhed. The garriſon conſiſted of a thouſand Spaniards, and ſix hundred French marines, commanded by colonel la Jonquiere, who imagined that the number of the be-
ſiegers amounted to at leaſt ten thouſand; ſo artfully
had they been drawn up in ſight of the enemy. The
batteries began to play, and in a little time demo-
liſhed four towers that ſerved as outworks to the fort:
then they made a breach in the outward wall, through
which brigadier Wade, at the head of the grenadiers,
ſtormed a redoubt, with ſuch extraordinary valour as
ſtruck the beſieged with conſternation. On the ſecond or third day they thought proper to beat a par-
ley, and capitulate, on condition, That they ſhould
march out with the honours of war: That the Spaniards ſhould be tranſported to Murcia, and the
French to Toulon. The Spaniſh governor was ſo
mortified when he learned the real number of the be-
ſiegers, that on his arrival at Murcia, he threw himſelf out of a window in deſpair, and was killed upon
the ſpot. La Jonquiere was confined for life, and all
the French officers incurred their maſter's diſpleaſure.
Fort St. Philip being thus reduced, to the amazement

of all Europe ; and the garrifon of Port Fornelles having furrendered themfelves prifoners to the admirals Leake and Whitaker, the inhabitants gladly fubmitted to the Englifh government.

During the courfe of this year the Englifh merchants fuftained no confiderable loffes by fea : the cruifers were judicioufly ftationed, and the trade was regularly fupplied with convoys. In the Weft Indies Commodore Wager deftroyed the admiral of the galleons, and took the rear-admiral on the coaft of Carthagene. Had the officers of his fquadron done their duty, the greateft part of the fleet would have fallen into his hands. At his return to Jamaica two of his captains were tried by a court-martial, and difmiffed . from the fervice.

On the twenty-eighth day of October prince George of Denmark died of an afthma and dropfy, with which he had been long afflicted. He was a prince of an amiable rather than a fhining character, brave, good-natured, modeft, and humane, but devoid of great talents and ambition. He had always lived in harmony with the queen, who, during the whole term of their union, and efpecially in his laft illnefs, approved herfelf a pattern of conjugal truth and tendernefs. At his death the earl of Pembroke was created lord high admiral.

As this war was profecuted chiefly on the continent, where the duke of Marlborough gained fuch glorious, though unprofitable advantages, over the French ; the events of that war rather furnifh materials for a general, than for a naval hiftory. Our fleets indeed were refpectable where-ever they were fent, and proved of great benefit to King Charles in his conteft for Spain : but to follow his fortunes would carry us into too wide a field ; and the convoys appointed for every fleet of merchantmen, would prove but tedious details, would our limits allow the mention of them. Thefe therefore we pafs over, as well as the unfuccefsful attempt on Quebec, under Sir

Hovenden

Hovenden Walker: two wars of a much more inter-esting nature call for our attention, we therefore pass on to the peace of Utrecht, which was privately signed April 1st, 1713, at the house of doctor Robinson, bishop of Bristol. In this treaty, though all was not obtained from France that might have been, after so long, and withal, successful a war; yet much was got by it, and greater advantages would certainly have attended it, had it not been for the disturbance given our ministers at home, by the opposition to their measures.

Not to insist on the adequate satisfaction, which was by this treaty stipulated for all our allies, it procured us, as a trading nation, far greater advantages. For Dunkirk having been put into our hands, we shall find what was to become of it from the ninth article of the treaty, by which it was stipulated as follows :—" The most Christian king shall take care that all the fortifications of the city of Dunkirk be razed; that the harbour be filled up; and that the sluices, or moles, which serve to cleanse the harbour, be levelled; and that, at the said king's own expence, within the space of five months, after the conditions of peace are concluded and signed: that is to say, the fortifications toward the sea, within the space of two months; and those toward the land, together with the said banks, within three months; on this express condition also, that the said fortifications, harbour, moles, or sluices, be never repaired again." This demolition was of vast importance, for lying but thirteen leagues from the South Foreland, any easterly wind which carries our ships down the channel, brings out those at Dunkirk to intercept them: the very situation of the place, furnishes the enemy with advantage; for the east end of the channel, which is exposed to Dunkirk, is but seven leagues broad, whence they may see our ships from side to side. So that by this demolition, six parts in nine of our trade from London, is freed from the hazards to which they were

exposed

expofed in time of war, while Dunkirk was open.
Befide, this was a heavy blow to the naval power of
France, and efpecially their trade to the Weft Indies;
and their fubmitting to this article, was not only a
clear proof of our fuperior force, but of the great diftrefs
they had then been plunged into.　They endeavoured
indeed to fhift off, and afterward mitigate the execution of this article; but the queen infifting on its demolition, according to the letter, it was done as effectually as could be defired.

To conclude; it may be obferved, that, upon the
clofe of the war, the French found themfelves totally
deprived of all pretenfions to the dominion of the fea.
Moft of our conquefts, indeed all of them that were
of any ufe to us, were made by, or at leaft chiefly by,
our fleets.　Sir George Rooke took Gibraltar, and
Sir John Leake reduced Minorca; and it is alfo evident, that it was our fleet alone that fupported king
Charles in Catalonia, and kept the king of Portugal
fteady to the grand alliance; which, befide the advantages it brought to the common caufe, fecured to
us the invaluable profits of our trade to that country:
and all this againft the fpirit, genius, and inclination
of the king of Portugal, and his minifters, who were
all, at that time, in the French intereft in their
hearts.

At the fame time, our fleets prevented the French
from fo much as failing on the Mediterranean, where
they had made a figure in the laft war; and kept many
of the Italian ftates in awe.　The very Algerines, and
other piratical ftates of Barbary, contrary to their natural
propenfity toward the French, were now obfequious
to us, and entertained no manner of doubt of the fuperiority of our flag.　The flacknefs of the Dutch, in
fending fhips to this part of the world, had, in this refpect, an effect happy enough for us, fince it occafioned our being confidered as the leading power, by
all who had any concerns with us and them.

The

The treaty of Utrecht, which put an end to our difputes abroad, proved the caufe of high debates, and great diftractions at home. The people grew uneafy, the miniftry divided, and the heats and vio- lence of party rofe to fuch a height, that her majefty found herfelf fo embarraffed, as not to be able either to depend upon thofe in power, or to venture to turn them out. The uneafinefs of mind, that fuch a per- plexed fituation of affairs occafioned, had a very bad effect upon her health, which had been in a declining condition from the time of prince George's death; and a quarrel between two of her principal minifters, in her prefence, proved, in fome meafure, the caufe of her death, which happened Auguft 1ft, 1714.

ABSTRACT of the ROYAL NAVY, as it ftood at the Death of QUEEN ANNE.

Rates.	Number.	Guns.	Men.
I.	7	714	5,312
II.	13	1,170	7,194
III.	39	2,890	16,089
IV.	66	3,490	16,058
V.	32	1,190	4,160
VI.	25	500	1,047
	182	9,954	49,860

Fire-fhips, &c. about —— 50

We now arrive at another change in our govern- ment, brought about by a ftatute made in the twelfth year of king William III. for limiting the fucceffion of the crown; by which, after the death of the queen, then princefs Anne, without iffue, it was to pafs to the moft illuftrious houfe of Hanover, as the next proteftant heirs: for the princefs Sophia, electrefs dowager of Hanover, was daughter to the queen of Bohemia, who, before her marriage with the elector Palatine, was ftiled the princefs Elizabeth of Great Britain,

Britain, daughter to James VI. of Scotland, and I. of England; in whom united all the hereditary claims to the imperial crown of these realms.

But, the princess Sophia dying a very little while before the queen, George-Lewis, elector of Hanover, her son, became heir of this crown, on the demise of queen Anne, and was accordingly called to the succession, in the manner directed by another statute, passed in the fourth year of her majesty's reign.

His majesty arriving from Holland on the 18th of September, and making his public entry on the 20th, took the reins of government into his own hands. A new parliament was summoned, and met at Westminster, March the 17th, 1715, and came to a resolution, to allow ten thousand seamen at four pounds a month; beside other large sums for other naval contingencies. These were thought necessary, because, at this juncture, the fleet of Great Britain was much decayed; and it was foreseen, that, notwithstanding the peace so lately concluded, new disputes were likely to arise.

Amongst these disputes, the most serious was that in which we were engaged with Sweden. This had begun before the queen's death, and was occasioned by the Swedish privateers taking many of our ships, which, with their cargoes, were confiscated; under a pretence that we assisted and supplied the Czar and his subjects, with ships, arms, ammunition, &c. contrary, as was suggested, to our treaties with the crown of Sweden. Several memorials had been presented upon this subject, without receiving any satisfactory answer; and, therefore, it was now thought expedient to send a strong squadron of men of war into the Baltic; the rather, because their high mightinesses the states-general, labouring under the same inconveniencies, found themselves obliged, after all pacific methods had been tried in vain, to have recourse to the same measures.

On

On the 18th of May a squadron of twenty sail was appointed for this service, under Sir John Norris, who arrived in the Sound on the 10th of June following: where, finding the Dutch squadron, it was resolved, that the combined fleet should proceed together, with the English and Dutch merchantmen under their convoy for their respective ports. About the middle of the month of August, the Danish fleet, consisting of twenty ships of the line, with the Russian squadron, resolved to sail up the Baltic, with the English and Dutch.

On the arrival of Sir John Norris in the Baltic, our minister presented a memorial, in which he set forth, the particular damages sustained by our merchants; for which he demanded satisfaction; and, at the same time, insisted on the repeal of an edict, which his Swedish majesty had lately published, and by which the commerce of the Baltic was wholly prohibited to the English. This memorial was presented, June 15, 1715, and in it, the nature of Sir John Norris's commission was explained; but he received a very unsatisfactory answer. Thus far, all this quarrel seems to arise from his majesty's care of the British commerce. But as elector of Hanover, he had also some disputes with his majesty of Sweden, of quite a different nature: for having purchased from the crown of Denmark the duchies of Bremen and Verden, which had been taken from the crown of Sweden, he found himself obliged, in quality of elector, to concur with the first-mentioned power, in declaring war against Sweden; and, even before this was done, some English ships joined the Danish fleet, in order to distress the Swedes. Of this, the Swedish minister here complained, by a memorial, in which he asserted, that the honour of the British flag had been prostituted to serve the interests of another state, and in order to create an intercourse between the king's regal and electoral dominions. The Dutch, though no less injured, no
less

lefs concerned in their trade than we, did not, however, think it neceffary to come to fuch extremities.

· The Swedes had, at this time, a very numerous fleet, and in good condition; but they were too wife to hazard it againft fuch an unequal force as that of the confederates; and, therefore, withdrew it into one of their own ports, till they could receive the king's abfolute orders. On the 9th of November, the Britifh men of war, from Dantzick, with the trade, joined Sir John Norris's fquadron at Bornholm, and the next day came all with him into the road of Copenhagen. On the 12th, arrived the Dutch trade, with their convoy, which had been obliged to ftay after ours at Dantzick, for provifions. A few days after, Sir John failed from the road of Copenhagen; and, notwithftanding his fleet, as well as the merchantmen under his convoy, were furprized by a violent ftorm, which difperfed them, and in which the Auguft, of fixty guns, and the Garland of twenty-four, were unfortunately loft; yet the reft, with all the trade, fafely arrived at the Trow, on the 29th of November, in the morning. Sir John Norris left feven fhips of war under the command of commodore Cleeland, in the Baltic, to act in conjunction with the Danes, and for the further fecurity of the Britifh trade, if neceffary.

During the time that this fquadron was employed in the Baltic, the rebellion was extinguifhed in Scotland; but with fo little affiftance from our naval force, that it fcarce deferves to be mentioned. The rebellion broke out under the influence and direction of the earl of Mar, who was foon joined by the clans; and the Duke of Argyll being fent down againft him, it quickly appeared how ill their meafures had been taken. His grace had, indeed, but a fmall number of regular troops under his command; but his intereft was fo extenfive, that he not only engaged many powerful families to declare for king George, but, which

perhaps

perhaps was the greater fervice of the two, engaged many more to remain quiet, who otherwife had joined the rebels. The bufinefs was decided by the battle of Sheriff Moore, near Dunblain, fought November 13, 1715, the fame day that general Fofter and the Eng-lifh, who were in arms, furrendered at Prefton. Yet, after this, the Chevalier de St. George ventured over into Scotland, in a very poor veffel; where, foon find-ing his affairs defperate, and his perfon in the utmoft danger, he contrived to make his efcape from the north, with the utmoft fecrecy; which he effected, by going on board a clean tallow'd French fnow, which failed out of the harbour of Montrofe, February the 3d, in fight of fome Englifh men of war, but kept fo clofe along fhore, that they foon found it was impof-fible to follow her.

We have already taken notice of what paft under Sir John Norris in the Baltic; and have, therefore, only to obferve, that this year fome of the piratical republics in Barbary having broke the peace, admiral Baker, who had the command of the Englifh fqua-dron in the Mediterranean, received orders to bring them to reafon; which he did, without any great difficulty.

In 1718, the king of England had ufed fome en-deavours to comprofife the difference between his imperial majefty and the Spanifh branch of the houfe of Bourbon. Mr. Stanhope had been fent to Madrid with a plan of pacification, which being rejected by Philip, as partial and iniquitous, the king determined to fupport his mediation by arms. Sir George Byng failed from Spithead on the 4th day of June, with twenty fhips of the line, two fire-fhips, two bomb-veffels, and ample inftructions how to act on all emer-gencies. He arrived off Cape St. Vincent on the 30th day of the month, when he difpatched his fe-cretary to Cadiz with a letter to Colonel Stanhope the Britifh minifter at Madrid, defiring him to inform his moft catholic majefty of the admiral's arrival in thofe

4   parts,

parts, and to lay before him his inftructions : which, when cardinal Alberoni perufed, he told colonel Stanhope with fome warmth, that his mafter would run all hazards, and even fuffer himfelf to be driven out of Spain, rather than recal his troops, or confent to a fufpenfion of arms. He faid the Spaniards were not to be frightened ; and he was fo well convinced that the fleet would do their duty, that in cafe of their being attacked by admiral Byng, he fhould be in no pain for the fuccefs. This interpofition could not but be very provoking to the Spanifh minifter, who had laid his account with the conqueft of Sicily ; and for that purpofe prepared an armament which was altogether furprifing, confidering the late fhattered condition of the Spanifh affairs. He feems to have put too much confidence in the ftrength of the Spanifh fleet. In a few days he fent back the admiral's letter to Mr. Stanhope, with a note under it, importing, that the chevalier Byng might execute the orders he had received from the king his mafter.

The admiral, in paffing by Gibraltar, was joined by vice-admiral Cornwal with two fhips. He proceeded to Minorca, where he relieved the garrifon of Portmahon. Then he failed for Naples, where he arrived on the firft day of Auguft, and was received as a deliverer : for the Neapolitans had been under the utmoft terror of an invafion from the Spaniards. Sir George Byng received intelligence from the viceroy count Daun, who treated him with the moft diftinguifhing marks of refpect, that the Spanifh army, amounting to thirty thoufand men, commanded by the marquis de Lede, had landed in Sicily, reduced Palermo and Meffina, and were then employed in the fiege of the citadel belonging to this laft city : that the Piedmontefe garrifon would be obliged to furrender, if not fpeedily relieved : that an alliance was upon the carpet between the emperor and the king of Sicily, which laft had defired the affiftance of the imperial troops, and agreed to receive them into the ci-

tadel

tadel of Meſſina. The admiral immediately reſolved to ſail thither, and on the 9th of Auguſt was in ſight of the Faro of Meſſina. He diſpatched his own captain with a polite meſſage to the marquis de Lede, propoſing a ceſſation of arms in Sicily for two months, that the powers of Europe might have time to concert meaſures for reſtoring a laſting peace. The Spaniſh general anſwered, that he had no powers to treat, conſequently ſhould obey his orders, which directed him to reduce Sicily for his maſter the king of Spain. The Spaniſh fleet had ſailed from the harbour of Meſſina on the day before the Engliſh ſquadron appeared. In doubling the point of Faro, he deſcried two Spaniſh ſcouts, that led him to their main fleet, which before noon he deſcried in line of battle, amounting to 27 ſail large and ſmall, beſide two fire-ſhips, four bomb-veſſels, and ſeven gallies. At ſight of the Engliſh ſquadron they ſtood away large, and Byng gave chace all the reſt of the day. In the morning, which was the 11th of Auguſt, the rear-admiral de Mari, with ſix ſhips of war, the gallies, fire-ſhips, and bomb-ketches, ſeparated from the main fleet, and ſtood in for the Sicilian ſhore. The Engliſh admiral detached captain Walton with five ſhips in purſuit of them ; and they were ſoon engaged. He himſelf continued to chace their main fleet ; and about ten o'clock the battle began. The Spaniards ſeemed to be diſtracted in their counſels, and acted in confuſion. They made a running fight ; and the admirals behaved with courage and activity, in ſpite of which they were all taken but Cammock, who made his eſcape with three ſhips of war and three frigates. In this engagement, which happened off Cape Paſſaro, captain Haddock of the Grafton ſignalized his courage in an extraordinary manner. On the 18th the admiral received a letter from captain Walton, dated off Syracuſe, intimating that he had taken four Spaniſh ſhips of war, together with a bomb-ketch, and a veſſel laden with arms ; and that he had burned

ed four ſhips of the line, a fire-ſhip, and a bomb-
veſſel.   This letter is juſtly deemed a curious ſpeci-
men of the laconic ſtyle.—" Sir, We have taken and
deſtroyed all the Spaniſh ſhips and veſſels which were
upon the coaſt, the number as per margin.   I am, &c.
G. Walton."

These ſhips that captain Walton thus thruſt into his
margin, would have furniſhed matter for ſome pages,
in a French relation.

Admiral Byng continued to aſſiſt the imperialiſts in
Sicily, during the beſt part of the winter, by ſcouring
the ſeas of the Spaniards, and keeping the communication open between the German forces and the Cala-
brian ſhore, from whence they were ſupplied with
proviſions.   He acted in this ſervice with equal conduct, reſolution, and activity.   He conferred with
the viceroy of Naples, and the other imperial generals, about the operations of the enſuing campaign;
and count Hamilton was diſpatched to Vienna, to lay
before the emperor the reſult of their deliberations:
then the admiral ſet ſail for Mahon, where his ſhips
might be refitted, and put in a condition to take the
ſea in the ſpring.

The deſtruction of the Spaniſh fleet was a ſubject
that employed the deliberations and conjectures of all
the politicians in Europe.   Spain exclaimed againſt
the conduct of England, as inconſiſtent with the rules
of good faith, for the obſervation of which ſhe had
always been ſo famous.   This was the language of
diſappointed ambition.   Nevertheleſs, it muſt be
owned, that the conduct of England on this occaſion
was rather irregular; and the Spaniards were not ſlow
in expreſſing their reſentments.   On the 1ſt of September, rear-admiral Guevara, with ſome ſhips under
his command, entered the port of Cadiz, and made
himſelf maſter of all the Engliſh ſhips that were there;
and, at the ſame time, all the effects of the Engliſh
merchants were ſeized in Malaga, and other ports of
Spain; which, as ſoon as it was known here, produced

duced reprifals on our part.   But it is now time to
leave the Mediterranean, and the affairs of Spain, in
order to give an account of what paffed in the northern
feas.

There remains only one tranfaction more of this
year, which a work of this kind requires to be mentioned ; which is the account of the reduction of the
pirates.   Captain Woodes Rogers, having been appointed governor of the Bahama iflands, failed for
Providence, which was to be the feat of his government, on the 11th of April ; and after a fhort and
eafy paffage, arriving there, he took poffeffion of the
town of Naffau, the fort belonging to it, and of the
whole ifland ; the people receiving him with all imaginable joy, and many of the pirates fubmitting immediately.   Some of them, it is true, rejected, at firft,
all terms, and did a great deal of mifchief on the
coaft of Carolina ; but, when they faw that governor
Rogers had thoroughly fettled himfelf at Providence,
and that the inhabitants of the Bahama iflands found
themfelves obliged, through intereft, to be honeft,
they began to doubt of their fituation, and thought
proper to go and beg that mercy which at firft they refufed ; fo that there were not above three or four veffels of thofe pirates who continued their trade, and
two of them being taken, and their crews executed,
the reft difperfed out of fear, and became thereby
lefs terrible.   Thus, in a fhort time, and chiefly
through the fteady and prudent conduct of governor
Rogers, this herd of villains were in fome meafure
difperfed, who for many years had frighted the Weft
Indies, and the northern colonies.

On the 17th of December 1718, a declaration of
war in form was publifhed againft the crown of Spain ;
as to the expediency of which, many bold things
were faid in the houfe of commons, efpecially with
regard to the pretenfions, and the intentions of thofe
who made this war.   The miniftry, however, continued the purfuit of their own fcheme, in fpite of op-

position, and took such vigorous measures for obliging Spain to accept the terms assigned her by the quadruple alliance, that she lost all patience, and resolved to attempt any thing that might either free her from this necessity, or serve to express her resentments against such as endeavoured to impose it upon her: with this view she drew together a great number of transports at Cadiz and Corunna; but the Spanish fleet, designed for this expedition, consisting of five men of war, and about forty transports, having on board the late duke of Ormonde, and upward of 5000 men, met with a violent storm, which entirely dispersed them. Thus, this design of the Spaniards, whatever it was, became abortive.

It may be proper, in this place, to take notice, that we acted now in such close conjunction with France, that the regent declared war against his cousin the king of Spain; and though many people here suspected that this war would produce no great effects, it proved quite otherwise; for the marquis de Silly advanced in the month of April as far as Port Passage, where he found six men of war just finished, upon the stocks, all which, prompted thereto by colonel Stanhope, (afterward earl of Harrington) he burned, together with timber, masts, and naval stores, to the value of half a million sterling; which was a greater real loss to the Spaniards, than that they sustained by our beating their fleet. Soon after, the duke of Berwick besieged Fontarabia; both which actions shewed, that the French were actually in earnest.

While the Spaniards were pleasing themselves with chimerical notions of invasions it was impossible to effect against us, our admiral in the Mediterranean was distressing them effectually; he continued there until he had seen the islands of Sicily and Sardinia evacuated by the Spaniards, and the mutual cessions executed between the emperor and the duke of Savoy. In a word, admiral Byng bore such a considerable

derable fhare in this war of Sicily, that the fate of the ifland depended wholly upon his courage, vigilance, and conduct.

The king of England, with a view to indemnify himfelf for the expence of the war, projected the conqueft of Corunna in Bifcay, and of Peru in South America. Four thoufand men, commanded by lord Cobham, were embarked at the Ifle of Wight, and failed on the 21ft day of September, under convoy of five fhips of war, conducted by admiral Mighels. Inftead of making an attempt upon Corunna, they reduced Vigo with very little difficulty. The expedition to the Weft Indies was prevented by the peace. Spain being oppreffed on all fides, and utterly exhaufted, Philip faw the neceffity of a fpeedy pacification. He was obliged at laft to accede to the quadruple alliance.

The pirates in the Weft Indies, who had received fome check from the vigorous difpofitions of governor Rogers, and other commanders in thofe parts, began to take breath again, and by degrees grew fo bold as even to annoy our colonies more than ever; owing to the encouragement they had met with of late from the Spaniards, and to the want of a fufficient force in the North American feas. There was among thefe pirates one Roberts, a man whofe parts deferved a better employment; he was an able feaman, and a good commander, and had with him two very ftout fhips, to which he foon added a third. With this force, Roberts had done a great deal of mifchief in the Weft Indies, before he failed for Africa, where he likewife took abundance of prizes, till in the month of April 1722, he was taken by the then captain, afterward Sir Chaloner Ogle.

Captain Ogle was then in the Swallow, and was cruifing off Cape Lopez, when he had intelligence of Roberts's being not far from him, and in confequence of this he went immediately in fearch of him, and foon after difcovered the pirates in a very convenient bay, where the biggeft and the leaft fhip were upon the heel, fcrubbing. Captain Ogle taking in his lower tier of guns, and lying at a diftance, Roberts took him for a merchantman, and immediately ordered his confort to flip his cable, and run out after him. Captain Ogle crouded all the fail he could to decoy the pirate to fuch a diftance, that his conforts might not hear the guns, and then fuddenly tacked, run out his lower tier, and gave the pirate a broadfide, by which their captain was killed: this fo difcouraged the crew, that after a brifk engagement, which lafted about an hour and a half, they furrendered. Captain Ogle returned then to the bay, hoifting the king's colours, under the pirates black flag with a death's head in it. This prudent ftratagem had the defired effect; for the pirates, feeing the black flag uppermoft, concluded the king's fhip had been taken, and came out full of joy to congratulate their confort on the victory. This joy of theirs was, however, of no long continuance, for captain Ogle gave them a very warm reception; and though Roberts fought with the utmoft bravery, for near two hours, yet being at laft killed, the courage of his men immediately funk, and both fhips yielded.

Peace affords no events of importance for naval hiftory; we therefore pafs on to the death of king George I. which happened at his brother's palace, in the city of Ofnaburg, June the 11th, 1727, in the thirteenth year of his reign, and in the fixty-eighth of his life. He was very well acquainted with the general intereft of all the princes in Europe, and particularly well verfed in whatever related to German affairs. He was allowed by the beft judges of military fkill, to be an excellent officer; was very capable of application, and underftood bufinefs as well as any prince of his time.

A LIST

A LIST of the ENGLISH NAVY, as it stood
    at the Accession of GEORGE II.

Rates.	Nº of Ships.	Men.	Guns.	Swivels.
I.	7	5,460	700	
II.	13	8,840	1,170	
III.	16	8,320	1,280	
	24	10,568	1,680	
IV.	24	37,600	1,440	
	40	17,200	2,000	
V.	24	4,800	960	
	1	155	30	
VI.	1	140	22	
	28	3,580	560	
Fire-ships	3	155	24	
Bombs	3	120	16	16
Store-ship	1	90	20	
Sloops	15	990	78	78
Yachts	7	260	64	
Ditto, small.	5	29	26	6
Hoys	11	87	12	2
Smacks	2	4		
Total	225	98,398	10,082	

After the accession of king George II. notwithstanding the seeming pacific disposition of the court
of Spain in Europe, and their engagements lately entered into, there was great reason to suspect, that their
governors in the West Indies had secret instructions to
carry on a depredatory war: for no sooner were our
men of war called off from action in those seas,
than our merchants severely felt the effects of a perfi-
dious treaty; and every ship from our colonies and
islands, brought fresh subject of complaint, concerning their depredations on our trade, and their cruelties to our sailors. Also in Europe, from the lessening of our naval force in the Mediterranean, the Sallee
rovers were encouraged to infest our navigation in the

C c 3   Streights

Streights and Weſtern ocean. Upon all this the parliament, which met on the 22d of January, agreed
to employ 15,000 ſeamen, at four pounds a man per
month, for thirteen months, for the current year;
and alſo voted 206,025 pounds, for the ordinary of the
navy during the ſame time.

The houſe of commons having examined the accounts of the Spaniſh depredations, came to the following reſolution; That ever ſince the peace of Utrecht,
concluded in 1713, to this time, the Britiſh trade
and navigation to and from the ſeveral colonies in
America, had been greatly interrupted by the continual depredations of the Spaniards; in manifeſt violation of the treaties ſubſiſting between the two crowns.
In conſequence of which reſolution, it was further
unanimouſly reſolved, that an humble addreſs be preſented to his majeſty, to deſire he would be graciouſly
pleaſed to uſe his utmoſt endeavours to prevent ſuch
depredations, to procure juſt and reaſonable ſatisfaction for the loſſes ſuſtained; and to ſecure to his ſubjects the free exerciſe of commerce and navigation, to
and from the Britiſh colonies in America. The conſequence was, an order for putting 27 ſhips in commiſſion; which joined to a Dutch ſquadron, were intended to act in conjunction under Sir Charles Wager.

This confederate fleet of the Engliſh and Dutch at
Spithead, raiſed expectations in the public, who now
imagined that ſome bold ſtroke was intended in favour of our merchants. But after ſpending above
three months in a pompous parade, the Dutch ſailed
homeward; and twelve of our largeſt ſhips were ordered to be laid up. This fleet, however, it is generally thought, accelerated the ſigning of the convention, and alſo the diſpatching thoſe orders which
were carried to Cuba, by the new governor of that
iſland; by virtue of which, he impriſoned his prede-
ceſſor, and even laid him in irons; at the ſame time
declaring, that his inſtructions were to live in amity
with the Engliſh. But all this, as appeared by the
conſe-

consequences, proved no more than grimace; for the guarda coftas continued their former depredations.

After the conclufion of the peace with Spain, Great Britain was drawn into an agreement, to carry Don Carlos, infant of Spain, and with the confent of the court of Vienna, to place him on the throne of Naples : notwithftanding which, every fhip from the W. Indies brought an account of a continued feries of Spanifh depredations and cruelties; a fhocking in-ftance of the latter, not to mention others, was the inhuman treatment of Robert Jenkins, mafter of the Rebecca, whofe ear they cut off, and, at the fame time, delivered it into his hands, infolently telling him to carry that prefent home to his mafter. Not-withftanding the pacific difpofition of the Britifh mi-niftry at that time, the popular clamours rofe very high on thefe and other acts of violence committed by the Spaniards; which year after year grew fo violent, that the Britifh miniftry was no longer able to ftem the current of national refentment fhewn by the daily petitions brought up from all parts of the kingdom, calling aloud for fatisfaction from Spain. His ma-jefty iffued a proclamation on the 10th of July, 1739, fetting forth the Spanifh depredations, the expiration of the term limited for the payment of 95,000 pounds compenfation, and on the non-payment of it, thereby au-thorizing general reprifals and letters of marque againft the fhips, goods, and fubjects of the king of Spain.

These orders, under his majefty's fign manual, dated June the 15th, had been difpatched above a month before their publication in London, to com-modore Brown, who then commanded a fquadron at Jamaica; in order to have an opportunity of making the beft ufe of them, before the Spaniards had notice of our defigns, and confequently prepared againft them. The commodore publifhed thefe orders on the 8th of Auguft. In the mean time the Britifh miniftry now forefeeing that a war with Spain could no longer be avoided, the firft thing they did, was to form a

refolution

resolution of endeavouring to preclude the Spaniards from the resources of their wealth in the West Indies and the South Seas.

With this view two squadrons were immediately ordered to be got ready with all expedition, the one to be put under the command of George Anson, Esq; who was then captain of his majesty's ship the Centurion, and the other under that of captain Cornwall. The particulars of Anson's voyage to the South Seas, are to be found in the third volume of this collection. Notwithstanding these preparations of war, Mr. Keene, the British minister at Madrid, declared to the court of Spain, that his master, although he had permitted his subjects to make reprisals, would not be understood to have broken the peace; and, that this permission would be recalled as soon as his catholic majesty should be disposed to make the satisfaction which had been so justly demanded. He was given to understand, that the king of Spain looked upon those reprisals as acts of hostility; and that he hoped, with the assistance of heaven and his allies, he should be able to support a good cause against his adversaries. He published a manifesto in justification of his own conduct. The French ambassador at the Hague declared, that the king his master was obliged by treaties to assist his catholic majesty by sea and land, in case he should be attacked: he dissuaded the states-general from espousing the quarrel of Great Britain; and they assured him they would observe a strict neutrality, though they could not avoid furnishing his Britannic majesty with such succours as he could demand, by virtue of the treaties subsisting between the two powers. The people of England were inspired with uncommon alacrity at the near prospect of war, for which they had so long clamoured; and the ministry seeing it unavoidable, began to be earnest and effectual in their preparations.

The great view of the nation now being to distress the Spaniards, another squadron was ordered to be fitted

fitted out for the Weſt Indies, and the command of it given to Edward Vernon, Eſq; then juſt made vice admiral of the blue, who, on account of the eminent ſervices he had formerly done his king and country in that part of the world, was looked on by all as the moſt proper perſon to be intruſted with ſo important an enterprize. He had withdrawn from employment, and on ſeveral accounts, had been diſguſted at the conduct of the miniſtry; yet upon the firſt application made to him to undertake the command of a ſquadron for the ſervice of his country, he immediately laid aſide all private animoſity, and ſacrificing all other conſiderations to the welfare of the public, very chearfully obeyed the ſummons, deſiring only a few days to ſettle his family affairs. He was counted a good officer, and his boiſterous manner ſeemed to enhance his character. As he had once commanded a ſquadron in Jamaica, he was perfectly well acquainted with thoſe ſeas; and in a debate upon the Spaniſh depredations, he chanced to affirm, that Porto Bello on the Spaniſh main might be eaſily taken: nay, he even undertook to reduce it with ſix ſhips only. This offer was echoed from the mouths of all the members in the oppoſition. Vernon was extolled as another Drake or Raleigh: he became the idol of a party, and his praiſe reſounded from all corners of the kingdom. The miniſter, in order to appeaſe the clamours of the people on this ſubject, ſent him as commander in chief to the Weſt Indies. He was pleaſed with an opportunity to remove ſuch a troubleſome cenſurer from the houſe of commons; and perhaps, he was not without hope, that Vernon would diſgrace himſelf and his party, by failing in the exploit he had undertaken. His catholic majeſty having ordered all the Britiſh ſhips in his harbours to be ſeized and detained, the king of England would keep meaſures with him no longer, but denounced war againſt him on the 23d day of October, 1739. Many Engliſh merchants began to equip privateers,

and

and arm their trading veffels, to protect their own commerce as well as to diftrefs that of the enemy.

On the 13th of March, 1740, a ship arrived from the Weft Indies, difpatched by admiral Vernon, with an account of his having taken Porto Bello, on the ifthmus of Darien, and demolifhed all the fortifications of the place. The Spaniards acted with fuch pufillanimity on this occafion, that their forts were taken almoft without bloodfhed. And though the admiral was not able to pufh his conquefts further up the country, yet the national advantage arifing from what he had already done was very confiderable: particularly as the traders of Jamaica had now a fair opportunity of opening an extenfive commerce with the Spaniards, who were fond of clandeftinely conveying their money from Panama over the ifthmus.

Sir Chaloner Ogle arrived at Jamaica on the 9th day of Jan. 1741; and admiral Vernon did not fail on his intended expedition to Carthagena, till toward the end of the month. He refolved to beat up againft the wind to Hifpaniola, in order to obferve the motion of the French fquadron, commanded by the marquis d' Antin: but the French admiral had failed for Europe in great diftrefs, for want of men and provifions, which he could not procure in the Weft Indies. Admiral Vernon, thus difappointed, fet fail for the continent of New Spain, and on the 4th of March anchored in Playa Grande, to the windward of Carthagena. There they lay inactive till the 9th, when the troops were landed on the ifland of Tierra Bomba, near the mouth of the harbour, known by the name of Boca-chica, or Little-mouth, which was furprifingly fortified with caftles, batteries, bombs, chains, cables, and fhips of war. The Britifh forces erected a battery on fhore, with which they made a breach in the principal fort, while the admiral fent in a number of fhips to divide the fire of the enemy, and co-operate with the endeavours of the army. Lord Aubrey Beauclerc, a gallant officer, who commanded

one

one of these ships, was slain on this occasion. The breach being deemed practicable, the forces advanced to the attack: but the forts and batteries were abandoned; the Spanish ships that lay athwart the harbour's mouth were destroyed or taken; the passage was opened, and the fleet entered without further opposition. Then the forces were reimbarked with the artillery, and landed within a mile of Carthagena, where they were opposed by about 700 Spaniards, whom they obliged to retire. The admiral and general had contracted a hearty contempt for each other, and took all opportunities of expressing their mutual dislike: far from acting vigorously in concert, each appeared more eager for the disgrace of his rival, than zealous for the honour of the nation: and this contributed in great measure to the ruin of the enterprize.

The forces mistook their rout, and advanced to the strongest part of the fortification, where they were moreover exposed to the fire of the town. Their number was so much reduced, that they could no longer maintain their footing on shore: beside, the rainy season had begun with such violence, as rendered it impossible for them to live in camp. They were therefore reimbarked; and all hope of further success immediately vanished.

The miscarriage of this expedition, which had cost the nation an immense sum of money, was no sooner known in England, than the kingdom was filled with murmurs and discontent; and the people were depressed, in proportion to that sanguine hope by which they had been elevated. Admiral Vernon, instead of undertaking any enterprize which might have retrieved the honour of the British arms, set sail from Jamaica with the forces in July, and anchored at the south-east part of Cuba, in a bay, on which he bestowed the appellation of Cumberland harbour. The troops were landed, and encamped at the distance of twenty miles farther up the river, where

where they remained totally inactive, and fubfifted chiefly on falt and damaged provifions, till the month of November; when, being confidérably diminifhed by ficknefs, they were put on board again, and reconveyed to Jamaica. He was afterward reinforced from England by four fhips of war, and about 3000 foldiers; but he performed nothing worthy of the reputation he had acquired.

While admiral Haddock, with twelve fhips of the line, lay at anchor in the bay of Gibraltar, the Spanifh fleet paffed the Streights in the night, and was joined by the French fquadron from Toulon. The Britifh admiral failing from Gibraltar, fell in with them in a few days, and found both fquadrons drawn up in line of battle. As he bore down upon the Spanifh fleet, the French admiral fent a flag of truce to inform him, that as the French and Spaniards were engaged in a joint expedition, he fhould be obliged to act in concert with his mafter's allies. This interpofition prevented an engagement, the combined fleets amounting to double the number of the Englifh fquadron. Admiral Haddock was obliged to defift; and proceeded to Portmahon, leaving the enemy to profecute their voyage without moleftation. The people of England were incenfed at this tranfaction, and did not fcruple to affirm, that the hands of the Britifh admiral were tied up by the neutrality of Hanover.

The court of Madrid feemed to have fhaken off that indolence and phlegm which had formerly difgraced the councils of Spain. They no fooner learned the deftination of commodore Anfon, who had failed from Spithead in the courfe of the preceding year, than they fent Don Pizarro, with a more powerful fquadron upon the fame voyage to defeat his defign. Their privateers were fo induftrious and fuccefsful, that in the beginning of this year, they had taken, fince the commencement of the war, 407 fhips, belonging to the fubjects of Great Britain, and valued

at

at near four millions of piasters. The traders had therefore too much cause to complain, considering the formidable fleets which were maintained for the protection of commerce. In the course of the sum-. mer, Sir John Norris had twice sailed toward the coast of Spain, at the head of a powerful squadron, without taking any effectual step for annoying the enemy; as if the sole intention of the ministry had been to expose the nation to the ridicule and contempt of its enemies. The inactivity of the British arms appears the more inexcusable, when we consider the great armaments which had been prepared. The land-forces of Great Britain, exclusive of Danish and Hessian auxiliaries, amounted to 60,000 men; and the fleet consisted of above 100 ships of war, manned by 54,000 sailors.

The new ministry in England (1742) had sent out admiral Matthews to assume the command of this squadron, which had been for some time conducted by Lestock, an inferior officer, as Haddock had been obliged to resign his commission on account of his ill state of health. Matthews was likewise invested with the character of minister plenipotentiary to the king of Sardinia and the states of Italy. Immediately. after he had taken possession of his command, he ordered captain Norris to destroy five Spanish gallies which had put into the bay of St. Tropez; and this service was effectually performed. In May he detached commodore Rowley with eight sail, to cruise off the harbour of Toulon; and a great number of merchant-ships belonging to the enemy fell into his hands. In August he sent commodore Martin with another squadron into the bay of Naples, to bombard that city, unless his Sicilian majesty would immediately recal his troops which had joined the Spanish army, and promise to remain neuter during the continuance of the war. Naples was immediately filled with consternation: the king subscribed to these conditions; and the English squadron rejoined the admiral in the road

5

of

of Hieres, which he had chofen for his winter-ftatiofl.
But before this period he had landed fome men at St.
Remo, in the territories of Genoa, and deftroyed the
magazines that were erected for the ufe of the Spanifh army.   He had likewife ordered two of his cruifers to attack a Spanifh fhip of the line, which lay at
anchor in the port of Ajacciò, in the ifland of Corfica; but, the Spanifh captain fet his men on fhore,
and blew up his fhip, rather than fhe fhould fall into
the hands of the Englifh.

In the courfe of this year admiral Vernon and general Wentworth made another effort in the Weft Indies.
They had received, in January, a reinforcement from
England, and planned a new expedition.   Their defign was to difembark the troops at Porto-Bello, and
march acrofs the ifthmus of Darien, to attack the
rich town of Panama.   They failed from Jamaica on
the 9th day of March, and on the 28th arrived at
Porto-Bello.   There they held a council of war, in
which it was refolved, that as the troops were fickly,
the rainy feafon begun, and feveral tranfports not yet
arrived, the intended expedition was become impracticable.   In purfuance of this determination, the armament immediately returned to Jamaica, exhibiting
a ridiculous fpectacle of folly and irrefolution.   Vernon and Wentworth received orders to return to England, with fuch troops as remained alive; and thefe
did not amount to a tenth part of the number which
had been fent abroad in that inglorious fervice.

In England the merchants ftill complained, that their
commerce was not properly protected; and the people
clamoured againft the conduct of the war.   They faid,
their burdens were increafed to maintain quarrels with
which they had no concern; to defray the enormous expence of inactive fleets and pacific armies.   The lord C.
had now infinuated himfelf into the confidence of his
fovereign, and engroffed the whole direction of public affairs.   The war with Spain was now become a
fecondary confideration, and neglected accordingly;
while

while the chief attention of the new minifter was turned upon the affairs of the continent.

The Britifh fleet commanded by admiral Matthews overawed all the ftates that bordered on the Mediterranean. About the end of June, 1743, underftanding that 14 xebecks, loaded with artillery and ammunition for the Spanifh army, had arrived at Genoa, he failed thither from the road of Hieres, and demanded of the republic, that they would either oblige thefe veffels with the ftores to quit their harbour, or fequefter their ladings until a general peace fhould be eftablifhed. After fome difpute, it was agreed, that the cannon and ftores fhould be depofited in the caftle of Bonifacio, fituated on a rock at the fouth end of Corfica: and, that the xebecks fhould have leave to retire without moleftation. Admiral Matthews, though he did not undertake any expedition of importance againft the maritime towns of Spain, continued to affert the Britifh empire at fea through the whole extent of the Mediterranean. The Spanifh army under Don Philip was no fooner in motion, than the Englifh admiral ordered fome troops and cannon to be difembarked for the fecurity of Villa-Franca; ftores having been landed at Civita-Vecchia for the ufe of the Spanifh forces under count Gages, Matthews interpreted this tranfaction into a violation of the neutrality which the pope had profeffed, and fent thither a fquadron to bombard the place. The city of Rome was filled with confternation; and the pope had recourfe to the good offices of his Sardinian majefty, in confequence of which the Englifh fquadron was ordered to withdraw. The captains of fingle cruifing fhips, by their activity and vigilance, wholly interrupted the commerce of Spain; cannonaded and burnt fome towns on the fea-fide, and kept the whole coaft in continual alarm.

In the Weft Indies fome unfuccefsful efforts were made by an Englifh fquadron, commanded by commodore Knowles. He attacked La Gueira, on the

coaft

coaft of Carraccas, in the month of February; but met with fuch a warm reception, that he was obliged to defift, and make the beft of his way for the Dutch ifland Curaçoa, where he repaired the damage he had fuftained. His fhips being refitted, he made another attempt upon Porto-Cavallo in April, which, like the former, mifcarried.

By the parliamentary difputes, the loud clamours, and general diffatisfaction of the people of Great Britain, the French miniftry were perfuaded, that the nation was ripe for revolt. This belief was corroborated by the affertions of their emiffaries in different parts of Great Britain and Ireland. They gave the court of Verfailles to underftand, that if the chevalier de St. George, or his eldeft fon Charles-Edward, fhould appear at the head of a French army in Great Britain, a revolution would inftantly follow in his favour. This intimation was agreeable to cardinal de Tencin, who had fucceeded Fleury, as prime minifter of France. He was of a violent interprifing temper. He had been recommended to the purple, by the chevalier de St. George, and was warmly attached to the Stuart family. His ambition was flattered with a profpect of giving a king to Great Britain; of and performing fuch eminent fervice to his benefactor, in reftoring him to the throne of his anceftors. He forefaw, that even if his aim fhould mifcarry, a defcent upon Great Britain would make a confiderable diverfion from the continent in favour of France, and embroil and embarrafs his Britannic majefty, who was the chief fupport of the houfe of Auftria and all its allies. Actuated by thefe motives, he concerted meafures with the chevalier de St. George at Rome; who being too much advanced in years to engage perfonally in fuch an expedition, agreed to delegate his pretenfions and authority to his fon Charles. Count Saxe was appointed by the French king commander of the troops defigned for this expedition, which amounted to 15,000. Charles departed from

Rome

Rome about the end of December, in the disguise of
a Spanish courier, attended by one servant only : and
prosecuting his journey to Paris, was indulged with
a private audience of the French king.   The British
ministry being apprised of his arrival in France, at
once comprehended the destination of the armaments
prepared at Brest and Boulogne.   Mr. Thomson, the
English resident at Paris, received orders to make a
remonstrance to the French ministry, on the violation
of those treaties by which the pretender to the crown
of Great Britain was excluded from the territories of
France.   But he was given to understand, that his
most christian majesty would not explain himself on
that subject, until the king of England should have
given satisfaction on the repeated complaints which
had been made to him, touching the infractions of
those treaties which had been so often violated by his
orders.

In the month of January, M. de Roquefeuille sailed
from Brest, directing his course up the English channel, with twenty ships of war.   Sir John Norris was
forthwith ordered to take the command of the squadron at Spithead, with which he sailed round to the
Downs, where he was joined by some ships of the
line from Chatham, and then he found himself at
the head of a squadron considerably stronger than that
of the enemy.

Several regiments marched to the southern coast of
England: all governors and commanders were ordered to repair immediately to their respective posts :
the forts at the mouth of the Thames and the Medway were put in a posture of defence.   A proclamation was issued for putting the laws in execution
against papists and nonjurors, who were commanded
to retire ten miles from London ; and every precaution taken which seemed necessary for the preservation of the public tranquillity.

Mean while the French court proceeded with their
preparations, at Boulogne and Dunkirk, under the

eye of the younger pretender; and 7000 men were actually embarked. M. de Roquefeuille sailed up the channel as far as Dungenels, a promontory on the coast of Kent, after having detached M. de Barreil with five ships, to hasten the embarkation at Dunkirk. While the French admiral anchored off Dungenels, he perceived, on the 24th day of February, the British fleet under Sir John Norris, doubling the South-Foreland from the Downs; and, though the wind was against him, taking the opportunity of the tide to come up and engage the French squadron. Roquefeuille, who little expected such a visit, could not be altogether composed, considering the great superiority of his enemies; but the tide failing, the English admiral was obliged to anchor two leagues short of the enemy. In this interval, M. Roquefeuille called a council of war; in which it was determined to avoid an engagement, to weigh anchor at sunset, and make the best of their way to the place from whence they had set sail. This resolution was favoured by a very hard gale of wind, which began to blow from the north-east, and carried them down the channel with incredible expedition. But the same storm which, in all probability, saved their fleet from destruction, utterly disconcerted the design of invading England. A great number of their transports was driven ashore and destroyed, and the rest so much damaged that they could not be speedily repaired.

The English were now masters at sea, and their coast was so well guarded, that the enterprise could not be prosecuted with any probability of success. The French generals nominated to serve in this expedition returned to Paris, and the pretender resolved to wait a more favourable opportunity. The French king no longer preserved any measures with the court of London: the British resident at Paris was given to understand, that a declaration of war must ensue; and this was actually published on the 20th day of

5 March,

March, 1744. The king of Great Britain was taxed
with having diffuaded the court of Vienna from en-
tertaining any thoughts of an accommodation ; with
having infringed the convention of Hanover ; with
having exercifed piracy upon the fubjects of France,
and even with blocking up the harbour of Toulon. On
the 31ft of March, a like denunciation of war againft
France was publifhed at London, amidft the acclamations of the people.

An action happened in the Mediterranean between
the Britifh fleet, commanded by admiral Matthews,
and the combined fquadrons of France and Spain,
which had been for fome time blocked up in the harbour of Toulon. On the 9th day of February, 1744,
they were perceived ftanding out of the road, to the
number of 34 fail : the Englifh admiral immediately
weighed from Hieres-bay ; and on the 11th, part of
the fleets engaged. Matthews attacked the Spanifh
admiral, Don Navarro, whofe fhip, the Real, was a
firft rate, mounted with above 100 guns. The rear-
admiral Rowley fingled out M. de Court, who commanded the French fquadron ; and a very few captains followed the example of their commanders :
but vice-admiral Leftock, with his whole divifion,
remained at a great diftance aftern ; and feveral captains, that were immediately under the eye of Matthews, behaved in fuch a manner as reflected difgrace
upon their country.

The whole tranfaction was conducted without order or deliberation. The French and Spaniards would
have willingly avoided an engagement, as the Britifh
fquadron was fuperior to them in ftrength and number. M. de Court therefore made the beft of his
way toward the Streights mouth, probably with intention to join the Breft fquadron : but he had orders
to protect the Spanifh fleet ; and as they failed heavily,
he was obliged to wait for them, at the hazard of
maintaining a battle with the Englifh. Thus circumftanced, he made fail and lay to by turns ; fo that

the British admiral could not engage them in proper
order; and as they out-failed his ships, he began to
fear they would escape him altogether should he wait
for vice-admiral Leftock, who was so far astern.
Under this apprehension, he made the signal for engaging, while that for the line of battle was still difplayed; and this inconsistency naturally introduced
confusion. The fight was maintained by the few who
engaged, with great vivacity. The Real being quite
disabled, and lying like a wreck upon the water, Mr.
Matthews sent a firefhip to destroy her; but the expedient did not take effect. The ship ordered to
cover this machine, did not obey the signal; so that
the captain of the firefhip was exposed to the whole
fire of the enemy. Nevertheless, he continued to
advance until he found the vessel finking; and being
within a few yards of the Real, he set fire to the fufees.
The ship was immediately in flames, in the midst of
which, he and his lieutenant, with twelve men, perifhed. This was likewife the fate of a Spanifh
launch, which had been manned with fifty failors to
prevent the firefhip from running on board the Real.
One ship of the line, belonging to the Spanifh fquadron, ftruck to captain Hawke, who fent a lieutenant to take poffeffion of her; fhe was afterward retaken by the French fquadron; but was found fo difabled, that they left her deferted, and fhe was next
day burned by order of admiral Matthews.

At night, the action ceafed; and the admiral found
his own ship fo much damaged, that he moved his
flag into another. Captain Cornwall fell in the engagement, after having exhibited a remarkable proof
of courage and intrepidity; but, the lofs of men was
very inconfiderable. Next day the enemy appeared
to leeward, and the admiral gave chafe till night,
when he brought to, that he might be joined by the
ships a-ftern. They were perceived again on the
13th at a confiderable diftance, and purfued till the
evening. In the morning of the 14th, 20 fail of
them

them were seen diſtinctly; and Leſtock with his diviſion had gained ground of them conſiderably, by noon; but admiral Matthews diſplayed the ſignal for leaving off chace, and bore away for Port-mahon, to repair the damage he had ſuſtained. Mean while, the combined ſquadrons continued their courſe toward the coaſt of Spain.

Admiral Matthews, on his arrival at Minorca, accuſed Leſtock of having miſbehaved on the day of action; ſuſpended him from his office, and ſent him priſoner to England; where, in his turn, he accuſed his accuſer. Long before the engagement, theſe two officers had expreſſed the moſt virulent reſentment againſt each other. Matthews was brave, open, and undiſguiſed; but proud, imperious, and precipitate. Leſtock had ſignalized his courage on many occaſions, and perfectly underſtood the whole diſcipline of the navy; but he was cool, and vindictive. He had been treated ſuperciliouſly by Matthews, and in revenge took advantage of his errors and precipitation. To gratify this paſſion, he betrayed the intereſt and glory of his country; for, it is not to be doubted, but that he might have come up in time to engage; and in that caſe, the fleets of France and Spain would in all likelihood have been deſtroyed: but he intrenched himſelf within the punctilios of diſcipline, and ſaw with pleaſure his antagoniſt expoſe himſelf to the hazard of death, ruin, and diſgrace. Matthews himſelf, in the ſequel, ſacrificed his duty to his reſentment, in reſtraining Leſtock from purſuing and attacking the combined ſquadrons on the third day after the engagement, when they appeared diſabled and in manifeſt diſorder, and would have fallen an eaſy prey, had they been vigorouſly attacked. One can hardly, without indignation, reflect upon thoſe inſtances, in which a community has ſo ſeverely ſuffered from the perſonal animoſity of individuals. The miſcarriage off Toulon became the ſubject of a parliamentary enquiry in England.

A court-martial was conſtituted, and proceeded to trial. Several commanders of ſhips were caſhiered : vice-admiral Leſtock was honourably acquitted, and admiral Matthews rendered incapable of ſerving for the future in his majeſty's navy. All the world knew that Leſtock kept aloof, and that Matthews ruſhed into the hotteſt part of the engagement : yet, the former triumphed on his trial, and the latter narrowly eſcaped ſentence of death for cowardice and miſconduct. Such deciſions are not to be accounted for, except from prejudice and faction.

After the action at Toulon, nothing of conſequence was atchieved by the Britiſh ſquadron in the Mediterranean ; and indeed the naval power of Great Britain was, during the ſummer, quite inactive. In the month of June, commodore Anſon returned from his voyage of three years and nine months, in which he had ſurrounded the terraqueous globe. Though this fortunate commander enriched himſelf by an occurrence that may be termed almoſt accidental, the Britiſh nation was not indemnified for the expence of the expedition, and the original deſign was entirely defeated. Had the Manilla ſhip eſcaped the vigilance of the Engliſh commodore, he might have been, at his return to England, laid aſide as a ſuperannuated captain, and died in obſcurity : but his great wealth inveſted him with conſiderable influence, and added luſtre to his talents. He ſoon became the oracle which was conſulted in all naval deliberations : and the king raiſed him to the dignity of a peerage.

In July, Sir John Balchen, an admiral of approved valour and great experience, ſailed from Spithead with a ſtrong ſquadron, in queſt of an opportunity to attack the French fleet at Breſt, under the command of M. de Rochambault. In the bay of Biſcay, he was overtaken by a violent ſtorm, that diſperſed the ſhips, and drove them up the Engliſh channel. Admiral Stewart, with the greater part of them, arrived at Plymouth ; but Sir John Balchen's own ſhip, the Victory, which

was

was counted the most beautiful first rate in the world, foundered at sea; and this brave commander perished with all his officers, volunteers, and crew, amounting to 1100 choice seamen.

The naval transactions of Great Britain were in the year 1745 remarkably spirited. In the Mediterranean, admiral Rowley had succeeded Matthews in the command; and Savona, Genoa, Finah, St. Remo, with Baftia the capital of Corsica, were bombarded: several Spanish ships were taken; but he could not prevent the safe arrival of their rich Havannah squadron, at Corunna. Commodore Barnet in the West Indies made prize of several French ships richly laden; and commodore Townshend, in the latitude of Martinico, took about 30 merchant-ships belonging to the enemy, under convoy of four ships of war, two of which were destroyed. The English privateers likewise met with uncommon success. But the most important atchievement was the conquest of Louisburgh, on the island of Cape-Breton, in North America; a place of great consequence, which the French had fortified at a prodigious expence. The scheme of reducing this fortress was planned in Boston, recommended by their general-assembly, and approved by his majesty; who sent instructions to commodore Warren, stationed off the Leeward Islands, to sail for the northern parts of America, and to co-operate with the forces of New England in this expedition. A body of 6000 men was formed under the conduct of Mr. Pepperel, a trader of Piscataway, whose influence was extensive in that country; though he was a man of little or no education, and utterly unacquainted with military operations. In April, Mr. Warren arrived at Canso with ten ships of war; and the troops of New England being embarked in transports, sailed immediately for the isle of Cape-Breton, where they landed without opposition. The enemy abandoned their grand battery, which was deta from the town; and the immediate seizure of it

D d 4   trit

tributed in a good meafure to the fuccefs of the enterprize. While the American troops, reinforced by
800 marines, carried on their approaches by land,
the fquadron blocked up the place by fea in fuch a
manner, that no fuccours could be introduced. A
French fhip of the line, with fome fmaller veffels,
deftined for the relief of the garrifon, were intercepted and taken by the Britifh cruifers; and indeed,
the reduction of Louifburgh was chiefly owing to
the vigilance and activity of Mr. Warren, one of the
braveft and beft officers in the fervice of England. The operations of the fiege were wholly conducted by the engineers and officers who commanded
the Britifh marines; and the Americans, being ignorant of war, were contented to act under their directions. The town being confiderably damaged by the
bombs and bullets of the befiegers, and the governor
defpairing of relief, capitulated on the 17th day of
June. The garrifon and inhabitants engaged, that
they would not bear arms for twelve months againft
Great Britain or her allies; and were tranfported to
Rochfort. In a few days after the furrender of Louifburgh, two French Eaft India fhips, and another from
Peru laden with treafure, failed into the harbour, on
the fuppofition that it ftill belonged to France; and
were taken by the Englifh fquadron*.

The poffeffion of Cape-Breton was, doubtlefs, a
valuable acquifition to Great Britain. It not only diftreffed the French in their fifhery and navigation, but
removed all fears of encroachment and rivalfhip from
the Englifh fifhers on the banks of Newfoundland.
It freed New England from the terrors of a dangerous neighbour; over-awed the Indians of that country; and fecured the poffeffion of Acadia to the crown
of Great Britain. The natives of New England acquired great glory from the fuccefs of this enterprife.
Britain, which had in fome inftances behaved like a
ftepmother to her own colonies, was now convinced

* See Ulloa's Voyage, in our firft volume, p. 484.

of their importance; and treated thofe as brethren whom fhe had too long confidered as aliens and rivals. Circumftanced as the nation is, the legiflature cannot too tenderly cherifh the interefts of the Britifh plantations in America. They are inhabited by a brave, hardy, induftrious people, animated with an active fpirit of commerce; infpired with a noble zeal for liberty and independence.

While the continent of Europe and the ifles of America were expofed to the ravages of war, Great Britain underwent a dangerous convulfion in her own bowels. The fon of the chevalier de St. George refolved to make another effort, which, though it might not be crowned with fuccefs, fhould at leaft aftonifh all Chriftendom. He was amufed with the promife of powerful fuccours from France, though the miniftry of that kingdom were never hearty in his caufe: neverthelefs they forefaw, that his appearance in England would embarrafs the government, and make a confiderable diverfion in their favour. Certain it is, that if he had been properly fupported, he could not have found a more favourable opportunity of exciting an inteftine commotion in Great Britain; for Scotland was quite unfurnifhed with troops, and the king was in Germany.

The young pretender accordingly embarked on board a frigate at Port Lazare in Brittany, and failed for Scotland on the 14th of July, 1745. The frigate was joined off Belleifle by the Elizabeth, a French man of war of fixty guns, which the miniftry had fitted out to convoy him in this expedition. As his defign was to fail round Ireland, and land in the north-weft of Scotland, the fhips fteered for the fouthern coaft of the former; but in their paffage were met by the Lion man of war, commanded by captain Brett, which, after a long engagement, fo effectually difabled the Elizabeth, that fhe was obliged to return to Breft. The frigate efcaped, and continued her courfe with fuch expedition, that on the 23d of July,

the

the young pretender found himself in the western isles of Scotland, where he continued cruising till the 26th between the islands of Bara and South Vist; but finding there was no hopes of being joined by the Elizabeth, the frigate stood in for the coast of Lochaber, one of the maritime counties on the north-west of Scotland, inhabited principally by papists; and on the 27th of July, landed the young pretender and his companions at Moidart, between the islands of Sky and Mull.

We shall not follow this young adventurer, as the subject is very foreign to a naval history; it being sufficient to observe, that his party was totally defeated by his royal highness the duke of Cumberland at Culloden, on the 16th of April, 1746, which put an end to this rebellion.

During these transactions, our ministry seemed determined to make an attempt on Quebec; and a large squadron was accordingly assembled at Portsmouth, and several regiments, under the command of lieutenant-general Sinclair, embarked: but after many delays, the expedition to Quebec was laid aside, and the fleet sailed to the coast of Brittany, and landed the troops in Quimperlay-bay, near Port l'Orient, which they besieged: but when the city was just going to surrender, they retreated in the night with the greatest precipitation, leaving behind them a mortar, and a considerable quantity of ammunition and stores. The Exeter man of war however engaged the Ardente, a 64 gun ship, forced her ashore and burnt her.

The French king, baffled in his projects upon Italy, in 1747, was not more fortunate in his naval operations. He had, in the preceding year, equipped an expensive armament, under the command of the duke d'Anville, for the recovery of Cape-Breton; but it was rendered ineffectual by storms, distempers, and the death of the commander. Not yet discouraged by these disasters, he resolved to renew his efforts against
the

the British colonies in North America, and their settlements in the East Indies. For these purposes two squadrons were prepared at Brest; one to be commanded by the commodore de la Jonquiere, and the other, destined for India, by monsieur de St. George. The ministry of Great Britain, being apprized of these measures, resolved to intercept both squadrons, which were to set sail together. For this purpose vice-admiral Anson and rear-admiral Warren took their departure from Plymouth with a formidable fleet, and steered their course to Cape Finisterre on the coast of Gallicia.

On the 3d day of May, they fell in with the French squadrons, commanded by la Jonquiere and St. George, consisting of six large ships of war, as many frigates, and four armed vessels equipped by their East India company, having under their convoy about thirty ships laden with merchandize. Those prepared for war immediately shortened sail, and formed a line of battle; while the rest, under the protection of the six frigates, proceeded on their voyage with all the sail they could carry. The British squadron was likewise drawn up in a line of battle: but Mr. Warren perceiving that the enemy began to sheer off, now their convoy was at a considerable distance, advised admiral Anson to haul in the signal for the line, and hoist another for giving chace and engaging, otherwise the French would in all probability escape by favour of the night. The proposal was embraced: and in a little time the engagement began with great fury, about four o'clock in the afternoon. The enemy sustained the battle with equal conduct and valour, until they were overpowered by numbers, and then they struck their colours. The admiral detached three ships in pursuit of the convoy, nine sail of which were taken; but the rest were saved by the intervening darkness. About seven hundred of the French were killed and wounded in this action. The English lost about five hundred; and among these,

captain

captain Grenville, commander of the ship Defiance.
The fuccefs of the Britifh arms, in this engagement,
was chiefly owing to the conduct, activity, and courage of the rear-admiral. A confiderable quantity
of bullion was found in the prizes, which were
brought to Spithead in triumph; and the treafure
being landed, was conveyed in twenty waggons to
the bank of London. Admiral Anfon was ennobled,
and Mr. Warren honoured with the order of the Bath.

About the middle of June, commodore Fox, with
fix fhips of war, cruifing in the latitude of Cape
Ortegal in Gallicia, took about forty French fhips,
richly laden from St. Domingo, after they had been
abandoned by their convoy. But the French king
fuftained another more important lofs at fea, in the
month of October. Rear-admiral Hawke failed from
Plymouth in the beginning of Auguft, with 14 fhips
of the line, to intercept a fleet of French merchant-
fhips bound for the Weft Indies. He cruifed for
fome time on the coaft of Bretagne; and at length,
the French fleet failed from the ifle of Aix, under
convoy of nine fhips of the line, befide frigates,
commanded by monfieur de Letenduer. On the 14th
day of October, the two fquadrons were in fight of
each other, in the latitude of Belleifle. The French
commodore immediately ordered one of his great
fhips and the frigates to proceed with the trading
fhips; while he formed the line of battle, and waited
the attack. At eleven in the forenoon, admiral
Hawke difplayed the fignal to chace, and in half an
hour both fleets were engaged. The battle lafted
till night, when all the French fquadron, except the
Intrepid and Tonant, had ftruck to the Englifh flag.
Thefe two capital fhips efcaped in the dark, and returned to Breft in a fhattered condition. The French
captains fuftained the unequal fight with uncommon
bravery and refolution, and did not yield until their
fhips were difabled. Their lofs in men amounted to
800: the number of Englifh killed in this engage-

ment

ment did not exceed 200, including captain Saumarez, a gallant officer, who had served under lord Anson in his expedition to the Pacific Ocean. Indeed, it muſt be owned, for the honour of that nobleman, that all the officers formed under his example, and raiſed by his influence, approved themſelves in all reſpects worthy of the commands to which they were preferred. Immediately after the action, admiral Hawke diſpatched a ſloop to commodore Legge, whoſe ſquadron was ſtationed at the Leeward Iſlands, with intelligence of the French fleet of merchant-ſhips, outward-bound, that he might take the proper meaſures for intercepting them in their paſſage to Martinique, and the other French iſlands. In conſequence of this advice, he redoubled his vigilance, and a good number of them fell into his hands.

In the Mediterranean, vice-admiral Medley blocked up the Spaniſh ſquadron in Carthagena; aſſiſted the Auſtrian general on the coaſt of Villa Franca; and intercepted ſome of the ſuccours ſent from France to the aſſiſtance of the Genoeſe. At his death, which happened in the beginning of Auguſt, the command of that ſquadron devolved upon rear-admiral Byng, who proceeded on the ſame plan of operation. Commodore Griffin had been ſent with a reinforcement of ſhips, to aſſume the command of the ſquadron in the Eaſt Indies; and although his arrival ſecured Fort St. David's, and the other Britiſh ſettlements in that country, from the inſults of monſieur de la Bourdonnais, his ſtrength was not ſufficient to enable him to undertake any enterpriſe of importance againſt the enemy: the miniſtry of England therefore reſolved to equip a freſh armament, that, when joined by the ſhips in India, ſhould be in a condition to beſiege Pondicherry, the principal ſettlement belonging to the French on the coaſt of Coromandel: For this ſervice, a ſtrong ſquadron was ſent, under the conduct of rear-admiral Boſcawen, an officer of unqueſ-

6   tioned

tioned valour and capacity. In the courſe of this year, the Britiſh cruiſers were ſo alert and ſucceſsful, that they took 644 prizes from the French and Spaniards; whereas the loſs of Great Britain, in the ſame time, did not exceed 550.

All the belligerant powers were, by this time, heartily tired of a war which had conſumed an immenſity of treaſure, had been productive of ſo much miſchief, and in the events of which; all, in their turns, had found themſelves diſappointed. Immediately after the battle of Laffeldt, the king of France had, in a perſonal converſation with Sir John Ligonier, expreſſed his deſire of a pacification; and afterward his miniſter at the Hague preſented a declaration on the ſame ſubject, to the deputies of the ſtatesgeneral. The ſignal ſucceſs of the Britiſh arms at ſea, confirmed him in theſe ſentiments, which were likewiſe reinforced by a variety of other conſiderations. His finances were almoſt exhauſted, and his ſupplies from the Spaniſh Weſt Indies rendered ſo precarious, by the vigilance of the Britiſh cruiſers, that he could no longer depend on their arrival. The trading part of his ſubjects had ſuſtained ſuch loſſes, that his kingdom was filled with bankruptcies; and the beſt part of his navy now contributed to ſtrengthen the fleets of his enemies. The election of a ſtadtholder had united the whole power of the ſtatesgeneral againſt him, in taking the moſt reſolute meaſures for their own ſafety: his views in Germany were entirely fruſtrated; the ſucceſs of his arms in Italy had not at all anſwered his expectation: and Genoa was become an expenſive ally. He had the mortification to ſee the commerce of Britain flouriſh in the midſt of war, while his own people were utterly impoveriſhed. The parliament of England granted, and the nation payed, ſuch incredible ſums as enabled their ſovereign, not only to maintain invincible navies and formidable armies, but likewiſe to give ſubſidies to all the powers of Europe. His moſt christian

christian majesty, moved by these considerations, made farther advances toward an accommodation, both at the Hague and in London; and the contending powers agreed to a congress, which was opened in March, 1748, at Aix-la-Chapelle, where peace was signed the 7th of October following.

The British fleet in the East Indies, under the command of admiral Boscawen, undertook the siege of Pondicherry; but after the most vigorous attempts to take the place, the admiral was obliged to raise the siege, and return to Fort St. David.

Thus have we brought this war to a conclusion; and shall conclude with observing, that the number of prizes taken by the English, from the beginning to the signing the preliminaries of peace, was 3434; namely, 1249 from the Spaniards, and 2185 from the French: and that they lost, during the war, 3238; 1360 being taken by the Spaniards, and 1878 by the French. Several of the ships taken from the Spaniards were immensely rich; so that the balance upon the whole amounted to almost two millions, in favour of the English.

Notwithstanding a general peace was signed, yet the French gave continual proofs of their intention to observe it no longer than was consistent with their interest; and that they intended to make themselves masters of some parts of our settlements in America. In order to which, they built a chain of forts on the back of our colonies, from the Mississippi to Canada, and gained over great part of the Indians to their interest.

Every method of negotiation was tried to put an end to these disputes; but the repeated and undoubted intelligence received from France, Holland, Italy, &c. of the great naval preparations making in every port of France, and of a great number of veteran troops drawn out of their several corps, and destined for America, convinced the British ministry, that nothing was to be hoped for from a negotiation.

Accord-

Accordingly a ftrong fleet was fitted out in 1754, to fruftrate the defigns of the enemy, and protect the Britifh colonies in America.

Whilft all Europe was in fufpence about the fate of the Englifh and the French fquadrons, preparations for a vigorous fea-war were going forward in England with an unparalleled fpirit and fuccefs. Other branches of the public fervice went on with equal alacrity; and fuch was the eagernefs of the people to lend their money to the government, that inftead of one million, which was to be raifed by way of lottery, three millions eight hundred and eighty thoufand pounds were fubfcribed immediately.

Admiral Bofcawen, with eleven fhips of the line and a frigate, having taken on board two regiments at Plymouth, failed in April for the banks of Newfoundland: and, in a few days after his arrival there, the French fleet from Breft came to the fame ftation, under the command of M. Bois de la Mothe. But the thick fogs, which prevail upon thefe coafts, efpecially at that time of the year, kept the two armaments from feeing each other; and part of the French fquadron efcaped up the river St. Lawrence, whilft another part of them went round, and got into the fame river through the ftreights of Belleifle, by a way which was never known to be attempted before by fhips of the line. However, whilft the Englifh fleet lay off Cape Race, which is the fouthernmoft point of Newfoundland, two French fhips, the Alcide, of 64 guns and 480 men, and the Lys, pierced for 64 guns, but mounting only 22, being feparated from the reft of their fleet in a fog, were both taken, with feveral confiderable officers and engineers, and about eight thoufand pounds in money.

Though the taking of thefe fhips, from which the commencement of the war may in fact be dated, fell greatly fhort of what was hoped for from this expedition; yet, when the news of it reached England, it was of infinite fervice to the public credit of every kind,

and

and animated the whole nation, who now faw plainly
that the government was determined to keep no farther meafures with the French; but juftly to repel
force by force, and put a ftop to their fending more
men and arms to invade the property of the Englifh
in America, as they had hitherto done with impu-
nity. The French, who, for fome time, did not
even attempt to make reprifals on our fhipping,
would gladly have chofen to avoid a war at that time;
and to have continued extending their encroachments
on our fettlements, till they had executed their grand
plan of fecuring a communication from the Miffifippi
to Canada by a line of forts: many of thefe they
had already erected, and had alfo deftroyed one of
ours on the Ohio; whilft they endeavoured to amufe
us with fruitlefs negotiations about the boundaries of
Nova Scotia.

The vaft increafe of the French marine of late
years, which in all probability would foon be employed againft Britain, very properly occafioned an
order for making reprifals general in Europe as well
as in America; and that all the French fhips, whether
outward or homeward bound, fhould be ftopt and
brought into Britifh ports. To give the greater
weight to thefe orders, it was refolved to fend out
thofe admirals who had diftinguifhed themfelves moft,
toward the end of the laft war. Accordingly, Sir
Edward Hawke failed on a cruife to the weftward,
with 18 fhips of the line, a frigate and a floop; but,
not meeting with the French fleet, thefe fhips returned
to England. Another fleet, confifting of 22 fhips
of the line, two frigates, and two floops, failed again
on a cruife to the weftward, under admiral Byng, in
hopes of intercepting the French fquadron under
Duguay, and likewife that commanded by La Mothe,
in cafe of its return from America. But this fleet
likewife returned to Spithead, without having been
able to effect any thing; though it was allowed, that

the admiral had acted judiciously in the choice of his stations.

In the mean time, the French trade was so annoyed by the English cruisers, that, before the end of this year, 300 of their merchant-ships, many of which, from St. Domingo and Martinico, were extreamly rich ; and 8000 of their sailors were brought into English ports. By these captures the British ministry answered many purposes : they deprived the French of a great body of seamen, and withheld from them a very large property, the want of which greatly distressed their people, and ruined many of their traders. The outward-bound merchant-ships were insured at the rate of 30 per cent. whilst the English paid no more than the common insurance. This intolerable burden was felt by all degrees of people amongst them : their ministry was publicly reviled, even by their parliaments ; and the French name, from being the terror, began to be the contempt of Europe.

Though the English continued to make reprisals upon the French, not only in the seas of America, but also in those of Europe, by taking every ship they could meet with ; yet the French, whether from a consciousness of their want of power by sea, or that they might have a more plausible plea to represent England as the aggressor, were so far from returning these hostilities, that their fleet, which escaped Sir Edward Hawke, having taken the Blandford man of war, with governor Lyttelton on board, going to Carolina, they set the governor at liberty, as soon as the court was informed of the ship's being brought into Nantes, and shortly after released both the ship and the crew. However, at the same time, their preparations for a land-war still went on with great diligence ; and their utmost arts and efforts were fruitlessly exerted to persuade the Spaniards and Dutch to join with them against Great Britain.

The

The Englifh navy, fo early as in the month of
September, 1755, confifted of one fhip of 110 guns,
five of 100 guns each, thirteen of 90, eight of 80,
five of 74, twenty-nine of 70, four of 66, one of
64, thirty-three of 60, three of 54, twenty-eight of
50, four of 44, thirty-five of 40, and forty-two of
20 ; four floops of war of 18 guns each, two of 16,
eleven of 14, thirteen of 12, and one of 10 ; befide
a great number of bomb-ketches, firefhips, and tenders : a force fufficient to oppofe the united maritime
ftrength of all the powers in Europe. Whilft that of
the French, even at the end of this year, and including the fhips then upon the ftocks, amounted to no
more than fix fhips of 80, twenty-one of 74, one of
72, four of 70, thirty-one of 64, two of 60, fix of
50, and thirty-two frigates.

Under the cloak of an invading armament, which
engroffed the attention of the Britifh nation, the
French were actually employed in preparations for an
expedition, which fucceeded according to their wifh.
In the beginning of the year 1756, advice was received that a French fquadron would foon be in a
condition to fail from Toulon, confifting of 12 or 13
fhips of the line, with a great number of tranfports ;
that they were fupplied with provifion for two months
only, confequently could not be intended for America. Notwithftanding thefe particulars of information, which plainly pointed out Minorca as the object of their expedition ; notwithftanding the extenfive and important commerce carried on by the fubjects of Great Britain in the Mediterranean ; no proper care was taken to fend thither a fquadron of fhips
capable to protect the trade, and fruftrate the defigns
of the enemy. Nay, the miniftry feemed to pay
little or no regard to the remonftrance of general
Blakeney, deputy-governor of Minorca, who, in repeated advices, reprefented the weaknefs of the garrifon which he commanded in St. Philip's caftle,

the chief fortrefs on the ifland.   Far from ftrengthen-
ing the garrifon with a proper reinforcement, they
did not even fend thither the officers belonging to it,
who were in England upon leave of abfence; nor gave
direction for any veffel to tranfport them, until the
French armament was ready to make a defcent upon
that ifland.   At laft their defign was fo univerfally
known, that the miniftry could not any longer defer
fending fuccours to a place of fo much importance to
the trade of Great Britain.   Accordingly vice-admiral
Byng was fent with ten fhips of the line to the Mediterranean in April; and war was declared in May.·

When admiral Byng arrived at Gibraltar, he found
captain Edgecumbe with the Princefs Louifa fhip of
war, and a floop; who informed him, that the French
armament, commanded by Mr. de la Galiffoniere, confifting of 13 fhips of the line, with a great number
of tranfports, having on board a body of 15,000
land-forces, had made a defcent upon the ifland of
Minorca; from whence he (captain Edgecumbe) had
been obliged to retire at their approach.

This admiral, being ftrengthened by Mr. Edgecumbe, and reinforced by a detachment from the
garrifon, fet fail from Gibraltar on the 8th day of
May, and was joined off Majorca by his majefty's fhip
the Phœnix, captain Hervey, who confirmed the intelligence he had already received.   When he approached Minorca, he defcried the Britifh colours
ftill flying at the caftle of St. Philip's, and feveral
bomb-batteries playing upon it from different quarters, where the French banners were difplayed.   The
French fleet appeared foon after, to the fouth-eaft,
and the wind blowing ftrong off fhore, he formed the
line of battle.   About fix o'clock in the evening, the
enemy, to the number of 17 fhips, 13 of which appeared to be very large, advanced in order; but
about feven tacked, with a view to gain the weather-
gage. Mr. Byng, in order to preferve that advantage,
as well as to make fure of the land-wind in the morning,

ing, followed their example, being then about five leagues from Cape Mola.

At day-light the enemy could not be defcried; but foon re-appearing, the line of battle was formed on each fide; and, about two o'clock, admiral Byng threw out a fignal to bear away two points from the wind, and engage. At this time his diftance from the enemy was fo great, that rear-admiral Weft, perceiving it impoffible to comply with both orders, bore away with his divifion feven points from the wind; and, clofing down upon the enemy, attacked them with fuch impetuofity, that the fhips which oppofed him were in a little time driven out of the line. Had he been properly fuftained by the van, in all probability the Britifh fleet would have obtained a compleat victory: but the other divifion did not bear down, and the enemy's center keeping their ftation, rear-admiral Weft could not purfue his advantage without running the rifque of feeing his communication with the reft of the line entirely cut off.

In the beginning of the action, the Intrepid, of Mr. Byng's divifion, was fo difabled in her rigging, that fhe could not be managed, and drove on the fhip that was next in pofition: a circumftance which obliged feveral others to throw all a-back, in order to avoid confufion; and for fome time retarded the action. Certain it is, that Mr. Byng, though accommodated with a noble fhip of 90 guns, made little or no ufe of his artillery; but kept aloof, either from an over-ftrained obfervance of difcipline, or timidity. When his captain exhorted him to bear down upon the enemy, he very coolly replied, That he would avoid the error of admiral Matthews, who, in his engagement with the French and Spanifh fquadrons off Toulon, during the preceding war, had broke the line by his own precipitation, and expofed himfelf fingly to a fire that he could not fuftain. Mr. Byng, on the contrary, was determined againft acting, except with the line entire; and, on pretence of

recti-

rectifying the diforder which had happened among fome of the fhips, hefitated fo long, and kept at fuch a wary diftance, that he never was properly engaged, though he received fome few fhots in his hull. Mr. de la Galiffoniere feemed equally averfe to the continuance of the battle: part of his fquadron had been fairly obliged to quit the line; and though he was rather fuperior to the Englifh in number of men and weight of metal, he did not chufe to abide the confequence of a clofer fight: he therefore took advantage of Mr. Byng's hefitation, and edged away with an eafy fail to join his van, which had been difcomfited. The Englifh admiral gave chace; but the French fhips being clean, he could not come up and clofe with them again, fo they retired at their leifure. Then he put his fquadron on the other tack, in order to keep the wind of the enemy; and next morning they were altogether out of fight.

While, with the reft of his fleet he lay to, at the diftance of ten leagues from Mahon, he detached cruifers to look for fome miffing fhips, which joined him accordingly, and made an enquiry into the condition of the fquadron. Three of the capital fhips were fo damaged in their mafts, that they could not keep the fea, with any regard to their fafety: a great number of the feamen were ill, and there was no veffel which could be converted into an hofpital for the fick and wounded. In this fituation, Mr. Byng called a council of war, at which the land-officers were prefent. He reprefented to them, that he was much inferior to the enemy in weight of metal and numbers of men; that they had the advantage of fending their wounded to Minorca, from whence at the fame time they were refrefhed and reinforced occafionally; that, in his opinion, it was impracticable to relieve St. Philip's fort, and therefore they ought to make the beft of their way back to Gibraltar, which might require immediate protection. They unanimoufly concurred with his fentiments, and thither he directed

his

his courfe accordingly. How he came to be fo well acquainted with the impracticability of relieving general Blakeney, is not eafy to determine, inafmuch as no experiment was made for that purpofe. Indeed, the neglect of fuch a trial feems to have been the leaft excufable part of his conduct ; for it afterward appeared, that the officers and foldiers belonging to the garrifon might have been landed at the Sally-port, without running any great rifk; and a gentleman, then in the fort, actually paffed and repaffed in a boat, unhurt by any of the enemy's batteries.

Mr. Byng's letter to the admiralty, containing a detail of this action, is faid to have arrived fome days before it was made public ; and when it appeared, was curtailed of divers expreffions and whole paragraphs, which either tended to his own juftification, or implied a cenfure on the conduct of his fuperiors. Whatever ufe might have been made of this letter, while it remained a fecret to the public, we fhall not pretend to explain : but fure it is, that on the 16th day of June, Sir Edward Hawke and admiral Saunders failed from Spithead to Gibraltar, to fuperfede the admirals Byng and Weft, in their commands of the Mediterranean fquadron ; and Mr. Byng's letter was not publifhed till the twenty-fixth day of the fame month : when it appeared, it produced all the effect which that gentleman's bittereft enemies could have defired. The populace took fire like a train of combuftibles, and broke out in fuch a clamour of rage againft the devoted admiral, as could not have been exceeded, if he had loft the whole navy of England, and left the coafts of the kingdom naked to invafion. In a word, he was devoted as the fcape-goat of the m——y, to whofe mifconduct the lofs of that important fortrefs was undoubtedly owing. Byng's mifcarriage was thrown out like a barrel to the whale, in order to engage the attention of the people, that it might not be attracted by the real caufe of the national misfor-

E e 4   tune.

tune. In order to keep up the flame which had been kindled againſt the admiral, recourſe was had to the loweſt artifices. Agents were employed to vilify his perſon in all public places of vulgar reſort; and mobs were hired at different parts of the capital to hang and burn him in effigy.

The two officers who ſucceeded to his command in the Mediterranean were accompanied by the lord Tyrawley, whom his majeſty had appointed to ſuper-ſede general Fowke in the government of Gibraltar; that gentleman having incurred the diſpleaſure of the miniſtry for not having underſtood an order which was unintelligible. Directions were diſpatched to Sir Edward Hawke, that Byng ſhould be ſent home under arreſt: and an order to the ſame purpoſe was lodged at every port in the kingdom. He was accompanied by Mr. Weſt, general Fowke, and ſeveral other offi-cers, who were alſo recalled in conſequence of having ſubſcribed to the council of war, which we have men-tioned above. When they arrived in England, Mr. Weſt met with ſuch a reception from his majeſty as was thought due to his extraordinary merit; but Mr. Byng was committed cloſe priſoner in an apartment of Greenwich hoſpital.

From thence Mr. Byng was ſent to Portſmouth, where he was tried by a court-martial; the ſum of whoſe opinion was, that he did not do his utmoſt to relieve Minorca; and that during the engagement he did not do his utmoſt to take, ſeize, and deſtroy the ſhips of the French king, and aſſiſt ſuch of his own ſhips as were engaged. That he therefore fell under part of the twelfth article of war, and the court ad-judged him to be ſhot: but as it appeared to the court that it was neither through cowardice or diſaffection, they unanimouſly recommended him to mercy. How-ever, notwithſtanding this recommendation of the court-martial to his majeſty's mercy, and notwith-ſtanding the interceſſion made for him, an order was ſent down for the execution of the ſentence; and he

was

was shot on board the Monarque at Portsmouth, pitied by all the dispassionate part of the nation.

The loss of Minorca was severely felt in England, as a national disgrace; but, instead of producing dejection and despondence, it excited an universal resentment, not only against Mr. Byng, who had retreated from the French squadron, but also in reproach of the administration.

Sir Edward Hawke, being disappointed in his hope of encountering la Galissoniere, and relieving the English garrison of St. Philip's, at least asserted the empire of Great Britain in the Mediterranean, by annoying the commerce of the enemy, and blocking up their squadron in the harbour of Toulon. Understanding that the Austrian government at Leghorn had detained an English privateer, and imprisoned the captain, on pretence that he had violated the neutrality of the port; he detached two ships of war to insist, in a peremptory manner, on the release of the ship, effects, crew, and captain: and they thought proper to comply with his demand, even without waiting for orders from Vienna. The person in whose behalf the admiral thus interposed, was one Fortunatus Wright, a native of Liverpool; who, though a stranger to a sea-life, had, in the last war, equipped a privateer, and distinguished himself in such a manner, by his uncommon vigilance and valour, that, if he had been indulged with a command suitable to his genius, he would have deserved an honourable place in the annals of the navy. An uncommon exertion of spirit was the occasion of his being detained at this juncture. While he lay at anchor in the harbour of Leghorn, commander of the St. George privateer of Liverpool, a small ship of twelve guns and eighty men; a large French xebeque, mounted with sixteen cannon, and nearly three times the number of his complement, chose her station in view of the harbour, in order to interrupt the British commerce. The gallant Wright could not endure this insult:

2   notwith-

notwithstanding the enemy's superiority in metal and number of men, he weighed anchor, hoisted his sails, engaged him within sight of the shore, and after a very obstinate dispute, in which the captain, lieutenant, and above threescore of the men belonging to the xebeque were killed on the spot, he obliged them to sheer off, and returned to the harbour in triumph. This brave corsair would, no doubt, have signalized himself by many other exploits, had not he, in the sequel, been overtaken by a dreadful storm, in which the ship foundering, he and all his crew perished.

Sir Edward Hawke, having scoured the Mediterranean, and insulted the enemy's ports, returned with the homeward-bound trade to Gibraltar; from whence, about the latter end of the year, he set sail for England with part of his squadron, leaving the rest in that bay for the protection of our commerce.

No action of great importance distinguished the naval transactions of this year on the side of America. In the beginning of June, captain Spry, who commanded a small squadron, cruising off Louisbourg, in the island of Cape Breton, took the Arc en Ciel, a French ship of 50 guns, having on board near 600 men, with a large quantity of stores and provisions for the garrison. He likewise made prize of another French ship, with stores of the like destination. On the 27th day of July, commodore Holmes, being in the same latitude, with two large ships and a couple of sloops, engaged two French ships of the line and four frigates, and obliged them to sheer off, after an obstinate dispute.

A great number of privateers were equipped in this country, as well as in the West India islands belonging to the crown of Great Britain; and as these seas swarmed with French vessels, their cruizes proved very advantageous to the adventurers.

Scenes of still higher import were this year acted by the British arms in the East Indies. The English and French companies on the peninsula of Indus,

profeprosecuted their operations, no longer as auxiliaries to the princes of the country, but as principals and rivals, both in arms and commerce. Major Laurence, who now enjoyed the chief command of the English forces, obtained divers advantages over the enemy; when the progress of his arms was interrupted by an unfortunate event at Calcutta, the cause of which is not easily explained. Surajah Doula, viceroy of Bengal, Bakar, and Orixa, taking umbrage at the refusal of certain duties, to which he had laid claim, being particularly incensed at the English governor of Calcutta, for having granted protection to one of his subjects, whom he had outlawed; and, moreover, irritated by other practices of the company, which we cannot pretend to unfold, levied a numerous army, and marching to Calcutta, invested the place, which was then in no posture of defence. The governor, intimidated by the number and power of the enemy, abandoned the fort; and the defence of the place devolved to Mr. Holwell the second in command, who, with the assistance of a few gallant officers, and a very feeble garrison, maintained it with uncommon courage and resolution, against several attacks, until he was over-powered by numbers, and the enemy had forced their way into the castle. He was then obliged to submit; and the suba, or viceroy, promised, on the word of a soldier, that no injury should be done to him or his garrison. Nevertheless, they were all driven, to the number of 146 persons of both sexes, into a place, called the Black-hole prison, a cube of about 18 feet, walled up to the eastward and southward, the only quarters from which they could expect the least refreshing air, and open to the westward by two windows strongly barred with iron, through which there was no perceptible circulation.

The humane reader will conceive with horror the miserable situation to which they must have been reduced, when thus stewed up in a close sultry night,

under

under fuch a climate as that of Bengal. In the morning, the fuba being informed that the greater part of the prifoners were fuffocated, enquired if the chief was alive; and being anfwered in the affirmative, fent an order for their immediate releafe, when no more than 23 furvived of 146 who had entered alive.

By the reduction of Calcutta, the Englifh Eaft India company's affairs were fo much embroiled in that part of the world, that perhaps nothing could have retrieved them but the interpofition of a national force and the good fortune of a Clive; whofe enterprizes were always crowned with fuccefs. In confequence of the company's reprefentations to the government, a fmall fquadron of large fhips was fent to the Eaft Indies, under the command of admiral Watfon; and in the courfe of this year arrived at Fort St. David's. The governor of that fortrefs having received intelligence, that Tullagee Angria, a piratical prince in the neighbourhood of Bombay, was on the eve of concluding a treaty with the nation of the Marahattas, which might prove prejudicial to the interefts of the Englifh company; a refolution was taken to drive him from his refidence at Geriah, which was well fortified, and formidable to all the trading fhips of Europe. He maintained a confiderable number of armed gallies, called Grabs, with which he often attacked the largeft fhips, when they happened to be becalmed on that part of the coaft of Malabar. He was in the fourth generation from the firft freebooter, who rendered himfelf independent, and lived like a fovereign prince. The undertaking againft Angria was originally concerted with the Marahattas, who likewife equipped an armament both by fea and land againft Geriah; but they acted entirely on their own fcore: and in the reduction of the place gave no manner of affiftance to the Englifh.

Admiral Watfon failed from the coaft of Coromandel to Bombay, where his fquadron was cleaned and refitted; and having on board a body of troops commanded

manded by colonel Clive, he failed on the 7th day of February, and found in the neighbourhood of Geriah the Marahatta fleet, lying to the northward of the place, in a creek called Rajipore; and a land-army of horse and foot, amounting to 7 or 8000 men, commanded by Rhamagee Punt, who had already taken one small fort, and was actually treating about the surrender of Geriah. Angria himself had quitted the place; but his wife and family remained under the protection of his brother-in-law; who, being summoned to surrender by a message from the admiral, replied, that he would defend the place to the last extremity. In consequence of this refusal, the whole English fleet, in two divisions, failed into the harbour; and a shell being thrown into one of Angria's armed vessels, set her on fire, and the flames communicating to the rest, they were all destroyed: the fort was set on fire by another shell; and as the magazine of the fort afterward blew up, the governor was at length obliged to submit. In this place, which was reduced with a very inconsiderable loss, the conquerors found above 200 cannon, six brass mortars, a large quantity of ammunition; with money and effects to the value of 130,000 pounds. The fleet which was destroyed, consisted of eight grabs, one ship finished, two upon the stocks, and a good number of gallivats. Among the prisoners, the admiral found Angria's wife, children, and mother, toward whom he demeaned himself with great humanity.

The admiral and Mr. Clive failed back to Madras in triumph, and there another plan was formed for restoring the company's affairs upon the Ganges; for recovering Calcutta, and taking vengeance on the cruel viceroy of Bengal: all which was happily executed.

In the course of the year 1756, the clamorous voice of dissatisfaction had been raised by a series of disappointments and miscarriages, which were imputed to want of intelligence, sagacity, and vigour in the administration:

tion : and the profpect of their acquiefcing in a con-
tinental war brought them ftill farther in contempt
and deteftation with the body of the people. In order to conciliate the good-will of thofe whom their
conduct had difobliged, to acquire a frefh ftock of
credit with their fellow fubjects, and remove from
their own fhoulders part of what future cenfure might
enfue ; they, in 1757, admitted into a fhare of the
adminiftration a certain fet of gentlemen, remarkable
for their talents and popularity, headed by Mr. Pitt
and Mr. Legge, the two moft illuftrious patriots of
Great Britain, alike diftinguifhed and admired for
their unconquerable fpirit and untainted integrity.
But the old junto found their new affociates very unfit for their purpofes. They could neither perfuade,
cajole, nor intimidate them into meafures which they
thought repugnant to the true intereft of their country : they were accordingly foon after difplaced.

What was intended as a difgrace to Mr. Pitt and
Mr. Legge, turned out one of the moft fhining circumftances of their character. The whole nation
feemed to rife up, as one man, in the vindication of
their fame ; every mouth was opened in their praife ;
and a great number of refpectable cities and corporations prefented them with the freedom of their refpective focieties, inclofed in golden boxes, as teftimo-
nials of their peculiar veneration. Nothing could be
more expreffive of that reverence which ever waits on
fuperior virtue, than the manner in which the nation
difplayed its refpect and affection for thofe two fellow
citizens; whofe names will always be dear to Britain,
while her fons are warmed with the flame of honefty
and freedom.

A great number of addreffes, dutifully and loyally
expreffed, follicited the king to reftore Mr. Pitt and
Mr. Legge to their former employments. Upon this
they refted the fecurity and honour of the nation, as
well as the public expectation of the fpeedy and fuccefsful iffue of a war, hitherto attended with difgraces

and

and misfortunes. Accordingly his majesty was graciously pleased to redeliver the seals to Mr. Pitt, appointing him secretary of state for the southern department, on the 29th day of June; and five days after, the office of chancellor of the exchequer was restored to Mr. Legge: promotions that afforded universal satisfaction.

The accumulated losses and disappointments of the preceding year, made it absolutely necessary to retrieve the credit of the British arms and councils, by some vigorous and spirited enterprize. A powerful fleet was ordered to be got in readiness to put to sea on the shortest notice, and ten regiments of foot were marched to the Isle of Wight. The naval armament, consisting of 18 ships of the line, beside frigates, fireships, bomb-ketches, and transports, was put under the command of Sir Edward Hawke, an officer, whose faithful services recommended him, above all others, to this command. Sir John Mordaunt was preferred to take the command of the land-forces; and both strictly enjoined to act with the utmost unanimity and harmony.

Europe beheld with astonishment these mighty preparations. The destination of the armament was wrapped in the most profound secrecy: it exercised the penetration of politicians, and filled France with very serious alarms. Various were the impediments which obstructed the embarkation of the troops for several weeks, while they expressed an eager impatience to signalize themselves against the enemies of the liberties of Europe: but the superstitious drew unfavourable presages from the dilatoriness of the embarkation.

At last the transports arrived, the troops were put on board with all expedition, and the fleet got under sail on the 8th day of September, attended with the prayers of every man warmed with the love of his country, and solicitous for her honour. The public, big with expectation, dubious where the stroke would fall, but confident of its success, were impatient for

I   tidings

tidings from the fleet; but it was not till the 14th, that even the troops on board began to conjecture that a defcent was meditated on the coaft of France near Rochfort, or Rochelle. But though fome dif-pofitions were made toward a difembarkation, no troops were landed, except on the little ifland of Aix, fituated in the mouth of the river Charente, leading up to Rochfort. After a parade of deftroying the for-tifications here, this grand fleet returned to England. Such was the iffue of an expedition that raifed the expectation of all Europe, threw the coafts of France into the utmoft confufion, and coft the people of Eng-land little lefs than a million of money.

The fleet was no fooner returned than the whole nation was in a ferment. Certain it was, that blame muft fall fomewhere, and the m——y refolved to acquit themfelves, and fix the accufation, by requeft-ing his majefty to appoint a board of officers of cha-racter and ability to enquire into the caufes of the late mifcarriage. This alone was what could ap-peafe the public clamours, and afford general fatis-faction. Sir John Mordaunt was alfo tried, by his own defire, and acquitted.

Befide the diverfion intended by a defcent on the coaft of France, feveral other methods were employed to amufe the enemy, as well as to protect the trade of the kingdom, fecure our colonies in the Weft In-dies, and infure the continuance of the extraordinary fuccefs which had lately bleffed his majefty's arms in the Eaft Indies: but thefe we could not mention be-fore, without breaking the thread of our narration.

In February, admiral Weft failed with a fquadron of men of war to the weftward; as did admiral Coates with the fleet under his convoy to the Weft Indies: and commodore Stevens with the trade to the Eaft Indies, in the month of March. Admiral Holbourn, and commodore Holmes, with eleven fhips of the line, a firefhip, a bomb-ketch, and fifty tranfports, failed from St. Helen's for America in April. The

admiral

admiral had on board 6200 effective men, exclusive
of officers, under the command of general Hopson,
assisted by lord Charles Hay. In May, admiral Osborne, forced back to Plymouth with his squadron
by stress of weather, set sail to the Mediterranean;
as did two ships of war sent to convoy the American
trade.

In the mean time the privateers fitted out by
private merchants, and societies, greatly annoyed the
French commerce. The Antigallican, a private ship
of war, equipped by a society of gentlemen who
assumed that name, took the Duke de Penthievre
Indiaman off the port of Corunna, and carried her
into Cadiz. The prize was estimated worth 200,000
pounds; and immediate application was made by
France to the court of Spain for restitution, as the
French East India company asserted, it was taken
within shot of a neutral port. The Penthievre was
wrested out of the hands of the captors, detained as
a deposit, with sealed hatches, and a Spanish guard
on board, till the claims of both parties could be
examined; and at last was adjudged to be an illegal
capture, and restored to the French. Beside the success
which attended a great number of other privateers, the
lords of the admiralty published a list of above thirty
ships of war and privateers taken from the enemy, in
the space of four months, by the English sloops and
men of war; exclusive of the Duke de Aquitaine
Indiaman, now fitted out as a ship of war; the Pondicherry Indiaman, valued at 160,000 pounds; and
above six privateers, which last were brought into
port by the diligent and brave captain Lockhart, and
for which he was honoured with a variety of presents
of plate by several corporations. This turn of good
fortune was not, however, without some retribution
on the side of the enemy, who, out of 21 ships,
homeward-bound from Carolina, made prize of 19;
whence the merchants sustained considerable damage,

and a great quantity of valuable commodities, indigo in particular, was loft to this country.

The operations at fea, during the courfe of the year 1757, either in Europe or America, were far from being decifive or important. The commerce of Great Britain fuftained confiderable damage from the activity and fuccefs of French privateers. The Greenwich fhip of war of 50 guns, and a frigate of 20, fell into the hands of the enemy, together with a very confiderable number of trading veffels. On the other hand, the Englifh cruifers and privateers acquitted themfelves with equal vigilance and valour. The Duc d'Aquitaine, of 50 guns, was taken; the Aquilon, of nearly the fame force, was driven on fhore and deftroyed. A French frigate, of 26 guns, called the Emeraude, was taken by a fhip of inferior force under the command of captain Gilchrift, a gallant officer. All the fea-officers feemed to be animated with a noble emulation, to diftinguifh themfelves in the fervice of their country; and the fpirit defcended even to the captains of privateers, who, inftead of imitating the former commanders of that clafs, in avoiding fhips of force, and centering their whole attention in advantageous prizes, now encountered the armed fhips of the enemy, and fought with the moft obftinate valour in the purfuit of national glory.

Perhaps hiftory cannot afford a more remarkable inftance of defperate courage, than that which was exerted in December of the preceding year, by the officers and crew of an Englifh privateer, of 26 guns and 200 men, called the Terrible, under the command of captain William Death. He engaged, and made prize of, a large French fhip from St. Domingo, with the lofs of his own brother and 16 feamen: he then directed his courfe to England; but in a few days he had the misfortune to fall in with the Vengeance, a privateer of St. Malo, carrying 36 large

cannon,

cannon, with 360 men. Their firſt ſtep was to attack the prize, which was eaſily retaken; then the two ſhips bore down upon the Terrible, which maintained ſuch a furious engagement againſt both, as can hardly be paralleled in the annals of Britain. The French commander and his ſecond were killed, with two-thirds of his company; but the gallant captain Death, with the greater part of his officers, and almoſt his whole crew, having met with the ſame fate, his ſhip was boarded by the enemy, who found no more than 26 perſons alive, 16 of whom were mutilated by the loſs of legs or arms, and the other 10 grievouſly wounded. The ſhip itſelf was ſo ſhattered that it could ſcarcely be kept above water; and the whole exhibited a ſcene of blood, horror, and deſolation. The victor itſelf lay like a wreck on the ſurface; and in this condition made ſhift, with great difficulty, to tow the Terrible into St. Malo, where ſhe was not beheld without aſtoniſhment and terror. This adventure was no ſooner known in England, than a liberal ſubſcription was raiſed for the ſupport of Death's * widow, and that part of the crew which ſurvived the engagement.

In this, and every ſea-rencounter that happened within the preſent year, the ſuperiority in ſkill and reſolution, was aſcertained to the Britiſh mariners: for even when they fought againſt great odds, their courage was generally crowned with ſucceſs. In the month of November, captain Lockhart, a young gentleman, who had already rendered himſelf a terror to the enemy, as commander of a ſmall frigate, now added conſiderably to his reputation, by reducing the Melampe, a French privateer of Bayonne, greatly ſuperior to his ſhip, in men and metal; and

* There was a ſtrange combination of names belonging to this privateer: the Terrible, equipped at Execution-Dock, commanded by captain Death, whoſe lieutenant was called Devil, and he had one Ghoſt for his ſurgeon. It may be added, that it was taken by the Vengeance.

alſo

also another French adventurer, called the Countess of Gramont. A third large privateer of Bayonne was taken by captain Saumarez, of the Antelope. In a word, the narrow seas were so well guarded, that in a little time scarce a French ship durst appear in the English channel, which the British traders navigated without molestation. The British cruisers kept the sea during all the severity of the winter, in order to protect the commerce of the kingdom, and annoy that of the enemy. They exerted themselves with such activity, and their vigilance was attended with such success, that the trade of France was almost totally extinguished. A very gallant exploit was atchieved by one captain Bray, commander of the Adventurer, a small armed vessel in the government's service: falling in with the Machault, a large privateer of Dunkirk, near Dungeness, he ran her aboard, fastened her boltsprit to his capstan, and after a warm engagement, compelled her commander to submit. A French frigate, of 36 guns, was taken by captain Parker, in a new fireship of inferior force. Divers privateers of the enemy were sunk, burned, or taken; and a great number of merchant-ships fell into the hands of the English.

Nor was the success of the British ships of war confined to the English channel. An action happened off the island of Hispaniola, between three English ships of war and a French squadron. Captain Forrest had, in the ship Augusta, sailed from Port Royal in Jamaica, accompanied by the Dreadnought and Edinburgh, under the command of the captains Suckling and Langdon, to cruize off Cape François: and this service he literally performed, in the face of a French squadron lately arrived at that place from the coast of Africa. The commander, piqued at seeing himself thus insulted by an inferior armament, resolved to come forth and give them battle; and that he might either take them, or at least drive them out of these seas, so as to afford a free passage to a

great

3

great number of merchant-ships then lying at the Cape, bound for Europe; he took every precaution which he thought neceffary to infure fuccefs. He weighed anchor and ftood out to fea, having under his command four large fhips of the line, and three ftout frigates. They were no fooner perceived advancing, than capain Forreft held a fhort council with his two captains. "Gentlemen, (faid he) you know our own ftrength, and fee that of the enemy : fhall we give them battle?" They replying in the affirmative, he added, "Then fight them we will; there is no time to be loft : return to your fhips, and get them ready for engaging." After this laconic confultation among thefe three gallant officers, they bore down upon the French fquadron without further hefitation, and between three and four in the afternoon the action began with great impetuofity. The enemy exerted themfelves with uncommon fpirit, confcious that their honour was peculiarly at ftake, and that they fought in fight, as it were, of their own coaft, which was lined with people expecting to fee them return in triumph. But notwithftanding all their endeavours, their commodore, after having fuftained a fevere engagement that lafted two hours and a half, found his fhip in fuch a fhattered condition, that he made fignal for one of his frigates to come and tow him out of the line. His example was followed by the reft of his fquadron, which, with the favour of the land-breeze and the approach of night, made fhift to accomplifh their efcape from the three Britifh fhips, that were too much difabled in their mafts and rigging to profecute their victory. They were fo much damaged, that, being unable to keep the fea, they returned to Jamaica; and the French commodore feized the opportunity of failing with a convoy for Europe.

The courage of captain Forreft was not more confpicuous in his engagement with the French fquadron near Cape François, than his conduct and fagacity in

a fuba fubfequent adventure near Port au Prince, a Freneh harbour, fituated at the bottom of a bay on the weftern part of Hifpaniola. After Mr. de Kerfin had taken his departure from Cape François for Europe, captain Forreft was commanded by admiral Cotes to cruize off the ifland of Gonave for two days only, enjoining him to return at the expiration of the time, and rejoin the fquadron at Cape Nicholas. Accordingly, captain Forreft, in the Augufta, proceeded up the bay, between the ifland Gonave and Hifpaniola, with a view to execute a plan which he had himfelf projected. Next day in the afternoon, though he perceived two floops, he forbore chafing, that he might not rifque a difcovery: for the fame purpofe he hoifted Dutch colours, and difguifed his fhip with tarpaulins. At five in the afternoon, he difcovered feven fail of fhips fteering to the weftward, and hauled from them to avoid fufpicion; but at the approach of night gave chace with all the fail he could carry. About ten, he perceived two fail, one of which fired a gun, and the other made the beft of her way for Leoganne, another harbour in the bay. At this period, captain Forreft reckoned eight fail to leeward, near another fort called Petit Goave: coming up with the fhip which had fired the gun, fhe fubmitted without oppofition, after he had hailed and told her captain what he was, produced two of his largeft cannon, and threatened to fink her if fhe fhould give the leaft alarm. He forthwith fhifted the prifoners from this prize, and placed on board of her 35 of his own crew, with orders to ftand for Petit Goave, and intercept any of the fleet that might attempt to reach that harbour. Then he made fail after the reft, and in the dawn of the morning, finding himfelf in the middle of their fleet, he began to fire at them all in their turns, as he could bring his guns to bear: they returned the fire for fome time; at length three of them ftruck their colours. Thefe, being fecured, were afterward ufed in taking the other five. Thus,

by

by a well-conducted stratagem, a whole fleet of nine sail were taken by a single ship in the neighbourhood of four or five harbours, in any one of which they would have found immediate shelter and security.

The ministry having determined, in 1758, to make vigorous efforts against the enemy in North America, admiral Boscawen was vested with the command of the fleet destined for that service, and sailed from St. Helen's on February, when the Invincible of 74 guns, one of his best ships, run aground and perished.

In the course of the succeeding month, Sir Edward Hawke steered into the bay of Biscay with another squadron, in order to intercept any supplies from France designed for Cape-Breton or Canada ; and about the same time, the town of Emden, belonging to his Prussian majesty, which had fallen into the hands of the enemy, was suddenly retrieved by the conduct of commodore Holmes, stationed on that coast. Admiral Osborne, while he cruised between Cape de Gatt and Carthagena, on the coast of Spain, fell in with a French squadron, commanded by the marquis du Quesne, consisting of four ships; namely, the Foudroyant of 80 guns, the Orphée of 64, the Oriflamme of 50, and the Pleiade frigate of 24, in their passage from Toulon to reinforce M. de la Clue, who had for some time been blocked up by admiral Osborne in the harbour of Carthagena. The enemy no sooner perceived the English squadron than they dispersed, and steered different courses : Mr. Osborne detached divers ships in pursuit of each, while he himself, with the body of his fleet, stood off for the bay of Carthagena, to watch the motions of the French squadron which there lay at anchor. About seven in the evening, the Orphée struck to captain Storr in the Revenge. The Monmouth of 64 guns, commanded by captain Gardener, engaged the Foudroyant, one of the largest ships in the French navy, under the command of the marquis du Quesne. The action was maintained with great fury on both fides; and the gallant captain Gardener loft his life : neverthelefs the fight was continued with unabating vigour by his lieutenant Mr. Carkett, and the Foudroyant difabled in fuch a manner, that her commander ftruck as foon as the other Englifh fhips, the Swiftfure and the Hampton-court, appeared. This mortifying ftep, however, he did not take until he faw his fhip lie like a wreck upon the water, and the decks covered with carnage. The Oriflamme was driven on fhore under the caftle of Aiglos, by the fhips Montague and Monarque, commanded by the captains Rowley and Montague, who could not compleat their deftruction without violating the neutrality of Spain. As for the Pleiade frigate, fhe made her efcape.

This was a fevere ftroke upon the enemy, who not only loft two of their capital fhips, but faw them added to the navy of Great Britain ; and the difafter was clofe followed by another, which they could not help feeling with equal fenfibility of mortification and chagrin. In the beginning of April, Sir Edward Hawke difcovered off the ifle of Aix a French fleet at anchor, confifting of five fhips of the line, with fix frigates, and forty tranfports, having on board 3000 troops, and a large quantity of ftores and provifion, intended as a fupply for their fettlements in North America. They no fooner faw the Englifh admiral advancing, than they began to flip their cables and fly in the utmoft confufion. Some of them efcaped to fea, but the greater number ran into fhoal water, where they could not be purfued ; and next morning they appeared aground, lying on their broadfides. Sir Edward Hawke, who had rode all that night at anchor abreaft of the ifle of Aix, furnifhed the fhips Intrepid and Medway, with trufty pilots, and fent them farther in when the flood began to make, with orders to found a-head, that he might know whether there was any poffibility of attacking the enemy ; but the want of a fufficient depth of

water

water rendered this scheme impracticable. In the mean time, the French threw overboard their cannon, stores, and ballast; and the boats and launches from Rochefort, were employed in carrying out warps to drag their ships through the soft mud, as soon as they should be waterborne by the flowing tide. By these means, their large ships of war, and many of their transports, escaped into the river Charente; but their loading was lost, and the end of their equipment totally defeated. Another convoy of merchant-ships, under the protection of three frigates, Sir Edward Hawke, a few days before, had chaced into the harbour of St. Martin's, on the isle of Rhé, where they still remained, waiting an opportunity for hazarding a second departure: a third, consisting of twelve sail, bound from Bourdeaux to Quebec, under convoy of a frigate and armed vessel, was encountered at sea by one British ship of the line and two fireships, which took the frigate and armed vessel; and two of the convoy afterward met with the same fate: but this advantage was over-balanced by the loss of captain James Hume, commander of the Pluto fireship, a brave accomplished officer, in an unequal combat with the enemy: and by the unfortunate burning of admiral Broderick's ship, the Prince George of 80 guns, which happened in his passage to the Mediterranean.

On the 29th day of May, the Raisonable, a French ship of the line, mounted with 64 cannon, having on board 630 men, commanded by the prince de Mombazon chevalier de Rohan, was, in her passage from Port l'Orient to Brest, attacked by captain Dennis in the Dorsetshire of 70 guns; and taken after an obstinate engagement, in which 160 men of the prince's complement were killed or wounded, and he sustained great damage in his hull, sails and rigging.

The king of Great Britain, being determined to renew his attempt upon the coast of France, ordered a formidable armament to be equipped for that purpole.

pofe. Two powerful fquadrons by fea were deftined for the fervices of this expedition: the firft, confifting of eleven great fhips, was commanded by Lord Anfon and Sir Edward Hawke; the other, compofed of four fhips of the line, feven frigates, fix floops, two firefhips, two bombs, ten cutters, twenty tenders, ten ftore-fhips, and one hundred tranfports, under the direction of commodore Howe. A body of troops, confifting of fixteen regiments, nine troops of lighthorfe, and fix thoufand marines, was affembled for the execution of this defign, and embarked under the command of the duke of Marlborough, affifted by lord George Sackville. The troops, having for fome time been encamped upon the Ifle of Wight, were embarked in the latter end of May, and the two fleets failed in the beginning of June for the coaft of Bretagne, leaving the people of England flufhed with the gayeft hopes of victory and conqueft.

The two fleets parted at fea: lord Anfon with his fquadron proceeded to the bay of Bifcay, in order to watch the motions of the enemy's fhips, and harrafs their navigation.; while commodore Howe, with the land forces, fteered directly toward St. Malo, on the coaft of Bretagne, againft which the purpofed invafion feemed to be chiefly intended. The town, however, was found too well fortified to admit of any attempt with profpect of fuccefs; and. therefore it was refolved to make a defcent in the neighbourhood. After the fleet had been, by contrary winds, detained feveral days in fight of the French coaft, it arrived in the bay of Cancalle, about two leagues to the eaftward of St. Malo; where the troops were landed without much oppofition. The duke of Marlborough immediately began his march toward St. Servan, with a view. to deftroy fuch fhipping and magazines as might be in any acceffible parts of the river; and this fcheme was executed with fuccefs. A great quantity of naval ftores, two fhips of war, feveral privateers, and about fourfcore veffels of different forts, were fet on fire, and reduced to afhes, almoft

under

under the cannon of the place; which, however, they could not pretend to befiege in form. His grace, having received repeated advices that the enemy were bufily employed in affembling forces to march againft him, returned to Cancalle; where Mr. Howe had made fuch a mafterly difpofition of the boats and tranfports, that the reimbarkation of the troops was performed with furprifing eafe and expedition.

The Britifh forces being reimbarked, the fleet was detained by contrary winds in the bay of Cancalle for feveral days; during which a defign feems to have been formed for attacking Granville, and afterward for landing at Havre de Grace, and at Cherbourg: neither of which took effect, from the tempestuoufnefs of the weather. The fleet therefore fteered for the Ifle of Wight, and anchored at St. Helen's.

Such was the iffue of an enterprize atchieved with confiderable fuccefs, if we confider the damage done to the enemy's fhipping, and the other objects which the miniftry had in view; namely, to fecure the navigation of the channel, and make a diverfion in favour of our German allies, by alarming the French king, and obliging him to employ a great number of troops to defend his coaft from infult and invafion: but whether fuch a mighty armament was neceffary for the accomplifhment of thefe petty aims, is left to the reader's own reflection.

The defigns upon the coaft of France, though interrupted by tempeftuous weather, were not as yet laid afide for the whole feafon: but, in the mean time, the troops were difembarked on the Ifle of Wight. The duke of Marlborough and lord George Sackville being appointed to conduct this Britifh corps upon the continent, the command of the marine expeditions devolved to lieutenant-general Bligh, an old experienced officer, who had ferved with reputation; and his royal highnefs prince Edward, afterward created Duke of York, entered as a volunteer

with

with commodore Howe, in order to learn the rudiments of the sea-service.

Every thing being prepared for the second expedition, the fleet sailed from St. Helen's on the first of August; and after a tedious passage, anchored on the 7th in the bay of Cherbourg. Here, though they met with opposition, the troops made good their landing, two miles from the town; the French retired, and the English forces marching to Cherbourg, found it abandoned; and the gates being open, entered it without opposition. The next morning, the place being reconnoitred, the general determined to destroy, without delay, all the forts and the bason; and the execution of this design was left to the engineers, assisted by the officers of the fleet and artillery. Great sums of money had been expended upon the harbour and bason of Cherbourg, which at one time was considered by the French court as an object of great importance, from its situation respecting the river Seine, as well as the opposite coast of England; but as the works were left unfinished, in all appearance the plan had grown into disreputation. While the engineers were employed in demolishing the works, the light horse scoured the country. About twenty pieces of brass cannon were secured on board the English ships; a contribution was exacted upon the town; and a plan of reimbarkation concerted: as it appeared from the reports of peasants and deserters, that the enemy, who encamped about four leagues off, were already increased to a formidable number. The forces marched from Cherbourg down to the beach, and reimbarked without the least disturbance from the enemy.

This service being happily performed, the fleet anchored in the bay of St. Lunaire, two leagues to the westward of St. Malo, against which it was determined to make another attempt. The troops landed on a fair open beach, and a detachment of grenadiers was sent to the harbour of St. Briac, above the

town

town of St. Malo, where they deftroyed above 15
fmall veffels. But St. Malo being properly furveyed,
appeared to be above infult, either from the land-
forces or the fhipping. The defign againft St. Malo
was therefore dropped; but the general being unwilling to reimbark without having taken fome ftep for
the further annoyance of the enemy, refolved to penetrate into the country; conducting his motions,
however, fo as to be near the fleet, which had, by
this time, quitted the bay of St. Lunaire, where it
could not ride with any fafety, and anchored in the
bay of St. Cas, about three leagues to the weftward.

General Bligh, with his little army, marched to
Guildo, at the diftance of nine miles, which he
reached in the evening. Next morning he proceeded
to the village of Matignon, where, after fome fmart
fkirmifhing, the French piquets appeared, drawn up
in order, to the number of two battalions; but having fuftained a few fhot from the Englifh field-pieces,
and feeing the grenadiers advance, they fuddenly difperfed. General Bligh continuing his route through
the village, encamped in the open ground about
three miles from the bay of St. Cas, which was this
day reconnoitred for reimbarkation: for he now received undoubted intelligence, that the duke d'Aiguil-
lon had advanced from Breft to Lambale, within fix
miles of the Englifh camp, at the head of twelve
regular battalions, fix fquadrons, two regiments of
militia, eight mortars, and ten pieces of cannon.
The bay of St. Cas was covered by an intrenchment
which the enemy had thrown up, to prevent or oppofe any difembarkation; and on the outfide of this
work, there was a range of fand-hills extending
along fhore, which could have ferved as a cover to
the enemy, from whence they might have annoyed
the troops in reimbarking: for this reafon, a propofal was made to the general, that the forces fhould be
reimbarked from a fair open beach on the left, between

tween St. Cas and Guildo; but this advice was rejected; and, indeed, the subsequent operations of the army favoured strongly of blind security and rash presumption.

Had the troops decamped in the night without noise, in all probability they would have arrived at the beach before the French had received the least intelligence of their motion : but instead of this cautious manner of proceeding, the drums were beaten at two o'clock in the morning, as if with intention to give notice to the enemy, who forthwith repeated the same signal. The troops were in motion before three, and though the length of the march did not exceed three miles, the halts and interruptions were so numerous and frequent, that they did not arrive on the beach of St. Cas till nine. Then the embarkation was begun, and might have been happily finished, had the transports lain near the shore, and received the men as fast as the boats could have conveyed them on board without distinction; but many ships rode at a considerable distance, and every boat carried the men on board the respective transports to which they belonged; a punctilio of disposition, by which a great deal of time was unnecessarily consumed.

The British forces had skirmished a little on the march, but no considerable body of the enemy appeared until the embarkation was begun; then they took possession of an eminence by a wind-mill, and forthwith opened a battery of ten cannon and eight mortars, from whence they fired with considerable effect upon the soldiers on the beach, and on the boats in their passage. Many swam toward the boats and vessels, which were ordered to give them all manner of assistance; but by far the greater number were either butchered on the beach, or drowned in the water. About 1000 chosen men of the English army were killed and taken prisoners on this occasion : nor was the advantage cheaply purchased by

the

the French troops, among whom the shot and shells from the frigates and ketches had done great execution.

The whole strength of Great Britain, during the campaign of 1758, was not exhausted in petty descents on the coast of France. The continent of America was the great theatre on which her chief vigour was displayed; nor did she fail to exert herself in successful efforts against the French settlements on the coast of Africa: there, a small squadron without much trouble, took possession of Fort Louis and the town of Senegal. But the attempt on Goree miscarried; though the failure was not attended with any great loss. This settlement was however taken afterward by a small squadron under commodore Keppel, after a warm but short dispute.

Scenes of still greater importance were acted in North America, where, exclusive of the fleet and marines, the government had assembled about 50,000 men, including 22,000 regular troops. About 12,000 of these were destined to undertake the siege of Louisbourg, on the island of Cape Breton. The reduction of Louisbourg, being an object of immediate consideration, was undertaken with all possible dispatch. Major-general Amherst, being joined by admiral Boscawen, with the fleet and forces from England, the whole armament, consisting of 157 sail, took their departure from the harbour of Halifax, in Nova Scotia; and on the 2d of June part of the transports anchored in the bay of Gabarus, about 7 miles to the westward of Louisbourg. The garrison of this place, commanded by the chevalier Drucour, consisted of 2500 regular troops, 300 militia, formed of the burghers; and toward the end of the siege, they were reinforced by 350 Canadians, including 60 Indians. The harbour was secured by six ships of the line, and five frigates, three of which the enemy sunk across the harbour's mouth, in order to render it inaccessible to the English shipping. The governor

nor had taken all the precautions in his power to prevent a landing, by establishing a chain of posts along
the most accessible parts of the beach : but there
were some intermediate places which, could not be
properly secured, and in one of these the English
troops were disembarked ; on which occasion brigadier Wolfe distinguished himself greatly.

The landing was not effected, however, without
an obstinate opposition : and the stores, with the artillery, being brought on shore, the town of Louisbourg was formally invested.   The difficulty of landing stores and implements in boisterous weather, and
the nature of the ground, which, being marshy, was
unfit for the conveyance of heavy cannon, retarded
the operations of the siege ; and Mr. Amherst made
his approaches with great circumspection.   A very
severe fire, well directed, was maintained against the
besiegers and their work, from the town, the island
battery, and the ships in the harbour ; and divers
sallies were made, though without much effect.   Beside the regular approaches to the town, conducted
by the engineers, under the immediate command and
inspection of general Amherst, divers batteries were
raised by the detached corps under brigadier Wolfe,
who exerted himself with amazing activity.   The
three great ships, the Entreprenant, Capricieux, and
Celebre, were set on fire by the bomb-shells, and
burned to ashes ; so that none remained but the Prudent and Bienfaisant, which the admiral undertook
to destroy.   For this purpose, the boats of the squadron were detached into the harbour in the night
time, through a terrible fire.   The Prudent, being
aground, was set on fire, and destroyed ; but the
Bienfaisant was towed out of the harbour in triumph.

In the prosecution of the siege, the admiral and
general co-operated with remarkable harmony : the
fire of the town was also managed with equal skill
and activity, and kept up with great perseverance ;
until, at length, their shipping being all taken or
destroyed,

deftroyed, and divers practicable breaches effected,
the governor was conftrained to fubmit.

Thus, at the expence of about 400 men killed or
wounded, the Englifh obtained poffeffion of the important ifland of Cape Breton, and the ftrong town
of Louifbourg; in which the victors found 221
pieces of cannon, 18 mortars, and a confiderable
quantity of ftores and ammunition. The lofs of
Louifbourg was the more feverely felt by the French
king, as it had been attended with the deftruction
of fo many confiderable fhips.

In the Eaft Indies the tranfactions of the war were
chequered with a variety of fuccefs; but, on the
whole, the defigns of the enemy were entirely defeated. The French king had fent a confiderable reinforcement to the Eaft Indies, under the command
of general Lally, with fuch a number of fhips as
rendered the fquadron of Mr. d'Apché fuperior to
that of admiral Pocock; who fucceeded after the
death of admiral Watfon, to the command of the
Englifh fquadron, ftationed on the coaft of Coromandel; which, in the beginning of this year, was
reinforced from England with feveral fhips, under
the direction of commodore Stevens. Immediately
after this junction, admiral Pocock, who had already
fignalized himfelf by his courage and conduct, failed
to intercept the French fquadron, of which he had
received intelligence. In two days he defcried in the
road of Fort St. David the enemy's fleet, confifting of
nine fhips; which immediately ftood out to fea, and
formed the line of battle a-head. The admiral took
the fame precaution, and, bearing down upon Mr.
d'Apché, the engagement began about three in the
afternoon. The French commodore, having fuftained a warm action for about four hours, bore away
with his whole fleet; and being joined by two fhips,
formed a line of battle again to leeward. Admiral
Pocock's own fhip, and fome others, being greatly
damaged in their mafts and rigging, two of his cap-

tains having mifbehaved in the action, and night coming on, he did not think it advifeable to purfue them clofely ; .neverthelefs, he followed them at a proper diftance, and maintained the weather gage, in cafe he fhould be able to renew the action in the morning. However, in the morning, not the leaft veftige of them appeared. Such was the iffue of the firft action between the Englifh and French fquadrons in the Eaft Indies, which, over and above the lofs of a capital fhip, difabled and run afhore, is faid to have coft the enemy about 500 men, whereas the Britifh admiral did not lofe one fifth part of that number.

In the mean time, Mr. Lally had difembarked his troops at Pondicherry, and, taking the field, immediately invefted the fort of St. David, while the fquadron blocked it up by fea ; two Englifh fhips being at anchor in the road when the enemy arrived, their captains, feeing no poffibility of efcaping, ran them on fhore, fet them on fire, and retired with their men into the fortrefs, which, however, was in a few days furrendered. Admiral Pocock having, to the beft of his power, repaired his fhips, fet fail again, in order to attempt the relief of Fort St. David's ; but notwithftanding his utmoft endeavours, could not reach it in time to be of any fervice. On the 30th day of May he came in fight of Pondicherry, from whence the French fquadron ftood away early next morning ; nor was it in his power to come up with them, though he made all poffible efforts for that purpofe. He failed a third time in queft of Mr. Apché, and in two days perceived his fquadron, confifting of eight fhips of the line and a frigate, at anchor in the road of Pondicherry. They no fooner defcried him advancing, than they ftood out to fea as before, and he continued to chace, in hope of bringing them to an engagement ; but all his endeavours proved fruitlefs, till the 3d day of Auguft, when, having obtained the weather-gage, he bore down upon them in order of battle. The engagement began

gan

gan with great impetuofity on both fides, but in little
more than ten minutes Mr. d'Apché fet his fore-
fail and bore away, his whole fquadron following his
example, and maintaining a running fight in a very
irregular line. The Britifh admiral then hoifted the
fignal for a general chace, which the enemy perceiving, thought proper to cut away their boats, and
croud with all the fail they could carry. They
efcaped by favour of the night into the road of Pondicherry, and Mr. Pocock anchored with his fquadron off Carical, a French fettlement; having thus
obtained an undifputed victory, with the lofs of 30
men killed. The French fleet was fo much damaged,
that their commodore failed for the ifland of Bourbon,
in the fame latitude with Madagafcar, in order to
refit; thus leaving the command and fovereignty of
the Indian feas to the Englifh admiral.

Previous to the more capital operations by fea, we
fhall fpecify the moft remarkable captures that were
made upon the enemy by fingle fhips of war, during
the courfe of the fummer and autumn, 1759. A
French privateer, belonging to Granville, called the
Marquis de Marigny, of 20 guns and 200 men, was
taken by captain Parker, of the Montague; who
likewife made prize of a fmaller armed veffel, from
Dunkirk, of 8 cannon and 60 men. About the
fame period, captain Graves, of the Unicorn, brought
in the Moras privateer of St. Malo, of 22 guns and
200 men. Two large merchant-fhips, loaded on the
French king's account, for Martinique, with ftores
for the troops on that ifland, were taken by captain
Lendrick, of the Brilliant. Captain Hood, of the
Veftal, belonging to a fmall fquadron commanded by
admiral Holmes, who had failed for the Weft Indies
in January, being advanced a confiderable way a-head
of the fleet, defcried and gave chace to the Bellona,
of 32 guns and 220 men. Captain Hood, having
made a fignal to the admiral, continued the chace
until he advanced within half mufket-fhot of the

enemy, and then poured in a broadside, which was immediately retorted. The engagement was maintained with great vigour on both sides, for the space of four hours; at the expiration of which, the Bellona struck, after having lost all her masts and rigging, with about 40 men killed in the action: nor was the victor in a much better condition. The Bellona had sailed in January from the island of Martinique, along with the Florissant, and another French frigate, from which she had been separated in the passage.

Immediately after this exploit, captain Elliot, of the Æolus frigate, accompanied by the Isis, made prize of French ship, the Mignonne, of 20 guns and 140 men; one of four frigates employed as a convoy to a large fleet of merchant-ships, near the island of Rhée.

In the month of March, the English frigates the Southampton and Melampe, commanded by the captains Gilchrist and Hotham, being at sea to the northward on a cruise, fell in with the Danae, of 40 cannon, and 330 men, which was engaged by captain Hotham in a ship of half the force, who maintained the battle a considerable time with admirable gallantry, before his consort could come to his assistance. As they fought in the dark, captain Gilchrist was obliged to lie by for some time, because he could not distinguish the one from the other; but no sooner did the day appear than he bore down upon the Danae, and soon compelled her to surrender.

Another remarkable exploit was about the same juncture achieved by captain Barrington, of the Achilles, of 60 cannon, who, to the westward of Cape Finisterre, encountered a French ship of equal force, called the Count de St. Florentin; who was obliged to strike after a close and obstinate engagement. Captain Falkner, in the Windsor, of 60 guns, cruising to the westward, discovered four large ships to leeward; which formed the line of battle a-head,

in

in order to give him a warm reception. He clofed
with the fternmoft fhip, which fuftained his fire about
an hour: then the other three bearing away, fhe
ftruck her colours, and was conducted to Lifbon.
She proved to be the Duc de Chartres, pierced for
60 cannon, though at that time carrying no more
than 24, with 300 men. She belonged, with the
other three that efcaped, to the French Eaft India
company, was loaded with gunpowder and naval
ftores, and bound for Pondicherry.

In the month of May, a French frigate, called
the Arethufa, of 32 guns, and well manned, fubmitted to two Britifh frigates, the Venus and the
Thames, commanded by the captains Harrifon and
Colby.

Several armed fhips of the enemy, and rich prizes,
were taken in the Weft Indies; particularly two
French frigates, and two Dutch fhips with French
commodities, all richly laden, by fome of the fhips
of the fquadron which vice-admiral Cotes commanded
in the Jamaica ftation. But notwithftanding the vigilance and courage of the Englifh cruizers in thofe
feas, the French privateers fwarmed to fuch a degree,
that, in the courfe of this year, they took above 200
fail of Britifh fhips, valued at 600,000 pounds fterling.
This their fuccefs is the more remarkable, as by this
time the ifland of Guadalupe was in poffeffion of the
Englifh, and commodore Moore commanded a numerous fquadron in thofe very latitudes.

Having taken notice of fome remarkable captures
that were made by fingle fhips, we fhall now proceed
to defcribe the actions that were performed in this period by the different fquadrons of Great Britain. Intelligence having been received, that the enemy meditated an invafion upon fome of the Britifh territories, and that a number of flat-bottomed boats were
prepared at Havre de Grace, for the purpofe of dif-
embarking troops; rear-admiral Rodney was detached with a fmall fquadron of fhips and bombs, to

Gg 3

over-

overawe that part of the coaft of France. He accordingly anchored in the road of Havre, and made a difpofition to execute the inftructions he had received.
The bomb veffels being placed in the narrow channel
of the river leading to Honfleur, began to throw their
fhells, and continued the bombardment for 52 hours,
without intermiffion; during which, a numerous body
of French troops was employed in throwing up entrenchments, erecting new batteries, and firing both
fhot and fhells upon the affailants.   The town was fet
on fire in feveral places, and burned with great fury;
fome of the boats were overturned, and a few of
them reduced to afhes, while the inhabitants forfook
the place in the utmoft confternation: neverthelefs,
the damage done to the enemy was too inconfiderable
to make amends for the expence of the armament,
and the lofs of 1900 fhells and 1100 carcaffes, which
were expended on this expedition.   Bombardments
of this kind are at beft but expenfive and unprofitable
operations, and may be deemed a barbarous method
of profecuting war; inafmuch as the damage falls
rather upon the innocent inhabitants, than on the
government.

The honour of the Britifh flag was much more
effectually afferted by the gallant admiral Bofcawen,
who was entrufted with the conduct of a fquadron in
the Mediterranean. It mult be owned, however,
that his firft attempt favoured of temerity.   Having
in vain difplayed the Britifh flag in fight of Toulon,
by way of defiance to the French fleet that there lay
at anchor; he ordered three fhips of the line, commanded by the captains Smith, Harland, and Barker, to advance and burn two fhips that lay clofe to
the mouth of the harbour.   They accordingly approached with great intrepidity, and met with a very
warm reception from divers batteries which they had
not before perceived: fo that they were towed off
with great difficulty, in a very fhattered condition.
The admiral feeing three of his beft fhips fo roughly
                                                handled

handled in this enterprize, returned to Gibraltar in
order to refit; and M. de la Clue, commander of
the fquadron at Toulon, feized this opportunity of
failing, in hope of paffing the Streights mouth un-
obferved; his fleet confifting of 12 large fhips and
3 frigates.   Admiral Bofcawen, who commanded 14
fail of the line, with 2 frigates, and as many firefhips,
having refitted his fquadron, detached 2 frigates to
keep a good look-out, and give timely notice in cafe
the enemy fhould approach.   On the 17th of Auguft,
in the evening, the Gibraltar frigate made a fignal
that 14 fail appeared on the Barbary fhore.   Upon
which the Englifh admiral immediately went to fea:
at day-light he defcried feven large fhips lying to;
but when the Englifh fquadron did not anfwer their
fignal, they difcovered their miftake, fet all their
fails, and made the beft of their way.   Even now
perhaps he might have efcaped, had he not been
obliged to wait for the Souveraine, which was a
heavy failer.   At noon the wind, which had blown a
frefh gale, died away; and it was fome time before
his headmoft fhips could clofe with the rear of the
enemy; which, though greatly out-numbered, fought
with uncommon bravery.   The Englifh admiral,
without waiting to return the fire of the fternmoft,
ufed all his endeavours to come with the Ocean,
which Mr. de la Clue commanded in perfon; and
about four o'clock in the afternoon, running athwart
her hawfe, poured into her a furious broadfide: thus
the engagement began with equal vigour on both
fides.   This difpute, however, was of fhort duration; in about half an hour admiral Bofcawen's
mizen-maft and topfail yards were fhot away; and
the enemy hoifted all the fail they could carry.   Mr.
Bofcawen, having fhifted his flag from the Namur to
the Newark, joined fome other fhips in attacking the
Centaur of 74 guns, which, being thus overpowered,
was obliged to furrender.   The Britifh admiral purfued them all night, during which the Souveraine

G g 4   and

and Guerrier altered their courfe, and deferted their
commander. At day-break, Mr. de la Clúe, whofe
left leg had been broke in the engagement, perceived
the Englifh fquadron crowding all their fails to come
up with him, and finding himfelf on the coaft of
Portugal, determined to burn his fhips rather than
they fhould fall into the hands of the victors. The
Ocean was run afhore two leagues from Lagos, near
the fort of Almadana, the commander of which fired
three fhots at the Englifh: another captain of the
French fquadron followed the example of his commander; and both endeavoured to difembark their
men: but the fea being rough, this proved a very
tedious and difficult attempt. The captains of the
Temeraire and Modefte, inftead of deftroying their
fhips, anchored as near as they could to the forts
Exavier and Lagres, in hope of enjoying their protection; but in this hope they were difappointed.
Mr. de la Clue had been landed, and the command of
the Ocean was left to the count de Carne; who having received one broadfide from the America, ftruck
his colours, and the Englifh took poffeffion of this
noble prize, the beft fhip in the French navy, mounted
with 80 cannon. Captain Bentley of the Warfpight,
who had remarkably fignalized himfelf by his courage
during the action of the preceding day, attacked the
Temeraire of 74 guns, and brought her off with
little damage. Vice-admiral Broderick, the fecond
in command, advancing with his divifion, burned the
Redoubtable of 74 guns, which was bulged and
abandoned by her men and officers; but they made
prize of the Modefte, carrying 64 guns, which had
not been much injured in the engagement. This
victory was obtained by the Englifh admiral at a very
fmall expence of men; the whole number of the
killed and wounded not exceeding 250 on board of
the Britifh fquadron; though the carnage among the
enemy muft have been much more confiderable: but
the moft fevere circumftance of this difafter was the

lofs

lofs of four capital fhips, two of which were deftroyed, and the other two brought in triumph to England, to be numbered among the beft bottoms of the Britifh navy. What augmented the good fortune of the victors, was, that not one officer loft his life in the engagement.

The court of Verfaille•, in order to embarrafs the Britifh miniftry, and divert their attention from all external expeditions, had, in the winter, projected a plan for invading fome part of the Britifh dominions; and, in the beginning of the year, had actually begun to make preparations on different parts of their coaft, for carrying this defign into execution. Every pre-cautionary ftep was, however, taken to fruftrate their intentions; but the adminiftration wifely placed their chief dependence upon the ftrength of the navy; part of which was fo divided and ftationed, as to block up all the harbours of France, in which the enemy were known to make any naval armament of confequence. Notwithftanding the difafter of Mr. de la Clue, the French miniftry perfifted in their defign: toward the execution of which, they had prepared another confiderable fleet, at the harbours of Roch-fort, Breft, and Port-Louis, to be commanded by Mr. de Conflans, and reinforced by a confiderable body of troops. Flat-bottomed boats, and tranf-ports to be ufed in this expedition, were prepared in different ports on the coaft of France; and a fmall fquadron was equipped at Dunkirk, under the com-mand of an enterprifing adventurer called Thurot, who had, in the courfe of the preceding year, figna-lized his courage and conduct in a large privateer called the Belleifle.

This man's name became a terror to the merchants of Great Britain; for his valour was not more re-markable in battle than his conduct in eluding the purfuit of the Britifh cruifers, who were fucceffively detached in queft of him. The court of Verfailles was not infenfible to his merit. He obtained a commiffion

miffion from the French king, and was vefted with the command of the fmall armament now fitting out in the harbour of Dunkirk.

The Britifh government, apprifed of all thefe particulars, took fuch meafures to defeat the propofed invafion, as muft have conveyed a very high idea of the power of Great Britain to thofe who confidered, that, exclufive of the force oppofed to this defign, they at the fame time carried on the moft vigorous and important operations of war in Germany, America, the Eaft and Weft Indies. Thurot's armament at Dunkirk was watched by an Englifh fquadron in the Downs, commanded by commodore Boys; the port of Havre was guarded by rear-admiral Rodney; Mr. Bofcawen had been ftationed off Toulon; and the coaft of Vannes was fcoured by a fmall fquadron detached from Sir Edward Hawke, who had, during the whole fummer, blocked up the harbour of Breft, where Conflans lay with his fleet, in order to be joined by the other divifions of the armament. Thefe different fquadrons of the Britifh navy were connected by a chain of feparate cruifers; fo that the whole coaft of France, from Dunkirk to the extremity of Bretagne, were diftreffed by an actual blockade.

The French miniftry being thus hampered, forbore their attempt upon Britain; and the projected invafion feemed to hang in fufpence, till the month of Auguft, in the beginning of which their army in Germany was defeated at Minden. Their defigns in that country being baffled by this difafter, they feemed to convert their chief attention to their fea-armament; the preparations were refumed with redoubled vigour: even after the defeat of La Clue, they refolved to try their fortune in a defcent upon Ireland: and the young pretender remained in the neighbourhood of Vannes incognito, in order once more to hazard his perfon, and countenance a revolt in the dominions of Great Britain.

The

The execution of this fcheme was, however, pre-vented by the vigilance of Sir Edward Hawke, who blocked up the harbour of Breft, with a fleet of 23 ca-pital fhips; while another fquadron of fmaller fhips and frigates, under the command of captain Duff, con-tinued to cruife along the French coaft from Port L'Orient in Bretagne to the point of St. Gilles in Poitou. At length, however, in the beginning of November, the Britifh fquadron were driven from the coaft of France by ftrefs of weather, and on the 9th day of the month anchored in Torbay. Admi-ral Conflans fnatched this opportunity of failing from Breft, with 21 fail of the line and 4 frigates, in hope of being able to deftroy the Englifh fquadron commanded by captain Duff, before the larger fleet could return from the coaft of England. Sir Edward Hawke, having received intelligence that the French fleet had failed from Breft, immediately ftood to fea, in order to purfue them; and, in the mean time, the government iffued orders for guarding all thofe parts of the coaft that were thought the moft expofed to a defcent.

While thefe meafures were taken with equal vigour and deliberation, Sir Edward Hawke fteered his courfe directly for Quiberon, on the coaft of Bretagne, which he fuppofed would be the rendezvous of the French fquadron. On the 20th of November, he fell in with them, as they were giving chace to cap-tain Duff's fquadron, which now joined the large fleet, after having run fome rifque of being taken. Sir Ed-ward Hawke, who had formed the line a-breaft, now perceiving that the French admiral endeavoured to efcape, threw out a fignal for feven of his fhips that were nearest the enemy to chace, and endeavour to detain them, until they could be reinforced by the reft of the fquadron. Confidering the roughnefs of the weather, the nature of the coaft, which is in this place very hazardous, and entirely unknown to the Britifh failors, it required extraordinary refolution in

the

the Englifh admiral to attempt hoftilities on this occafion. With refpect to his fhips of the line, he had
but the advantage of one in point of number, and
no fuperiority in men or metal; confequently Mr.
de Conflans might have hazarded a fair battle in the
open fea, without any imputation of temerity: but
he thought proper to play a more artful game, and
retired clofe in fhore, with a view to draw the Englifh fquadron among the fhoals and iflands, while he
and his officers, who were perfectly acquainted with
the navigation, could either ftay, and take advantage of their difafter, or, if hard preffed, retire through
channels unknown to the Britifh pilots.

At half an hour after two, the van of the Englifh
fleet began the engagement with the rear of the enemy, in the neighbourhood of Belleifle. Every fhip
as fhe advanced poured in a broadfide on the fternmoft of the French, and bore down upon their van,
leaving the rear to thofe that came after. Sir Edward
Hawke, in the Royal George of 110 guns, referved
his fire in paffing through the rear of the enemy, and
ordered his mafter to bring him along-fide of the
French admiral, who commanded in perfon on board
of the Soleil Royal, of 80 guns and 1200 men.
When the pilot remonftrated that he could not obey
his command, without the moft imminent rifque of
running upon a fhoal, the brave veteran replied,
" You have done your duty in fhewing the danger ;
now you are to comply with my order, and lay me
along-fide the Soleil Royal." His wifh was gratified:
the Royal George ranged up with the French admiral. The Thefée, another large fhip of the enemy,
running up between the two commanders, fuftained
the fire referved for the Soleil Royal ; but in returning the firft broadfide foundered, in confequence of
the high fea that entered her lower deck-ports, and
fill'd her with water. Notwithftanding the boifterous weather, a good number of fhips on both fides
fought with equal fury and dubious fuccefs, till about

four

four in the afternoon, when the Formidable ftruck her colours. -The Superbe fhared the fate of the Thefée in going to the bottom. The Heros hauled down her colours in token of fubmiffion, and dropped anchor; but the wind was fo high, that no boat could be fent to take poffeffion. By this time day-light began to fail, and the greater part of the French fleet efcaped under colour of the darknefs.

Night approaching, the wind blowing with augmented violence on a lee-fhore, and the Britifh fquadron being intangled among unknown fhoals and iflands, Sir Edward Hawke made the fignal for anchoring to the weftward of the fmall ifland Dumet; and here the fleet remained all night in a very dangerous riding, alarmed by the fury of the ftorm, and inceffant firing of guns of diftrefs, without their knowing whether it proceeded from friend or enemy. The Soleil Royal had, under favour of the night, anchored alfo in the midft of the Britifh fquadron; but at day-break, Mr. de Conflans ordered her cable to be cut, and fhe drove afhore to the weftward of Crozie. The Englifh admiral immediately made fignal to the Effex to flip her cable and purfue her; but in obeying this order, fhe ran unfortunately on a fandbank, called Lefour, where the Refolution, another fhip of the Englifh fquadron, was already grounded. Here they were both irrecoverably loft, in fpite of all the affiftance that could be given: but all their men, and part of their ftores, were faved, and the wrecks burnt. He likewife detached the Portland, Chatham, and Vengeance, to deftroy the Soleil Royal, which was burned by her own people, before the Englifh fhips could approach; but they arrived time enough to reduce the Heros to afhes on Lefour, where fhe had been alfo ftranded: and the Jufte, another of their great fhips, perifhed in the mouth of the Loire.

The admiral perceiving feven large fhips of the enemy riding at anchor between Point Penvas and
the

the mouth of the river Vilaine, made the fignal to
weigh, in order to attack them; but the fury of the
ftorm increafed to fuch a degree, that he was obliged
to remain at anchor, and even ordered the top-gallant-
mafts to be ftruck.

In the mean time, the French fhips being lighten-
ed of their cannon, their officers took advantage of
the flood, and a more moderate gale under the land,
to enter the Vilaine; where they lay within half a
mile of the entrance, protected by fome occafional
batteries erected on the fhore, and by two large frigates, moored acrofs the mouth of the harbour.
Thus they were effectually fecured from any attempts
of fmall veffels; and as for large fhips, there was
not water fufficient to float them within fighting diftance of the enemy.

On the whole, this battle, in which a very inconfiderable number of lives were loft, may be confidered as one of the moft perilous and important actions that ever happened in any war between the two
nations: for it not only defeated the projected invafion, which had hung menacing fo long over the apprehenfions of Great Britain; but it gave the finifh-
ing blow to the naval power of France, which was
totally difabled from undertaking any thing of confequence in the fequel.

By this time, indeed, Thurot had efcaped from
Dunkirk, and directed his courfe to the North Sea,
whither he was followed by commodore Boys, who
neverthelefs was difappointed in his purfuit; but the
fate of that adventurer falls under the occurrences of
the enfuing year.

As for Sir Edward Hawke, he continued cruifing
off the coaft of Bretagne for a confiderable time after
the victory he had obtained, taking particular care
to block up the mouth of the river Vilaine, that the
feven French fhips might not efcape, and join Mr.
Conflans, who made fhift to reach Rochfort with the
fhattered remains of his fquadron. Indeed, this fervice

vice became such a considerable object in the eyes of
the British ministry, that a large fleet was maintained
upon this coast, apparently for no other purpose,
during a whole year; and, after all, the enemy
eluded their vigilance.

A plan had been formed for improving the success
of the preceding year in North America, by carrying
the British arms up the river St. Laurence, and be-
sieging Quebec, the capital of Canada. The armament employed against the French islands of Martinique and Guadalupe, constituted part of this design; inasmuch as the troops embarked on that expedition were, in case of a miscarriage at Martinique,
intended to reinforce the British army in North America, which was justly considered as the chief seat of
the war. Martinique was reduced to great distress
by the ruin of its trade, and by want of all, even necessary provisions, when the inhabitants every day
expected a visit from the British armament, whose
progress we are now to relate. In November of the
preceding year, captain Hugh's sailed from St. Helen's, with eight sail of the line, one frigate, four
bomb-ketches, and a fleet of transports, containing
land forces, under the command of major-general
Hopson. At Barbadoes they joined commodore
Moore, who now assumed the command of the united
squadrons, amounting to ten ships of the line, beside
frigates and bomb-ketches.

After an unsuccessful attempt on Martinique, the
failure of which it is not easy to account for, the
whole armament directed their course to Guadalupe,
another of the French Carribbee islands, lying 30
leagues to the westward. Having arrived at Basse-
terre, a council of war was held on board the commodore's ship; where it was resolved to make a general
attack by sea, upon the citadel, the town, and other
batteries by which it was defended. A disposition
being made for this purpose, the large ships took
their

their refpective ftations next morning, being the 23d
of January.

In this prefent attack, all the fea commanders behaved with extraordinary fpirit and refolution, particularly the captains Leflie, Burnet, Gayton, Jekyl,
Trelawney, and Shuldam; who, in the hotteft tumult of the action, diftinguifhed themfelves equally by their courage, impetuofity, and deliberation.
The four bombs being anchored near the fhore, began to ply the town with fhells and carcaffes; fo that
in a little time the houfes were in flames, the magazines of gunpowder blew up with the moft terrible
explofion, and about ten o'clock the whole place
blazed out one general conflagration.

Next day at two in the afternoon, the fleet come
to an anchor in the road of Baffeterre, where they
found the hulls of divers fhips which the enemy had
fet on fire at their approach : feveral fhips turned out
and endeavoured to efcape, but were intercepted and
taken by the Englifh fquadron. At five, the troops
landed without oppofition, and took poffeffion of the
town and citadel, which they found entirely abandoned.   They learned from a Genoefe deferter, that
the regular troops of the ifland confifted of five companies only, the number of the whole not exceeding
100 men; and that they had laid a train to blow up
the powder-magazine in the citadel : but had been
obliged to retreat with fuch precipitation, as did not
permit them to execute this defign.   The train was
immediately cut off, and the magazine fecured. The
nails with which they had fpiked up their cannon
were drilled out by the matroffes; and in the mean
time, the Britifh colours were hoifted on the parapet.
Part of the troops took poffeffion of an advantageous
poft on an eminence, and part entered the town,
which ftill continued burning with great violence.

In the morning, at day-break, the enemy appeared, to the number of 2000, about four miles from
the

the town, and began to throw up intrenchments in the neighbourhood of a houſe where the governor had fixed his head-quarters, declaring he would maintain his ground to the laſt extremity. In the mean time, the reduction of the iſlanders on the ſide of Guadalupe appearing more and more impracticable, the general reſolved to transfer the ſeat of war to the eaſtern and more fertile part of the iſland, called Grand-Terre; which, as we have already obſerved, was defended by a ſtrong battery, called Fort Louis. In purſuance of this determination, the great ſhips were ſent round to Grand-terre, in order to reduce this fortification, which they accordingly effected on the 13th of February. After a ſevere cannonading, which laſted ſix hours, a body of marines being landed, with the highlanders, they drove the enemy from their intrenchments ſword in hand, and, taking poſſeſſion of the fort, hoiſted the Engliſh colours.

In a few days after this exploit, general Hopſon dying at Baſſe-terre, the chief command devolved to general Barrington, who reſolved to proſecute the final reduction of the iſland with vigour and diſpatch.

In the mean time, commodore Moore having received certain intelligence that Monſ. de Bompart had arrived at Martinique with a ſquadron, conſiſting of eight ſail of the line and three frigates, having on board a whole battalion of Swiſs, and ſome other troops, to reinforce the garriſons of the iſlands; he called in his cruiſers, and ſailed immediately to the bay of Dominique, an iſland to the windward, at the diſtance of nine leagues from Guadalupe; whence he could always ſail to oppoſe any deſigns which the French commander might form againſt the operations of the Britiſh armaments.

Without entering into a detail of the proceedings of the land-forces, toward a reduction of the internal parts of the iſland, which was a work of ſome time; it is ſufficient to obſerve, that the inhabitants capitulated on May 1ſt, 1759, at the very time that

a confiderable reinforcement from Martinique had
landed on another part of the ifland; which on knowlege of this event, returned directly.

The town of Baffe-terre being reduced to a heap
of afhes, the inhabitants began to clear away the rubbifh, and erected occafional fheds, where they refumed their feveral occupations with that good humour fo peculiar to the French nation; and general
Barrington humanely indulged them with all the affiftance in his power.

Immediately after the capitulation of Guadalupe,
he fummoned the iflands called Santos and Defeada
to furrender; and they, together with Petit-terre,
fubmitted on the fame terms which he had granted to
the great ifland: but his propofal was rejected by the
inhabitants of Marigalante, which lies about three
leagues to the fouth-eaft of Grand-terre, extending
20 miles in length, 15 in breadth, flat and fertile,
but poorly watered, and ill-fortified. The general,
refolving to reduce it by force, embarked a body of
troops on board of tranfports, which failed thither
under convoy of three fhips of war and two bomb
veffels from prince Rupert's Bay; and at their appearance the iflanders fubmitting, received an Englifh
garrifon.

Three regiments were allotted as a fufficient guard
for the whole ifland, and the other three were embarked for England. General Barrington himfelf
went on board the Roebuck in the latter end of June,
and with the tranfports, under convoy of captain
Hughes, and a fmall fquadron, fet fail for Great Britain; while commodore Moore, with his large fleet,
directed his courfe to Antigua.

The reduction of Niagara, and the poffeffion of
Crown-point, were exploits much more eafily atchieved than the conqueft of Quebec, the great object to which all thefe operations were fubordinate.
Of that we now come to give the detail, fraught with
fingular events; in the courfe of which a noble fpirit
of

of enterprize was difplayed. It was about the middle
of February that a confiderable fquadron failed from
England for Cape Breton, under the command of the
admirals Saunders and Holmes : but the harbour was
blocked up with ice in fuch a manner, that they were
obliged to bear away for Halifax in Nova Scotia.
From hence admiral Saunders arrived at Louifbourg;
and the troops being embarked, to the number of
8000, proceeded up the river without further delay.
The operations at land were intrufted to the conduct
of major-general James Wolfe, whofe talents had
fhone with fuch fuperior luftre at the fiege of Louifbourg; and his fubordinates in command were the
brigadiers Monckton, Townfhend, and Murray.

The armament intended for Quebec failed up the
river St. Laurence, without having met with any interruption, or having perceived any of thofe difficulties and perils with which it had been reported that
the navigation of it was attended. Their good fortune in this particular, indeed, was owing to fome
excellent charts of the river, which had been found
in veffels taken from the enemy. About the latter
end of June the land-forces were difembarked in two
divifions upon the ifle of Orleans, fituated a little below Quebec. General Wolfe no fooner landed on
the ifland of Orleans than he diftributed a manifefto
among the French colonifts, explaining the nature of
the undertaking; that the hoftilities were intended
againft the fettlements and forces of the king of
France, but not againft the innocent inhabitants; af-
furing them of his protection while they gave him no
difturbance, which he fhewed them muft be ineffectual, and would only expofe them to his refentment.
This declaration produced no immediate effect; nor,
indeed, did the Canadians depend upon the fincerity
and promifed faith of a nation, whom their priefts had
induftrioufly reprefented as the moft favage and cruel
enemy on earth. Poffeffed of thofe notions, which
prevailed even among the better fort, they chofe to

abandon

abandon their habitations, and expose themselves and families to certain ruin, in provoking the English by the most cruel hostilities, rather than to be quiet, and confide in the general's promise of protection : so that Mr. Wolfe, in order to intimidate the enemy into a cessation of these outrages, found it necessary to connive at some irregularities in the way of retaliation.

Mr. de Montcalm, who commanded the French troops, though superior in number to the invaders, very wisely resolved to depend upon the natural strength of the country, which appeared almost insurmountable, and had carefully taken all his precautions of defence. The city of Quebec was skilfully fortified, secured with a numerous garrison, and plentifully supplied with provision and ammunition. Montcalm had reinforced the troops of the colony, and had taken the field, in a very advantageous situation, encamped along the shore of Beaufort, from the river St. Charles to the falls of Montmorenci; every accessible part being deeply intrenched. To undertake the siege of Quebec against such odds and advantages, was not only a deviation from the established maxims of war, but seemingly a rash enterprize : Mr. Wolfe was well acquainted with the difficulties of the undertaking; but he knew at the same time he should always have it in his power to retreat, in case of emergency, while the British squadron maintained its station in the river; and he was not without hope of being joined by general Amherst. Understanding that there was a body of the enemy posted, with cannon, at the Point of Levi, on the south shore, opposite to the city of Quebec, he detached against them brigadier Monckton, at the head of four battalions, who passed the river at night; and next morning, having skirmished with some of the enemy's irregulars, obliged them to retire from that post, which the English immediately occupied. At the same time colonel Carlton, with another detachment,

tachment, took poffeffion of the weftern point of the
ifland of Orleans; and both thefe pofts were fortified,
in order to anticipate the enemy, who, had they kept
poffeffion of either, might have rendered it impoffible
for any fhip to lie at anchor within two miles of
Quebec. Befide, the Point of Levi was within can-
non-fhot of the city, againft which a battery of mortars and artillery was immediately erected. Montcalm, forefeeing the effect of this expedient, detached
a body of fixteen hundred men acrofs the river, to
attack and deftroy the works before they were com-
pleted: but this detachment fell into diforder, fired
upon each other, and retired in confufion. The battery being finifhed, without further interruption, the
cannon and mortars began to play with fuch fuccefs,
that in a little time the upper town was confiderably
damaged, and the lower town reduced to a heap of
rubbifh.

In the mean time the fleet was expofed to the moft
imminent danger. Immediately after the troops had
been landed on the ifland of Orleans, the wind increafed to a furious ftorm, which blew with fuch
violence, that many tranfports ran foul of one another, and were difabled; a number of boats and
fmall craft foundered, and divers large fhips loft their
anchors. The enemy refolving to take advantage of
the confufion which they imagined this difafter muft
have produced, prepared feven firefhips, and at midnight fent them down from Quebec among the tranfports, which lay fo thick as to cover the whole fur-
face of the river. The fcheme, though well contrived, and feafonably executed, was entirely defeated by the deliberation of the Britifh admiral, and
the dexterity of his marines, who refolutely boarded
the firefhips, and towed them faft a-ground; where
they lay burning to the water's edge, without having
done the leaft prejudice to the Englifh fquadron. On
the very fame day of the fucceeding month, they fent

down a raft of firefhips, or radeaus, which were likewife confumed, without producing any effect.

The works for the fecurity of the hofpital, and the
ftores on the ifland of Orleans, being finifhed, the
Britifh forces croffed the north channel in boats, and
landing under the cover of two floops, encamped on
the fide of the river Montmorenci, which divided
them from the left of the enemy ; and next morning
a company of rangers, pofted in a wood to cover fome
workmen, were attacked by the French Indians, and
totally defeated : however, the neareft troops advancing, repulfed the Indians in their turn with confiderable lofs. On the 18th day of July, the admiral, at
general Wolfe's requeft, fent two fhips of war, two
armed floops, and fome tranfports, having troops on
board, up the river; and they paffed the city of
Quebec, without having fuftained any damage. The
general, being on board of this little armament, carefully obferved the banks on the fide of the enemy,
which were extreamly difficult from the nature of the
ground ; and thefe difficulties were redoubled by the
forefight and precaution of the French commander.
Though a defcent feemed impracticable between the
city and Cape Rouge, where it was intended, general
Wolfe, in order to divide the enemy's force, and procure intelligence, ordered a detachment, under the
command of colonel Carlton, to land higher up at the
Point Au Tremble; to which place he was informed,
a good number of the inhabitants of Quebec had retired with their moft valuable effects. This fetvice
was performed with little lofs, and fome prifoners
were brought away ; but no magazine was difcovered.

The general, thus difappointed in his expectation,
returned to Montmorenci, where brigadier Townfhend had, by maintaining a fuperior fire acrofs that
river, prevented the enemy from erecting a battery,
which would have commanded the Englifh camp :
and now he refolved to attack them, though pofted

to

to great advantage, and every where prepared to give him a warm reception. His defign was, firft to reduce a detached redoubt clofe to the water's edge; feemingly fituated without gun-fhot of the intrenchment on the hill. Should this fortification be fupported by the enemy, he forefaw that he fhould be able to bring on a general engagement: on the contrary, fhould they remain tame fpectators of its reduction, he could afterward examine their fituation at leifure, and determine the place at which they could be moft eafily attacked. Preparations were accordingly made for ftorming the redoubt: which was undertaken with great bravery, but the fire of the French was fo hotly maintained, that the Englifh were for that time obliged to give up the conteft. Had the attack fucceeded, the lofs of the Englifh muft have been very heavy, and that of the French inconfiderable; becaufe the neighbouring woods afforded them immediate fhelter: finally, the river St. Charles ftill remained to be paffed, before the town could be invefted.

Immediately after this mortifying check, in which above five hundred men, and many brave officers were loft, the general detached brigadier Murray, with twelve hundred men, in tranfports above the town, to co-operate with rear-admiral Holmes, whom the admiral had fent up with fome force againft the French fhipping, which he hoped to deftroy. The brigadier was likewife inftructed to feize every opportunity of fighting the enemy's detachments, and even of provoking them to battle. In purfuance of thefe directions, he twice attempted to land on the north fhore; but thefe attempts were unfuccefsful: the third effort was more fortunate; he made a fudden defcent at Chambaud, and burned a confiderable magazine, filled with arms, cloathing, provifion, and ammunition.

The difafter at the falls of Montmorenci made a deep impreffion on the mind of general Wolfe; he

H h 4   knew

knew the character of the English people, rash, impatient, and capricious; elevated to exultation by the least gleam of success, dejected even to despondency by the most inconsiderable frown of adverse fortune. Among those who shared his confidence, he was often seen to sigh, he was often heard to complain, and even in the transports of his chagrin, declare, that he would never return without success, to be exposed, as other unfortunate commanders had been, to the censure and reproach of an ignorant populace. This tumult of the mind, added to the fatigues of body he had undergone, produced a fever and dysentery; by which, for some time, he was totally disabled.

When we consider the situation of this place, and the fortifications with which it was secured; the natural strength of the country; the great number of vessels and floating batteries they had provided for the defence of the river; the skill, valour, superior force, and uncommon vigilance of the enemy; their numerous bodies of savages continually hovering about the posts of the English, to surprize parties and harrass detachments; we must own that there was such a combination of difficulties, as might have discouraged and perplexed the most resolute and intelligent commander.

As no possibility appeared of annoying the enemy above the town, the scheme of operations was totally changed. The three brigadiers formed, and presented a plan for conveying the troops farther down in boats, and landing them in the night within a league of Cape Diamond, in hope of ascending the heights of Abraham, which rise abruptly, with a steep ascent from the banks of the river; that they might take possession of the ground on the back of the city, where it was but indifferently fortified. The dangers and difficulties attending the execution of this design were so peculiarly discouraging, that one would imagine it could not have been embraced but by a spirit

of

of enterprize that bordered on defperation. The
ftream was rapid; the fhore fhelving; the bank of
the river lined with centinels; the landing place fo
narrow as to be eafily miffed in the dark; and the
ground fo difficult as hardly to be furmounted in the
day-time, had no oppofition been expected.

The previous fteps being taken, and the time fixed
for this hazardous attempt, admiral Holmes moved
with his fquadron farther up the river, about three
leagues above the place appointed for the difembarkation; that he might deceive the enemy, and
amufe Mr. de Bougainville, whom Montcalm had
detached with 1500 men to watch the motions of
that fquadron: but the Englifh admiral was directed
to fail down the river in the night, fo as to protect the
landing of the forces; and thefe orders he punctually
fulfilled. On the 12th of September, an hour after
midnight, the firft embarkation, confifting of four
compleat regiments, the light infantry, commanded
by colonel Howe, a detachment of Highlanders, and
the American grenadiers, was made in flat-bottomed
boats, under the immediate command of the brigadiers Monckton and Murray. Without any diforder
the boats glided gently along; but, by the rapidity
of the tide, and darknefs of the night, they overfhot
the mark, and the troops landed a little below the
place at which the difembarkation was intended.

How far the fuccefs of this attempt depended upon
accident, may be conceived from the following particulars.—In the twilight two French deferters were
carried on board a fhip of war, commanded by captain Smith, and laying at anchor near the North
fhore. They told him, that the garrifon of Quebec
expected that night to receive a convoy of provifions,
fent down the river in boats, from the detachment
above, commanded by Mr. de Bougainville. Thefe
deferters ftanding upon deck, and perceiving the
Englifh boats, with the troops, gliding down the river
in the dark, began to fhout, and make a noife; declaring

claring they were part of the expected convoy. Captain Smith, who was ignorant of general Wolfe's design, believing their affirmation, had actually given orders to point the guns at the British troops; when the general perceiving a commotion on board, rowed along-side in person, and prevented the discharge, which would have alarmed the town, and entirely frustrated the attempt.

The French had posted sentinels along-shore, to challenge boats and vessels, and give the alarm occasionally. The first boat that contained the English troops, being questioned accordingly, a captain of Fraser's regiment, who had served in Holland, and who was perfectly well acquainted with the French language and customs, answered, without hesitation, to *Qui vit?* which is their challenging word, *la France:* nor was he at a loss to answer the second question, which was much more particular and difficult. When the sentinel demanded *a quel regiment?* of what regiment? the captain replied, *de la Reine,* which he knew, by accident, to be one of those that composed the body commanded by Bougainville. The soldier took it for granted, this was the expected convoy; and saying *passe,* allowed all the boats to proceed without further question. In the same manner the other sentinels were deceived; though one more wary than the rest, came running down to the water's edge, and called, *pourquoy est que vous ne parlez plus haut?* "Why don't you speak aloud?" To this interrogation, which implied doubt, the captain answered with admirable presence of mind, in a soft tone of voice, *Tai tai, nous serons entendues!* "Hush! we shall be overheard and discovered." Thus cautioned, the sentinel retired without farther altercation. The midshipman who piloted the first boat, passing by the landing-place in the dark, the same captain, who knew from his having been posted formerly with his company on the other side of the river, insisted upon the pilot's being mistaken, and commanded the

rowers

rowers to put afhore in the proper place, or at leaft very near it.

As the troops landed, the boats were fent back for the fecond embarkation, which was fuperintended by brigadier Townfhend. In the mean time colonel Howe, with the light infantry and the Highlanders, afcended the woody precipices with admirable courage and activity; and diflodged a captain's guard, which defended a fmall intrenched narrow path, by which alone the reft of the forces could reach the fummit. Then they mounted, without further moleftation from the enemy, and the general drew them up in order, as they arrived. Monfieur de Montcalm no fooner underftood that the Englifh had gained the heights of Abraham, which in a manner commanded the town on its weakeft part, than he refolved to hazard a battle, and began his march without delay; after having collected his whole force from the fide of Beauport.

General Wolfe, perceiving the enemy croffing the river St. Charles, began to form his own line; the French had lined the bufhes and corn-fields in their front with 1500 of their beft markfmen, who kept up an irregular galling fire, which proved fatal to many brave officers, thus fingled out for deftruction. This fire, indeed, was in fome meafure checked by the advanced pofts of the Britifh line; who piqueered with the enemy for fome hours before the battle began. Both armies were deftitute of artillery, except two fmall pieces on the fide of the French, and a fingle gun, which the Englifh feamen had made fhift to draw up from the landing-place. This was very well ferved, and galled their column feverely. General Wolfe was ftationed on the right, at the head of Bragg's regiment, and the Louifbourg grenadiers, where the attack was moft warm. As he ftood confpicuous in the front of the line, he had been aimed at by the enemy's markfmen; and received a fhot in the wrift, which, however, did not oblige him to

quit

quit the field. Having wrapped a handkerchief round his hand, he continued giving orders without the least emotion; and advanced at the head of the grenadiers, with their bayonets fixed, when another ball unfortunately pierced the breast of this young hero, who fell in the arms of victory, just as the enemy gave way! For, at this very instant, every separate regiment of the British army seemed to exert itself for the honour of its own peculiar character. General Wolfe being slain, and, at the same time, Mr. Monckton dangerously wounded at the head of Lascelles's regiment, where he distinguished himself with remarkable gallantry, the command devolved to brigadier Townshend, who hastened to the centre; and finding the troops disordered in the pursuit, formed them again with all possible expedition. This necessary task was scarce performed, when M. de Bougainville, with a body of 2000 fresh men, appeared in the rear of the English. He had begun his march from Cape Rouge, as soon as he received intelligence that the British troops had gained the heights of Abraham; but did not come up in time to have any share in the battle.

Mr. Townshend immediately ordered two battalions, with two pieces of artillery, to advance against this officer, who retired, at their approach. The French general Mr. de Montcalm was mortally wounded in the battle, and conveyed into Quebec; from whence, before he died, he wrote a letter to general Townshend, recommending the prisoners to that generous humanity by which the British nation is distinguished. His second in command was left wounded on the field, and next day expired on board an English ship, to which he had been conveyed. About one thousand of the enemy were made prisoners, including a great number of officers; and about five hundred were slain on the field of battle. The wreck of their army, after they had reinforced

the

the garrifon of Quebec, retired to Trois Rivieres and Montreal.

This important victory was obtained at the expence of fifty men killed, including nine officers; and of about 500 men wounded; but the death of general Wolfe was a national lofs, and univerfally lamented.

Immediately after the battle of Quebec, admiral Saunders fent up all the boats of the fleet, with artillery and ammunition; and failed up, with all the fhips of war, in a difpofition to attack the lower town; while the upper part fhould be affaulted by general Townfhend. But on the 17th of September, before any battery could be finifhed, a flag of truce was fent from the town, with propofals of capitulation; which, being maturely confidered by the general and admiral, were accepted and figned at eight next morning.

They granted the more favourable terms, as the enemy continued to affemble in the rear of the Britifh army; as the feafon was become wet, ftormy, and cold; threatening the troops with ficknefs, and the fleet with accident; and as a confiderable advantage would refult from taking poffeffion of the town while the walls were in a ftate of defence.

The capitulation was no fooner ratified, than the Britifh forces took poffeffion of Quebec, and guards were pofted in different parts of the town, to preferve order and difcipline. The death of Montcalm, which was indeed an irreparable lofs to France, in all probability, overwhelmed the enemy with confternation; and confounded all their councils: otherwife we cannot account for the tame furrender of Quebec to a handful of troops, even after the victory they had obtained: for the feafon was fo far advanced, that the Britifh forces in a little time muft have been forced to defift, by the feverity of the weather, and even retire with their fleet before the approach of winter, which never fails to freeze up the river St. Laurence.

The

The city of Quebec being reduced, together with great part of the circumjacent country, brigadier Townshend, who had accepted his commission with the express proviso, that he should return to England at the end of the campaign, left a garrison of 5000 effective men, victualled from the fleet, under the command of brigadier Murray; and embarking with admiral Saunders, arrived in Great Britain about the beginning of winter. As for brigadier Monckton, he was conveyed to New York, where he happily recovered of his wounds.

While the arms of Great Britain triumphed in Europe and America, her interest was not suffered to languish in other parts of the world. This was the season of ambition and activity, in which every separate armament seemed to exert themselves with the most eager appetite of glory. The East Indies, which, in the course of the preceding year, had been the theatre of operations carried on with various success, exhibited nothing now but a succession of trophies to the English commanders. During the operations by land, the superiority at sea was still disputed between the English and French admirals. On the 1st day of September, vice-admiral Pocock sailed from Madrass to the southward, in quest of the enemy; and next day descried the French fleet, consisting of fifteen sail, standing to the northward. He used his utmost endeavours to bring them to a battle, which they still declined, and at last they disappeared. He then directed his course to Pondicherry, on the supposition that they were bound to that harbour; and on the 8th day of the month, perceived them standing to the southward: but he could not bring them to an engagement till the 10th, when Mr. d'Apche, about two in the afternoon, made the signal for battle, and the cannonading began without further delay. The British squadron did not exceed nine ships of the line; the enemy's fleet consisted of eleven;

eleven; but they had ſtill a greater advantage in number of men and artillery. Both ſquadrons fought with great impetuoſity, till about ten minutes after four, when the enemy's rear began to give way: this example was ſoon followed by their centre: and finally the van, with the whole ſquadron, bore to the ſouth ſouth-eaſt, with all the canvas they could ſpread. The Britiſh ſquadron was ſo much damaged in their maſts and rigging, that they could not purſue; ſo that M. d'Apche retreated at his leiſure unmoleſted. On the 15th, admiral Pocock returned to Madraſs, where his ſquadron being prepared by the 26th, he ſailed again to Pondicherry, and in the road ſaw the enemy lying at anchor in line of battle. The wind being off ſhore, he made the line of battle a-head, and for ſome time continued in this ſituation. At length the French admiral weighed anchor, and came forth; but inſtead of bearing down upon the Engliſh ſquadron, which had fallen to leeward, he kept cloſe to the wind, and ſtretched away to the ſouthward. Admiral Pocock finding him averſe to another engagement, and his own ſquadron being in no condition to pur-ſue, he, with the advice of his captains, deſiſted, and meaſured back his courſe to Madraſs; while the French ſquadron made the beſt of their way to the iſland of Mauritius, in order to be refitted, having on board general Lally, and ſome other officers. Thus they left the Engliſh maſters of the Indian coaſt; a ſuperiority ſtill more confirmed by the arrival of rear-admiral Corniſh with four ſhips of the line, who had ſet ſail from England in the beginning of the year, and joined admiral Pocock at Madraſs on the 18th day of October.

The French were not the only enemies with whom the Engliſh had to cope in the Eaſt Indies. The great extenſion of their trade in the kingdom of Bengal, had excited the envy and avarice of the Dutch factory, who poſſeſſed a ſtrong fort at Chinchura in the river of Bengal; and reſolved, if poſſible, to engroſs the

whole falt-petre branch of commerce. Their fcheme
was approved by the governor of Batavia, who
charged himfelf with the execution of it; and for that
purpofe, chofe the opportunity when the Britifh fquadron had retired to the coaft of Malabar. On pretence of reinforcing the Dutch garrifens in Bengal, he
equipped an armament of feven fhips, having on
board 500 European troops, and 600 Malayefe, under the command of colonel Ruffel. This armament
having touched at Negapatam, proceeded up the
bay, and arrived in the river of Bengal about the beginning of October. Colonel Clive, who then refided at Calcutta, had received information of their
defign, which he was refolved, at all events, to defeat.
He complained to the Subah, who, upon fuch application, could not decently refufe an order to the director and council of Hughley, implying, that this
armament fhould not proceed up the river. The colonel at the fame time fent a letter to the Dutch commodore, that as he had received information of their
defign, he could not allow them to land forces, and
march to Chinchura. In anfwer to this declaration,
the Dutch commodore, whofe whole fleet had not yet
arrived, affured the Englifh commander that he had
no intention to fend any forces to Chinchura; and
begged liberty to land fome of his troops for refrefh-
ment; a favour that was granted, on condition that
they fhould not advance. Notwithftanding the Subah's order, and his own engagement to this effect,
the reft of the fhips were no fooner arrived, than he
proceeded up the river to the neighbourhood of Tan-
nah-fort, where his forces being difembarked, began
their march to Chinchura. In the mean time, by
way of retaliating the affront he pretended to have
fuftained, in being denied a paffage to their own
factory, he took feveral fmall veffels on the river belonging to the Englifh company: and the Calcutta
Indiaman, commanded by captain Wilfon, homeward-bound, failing down the river, the Dutchman
gave

gave him to underftand, that if he prefumed to pafs, he would fink him without further ceremony. The Englifh captain feeing them run out their guns, as if really refolved to put the threats in execution, returned to Calcutta, where two other India fhips lay at an anchor; and reported his adventure to colonel Clive, who forthwith ordered the three fhips to prepare for battle, and attack the Dutch armament. The fhips being properly manned, and their quarters lined with falt-petre, they fell down the river, and found the Dutch fquadron drawn up in line of battle, in order to give them a warm reception; for which indeed they feemed well prepared; for three of them were mounted with 36 guns each; three of them with 26; and the feventh carried 16. The duke of Dorfet, commanded by captain Forrefter, being the firft that approached them, dropped anchor clofe to their line, and began the engagement with a broadfide, which was immediately returned. A dead calm unfortunately intervening, this fingle fhip was for a confiderable time expofed to the whole fire of the enemy; but a fmall breeze fpringing up, the Calcutta and the Hardwick advanced to her affiftance, and a fevere fire was maintained on both fides, till two of the Dutch fhips flipping their cables, bore away, and a third was driven afhore. Their commodore thus weakened, after a few broadfides, ftruck his flag to captain Wilfon; and the other three followed his example. The victory being thus obtained, without the lofs of one man on the fide of the Englifh, captain Wilfon took poffeffion of the prizes, the decks of which were ftrewed with carnage, and fent the prifoners to colonel Clive at Calcutta. The detachment of troops, which they had landed to the number of 1100 men, was not more fortunate in their progrefs. Colonel Clive no fooner received intelligence that they were in full march to Chinchura, than he detached colonel Forde, with 500 men from Calcutta, in order to put a ftop to their march. The Dutch advanced to the charge with great refolution and activity; but found the fire of the Englifh artillery and battalion fo intolerably hot, that they foon gave way, and were totally defeated.

In the mean time, propofals of accommodation being fent to him by the directors and council of the Dutch factory at Chinchura, a negotiation enfued, and a treaty was concluded to the fatisfaction of all parties. Above 300 of the prifoners entered into the fervice of Great Britain: the reft embarked on board their fhips, which were reftored as foon as the peace was ratified, and fet out on their return for Batavia.

The navy in 1760 amounted to 120 fhips of the line, befide frigates, firefhips, floops, bombs, and tenders. Of thefe fhips 17 were ftationed in the Eaft Indies, 20 for the defence of the Weft Indian iflands, 12 in North America, 10 in the Mediterranean, and 61 either on the coaft of France, in the harbours of England, or cruifing in the Englifh feas for the protection of the Britifh commerce. Notwithftanding thefe numerous and powerful armaments, the enemy, who had not a fhip of the line at fea, were fo alert with their fmall privateers and armed veffels, that, in the beginning of this year, from the 1ft of March to the 10th of June, they had made prize of 200 veffels belonging to Great Britain and Ireland. The prodigious number of Britifh veffels, taken by their petty coafting privateers, in the face of fuch mighty armaments, numerous cruifers, and convoys, feems to argue, that either the Englifh fhips of war were inactive or improperly difpofed; or that the merchants hazarded their fhips without convoy. Certain it is, in the courfe of this year we find fewer prizes taken from the enemy, and fewer exploits atchieved at fea, than we had occafion to record in the annals of the paft.

Not that the prefent year is altogether barren of events, which redound to the honour of our marine commanders. We have, in recounting the tranfactions

actions of the preceding year, mentioned a small armament equipped at Dunkirk, under the command
of Mr. de Thurot; who, in spight of all the vigilance
of the British commander stationed in the Downs,
found means to escape from the harbour in the month
of October, and arrived at Gottenburgh in Sweden, from whence he proceeded to Bergen in Norway. His instructions were to make occasional descents upon the coast of Ireland; and, by dividing
the troops, and distracting the attention of the government in that kingdom, to facilitate the enterprize
of Mr. de Conflans, the fate of which we have already narrated. The original armament of Thurot
consisted of five ships, one of which, called the Ma-
reschal de Belleisle, was mounted with 44 guns; the
Begon, the Blond, the Terpsichore, had 30 guns
each; and the Marante carried 24. The number of
soldiers put on board this little fleet, did not exceed
1270, exclusive of mariners to the number of 700 :
but in their voyage between Gottenburgh and Bergen
they lost company of the Begon, during a violent
storm. The intention of Thurot was to make a descent about Derry; but before this design could be
executed, the weather growing tempestuous, they
were driven out to sea, and, in the night, lost sight
of the Marante, which never joined them in the sequel. After having been tempest-beaten for some
time, the officers requested of Thurot, that he would
return to France, lest they should all perish by famine;
but he lent a deaf ear to this proposal, and frankly
told them, he could not return to France, without
having struck some stroke for the service of his country. Nevertheless, in hope of meeting with some re-
freshment, he steered to the island of Isla, where
the troops were landed; and here they found black
cattle, and a small supply of oatmeal, for which they
payed a reasonable price; and it must be owned,
Thurot himself behaved with great moderation and
generosity.

While

While this fpirited adventurer ftruggled with thefe wants and difficulties, his arrival in thofe feas filled the whole kingdom with alarm. Bodies of regular troops and militia were pofted along the coafts of Ireland and Scotland; and befide the fquadron of commodore Boys, who failed to the northward on purpofe to purfue the enemy, other fhips of war were ordered to fcour the Britifh channel, and cruize between Scotland and Ireland. The weather no fooner permitted Thurot to purfue his deftination, than he failed from Ifla to the bay of Carrickfergus in Ireland, and made all the neceffary preparations for a defcent; which was accordingly effected, with 600 men, on the 21ft day of February. Lieutenant colonel Jennings commanded four companies of raw undifciplined men at Carrickfergus. A regular attack was carried on, and a fpirited defence made, until the ammunition of the Englifh failed: then colonel Jennings retired in order to the caftle; which, however, was in all refpects untenable. Neverthelefs, they repulfed the affailants in their firft attack, even after the gate was burft open; and fupplied the want of fhot with ftones and rubbifh. At length, the colonel and his troops were obliged to furrender, on condition that they fhould not be fent prifoners to France, but be ranfomed. The enemy, after this exploit, did not prefume to advance farther into the country; a ftep which indeed they could not have taken, with any regard to their own fafety: and the defeat of Conflans, which they had alfo learned, obliged them to reimbark with fome precipitation, after having laid Carrickfergus under moderate contribution.

The fate they efcaped on fhore, they foon met with at fea. Captain John Elliot, who commanded three frigates at Kinfale, was informed by a difpatch, that three of the enemy's fhips lay at anchor in the bay of Carrickfergus; and thither he immediately fhaped his courfe in the fhip Æolus, accompanied by the Pallas
and

and Brilliant, under the command of the captains
Clements and Logie. On February the 28th they
defcried the enemy, and gave chace, in fight of the
Ifle of Man; and about nine in the morning captain
Elliot, in his own fhip, engaged the Belleifle, commanded by Thurot, although confiderably his fuperior in ftrength of men, number of guns, and
weight of metal. In a few minutes his conforts were
alfo engaged with the other two fhips of the enemy.
After a warm action maintained with great fpirit on
all fides for an hour and a half, in which Thurot
was killed; captain Elliot's lieutenant boarded the
Belleifle, and, ftriking her colours with his own hand,
the commander fubmitted : his example was immediately followed by the other French captains; and
the Englifh commodore, taking poffeffion of his
prizes, conveyed them into the bay of Ramfay in the
Ifle of Man, that their damage might be repaired.
The name of Thurot was become terrible to all the
trading fea-ports of Britain and Ireland; and therefore the defeat and capture of his fquadron were
celebrated with as hearty rejoicings, as the moft important victory could have produced.

The incidents of the war were much more impor-
tant and decifive in America. Brigadier-general
Murray had been left to command the garrifon of
Quebec, amounting to about 6000 men; a ftrong
fquadron of fhips was ftationed at Halifax in Nova
Scotia, under the direction of lord Colvil, an able and
experienced officer, who had inftructions to revifit
Quebec in the beginning of fummer, as foon as the
river St. Laurence fhould be navigable : and general
Amherft, the commander in chief of the forces in
America, wintered in New York, that he might be at
hand to affemble his troops in the fpring, and recom-
mence his operations for the entire reduction of Canada. The garrifon, however, within the walls of
Quebec, fuffered greatly from the exceffive cold in
the winter, and the want of vegetables and frefh pro-

vifion, infomuch that, before the end of April, 1000
foldiers were dead of the fcurvy, and twice that number rendered unfit for fervice. Such was the fituation of the garrifon, when Mr. Murray received undoubted intelligence, that the French commander,
the chevalier de Levis, was employed in affembling
his army, which had been cantoned in the neighbourhood of Montreal; and determined to undertake the
fiege of Quebec, whenever the river St. Laurence
fhould be fo clear of ice, that he might ufe his four
frigates, and other veffels, by means of which he
was entirely mafter of the river.

The French accordingly landed, and Mr. Murray
was defeated in an engagement with them. The
French therefore formed the fiege of the place.

Lord Colvil had failed from Halifax, with the
fleet under his command, but was retarded in his paffage by thick fogs, contrary winds, and great fhoals
of ice floating down the river. Commodore Swanton,
who had failed from England with a fmall reinforcement, arrived about the beginning of May at the Ifle
of Bec, in the river St. Laurence; where, with two
fhips, he purpofed to wait for the reft of his fquadron,
which had feparated from him in the paffage: but
one of thefe, the Loweftoffe, commanded by captain
Deane, had entered the harbour of Quebec on the
9th day of May, and communicated to the governor
the joyful news that the fquadron was arrived in the
river. Commodore Swanton no fooner received intimation that Quebec was befieged, than he failed up
the river with all poffible expedition, and anchored
above Point Levi. The brigadier expreffing an earneft defire, that the French fquadron above the town
might be removed, the commodore ordered captain
Schomberg of the Diana, and captain Deane of the
Loweftoffe, to flip their cables early next morning,
and attack the enemy's fleet, confifting of two frigates, two armed fhips, and a good number of fmaller
veffels. They were no fooner in motion than the
French

French fhips fled in the utmoft diforder. One of their frigates was driven on the rocks above Cape Diamond; the other ran afhore, and was burned at Point au Tremble, about ten leagues above the town; and all the other veffels were taken or deftroyed.

The enemy were fo confounded and difpirited by this difafter, and the certain information that a ftrong Englifh fleet was already in the river of St. Laurence, that in the following night they raifed the fiege of Quebec, and retreated with great precipitation. The reduction of Montreal followed foon after.

The French miniftry had attempted to fuccour Montreal, by equipping a confiderable number of ftorefhips, and fending them out in the fpring under convoy of a frigate; but as their officers underftood that the Britifh fquadron had failed up the river St. Laurence before their arrival, they took fhelter in the bay of Chaleurs on the coaft of Acadia, where they did not long remain unmolefted. Captain Byron, who commanded the fhips of war that were left at Louifbourg, having received intelligence of them, failed thither with his fquadron, and found them at anchor. The whole fleet confifted of one frigate, two large ftore-fhips, and nineteen fail of fmaller veffels, the greater part of which had been taken from the merchants of Great Britain : all thefe were deftroyed, together with two batteries which had been raifed for their protection. The French town, confifting of 200 houfes, was demolifhed, and the fettlement totally ruined.

The conqueft of Canada being atchieved, nothing now remained to be done in North America, except the demolition of the fortifications of Louifbourg on the ifland of Cape Breton; for which purpofe, fome able engineers had been fent from England with the fhips commanded by captain Byron. By means of mines artfully difpofed and well conftructed, the fortifications were reduced to a heap of rubbifh; the

I i 4

glacis

glacis was levelled, and the ditches were filled. All
the artillery, ammunition, and implements of war,
were conveyed to Halifax; but the barracks were
repaired fo as to accommodate 300 men occafionally;
and the hofpital, with the private houfes, were left
ftanding.

Rear-admiral Holmes, who commanded at fea, in
the Weft Indies, took every precaution to fecure the
ifland of Jamaica from infult or invafion, and alfo
contrived fchemes for annoying the enemy. Having,
in the month of October, received intelligence that
five French frigates were equipped at Cape Francois
on the ifland of Hifpaniola, in order to convoy a fleet
of merchant-fhips to Europe, he ftationed the fhips
under his command in fuch a manner as was moft
likely to intercept this fleet: and by the prudent difpofition of the admiral, fupported by the gallantry of
his captains, two large frigates of the enemy were
taken, viz. the Sirenne and the Valeur; and three
deftroyed.

The fpirit of the officers was happily fupported by
an uncommon exertion of courage in the men, who
chearfully engaged in the moft dangerous enterprizes.
Immediately after the capture of the French frigates,
eight of the enemy's privateers were deftroyed or
brought into Jamaica.

The fame activity and refolution diftinguifhed the
captains and officers belonging to the fquadron commanded by Sir James Douglas off the Leeward iflands.
In the month of September, the captains Obrien and
Taylor, of the fhips Temple and Griffin, being on a
joint cruife off the iflands Granadas, received intelligence that the Virgin, formerly a Britifh floop of war,
which had been taken by the enemy, then lay at anchor, together with three privateers, under protection
of three forts on the ifland; he failed thither in order
to attack them; and the enterprize was crowned with
fuccefs. After a warm engagement, that lafted feveral hours, the enemy's batteries were demolifhed,
and

and the English captains took possession of the four prizes. They afterward entered another harbour of that island, having first demolished another fort; and carried off three more prizes. In their return to Antigua, they fell in with thirteen ships bound to Martinique with provisions, and took them all without resistance. About the same time, eight or nine privateers were taken by the ships which commodore Douglas employed in cruising round the island of Guadaloupe; so that the British commerce in those seas flourished under his care and protection.

No action of importance was in the course of this year atchieved by the naval forces of Great Britain in the seas of Europe. A powerful squadron still remained in the bay of Quiberon, in order to amuse and employ a body of French forces on that part of the coast; and interrupt the navigation of the enemy: though the principal aim of this armament seems to have been to watch and detain the few French ships, which had run into the river Villaine, after the defeat of Conflans; an object the importance of which will doubtless astonish posterity.

Admiral Rodney still maintained his former station off the coast of Havre de Grace, to observe what should pass at the mouth of the Seine. In the month of July, while he hovered in this neighbourhood, five large flat-bottomed boats loaded with cannon and shot, set sail from Harfleur in the middle of the day, with their colours flying, as if they had set the English squadron at defiance; for the walls of Havre de Grace, and even the adjacent hills were covered with spectators, assembled to behold the issue of this adventure. Having reached the river of Caen, they stood backward and forward upon the shoals, intending to amuse Mr. Rodney till night, and then proceed under cover of the darkness. He perceived their drift, and gave directions to his small vessels as soon as day-light failed, to make all the sail they could to cut off the enemy's retreat; while he himself
stood

ftood with the larger fhips to the fteep coaft of Port
Baffin. The fcheme fucceeded to his wifh. The
enemy, feeing their retreat cut off, ran afhore at Port
Baffin, where the admiral deftroyed them, together
with the fmall fort which had been erected for the
defence of this harbour. Each of thofe veffels was
100 feet in length, capable of containing 400 men for
a fhort paffage. What their deftination was, we cannot pretend to determine : but the French had provided a great number of thefe tranfports ; for ten
efcaped into the river Orne leading to Caen ; and in
confequence of this difafter 100 were unloaded and
fent up again to Rouen. The cutters belonging to
Mr. Rodney's fquadron fcoured the coaft toward
Dieppe, where a confiderable fifhery was carried on,
and where they took or deftroyed near 40 veffels of
confiderable burden.

Of the domeftic tranfactions relating to the war, the
moft confiderable was the equipment of a powerful
armament deftined for fome fecret expedition. The
troops were actually embarked with a great train of
artillery ; and the eyes of the whole nation were attentively fixed upon this armament, which could not
have been prepared without incurring a prodigious
expence. Notwithftanding thefe preparations, the
whole fummer was fpent in idlenefs and inaction ; and
at the end of the feafon the undertaking was laid
afide.

We fhall now turn our attention to the progrefs of
the Britifh arms in the Eaft Indies. Colonel Coote,
after having defeated the French general Lally in the
field, and reduced divers of the enemy's fettlements
on the coaft of Coromandel, at length cooped them
up within the walls of Pondicherry, the principal feat
of the French Eaft India company. In the month of
October admiral Stevens failed from Trincamaley with
all his fquadron, in order to its being refitted, except
five fail of the line, which he left under the command
of captain Haldane, to block up Pondicherry by fea,

while

while Mr. Coote fhould carry on his operations by land. By this difpofition, and the vigilance of the Britifh officers, the place was fo hampered as to be greatly diftreffed for want of provifions, even before the fiege could be undertaken in form; for the rainy feafon rendered all regular approaches impracticable. Lally made a gallant defence, and had he been properly fupplied with provifion, the conqueft of the place would not have been fo eafily atchieved. He was obliged, however, to furrender the place at difcretion.

By the reduction of Pondicherry the French intereft was annihilated on the coaft of Coromandel, and therefore it was of the utmoft importance to the Britifh nation. It may be doubted, however, whether colonel Coote, with all his fpirit, vigilance, and military talents, could have fucceeded in this enterprize, without the affiftance of the fquadron, which co-operated with him by fea, and effectually excluded all fuccours from the befieged. It muft be owned, for the honour of the fervice, that no incident interrupted the good underftanding which was maintained between the land and fea-officers; who vied with each other in contributing their utmoft efforts toward the fuccefs of the expedition.

While the arms of great Britain ftill profpered in every effort tending to the real intereft of the nation, an event happened which, for a moment, obfcured the fplendour of her triumphs. On the 25th day of October, 1760, George II. king of Great Britain, without any previous diforder, died fuddenly in his palace at Kenfington; at the age of feventy-feven, after a long reign of thirty-three years, diftinguifhed by a variety of important events, and chequered with a viciffitude of character and fortune. He loved war as a foldier; he ftudied it as a fcience; and correfponded on the fubject with fome of the greateft officers whom Germany had produced. The extent of his underftanding, and the fplendour of his virtue, we

4   fhall

shall not presume to ascertain, nor attempt to display. With respect to his government, it very seldom deviated from the institutions of law; encroached upon private property; or interfered with the common administration of justice. The circumstances that chiefly mark his public character, were a predilection for his native country, and a close attention to the political interests of the Germanic body: points and principles to which he adhered invincibly.

We postpone giving the state of the navy at this period; proposing to give a particular list of the British navy as it stood at the ensuing peace.

The demise of the crown was no sooner signified to the secretaries of state, than Mr. Pitt repaired to Kew, and communicated these tidings to his new sovereign George III. grandson to the late king, who thus ascended the throne in the 23d year of his age. How much soever the new king might have disapproved of those measures which had involved the nation in such an expensive war on the continent of Europe, affairs were so situated, that he could not abruptly renounce that system of politics, with any regard to the dignity of his crown, or to the honour of the public faith, which was in some measure engaged to support the German allies of Great Britain. With the crown he inherited a war, which he thought it his duty to prosecute with vigour, until it could be terminated by a general peace; in which the honour and advantage of the nation might be equally consulted. It was therefore agreed, that the armament then preparing at Portsmouth should proceed on the expedition for which it was originally intended; but it was countermanded in the sequel.

The chief command of the army in Great Britain rested in the person of lord Ligonier. The German army in Westphalia, payed by England, remained under the auspices of prince Ferdinand of Brunswick: the marquis of Granby commanded the British forces on that service; and the direction of the troops in

Ame-

America was still retained by Sir Jeffery Amherst.
Neither was any material change produced in the disposition of the different squadrons which constituted
the navy of Great Britain. Admiral Holborne's flag
continued flying at Spithead. Sir Edward Hawke
and Sir Charles Hardy were stationed in the bay of
Quiberon. Sir Charles Saunders kept the sea in the
Mediterranean. The rear-admirals Stevens and Cor-
nish commanded one squadron in the East Indies ;
rear-admiral Holmes another at Jamaica ; Sir James
Douglas a third at the Leeward Islands ; Lord Colvil a fourth at Halifax in Nova Scotia. These were
stationary ; but other squadrons were equipped occasionally, under different commanders ; beside the
single ships that cruised in and about the Channel,
and those that were stationed to protect the trade of
Great Britain in different parts of the world.

Even from the beginning of winter, the single
ships that cruised in the Channel were conducted
with such care and dexterity, that they made prize
of a great number of French privateers ; a circumstance that evinced their own vigilance and the enemy's activity. In the month of January, captain
Elphinston, of the Richmond, of 32 guns, fell in
with the Felicite, a French frigate, of the same
force, off the coast of Holland : a severe engagement began about ten in the morning, near Grave-
sande, about eight miles from the Hague, to which
place the prince of Orange, general Yorke the British
envoy, and the count d'Affry the French ambassador,
repaired, with a great multitude of people, to behold the conflict. About noon both ships ran ashore ;
nevertheless the action was still maintained, until the
enemy deserted their quarters : they afterward abandoned the ship, which was entirely destroyed, after
having lost their captain and about 100 men, who
fell in the dispute. The Richmond soon floated,
without any damage ; and the victory cost but three
men killed, and thirteen wounded. The French

court

court loudly exclaimed againſt this attack as a violation of the Dutch neutrality, and demanded ſignal ſatisfaction for the inſult and damage they had ſuſtained. Accordingly the States General made ſome remonſtrances to the court of London, which found means to remove all cauſe of miſunderſtanding on this ſubject. The Felicite was bound for Martinique, with a valuable cargo, in company with another frigate of the ſame force, which ſuffered ſhipwreck on the coaſt of Dunkirk.

In the courſe of the ſame month, captain Hood, in the Minerva frigate, cruiſing in the chops of the channel, deſcried a great ſhip of two decks ſteering to the weſtward, and found it to be the Warwick, an Engliſh ſhip, which had carried ſixty cannon, and been taken by the enemy. She was now mounted with thirty-five guns, and commanded by Mr. le Verger de Belair, with a commiſſion from the French king. Her crew amounted to about 300 men, including a detachment of ſoldiers; and he was bound to Pondicherry in the Eaſt Indies. Captain Hood, notwithſtanding her ſuperior ſize, attacked her without heſitation, and was very warmly received. In the iſſue the captain of the Warwick ſtruck his colours, having loſt about 14 men killed outright, beſide 35 wounded. The loſs in number of men was equal on board the Minerva, and all her maſts went by the board : neverthelefs the prize was brought in triumph to Spithead. In the progreſs of the ſame cruize, captain Hood had alſo taken the Ecurneil privateer from Bayonne, of 14 guns, and 122 men.

In March, another French ſhip, called the Entreprenant, pierced for 44 guns, but mounted with 26 only, having 200 men on board, and a rich cargo, bound for St. Domingo, was encountered near the Land's-end by the Vengeance frigate of 26 guns, commanded by captain Nightingale. The action was maintained on both ſides with uncommon fury, until the Vengeance being ſet on fire by the enemy's wadding ;

ding; the French refolved to take advantage of the confufion produced by this accident, and, running their boltfprit upon the taffaril of the Englifh frigate, attempted to board her.   In this defign, however, they mifcarried, through the courage and activity of captain Nightingale; who found means to difengage himfelf, and fheered off to repair his rigging, which had greatly fuffered in the engagement. The fhip was no fooner in proper condition, than he ranged up again clofe to the enemy, and renewed the conteft, which lafted a full hour : then the Entreprenant bore away.   Captain Nightingale, though a fecond time difabled in his mafts and rigging, wore fhip, ran within piftol-fhot, and began a third vigorous attack, which lafted an hour and a half before the enemy called for quarter.   Fifteen of their men were killed, and about twice that number wounded. The victors loft about half as many.   The iffue of all thefe engagements between fingle fhips, proves, to demonftration, that the French mariners neither work their fhips nor manage their artillery with that fkill and dexterity which appear in the Englifh navy: a circumftance the more remarkable, as all the French feamen are regularly taught the practical part of gunnery; whereas no fuch pains are taken with the failors of Great Britain.

In April, another French frigate, called the Comete, of 32 guns, and 250 men, juft failed from Breft, was taken to the weftward of Ufhant by the Bedford, captain Deane.   About the fame period, and near the fame place, a fourth frigate of the enemy, called the Pheafant, manned with 125 mariners, was taken by captain Brograve, of the Albany floop; whofe victory was the cheaper, as the crew of the Pheafant had thrown 14 of her guns over-board during the chace.   In the courfe of the fame month, a large Eaft India fhip, fitted out from France, with 28 guns, and 350 men, fell in with the Hero and the

Venus,

Venus, commanded by the captains Fortescue and Harrison, and were taken without opposition.

The cruizers belonging to the squadron commanded by vice-admiral Saunders in the Mediterranean, were distinguished by the same spirit of enterprize and activity. In the beginning of this very month, the Oriflamme, a French ship of 40 guns, being off Cape Tres Foreas, was taken by the Isis, captain Wheeler, who being unfortunately killed in the beginning of the action, the command devolved to lieutenant Cunningham: she was brought into the bay of Gibraltar. In July another exploit was performed by a small detachment from the squadron commanded by the same admiral. Captain Proby, in the Thunderer, together with the Modeste, Thetis and Favourite sloop, being ordered to cruise upon the coast of Spain with a view to intercept the Achilles and Bouffon, two French ships of war, which lay in the harbour of Cadiz; they at length ventured to come forth, and were descried by the British cruizers. About midnight, the Thunderer came up with the Achilles, which struck, after a warm engagement of half an hour. The Thetis engaged the Bouffon, and the fire was maintained on both sides with great vivacity for half an hour, when the Modeste ranging up, and firing a few guns, the French captain submitted. His ship and her consort suffered considerably, both in their crews and rigging; nevertheless, the victors carried them safely into the bay of Gibraltar.

One of the most remarkable and shining actions that distinguished this war, and 'proved, beyond all contradiction, the superiority which the English claimed over the French in point of naval discipline, was an incident which we shall now relate. August 10th, captain Faulkner of the Bellona, a ship of the line, and captain Logie of the Brilliant, a frigate, sailed from the Tagus for England, having on board a considerable sum of money for the merchants of London.

In

In the afternoon, being then off Vigo, they discovered three sail of ships standing in for the land, one of the line of battle, and two frigates. They no sooner descried captain Faulkner, than they bore down upon him, until within the distance of seven miles, when, seeing the Bellona and a frigate through the magnifying medium of a hazy atmosphere, they mistook them both for two-decked ships, and dreading the issue of an engagement, resolved to avoid the encounter. For this purpose, they suddenly wore round, filled their sails, and crouded away. Captain Faulkner, being by this time convinced of their size, and conjecturing, from the intelligence he had received, that the large ship was the Courageux (in which particular he was not mistaken) he hoisted all the canvas he could carry, and gave chace until sunset; when one of the French frigates hauling out in the offing, he displayed a signal to the Brilliant to pursue in that direction, and his order was immediately obeyed. They kept sight of the enemy during the whole night, and at sun-rise had gained but about two miles upon them in a chace of fourteen hours; so that the French commodore might have still avoided an engagement for the whole day, and enjoyed the chance of escaping in the darkness of the succeeding night; but he no longer declined the action. The air being perfectly serene, he now perceived that one of the English ships was a frigate; and the Bellona herself which was one of the best constituted ships in the English navy, lay so flush in the water as to appear at a distance considerably smaller than she really was. The French commodore, therefore, hoisted a signal for his two frigates to close with and engage the Brilliant. At the same time he wore round, and stood for the Bellona under his topsails; while captain Faulkner advanced toward her with an easy sail, and ordered his quarters to be manned. The sea was undulated by a gentle breeze, which facilitated the working of the ships, and at the same time per-

Vol. VII.   K k   mitted

.mitted the full use of their heavy artillery.   The
two ships were equal in burden, in number of guns,
and in weight of metal.   The crew on board the
Courageux amounted to 700 men, able to stand to
their quarters; and they were commanded by M. du
Guy Lambert, an officer of approved valour and
ability.   The Bellona's compliment confisted of 550
chosen men, accustomed to discipline, and inured to
service.   All the officers were gentlemen of known
merit, and the commander had on many occasions
diftinguished himself by his bravery and conduct.
The fire on both sides was suspended till they were
wit in musket-shot of each other, and then the engagement began with a dreadful difcharge of fire-arms
and artillery.   In less than nine minutes, all the Bellona's braces, bowlings, shrowds, and rigging, were
cut and shattered by the shot, and the mizen-maft fell
over the stern, with all the men on the round-top;
who, nevertheless, saved their lives, by clambering
into the port-holes of the gun-room.   Captain Faulkner, apprehensive that the enemy would seize the
opportunity of his being difabled, and endeavour to
efcape, gave orders for immediate boarding; an attempt which the position of the two ships soon rendered altogether impracticable.   The Courageux was
now falling athwart the fore-foot, or bows of the
Bellona, in which case the English ship must have
been raked fore and aft with great execution.   The
haul-yards, and moft of the other ropes by which
the Bellona could be worked, were already shot away.
Captain Faulkner, however, with the affiftance of
his mafter, made use of the ftudding fails with such
dexterity, as to ware the ship quite round, and fall
upon the opposite quarter of the Courageux.   His
presence of mind and activity in this delicate fituation, were not more admirable than the discipline
and difpatch of his officers and men, who, perceiving this change of their fituation, flew to the guns on
the other fide, now oppofed to the enemy, from
                                    whence

whence they poured in a moſt terrible diſcharge, and maintained it without intermiſſion or abatement. Every ſhot took place, and bore deſtruction along with it. The ſides of the Courageux were ſhattered and torn by every ſucceſſive broadſide, and her decks were ſtrewed with carnage. About twenty minutes did the enemy ſuſtain the havock made by this battery, ſo inceſſantly plied and ſo fatally directed. At length it became ſo intolerable, that the French enſign was hauled down : the rage of battle ceaſed ; the Engliſh mariners had left their quarters, and the officers congratulated each other on the ſucceſs of the day. At this juncture, a ſhot being unexpectedly fired from the lower tire of the Courageux, the Britiſh ſeamen ran to their quarters, and, without orders, poured in two broadſides upon the enemy, who now called for quarter, and an end was put to the engagement. The damage done to the rigging of the Bellona was conſiderable ; but ſhe ſuffered very little in the hull, and the number of the killed and wounded did not exceed forty. The caſe was very different with the Courageux, which now appeared like a wreck upon the water. Nothing was ſeen ſtanding but her foremaſt and boltſprit ; large breaches were made in her ſides ; her decks were torn up in ſeveral parts ; many of her guns were diſmounted ; and her quarters filled with the mangled bodies of the dying and the dead. Above 220 were killed outright, and half that number was brought aſhore wounded to Liſbon, to which place the prize was conveyed. Captain Faulkner was not more commendable for his gallantry in the action, than for the humanity and politeneſs with which he treated his priſoners ; whoſe grateful acknowlegment, and unſolicited applauſe, conſtitute the faireſt teſtimony that a man of honour can enjoy. Nor ought captain Logie of the Brilliant to be forgotten, whoſe valour and dexterity, in a great meaſure, contributed to the ſucceſs of his commodore. The two Engliſh captains

joined

joined in a liberal fubfcription with the Britifh factory at Lifbon, for the relief of the wounded French pri- foners, who, without this generous interpofition, muft have ftarved, as no provifion was made by their fovereign.

In the Weft Indies, rear-admiral Holmes, com- mander of the fquadron at Jamaica, planned his cruizes with equal judgment and fuccefs. Having received intelligence in the beginning of June, that feveral fhips of war belonging to the enemy had failed from Port Louis, and in particular, that the St. Anne had juft quitted Port au Prince; he forthwith made fuch a difpofition of his fquadron as was moft likely to intercept them. He fell in with and took the St. Anne, a beautiful new fhip, pierced for 64 cannon, but mounting only 40, manned with near 400 mari- ners and foldiers; and loaded with a rich cargo of coffee, indigo, and fugar. Nor was the fquadron ftationed off the Leeward Iflands, under the direction of Sir James Douglas, lefs alert and effectual in pro- tecting the Britifh traders, and fcouring thofe feas of the Martinico privateers, of which he took a great number.

The ifland of Dominique, which the French had fettled and put in a pofture of defence, was attacked and reduced by a fmall body of troops, commanded by lord Rollo, and conveyed thither from Guadalupe by Sir James Douglas, with four fhips of the line, and fome frigates.

According to the laudable cuftom of thefe latter times, a powerful fquadron had been ftationed all the winter in the bay of Quiberon, under the command of Sir Edward Hawke and Sir Charles Hardy. In January, they took two fmall French frigates, bound to the coaft of Guinea, and a few merchant-fhips of little value; and in March, the two admirals returned to Spithead: but another fquadron was afterward fent to occupy the fame ftation. In July, while the Eng- lifh were employed in demolifhing the fortifications

on

on the isle of Aix, the great ships that protected this service were attacked by a French armament from the Charante, consisting of six prames *, a few row-gallies, and a great number of launches crouded with men. They dropped down with the ebb, and placing themselves between the isle of d'Enet and Fort Fouras, played upon the English ships in Aix road, with 12 mortars, and 70 large cannon : but they met with such a warm reception from the British squadron, that in a few hours they retreated to their former station, where the water was too shallow for the English ships to return the attack.

These were part of that armament which had loitered in the preceding year at Spithead, until the season for action was elapsed. It had been a favourite scheme of the minister, to reduce the island of Belleisle on the coast of Brittany, and this was the aim of the expedition. Belleisle lies about four leagues from the point of Quiberon, about half way between Port Louis and the mouth of the Loire. It extends about six leagues in length, and little more than two in breadth; contains a pretty large town, called Palais, fortified with a citadel, beside a good number of villages: and the whole number of inhabitants, exclusive of the garrison, may amount to 6000, chiefly maintained by the fishery of pilchards. It was supposed the reduction of this island would be easily atchieved, and the conquest attended with manifold advantages.

The squadron equipped for this enterprize consisted of ten ships of the line, several frigates, two fireships, and two bomb-ketches, commanded by commodore Kepple, brother to the earl of Albemarle, a gallant officer, who had signalized himself on several occasions, in the course of this and the last

* A prame is a long broad vessel of two decks, mounted with 26 large cannon below, and 3 mortars above. They are rigged like ketches, and draw very little water.

K k 3

war.

war. The whole armament came to anchor in the
g eat road of Belleisle April 7th, where a disposition
was made for landing the forces. This attempt failed,
with the loss of near 500 men, and about 50 mariners. Notwithstanding this unfavourable beginning,
another scheme was laid, and the execution of it
crowned with success. On the 22d day of the month
in the morning, the troops were disposed in the flat-
bottomed boats, and rowed to different parts of the
island, as if they intended to land in different places:
thus the attention of the enemy was distracted in such a
manner, that they knew not where to expect the descent, and were obliged to divide their forces at ran-
dom. Mean while brigadier Lambert pitched upon
the rocky point of Lomaria, where captain Paterson,
at the head of Beauclerk's grenadiers, and captain
Murray, with a detachment of marines, climbed the
precipice with astonishing intrepidity, and sustained
the fire of a strong body of the enemy, until they
were supported by the rest of the English troops.
Then the French abandoned their batteries, and retired with precipitation : but this advantage was not
gained without bloodshed. The landing was followed
by the reduction of the citadel. A conquest which
could in no respect be considered as a compensation
for the expence of the armament, and the lives of
about 2000 men, who might have been much better
employed.

A negociation was now entered into toward a peace,
but the intervention of some Spanish claims, which
led to the discovery of a private family-compact entered into between France and Spain, frustrated it;
and Mr. Pitt, disgusted that his advice for rigorous
measures with Spain was disapproved, resigned his
posts.

A plan for the conquest of Martinique was already
formed. In the month of October, rear-admiral
Rodney sailed from England with a squadron of ships,
having under convoy a number of transports, with

for

four battalions from Belleiſle, to join at Barbadoes a ſtrong body of forces from North America, together with ſome regiments and volunteers from Guadalupe and the Leeward Iſlands; thence to proceed, in conjunction with the fleet already on that ſtation, to the execution of the projected invaſion. This was doubtleſs an object of great importance, and might have been eaſily accompliſhed in the firſt attempt under the conduct of general Hopſon; but now the enterprize was encumbered by many difficulties. The iſland was ſtrengthened with new fortifications, a ſtrong body of troops, a numerous regulated militia, experienced officers, and plenty of proviſion, artillery, and ammunition.

War againſt Spain was declared January 4th, 1762.

The armament from North America and England, under the command of major-general Monckton and rear-admiral Rodney, amounting to 18 battalions, and as many ſhips of the line, beſide frigates, bombs, and fireſhips; which having rendezvouſed at Barbadoes in the month of December, proceeded from thence and anchored in St. Anne's Bay, in the eaſtern part of Martinique, after the ſhips of war had ſilenced ſome batteries which the enemy had erected on that part of the coaſt. In the courſe of this ſervice, the Raiſonable, a ſhip of the line, was, by the ignorance of the pilot, run upon a reef of rocks, from whence ſhe could not be diſengaged, though the men were ſaved, together with her ſtores and artillery.

The troops being landed at Cas des Navires, and reinforced with two battalions of marines, which were ſpared from the ſquadron, the general reſolved to beſiege the town of Fort-Royal; which was proſecuted with great bravery. The governor of the citadel, perceiving the Engliſh employed in erecting batteries on the different heights by which he was commanded, ordered the chamade to be beat, and ſurrendered the place by capitulation, on the 4th of February. The

K k 4   moſt

moft remarkable circumftance of this enterprize was the furprifing boldnefs and alacrity of the feamen, who, by force of arm, drew a number of heavy mortars and fhips cannon up the fteepeft mountains to a confiderable diftance from the fea, and acrofs the enemy's line of fire, to which they expofed themfelves with amazing indifference. Fourteen French privateers were found in the harbour of Port Royal; and a much greater number, from other parts of the ifland, were delivered up to admiral Rodney, in confequence of the capitulation with the inhabitants, who, in all other refpects, were very favourably treated.

The French were now expelled from all their fettlements in North America, except that of Louifiana, which was deemed an object of little or no importance: the feat of war was transferred from that continent to the French iflands, the conqueft of which we have already defcribed; and it was now refolved to make a vigorous impreffion upon Spain, not only by attempting the reduction of the Havanna, which may be confidered as the key of the bay of Mexico; but alfo by making a defcent on the ifland of Manilla, in the Eaft Indies, a country in which the French had now nothing left to be conquered.

The firft of thefe expeditions was entrufted to the conduct of the earl of Albemarle, commander of the land-forces, recommended for this fervice by the duke of Cumberland, under whofe aufpices he had been formed to war; and the fhips of war, deftined to cooperate in the attack, were commanded by admiral Sir George Pococke, who had already diftinguifhed himfelf by his gallantry in the Eaft Indies: his fecond was Mr. Keppel, brother to the earl, an able officer, who had reduced the Ifle of Goree, on the coaft of Africa. They failed from Portfmouth in the beginning of March; and reached the place of their deftination without accident or obftruction. Their proceedings fhall be particularized in their proper place.

The

The defign againft Manilla was executed by rear-admiral Cornifh, which we fhall recount.

, For the defence of the Britifh coaft, and in order to anfwer the emergencies of war, a powerful fqua-dron was kept in readinefs at Spithead, under the di-rection of Sir Edward Hawke; another rode at an-chor in the Downs, under the command of rear-ad-miral Moore; and from thefe two were occafionally detached into the channel, and all around the coafts of the ifland, a number of light cruizers, which act-ed with fuch vigilance and activity, that not a fhip could venture from any of the French fea-ports, without running the moft imminent rifque of being taken.

Sir Charles Saunders was reinforced in fuch a man-ner, as enabled him to give law in the Mediterranean, and either to prevent a junction of the French and Spanifh fleets, or, if that fhould be found impracti-cable, to give them battle when joined.   Lord Col-ville was continued in the command of the fquadron at Halifax in Nova Scotia, in order to protect the coaft of North America, and the new conquefts, in the gulph and river of St. Laurence.   Sir James Douglas ftill commanded the fhips of war appointed for the defence of the Leeward Iflands; and captain Forreft, fince the death of admiral Holmes, directed the fmall fquadron at Jamaica.   Such was the general difpofition for the offenfive as well as the defenfive meafures of the campaign; and the greateft enemies of the miniftry muft allow it was planned with faga-city, and maintained with refolution.

A fruitlefs attempt had been made by the enemy to burn the Britifh fhips of war at anchor in the road of Bafque.   They prepared three fire-veffels, which being chained together, were towed out of the port, and fet on fire with a ftrong breeze that blew directly on the Englifh fquadron.   This attempt, however, was made with hurry and trepidation; and the wind luckily fhifting, drove them clear of the

fhips

fhips they were intended to deftroy. They continued burning for fome time, after having blown up with a terrible explofion, and every perfon on board perifhed.

Captain Gambier, of the Burford, arrived at Plymouth in April with a large French Eaft India fhip from the Ifle of Bourbon, laden with coffee and pepper, which had been taken by one of Sir George Pococke's fquadron. In May, two Britifh frigates, cruifing off Cape St. Vincent, made prize of the Hermione, a Spanifh regifter fhip, bound from Lima to Cadiz, loaded with treafure and valuable effects, by which all the captors were enriched. Her cargo amounted to about one million fterling, which was confiderably more than had ever before been taken in any one bottom : and the lofs of fo much treafure, in the beginning of fuch an expenfive war, muft have been a fevere ftroke on the court of Madrid. The prize was brought from Gibraltar to England, and the gold and filver being conveyed in covered waggons to London, was carried in proceffion to the bank ; happening to arrive the fame morning the prince of Wales was born, which was the 12th of Auguft.

About the latter end of May, a French fquadron, under the command of Mr. de Ternay, efcaped from Breft in a fog. The French commander fteered his courfe to Newfoundland, and entered the bay of Bulls, where he landed fome troops without oppofition. Having taken poffeffion of an inconfiderable Englifh fettlement in that bay, they advanced to the town of St. John's, which being in no condition of defence, was furrendered upon capitulation. They alfo took the officers and crew of the Gramont floop which was in the harbour, with feveral other veffels ; and did confiderable damage to the Englifh fifhers and fettlers on different parts of the coaft. The miniftry were no fooner informed of this fmall check, which it was impoffible either to forefee or prevent, than
they

they took meafures for retrieving the lofs; and this petty triumph of the enemy was of very fhort duration. The armament fitted out in England for re-taking Newfoundland, was rendered unneceffary by the vigilance and activity of Sir Jeffery Amherft and lord Colville, who commanded by land and fea in North America.

In September, the Hunter floop of war, one of admiral Moore's cruizers, falling in with four Dutch merchant fhips in the Channel, under convoy of a frigate of 36 guns, the Englifh captain prepared to examine the lading of the Dutch veffels, when the commander of the frigate interpofing, declared he would not fuffer any fuch fearch to be made. The other infifted upon the examination, but being prevented by fuperior force, made a fignal to the Diana and Chefter fhips of war, which happened to be in fight, and they advanced accordingly. After fome expoftulation, the Dutch captain continuing obftinate, the Diana fired a gun to bring him to, and he returned a whole broadfide. An engagement immediately enfued, and was maintained with great vivacity for about fifteen minutes, when the Dutchman thought proper to ftrike his colours, having loft his own nofe, and nine or ten men in the action. He was brought into the Downs, together with his convoy, which were found laden with contraband merchandize from Havre to Breft. The Zephyr, a French frigate of 32 guns, bound to Newfoundland, with troops, artillery, ftores, and ammunition, was alfo taken in the channel, by the Lion fhip of war. In the beginning of November, a French fhip of 20 guns, was taken by captain Ruthven, of the Terpfichore, after a fharp action, in which he himfelf was wounded. The enemy loft likewife the Oifeau, another frigate of 26 guns, which fell in with captain Tonyn of the king's fhip the Brune. A third French frigate, called the Minerve, was wrecked in the harbour of Villa Franca, through the pride, precipita-

tion,

tion, and ignorance of her commander. She had, in company with four French ſhips of war, given chace to the Sheerneſs frigate, captain Clarke, from Gibraltar, who took refuge in the harbour of Villa Franca, and there anchored, the wind blowing freſh. He was immediately followed by the enemy, when the captain of the Minerve, actuated by an idle ſpirit of vanity and inſolence, reſolved to lie between him and the ſhore, and ran his ſhip upon the rocks that bound the eaſtern ſide of the harbour. On this melancholy occaſion, captain Clarke, forgetting they were enemies, obeyed the dictates of humanity, by exerting himſelf for their relief. He ſent his boats manned to their aſſiſtance, and actually ſaved the lives of the greater part of their company : an act of generous benevolence, for which he was thanked in perſon by the French commodore.

About the end of Auguſt, captain Hotham of the Æolus, chaced two Spaniſh ſhips into the bay of Aviles, in the neighbourhood of Cape Pinas; and ſtanding into the bay, came to an anchor in ſuch a ſituation, as to bring his guns to bear, not only upon one of the ſhips, but alſo upon a ſmall battery ſituated upon an eminence. After a ſhort conteſt, both the battery and the ſhip were abandoned : but before captain Hotham could take poſſeſſion of his prize, ſhe ran aground, and bulging, was burned by the captors : the other eſcaped in the night. Captain Hotham afterward fell in with a French ſquadron, conſiſting of ſeven ſail, between St. Andero and Bilboa, and kept company with them till the 16th, as far to the weſtward as Cape Finiſterre, when he returned to his ſtation. By a ſloop from Bourdeaux, which he took, he underſtood that this ſquadron had a body of troops on board for St. Domingo.

The navy of France was by this time reduced to ſuch a ſmall number, that their miniſtry was obliged to ſend reinforcements to their ſettlements abroad in ſingle ſhips; ſome of which were intercepted by the

6   Britiſh

British cruifers, particularly one tranfport, containing the beft part of a regiment, defigned to reinforce their colony of Louifiana, which had engaged a good fhare of their attention fince the reduction of Canada.

The cruizers of Great Britain were not lefs alert in the feas of America. Captain Ourry of the Actæon, in the latitude of Tobago, took a large Spanifh regifter fhip, bound to Lagueira, laden with artillery, ftores, and ammunition. A fleet of 25 fail of French merchant-fhips, richly laden with fugar, coffee and indigo, took their departure from Cape François for Europe, under convoy of four frigates. Five of thefe veffels were furprifed and taken in the night by fome privateers of New York and Jamaica. Next day it was their misfortune to fall in with commodore Keppel, who made prize of their whole fleet and convoy, which were carried into the harbour of Port-Royal in Jamaica.

In the courfe of this war the French nation loft 37 fhips of the line, and 55 frigates; of thefe the Englifh took 18 capital fhips of war, and 36 frigates; and deftroyed 14 of the line, and 13 frigates; five large fhips and fix frigates they loft by accidents. On the other hand, the French took two, and deftroyed three Englifh frigates; and 13 capital Britifh fhips, and 14 frigates, were loft by accident. Of merchant fhips belonging to Great Britain, the enemy took 812, from the commencement of the war to the ceffation of arms.

In September, the honourable Auguftus Hervey and captain Nugent, arrived in London with difpatches from the earl of Albermarle and fir George Pococke. We have already obferved that the armament under the conduct of thofe two commanders had failed from Portfmouth in March; and, according to the general opinion, was deftined to act againft the ifland of Cuba. They were joined by a detachment of the fleet from Martinique, under Sir James Douglas; and, in confequence of this junction, their
whole

whole force confifted of 19 fail of the line, 18 fmaller
fhips of war, and about 150 tranfports, having on
board about 10,000 land forces and marines. Without accident or danger, on July 6th, the admiral lay
to, about five leagues to the eaftward of the Havanna,
after having taken a Spanifh frigate and a ftore-fhip
in the paffage. Having iffued directions to the mafters
of the tranfports, with refpect to the difembarkation
of the army, and left commodore Keppel to fuper-
intend this fervice, with fix fail of the line and fome
frigates, he bore away with the reft of the fleet, and
ran down off the harbour, where he defcried 12 Spanifh fhips of the line, with feveral trading veffels. .
Next morning he embarked his marines in boats, and
made a fhew of landing about four miles to the weftward of the Havanna; while the earl of Albemarle
landed with the whole army, between the rivers Boca-
nao and Coxemar, about fix miles to the eaftward of
the Moro Caftle, which was the enemy's chief fortrefs for the defence of the town and harbour. Three
bomb-veffels being anchored in fhore, began to throw
fhells into the town. Though this invafion of the
Englifh was altogether unexpected, the place being
ftrongly fortified and well fupplied, preparations were
inftantly made for a vigorous defence, by Don Juan
de Prado, governor of the city, and the marquis
del Real, commodore of the fhipping; affifted by the
counfels and experience of the viceroy of Peru and
the governor of Carthagena, who happened to be at
the Havanna, in the way to or from their refpective
governments. The attack of the Moro was commanded by major-general Keppel, brother to the
earl of Albemarle; and the chief engineer was Mr.
Mackellar, who difplayed uncommon abilities at the
fiege of Louifbourg, and on many other occafions
both in this and the laft war.

Fafcines, ftores, and artillery, being landed from
the fhips with great expedition by the feamen, the
engineers began to erect batteries of bombs and cannon,

son, while a body of pioneers were employed to cut parallels in the wood, and form a line with fascines to secure the guards from the fire of the enemy, which began to be very troublesome. About 1000 chosen men of the enemy, with a detachment of armed negroes and mulattoes, landed on two divisions to the right and left of the Moro, in order to destroy the works of the besiegers: but they were repulsed by the piquets and advanced posts, and retreated in great confusion, with the loss of 200 men, killed and taken.

The admiral's cruizers, who scoured the sea round the whole island, brought in the Venganza frigate of 26 guns, the Marté of 18, and a schooner, laden with coffee. Sir James Douglas, who had parted from the admiral immediately after their junction, and steered his course to Jamaica, in a single ship, now arrived off the Havanna, having under his convoy a fleet of merchant ships bound for England.

The parapet of Fort Moro was all of masonry; the ditch of the front attacked, was seventy feet deep from the edge of the counterscarp, and more than forty feet of that depth sunk in the rock. The soil of the country in the neighbourhood, being very thin, afforded little earth; and as it was thought necessary to carry on the approaches by sap, this method might have been found altogether impracticable, had not Sir James supplied the engineers with cotton bags, from some ships of his convoy, which were partly loaded with this commodity. Mean while, the enemy made such a vigorous defence, that the siege was protracted beyond expectation; a considerable delay was likewise occasioned by an unlucky accident. On July 3d, the principal battery of the besiegers, chiefly constructed of timber and fascines, being dried by the heat of the weather and the continual cannonade, took fire, and the flames raged with such violence, that almost the whole work was consumed. The besiegers were subjected to various other

5

other difcouragements. Epidemical diftempers, fuch as never fail to attack the natives of Britain who vifit thofe countries, began to make great havock, both in the army and the navy. Thefe were rendered more fatal by the want of neceffaries and refrefh-ments. The provifion was bad; and the troops were ill fupplied with water. The great number of the fick rendered the duty more fatiguing to thofe that were well. In thofe warm climates, the human body being in a ftate of relaxation, is incapable of fuch a degree of labour as it can bear in more northern la-titudes; and the men are fubject to a fpecies of de-jection, which always augments the general morta-lity: this was now increafed by the delay of the troops from North America, which they had long expected to no purpofe.

On the 2d of Auguft, the fecond divifion of the tranfports, with the troops from North America, ar-rived; and this reinforcement added frefh vigour to the operations of the fiege. In a few days, the fea-men and foldiers belonging to four of the American tranfports, which had been wrecked in the ftraights of Bahama, were brought off in five floops, detached by the admiral on this fervice: but, at the fame time, he received information that five other tranfports, having on board 350 foldiers of Anftruther's regi-ment, and 150 provincial troops, were taken by a French fquadron, near the paffage between Maya Gu-anna, and the North Caicos. All the reft of the troops, however, arrived in perfect health.

July 19th the befiegers took poffeffion of the co-vered-way, before the point of the right baftion, and a new fap was begun at this lodgment. The only place by which the foot of the wall was acceffible, happened to be a thin ridge of rock, left at the point of the baftion, to cover the extremity of the ditch, which would otherwife have been open to the fea. Along this ridge the miners paffed, without cover, to the foot of the wall, where they made a lodgment

with

with little lofs.   Mean while, they funk a fhaft without the covered-way, in order to form a mine for
throwing the counterfcarp into the ditch, fhould it be
found neceffary to fill it; and continued their former
fap along the glacis.   In the night of the 21ft a fer-
geant and 12 men fcaled the walls by furprize; but,
the garrifon being alarmed before they could be fuftained, they were obliged to retreat with precipitation.
Next day, at four in the morning, a fally was made
from the town, by 1500 men, divided into three detachments, who attacked the befiegers in three different places, while a warm fire was kept up in their
favour from the forts and their fhipping in the harbour.   After a warm difpute, which coft the Englifh
about fifty men killed or wounded, all their three
parties were repulfed, and fled with fuch precipitation, that a confiderable number was drowned in the
hurry of their retreat.   On the 30th day of the
month, about two in the morning, a floating battery
was towed out into the harbour, and fired with grape-
fhot and fmall arms into the ditch, though without
any great interruption to the miners; and the clofe
fire of the covering party foon compelled the enemy
to retire.

In the afternoon, two mines were fprung by the
befiegers, with fuch effect, that a practicable breach
was made in the baftion; and orders were immediately given for the affault.   The troops mounted with
great intrepidity, and, forming on the top of the
breach, drove the enemy from every part of the ram-
parts, after a fhort, though very warm, difpute; in
which about 130 Spaniards were killed, including feveral officers of diftinction.   Don Louis de Velafco,
governor of the fort, had diftinguifhed himfelf from
the beginning of the fiege, by fuch activity and courage, as attracted the admiration and efteem even of
his enemies.   In this laft action, he did all that could
be expected from the moft romantic gallantry; and
fell by a fhot he received in defending the colours of

VOL. VII.   L l   Spain.

Spain. The marquis Gonzales, who was fecond in
command, likewife loft his life on this occafion.
About 400 of the garrifon threw down their arms, and
were made prifoners: the reft were either killed or
drowned, in attempting to efcape to the Havanna.
Lieutenant-colonel Stuart, who commanded the attack, loft but 2 lieutenants, and 12 men.

The reduction of the Moro was not immediately
attended with the furrender of the Havanna; on the
contrary, the governor of the place now directed his
chief fire againft the fortrefs which they had loft. On
the 11th of Auguft, at day-break, about 45 cannon
and 8 mortars began to play againft the town and the
Punta, which laft was filenced before ten; in another
hour the north baftion was almoft difabled. About
two in the afternoon, white flags were hung out all
round the place, as well as on board the admiral's
fhip in the harbour; and, in a little time, a flag of
truce arrived at the head quarters, with propofals of
capitulation. The governor ftickled hard to obtain
permiffion to fend the fhips to Spain, and to have the
harbour declared neutral: but neither of thefe points
could be given up, and hoftilities were ordered to be
renewed; when the enemy thought proper to recede
from their demands. By the capitulation, which was
figned on the 13th, the inhabitants were fecured in
their private property, in the enjoyment of their own
laws and religion; and next day the Englifh troops
took poffeffion of this important conqueft. As for
the Spanifh garrifon, which amounted to about 900,
including officers, they were indulged with the honours of war; and it was ftipulated, that they and
the failors fhould be conveyed to Old Spain. In the
progrefs of the fiege, about 500 of the Britifh troops,
including 15 officers, were killed out-right or died of
their wounds; and about 700, comprehending 39
officers, were cut off by diftemper, which raged with
redoubled violence after the reduction of the place.

So

So much-treasure intercepted by the English, first in the ship Hermione, and now in the island of Cuba, must have been a severe stroke upon the king of Spain: but the ruin of his navy was of much greater importance, and even that but a trifle in comparison to the loss of the Havanna; the port at which all their galleons and flota, loaded with the riches of Mexico and Peru, rendezvoufed in their return to Old Spain; the port which abfolutely commanded the only paffage by which their ships could fail from the bay of Mexico to Europe. The reduction of the Havannah, therefore, was an acquisition, that not only diftreffed the Spaniards in the moft effential manner, by ftopping the fources of their wealth, but likewife opened to the conquerors an eafy avenue to the centre of their American treafures. In no former war had Great Britain acquired fuch large fums at the expence of her enemies. Her fuccefs in the Eaft Indies is faid to have brought into England near fix millions in treafure and jewels, fince the commencement of hoftilities: but every million thus acquired, fhe expended tenfold in the courfe of her fubfidies and expeditions.

The lofs of the Havanna, with the ships and treafure there taken, was not the only difafter fuftained by Spain in the fhort courfe of the war, which fhe had fo imprudently declared againft Great Britain. She received another dangerous wound in the Eaft Indies by the lofs of Manilla, a confiderable fettlement on Luconia, the largeft of the Philippine iflands. This city is the centre of the Spanish trade, from whence two large ships are fent annually acrofs the vaft Pacific ocean to Acapulco, on the coaft of Mexico, laden with the fpices, ftuffs, jewels, and other rich merchandize of India. (See our account of the Spanish American trade, in vol. 1. and Anfon's voyage in vol. 3.)

Againft this fettlement, a plan of attack was formed at Madrafs, to be executed by part of the fquadron of vice-admiral Cornifh, and a few battalions under the command of brigadier-general Draper, who had

figna-

fignalized himfelf in the defence of Madrafs, when it was befieged by the .enemy. Vice-admiral Cornifh fupplied a ftrong battalion of feamen and marines; fo that the whole force amounted to 2300 effective men.

The forces, with the ftores and artillery, being embarked, the admiral failed in two divifions about the beginning of Auguft, and on the 23d of September anchored in the bay of Manilla, where they found the enemy but ill prepared for a fiege, and much alarmed at this unexpected vifit. The governor was the archbifhop, who ftiles himfelf captain-general of the Philippine iflands : but the garrifon, amounting to 800 men of the royal regiment, was commanded by the marquis de Villa-Medina, a brigadier-general, who now reinforced it with a body of 10,000 Indians, from the province of Pampanga, a fierce and favage nation.

The admiral, having founded the coaft, difcovered a convenient place for landing the troops, about two miles to the fouthward of Manilla. The proper difpofitions being made, and the three frigates, Argo, Sea-horfe, and Seaford, moored very near the fhore, to cover the defcent; three divifions of the forces were put on board the boats of the fleet, and landed at the church and village of Malata, not without fome difficulty from a great furf that rolled on the beach. The enemy began to affemble in great numbers, both horfe and infantry, to oppofe the defcent; but the frigates maintained fuch a warm fire of cannon, to the right and left, that they foon difperfed; and the general difembarked his troops without the lofs of one man; while the Spanifh garrifon were employed in burning the fuburbs of Manilla.

The governor had been already twice fummoned to furrender, but returned a refolute refufal; and, indeed, if the valour of his troops had correfponded with the vigour of his declaration, he had but little to apprehend from an handful of enemies, who, far from

from being in a condition to inveft the city on all fides, were obliged to confine their operations to one corner, leaving two thirds of it open to all manner of fupplies. The front, which the general refolved to attack, was defended by the baftions of St. Diego, and St. Andrew; a ravelin, which covered the royal gate, a wet ditch, a covered way, and a glacis. The baftions were in good order, mounted with a great number of fine brafs cannon: but the ravelin was not armed; nor the covered way in good repair: the glacis was too low, and the ditch was not carried round the capital of the baftion of St. Diego. The breadth of the ditch was about thirty yards, but the depth of water did not exceed five feet. It was founded by a detachment, headed by captain Fletcher, who begged leave to undertake this dangerous enterprize, which he atchieved in the midft of the enemy's fife, with the lofs of three men. Some ftraggling feamen having been murdered by the favages, the governor fent out a flag of truce on the 27th, to apologize for thefe barbarities, and requeft the releafe of his own nephew, who had been lately taken in the bay, by the boats of the fleet. Next day, while lieutenant Fryar, with a flag of truce, conducted this prifoner to the town, a detachment of the garrifon, intermixed with Indians, fallied out to attack one of the pofts of the befiegers: when the favages, without refpecting the law of nations, or the facred character of an officer, under the protection of a flag of truce, fell upon Mr. Fryar, with the moft inhuman fury, murdered him on the fpot, and mortally wounded the Spanifh gentleman who endeavoured to protect his conductor. In their attack, they were foon repulfed by the Britifh party that defended the poft, who were fo exafperated by their barbarity, that they gave them no quarter.

Meanwhile feveral mortars bombarded the town day and night, without ceafing; and the engineers were employed in erecting batteries to play upon their

works.

works. At length the greater part of their Indians, difcouraged by repeated defeats, returned to their own habitations. The fire from the garrifon grew faint; and all their defences appeared to be in a ruinous condition. On the 5th of October, the fire of the befiegers was fo well directed, that the breach became practicable; and it was hoped the garrifon would demand a capitulation: but they feemed to be obftinate and fullen, without courage or activity: they had not exerted themfelves in repairing their works; and now they neglected all means of obtaining favourable terms, without having taken the refolution to defend the breach; fo that the Englifh general made a difpofition for ftorming the town.

On the 6th, at four o'clock in the morning, the troops deftined for this fervice, filed off from their quarters, in fmall bodies, to avoid fufpicion, and gradually affembling at the church of St. Jago, concealed themfelves in the place of arms, and the parallel between the church and the battery. Meanwhile, major Barker maintained a clofe fire upon the works of the enemy, and thofe places where they might be lodged or intrenched; the mortars co-operating in the fame fervice. At day-break, a large body of Spaniards was feen formed on the baftion of St. Andrew, as if they had received intimation of the intended affault, and had refolved to annoy the affailants with mufquetry and grape-fhot from the retired flank of the baftion, where they had ftill two cannon fit for fervice; but a few fhells falling among them, they retired in confufion. The Britifh troops feized this opportunity, and, directed by the fignal of a general difcharge from the artillery and mortars, rufhed on to the affault, under cover of the thick fmoke which blew directly on the town. According to colonel Draper's own account, the total of the troops with which he entered Manilla amounted to little more than 2000, a motley compofition of feamen, foldiers, Sepoys, Cafres, Lafcars, Topafees, with French and German

man

man deferters. Thefe affailants mounted the breach
with incredible courage and rapidity; while the Spaniards, on the baftion, retired fo fuddenly, that it
was imagined they depended entirely on their mines.
Captain Stephenfon was immediately ordered to examine the ground; but this precaution was needlefs.
The Englifh troops penetrated into the town with
very little oppofition, the governor, with the principal magiftrates, retiring into the citadel. This retreat was in itfelf imprudent, becaufe they did not fo
much as attempt either to defend themfelves or to
make their efcape; and it was accordingly attended
with the moft difagreeable confequences. Colonel
Draper, having no offer of capitulation or furrender
made him, could not prevent his troops, for fome
hours, from making the city feel all the rapacioufnefs
to which a city taken by ftorm is fubjected from the
common men; and thofe he commanded, we may
eafily fuppofe, excepting the few regulars among
them, were of the moft unruly kind. At laft, the citadel being in no condition of defence, the archbifhop and the magiftrates furrendered themfelves
prifoners at difcretion. The marquis de Villa-Medina, with the reft of the Spanifh officers, were admitted as prifoners of war, on their parole of honour;
and all the Indians were difmiffed in fafety. The fuccefs of the victors was the more agreeable, as it was
obtained with very little bloodfhed; their lofs in the
action not exceeding 20 men.

Manilla was no fooner poffeffed by the Britifh
forces, than the admiral went on fhore to confult with
general Draper on this great event; and to fettle a capitulation, that might fave fo fine a city from deftruction: but a draught of terms, in the name of the
archbifhop, the royal audience, and the city and
commerce of Manilla, was prefented, which were fo
unfuitable to their defperate fituation, that they were
rejected as unfatisfactory and inadmiffible. The Englifh commanders then took the pen, and dictated the

L l 4   conditions

conditions on which the city of Manilla should be preferved from plunder, and the inhabitants maintained in their religion, liberties, and properties; to which the Spaniards confented. In confequence of this capitulation, the town and port of Cavite, with the iflands and forts depending upon Manilla, were to be furrendered to his Britannic majefty; and four millions of dollars paid as a ranfom for the city of Manilla, and the effects of the inhabitants. All the Britifh forces employed in this expedition were but barely fufficient to garrifon thefe important conquefts, which were atchieved with fo little lofs, that not above one hundred men were killed in the whole fervice.

The acquifition of Luconia, with its towns, treafures, artillery, ftores, iflands, and dependencies, was rendered compleat by another fortunate event. Admiral Cornifh no fooner underftood by letters taken in the galley with the Spanifh governor's nephew, that the galleon Philippina was arrived from Acapulco at Cajayagan, than he fent the Panther and Argo in queft of her. On the 30th of October, being off the ifland Capul, near the entrance of the Embocadero, they defcried a fail ftanding to the northward; they came up with, and engaged her: after having been cannonaded two hours at a very fmall diftance, fhe ftruck their colours and furrendered. But they were not a little furprifed, when the Spanifh general came on board, to learn, that, inftead of the St. Philippina, they had taken the Santiffima Trinidad, which had departed from Manilla on the 1ft day of Auguft, bound for Acapulco. She was a very large fhip, fo thick in the fides, that the fhot of the Panther did not penetrate any part of her, except the upper works. She had 800 men on board; was pierced for fixty cannon, but no more than 13 were mounted. The merchandize on board was regiftered to the amount of one million and a half of dollars, and the whole cargo fuppofed to be worth double that fum; fo that this capture

capture was a valuable addition to the conqueft, and a frefh wound to the enemy.

At no period of time had the Spanifh monarchy fuffered fuch grievous and mortifying difafters, as thofe fhe fuftained in the courfe of this year, from a war into which fhe was precipitately plunged, againft all the dictates of found policy and caution, meerly to gratify the private inclinations of her fovereign.

The recovery of St. John's, in Newfoundland, was likewife numbered among the fucceffes which gave a luftre to the Britifh arms in the courfe of this autumn; and was regained without much trouble or lofs.

Thus the operations of war were profecuted with unremitting ardour in the Eaft and Weft Indies; while the king ftill perfifted in his refolution to embrace the firft opportunity of re-eftablifhing peace, which, exclufive of motives of humanity, he thought abfolutely neceffary for the advantage of his own people. He faw them exhaufting their blood and treafure in quarrels, not their own, upon the continent of Germany; and that this fatal drain could not be effectually ftopped, but by a general pacification. The national debt was encreafed to fuch an enormous burden, as feemed to threaten the immediate ruin of public credit, which a peace alone could prevent. The original fcope of the war, namely, the fecurity of the Britifh colonies in America, was fully accomplifhed; forty fhips of the line were rendered ufelefs by hard fervice: 30,000 recruits were wanted for the army; and the war had occafioned fuch a fcarcity of men, that, during the preceding year, it had been found impracticable to raife above 1500 recruits for the eftablifhed regiments, though great premiums had been offered to engage men in the fervice. Thefe confiderations reinforced the other reafons which induced his majefty to wifh for peace; and his fentiments were warmly efpoufed by all the members of his council.

The

The king of Sardinia is faid to have offered his beft offices for reviving the negotiation between the courts of London and Verfailles; and, in all probability, his mediation was cordially embraced by both. Certain it is, they agreed to treat in good earneft, and to fend mutually to each other, a perfon of the firft rank, vefted with the powers and character of ambaffador and plenipotentiary. The duke of Bedford being chofen for this purpofe, by the king of Great Britain, fet out for France in the beginning of September; and, at the fame time, the duke de Nivernois arrived in England with the fame character from his moft chriftian majefty. Many difficulties were levelled by the hearty defire of peace, which animated both monarchs. The humours and interefts of their German allies no longer obftructed the progrefs of the negotiation, which now turned only upon the re-eftablifhment of peace between England and the houfes of Bourbon. The king of Pruffia delivered from two formidable enemies, in confequence of his late accommodation with Ruffia and Sweden, was now in a condition to take care of himfelf: befide, that fyftem was changed, by which his interefts had been fo warmly efpoufed at the court of London. In fettling the preliminaries, which were difcuffed in concert with the kings of Spain and Portugal, the belligerant powers made allowances for what might have happened in the Eaft and Weft Indies, and regulated the conceffions to be made in proportion to the fuccefs or mifcarriage that might attend the Britifh armaments.

We have now nothing remaining unnoticed, but an unfortunate affair which was the laft tranfaction of the war; and which ftands in a manner unconnected with any other. Upon the difpute with Spain, fome private merchants and adventurers had fitted out two fhips called the Lord Clive and the Ambufcade privateers. The former, being equal in force to a fhip of 50 guns, was commanded by one captain M'Namara, who was efteemed as a brave experienced officer,

officer, and he was to be joined by other ships, particularly a Portuguese frigate, to proceed on an expedition to the South Seas. In December 1762, the whole squadron arrived in the river Plata; which they found much better prepared to receive them than they had imagined. The expedition was originally planned for getting possession of Buenos Ayres; but finding the navigation of the river very difficult, they resolved, before they proceeded farther, to attack Nova Colonia; a colony on the north side of the river Plate, which the Spaniards had some time before taken from the Portuguese: an English pilot, whom they found on board a Portuguese ship, undertaking to bring the commodore within pistol-shot of the chief battery on shore. On the 6th of January 1763, the Lord Clive made the signal for engaging, and soon after anchored under the fire of the eastmost battery of the place, while the Ambuscade was severely handled by the fire of the middle and westmost batteries, and from some Spanish frigates. A most fierce cannonading began on both sides, which lasted from eleven in the forenoon till three in the afternoon; when the enemy's fire, that had been before kept up very steadily, began to flag, and they themselves to retire to the eastmost battery, as the place of greatest safety. In this state of the engagement, when the English expected every moment to see the Spanish colours struck, the Lord Clive was found to be on fire. No sooner did the flames appear, than it was easy to perceive that it was impossible to extinguish them. In an instant the attack was discontinued: the Ambuscade, with vast difficulty, got clear of the other ship's flames, but was little better than a wreck, having received a great number of shot between wind and water. As to the crew of the Lord Clive, some perished in the water, some in the flames, and many by the enemy's fire, which recommenced on the occasion: so that no more than 78 of 340, the complement of the ship when the engagement began, escaped with their lives, the ship

6   blowing

blowing up about eight in the evening. The fate of
the unhappy fufferers was the more affecting, as it
would have been certain deftruction for any of the
other ſhips to have moved to their relief. The Am-
buſcade, in danger of finking every moment, found
means to ſtop her leaks in the river Plate, and to
eſcape to the Portugueſe ſettlement of Rio de Janeiro,
with the loſs of 24 killed. It ought however to be
confeſſed, that ſuch of the Lord Clive's crew as
reachêd the ſhore, were humanely received, treated,
and cloathed, by the Spaniards, whoſe reſentment
ſeemed to be extinguiſhed in the calamity of their
enemies.

The definitive treaty of peace was figned at Paris
on February 10th, 1763; and the terms of it were
more advantageous to Great Britain and her allies,
than thoſe which were agreed to by the late miniſter.
It muſt be acknowleged that Great Britain, by extending the frontiers of Canada, to the middle of the
Miſſiſippi, gained a large tract of fertile country
lying on the banks of that river, befide the advantage
of a free navigation upón it, and the poſſeſſion of the
port of Mobile : but, in order to ſecure the Engliſh
American colonies from all poſſibility of diſturbance
from the French, that reſtleſs nation ought to have
been expelled from the whole country of Louiſiana.

England, by this peace, likewiſe gained an acceſ-
ſion, in France's ceding to her the iſland of Grenada ;
which, when fully cultivated and peopled, may be
of ſome conſequence. She moreover acquired the
unſettled iſlands of Dominica, Tobago, and St.
Vincent ; but yielded to France the iſland of St.
Lucie, ſaid to be worth all the reſt. She retains the
ſettlement of Senegal on the coaſt of Africa, by
which ſhe engroſſes the whole gum trade of that
country ; as for the rock of Goree, which ſhe re-
ſtored, it was no great ſacrifice. The article that
relates to the Eaſt Indies, was dictated by the directors of the Engliſh company ; and ſurely the French
have

have no reason to complain of its severity, as it restores them to the possession of all the places they had at the beginning of the war, on condition that they shall maintain neither forts nor forces in the kingdom of Bengal: thus they will enjoy all their former advantages in trade, without the temptation and expence of forming schemes of conquest and dominion.

The demolition of the works belonging to the harbour of Dunkirk, is no doubt a sensible mortification to France, though of little consequence to England, while a squadron of ships is kept at anchor in the Downs. It became an object of some consideration in the war of queen Anne, as a nest of privateers that infested the channel; and was afterward used as an inflammatory term of faction. The danger that may threaten England from Dunkirk, does not depend upon vessels which could be received into the harbour; but must arise from a strong squadron of ships of the line, which may always lie at anchor in the road.

The liberty of cutting logwood in the bay of Honduras, granted to the subjects of Great Britain, was undoubtedly a great point gained in their favour; but their obliging themselves to demolish their fortifications on that coast, was a tacit acknowlegement that the privilege was not founded upon right, but derived from favour. The cession of Florida, with the forts of St. Augustine and Pensacola, to Great Britain, was an object of much greater importance. It extended the British dominions along the coast to the mouth of the Mississippi. It removed an asylum for the slaves of the English colonies, who were continually making their escape to St. Augustine. It deprived the Spaniards of an easy avenue, through which they had it in their power to invade Georgia and Carolina; it afforded a large extent of improveable territory, a strong frontier, and a good port in the bay of Mexico, both for the convenience of trade,

5   and

and the annoyance of the Spaniards in any future conteft. But neither the ceffion of Florida, nor the renunciation of the right to the fifhery, nor the per-miffion granted to the Englifh logwood cutters, nor the evacuation of Portugal; nor all thefe articles to-gether, can ever be efteemed equivalent to the refti-tution of the Havanna; for which, indeed, the Spa-nifh monarch had no fuitable compenfation to make, without difmembring his kingdom; unlefs he had thrown into the fcale with his other conceffions, that of a free navigation, without fearch, to the Britifh traders on the coaft of New Spain. The crown of Spain was much favoured by the article which fti-pulates, that the conquefts, not included in the treaty either as ceffions or reftitutions, fhould be reftored without compenfation. Neither France nor Spain had any armament on foot, from which they could expect the leaft acquifition or fuccefs; whereas the miniftry of England had great reafon to believe that the ifland of Luconia was already reduced.

On the whole, the treaty, though it might have been more favourable in fome articles, certainly confirmed great and folid advantages to Great Britain; and will remain as an eternal monument of that mo-deration which forms the moft amiable flower in the wreath of conqueft.

Such was the iffue of a war, fanguinary beyond ex-ample, which had raged with uncommon fury in the four quarters of the globe; which had ruined many fair provinces; and, in the fpace of feven years, de-ftroyed above a million of lives; which had coft Great Britain, in particular, above two hundred and eighty thoufand men, including a great number of brave and able officers, with an incredible quantity of treafure; and increafed the burthen of her national debt, from fourfcore, to one hundred and thirty millions fterling.

The

The Royal Navy of GREAT BRITAIN as it ſtood at the cloſe of the Year 1762.

N. B. Thoſe in *Italics* were taken from the French or Spaniards.

FIRST RATES.

Guns	
100	Britannia
100	Royal George
100	*R. Sovereign*

SECOND RATES.

Guns	
90	Blenheim
90	Duke
90	St. George
90	Namur
90	*Neptune*
90	Ocean
90	Prince
90	Princeſs Royal
84	Royal William
90	Sandwich
90	Union

THIRD RATES.

Guns	
64	Africa
64	*Alcide*
74	Arrogant
64	Bedford
64	*Belliqueux*
74	Bellona
64	Belleiſle
64	*Bienfaiſant*
70	Buckingham
70	Burford
80	Cambridge
64	Captain
74	*Centaur*
70	Chicheſter
74	Cornwall
74	Culloden
64	Defiance
66	Devonſhire
70	Dorſetſhire
74	Dragon
74	Dublin
64	Elizabeth
64	Eſſex
74	Fame
80	*Foudroyant*
70	Grafton
64	Hampton-Court
74	Hercules
74	Hero
74	Kent
74	Lenox
74	*Magnanime*

Guns	
68	Marlborough
74	Mars
64	*Modeſte*
64	Monmouth
64	Naſſau
80	Newark
74	Norfolk
70	Northumberland
70	Orford
64	Pr. Frederick
80	Princeſs Amelia
60	Princeſs Mary
64	Revenge
74	Shrewſbury
70	Somerſet
74	Sterling-Caſtle
74	*Superb*
70	Swiftſure
74	*Temeraire*
70	Temple
74	Terrible
74	Thunderer
74	Torbay
64	*Trident*
74	Valiant
70	Vanguard
74	Warſpight

FOURTH RATES.

Guns	
60	Achilles
60	America
60	Anſon
50	Antelope
50	Aſſiſtance
50	Centurion
50	Chatham
50	Cheſter
	Dreadnought
60	Deptford
60	Dunkirk
60	Edgar
50	Falkland
50	Falmouth
60	*Firme*
60	*Florentine*
50	Guernſey
50	Hampſhire
60	Jerſey
60	*Irrreſide*
50	*Iſis*
60	Lion
60	Medway
60	Montague

Guns	
50	Norwich
60	Nottingham
50	*Oriflame*
60	Panther
60	Pembroke
50	Portland
50	Preſton
60	Prince of Orange
60	Rippon
50	Romney
50	Rocheſter
50	Saliſbury
50	Sutherland
60	Weymouth
50	Wincheſter
60	Windſor
60	York

FIFTH RATES.

Guns	
32	Adventure
32	Alarm
32	*Arethuſa*
32	Æolus
32	*Bologne*
32	Boſton
32	*Blonde*
36	Brilliant
32	*Creſcent*
38	*Danae*
32	Diana
44	Dover
32	*Emerald*
44	Enterprize
32	*Flora*
44	Goſport
32	Juno
32	Lark
44	Launceſton
30	Looe
44	Lyme
36	*Melampe*
32	Minerva
32	Montreal
32	*Niger*
36	Pallas
44	Penzance
44	Phœnix
44	Prince Edw.
32	Quebec
44	*Rainbow*
36	Renown
32	Repulſe
32	Richmond
32	Saphire

Guns	
32	Southampton
32	Stagg
32	Thames
32	*Thetis*
30	Torrington
32	Tweed
36	Venus
32	*Veſtal*
44	Woolwich

SIXTH RATES.

Guns	
28	Actæon
28	*Active*
20	Aldborough
24	*Amazon*
28	*Aquilon*
28	Argo
24	Arundel
28	Boreas
28	Cerberus
24	Coventry
20	Deal-Caſtle
24	Dolphin
24	Echo
20	Flamborough
24	Fowey
24	Garland
20	Gibraltar
20	Glaſgow
20	Greyhound
24	Hind
24	Kennington
28	Levant
24	Lively
28	Liverpool
28	Lizard
24	Ludlow Caſtle
28	Maidſtone
24	Mercury
28	Milford
24	Nightingale
24	Portmahon
20	Roſe
24	Rye
20	Scarborough
20	Seaford
20	Seahorſe
28	Shannon
24	Sheerneſs
24	Solebay
20	*Syren*
24	Surprize
28	Tartar
4	*Terpſichore*
28	Trent

Guns:	Guns.	Guns.	Infernal
28 Trent	14 Grampus	8 Savage	*Fire-Sh.* no Guns.
28 *Valeur*	10 Granado	14 Senegal	Ætna
28 Unicorn	8 Goree	14 Sardome	Cormorant
24 Wager	8 Happy	8 Speedwell	Grampus
SLOOPS.	8 Hazard	10 Spy	Lightning
14 Albany	14 Hornet	14 Swallow	Pluto
10 Alderney	14 Hound	14 Swift	Raven
10 Antigua	10 Hunter	14 Swan	Roman Emperor
12 Badger	14 Jamaica	16 Tamer	Proserpine
16 Baltimore	10 King's Fisher	Terror	Salamander
10 Barbadoes	8 Laurel	10 Thunder	Strombolo
10 Bonetta	6 Lurcher	14 Trial	Vesuvius
8 Cruizer	18 Merlin	14 Vulture	**YACHTS.**
18 Cygnet	16 Mortar	8 Wasp	10 Dorset
10 Diligence	18 Nautilus	16 Weazle	8 Fubbs
14 Dispatch	8 Peggy	8 Wolf	8 Katherine
10 Druid	10 Pomona	10 *Zephir*	Augusta
14 Escorte	10 Otter	**BOMB Vessels.**	**STORESHIPS.**
16 Favourite	14 Pelican	Basilisk	10 Crown
18 Ferret	14 Porcupine	Blast	24 South-Sea Castle
8 *Flambro's Prize*	18 Postillion	Carcass	
8 Fly	8 Ranger	Firedrake	
14 Fortune	Racehorse	Furnace	
	14 Saltash		

Ships out of Commission and building.

Rates.	Guns.	Names.	Rates.	Guns.	Names.	Rates.	Guns.	Names.
3	74	Albion	5	44	Eltham	3	84	Ramillies
3	64	Asia	5	44	Expedition	3	64	Royal Oak
4	60	Augusta	3	80	*Formidable*	4	60	Rupert
5	44	Anglesea	4	50	Gloucester	4	50	Ruby
5	32	Aurora	5	44	Glory			R. Charlotte Yacht
2	90	*Ba-fleur*	6	28	Guadalupe			
		Ditto, a new ship	5	44	Hastings	3	64	Suffolk
3	80	Boyne	5	44	Hector	4	60	St. Albans
4	50	Bristol	5	30	Jason	6	24	Sphinx
6	24	Blandford	2	90	London	3	74	Triumph
	90	Blenheim	5	44	Mary Galley		28	Vengeance
		Hospital-ship			Martin Sloop		10	Viper
3	74	Canada			Mary Yacht	1	100	Victory
4	60	Canterbury	3	74	Monarch			Vulture Sloop
3	74	*Courageux*	4	50	Nonsuch	4		Warwick
4	50	Colchester	3	80	Pr. Caroline	5		Winchelsea
3	74	Defiance	4	60	Pr. Louisa	4	60	Worcester
6	24	Experiment	4	60	Plymouth			William and
4	60	Eagle	5	44	Poole			Mary Yacht
3	64	Edinburgh	1	90	Queen	3	64	Yarmouth
4	60	Exeter	1	100	Royal Ann			

Complement of Men, and Weight of Metal, in the Royal Navy.

Guns.	Men.	Metal.				Guns.	Men.	Metal.		
Ships of three Decks.						60	420	24	12	6
100	850	42	24	12	6	60	400	24	9	6
90	750	32	18	12	6	50	350	24	12	6
80	600	32	18	9	6	50	300	18	9	6
Ships of two Decks.						44 40	250	18	9	6
80 74	600	32	18	9		*Frigates of one Deck.*				
70	520	32	18	9		36	240	12	6	
68	Ditto					32	220	12	6	
66	Ditto					28	200	9	4	
64	480	24	12	6		20	160	9	4	

The End of the SEVENTH VOLUME.